# OXFORD THEOLOGICAL MONOGRAPHS

*Editorial Committee*

*Oxford Theological Monographs*

THE PRINCIPLE OF RESERVE IN THE WRITINGS OF JOHN HENRY
NEWMAN
By R. C. SELBY. 1975

GELASIAN SACRAMENTARIES OF THE 8TH CENTURY
By M. B. MORETON. 1975

THREE MONOPHYSITE CHRISTOLOGIES
By R. C. CHESNUT. 1976

RITUALISM AND POLITICS IN VICTORIAN BRITAIN
By J. BENTLEY. 1978

THE ONTOLOGY OF PAUL TILLICH
By A. THATCHER. 1978

BECOMING AND BEING
By C. E. GUNTON. 1978

CALVIN AND ENGLISH CALVINISM TO 1649
By R. T. KENDALL. 1979

NEWMAN AND THE GOSPEL OF CHRIST
By RODERICK STRANGE. 1981

HAMANN ON LANGUAGE AND RELIGION
By TERENCE J. GERMAN. 1981

# The Cosmic Christ
# in Origen and
# Teilhard de Chardin

## A COMPARATIVE STUDY

BY
J. A. LYONS

OXFORD UNIVERSITY PRESS
1982

Oxford University Press, Walton Street, Oxford OX2 6DP
London Glasgow New York Toronto
Delhi Bombay Calcutta Madras Karachi
Kuala Lumpur Singapore Hong Kong Tokyo
Nairobi Dar es Salaam Cape Town
Melbourne Auckland
and associate companies in
Beirut Berlin Ibadan Mexico City

Published in the United States by
Oxford University Press, New York

© *The Australian Province of the Society of Jesus 1982*

*British Library Cataloguing in Publication Data*
Lyons, J. A.
The Cosmic Christ in Origen and Teilhard de
Chardin.—(Oxford theological monographs)
1. Jesus Christ    2. Origen    3. Teilhard
de Chardin, Pierre
1. Title
232'. 092'4    BT198
ISBN  0-19-826721-5

*Photo Typeset by
MacMillan India Ltd., Bangalore
and printed in Great Britain
at the University Press, Oxford
by Eric Buckley
Printer to the University*

# FOREWORD

BY PROFESSOR M F WILES, D.D.

FR James Lyons died of cancer on 18 July 1979, at the age of 45. A member of the Society of Jesus, he was ordained priest in Adelaide in 1968, where he had been born 35 years earlier. When the theologate of the Australian Province of the Society of Jesus moved to a site adjacent to the University of Melbourne, where he himself took an honours degree in English Language and Literature, he played a major role in moving the large Jesuit library to Melbourne and integrating it with the libraries of the other theological colleges. In 1971 he came to Oxford to undertake graduate work in theology. From the outset he showed himself a student of unusual diligence and persistence. His research was done under the supervision of myself and Dr A. O. Dyson, now of Manchester University. When illness overtook him, his work was well on its way to completion. The last stages were written with indomitable courage in spite of much pain and weakness. At the time of his death only the last part of chapter 8 remained to be put into its final form from a much fuller first draft. I did that myself in line with the intentions which he dictated to me a week before he died. Fr Lyons received his Doctorate of Philosophy from the University of Oxford posthumously. In preparing the manuscript for publication, the thesis that was submitted and which is now available in the Bodleian Library has been abbreviated in two ways. Parts of Fr Lyons' discussion of Origen's background and teaching have been omitted, and some of his extremely thorough notes have been either omitted or substantially shortened. Otherwise the structure and text of the original thesis have been retained. I have received generous help from Dr E. J. Yarnold, S. J., who assisted with the reading of the proofs, and from Miss Margaret Pellow, who compiled the index.

# ACKNOWLEDGEMENTS

M. Claude Cuénot, Paris, for assistance with Teilhardian source material.

Rév. Henri de Lubac, S. J., Paris, for advice on Teilhardian background material.

Rév. Christian d'Armagnac, S. J., 'Les Fontaines', Chantilly, for assistance with and advice on Teilhardian source material.

Mr W. F. Toporowski, Oxford, for translating from Polish.

Mlle Jeanne Mortier, Fondation Teilhard de Chardin, Paris, for making available Teilhardian source material.

Mme S. Clair, Fondation Teilhard de Chardin, Paris, for assistance with Teilhardian source material.

Rév. Paul Mech, S. J., Centre-Sèvres, Paris, for library assistance.

Rév. Robert Brunet, S. J., 'Les Fontaines', Chantilly, for library assistance.

The Revd A. Meredith, S. J., Campion Hall, Oxford, for assistance in the background to Patristic studies.

The Revd B. Byrne, S. J., Campion Hall, Oxford, for assistance in New Testament studies.

The Revd A. Hamilton, S. J., Campion Hall, Oxford, for assistance in the background to Patristic studies.

The Revd J. Gill, S. J., Campion Hall, Oxford, for advice on stylistic matters.

The Revd Professor M. F. Wiles, Christ Church, Oxford, for directing the thesis.

The Revd Professor A. O. Dyson, University of Manchester, for assisting in the directing of the thesis.

Dr Karl Schmitz-Moormann, Bochum, for assistance with Teilhardian sources.

Professor Paul L'Archevêque, Université Laval, Québec, for assistance with the indexing of Teilhard's works.

The Revd Jerome Vereb, C. P., Campion Hall, Oxford, for assistance in ecumenical studies.

Margaret Koch, librarian, Institut Oecumenique, Château de Bossey, for information concerning a seminar conducted by Karl Barth.

The Very Reverend Henri Madelin, Provincial of the French Province of the Society of Jesus, for permission to quote from Teilhard de Chardin's unpublished journals and lectures.

# CONTENTS

# ABBREVIATIONS USED IN REFERRING TO THE WORKS OF TEILHARD de CHARDIN

| | |
|---|---|
| *AE* | *Activation of Energy* |
| *AM* | *The Appearance of Man* |
| *BT* | *Correspondence: Pierre Teilhard de Chardin and Maurice Blondel* |
| *CE* | *Christianity and Evolution* |
| *ETG* | *Écrits du temps de la Guerre (Grasset)* |
| *FM* | *The Future of Man* |
| *GP* | *Genèse d'une pensée* |
| *HE* | *Human Energy* |
| *HM* | *The Heart of Matter* |
| *HU* | *Hymn of the Universe* |
| *LE* | *Letters from Egypt, 1905–1908* |
| *LHP* | *Lettres d'Hastings et de Paris* |
| *LI* | *Lettres Intimes* |
| *LLZ* | *Letters to Leontine Zanta* |
| *LP* | *Letters from Paris, 1912–1914* |
| *LT* | *Letters from a Traveller, 1923–1955* |
| *LTF* | *Letters to Two Friends, 1926–1952* |
| *MD* | *Le Milieu Divin* |
| *MM* | *The Making of a Mind: Letters from a Soldier Priest* |
| *MPN* | *Man's Place in Nature* |
| *PM* | *The Phenomenon of Man* |
| *SC* | *Science and Christ* |
| *TF* | *Toward the Future* |
| *VP* | *The Vision of the Past* |
| *WTW* | *Writings in Time of War* |

# INTRODUCTION

DURING the 1960s the term 'cosmic Christ' and related expressions became widespread in theological discussion. The interest which the idea of a cosmic Christ then aroused has to a large extent subsided, leaving behind several problems only partially considered. The problems concern the meaning and application of 'cosmic Christ' and the effect which the idea of a cosmic Christ could have on Christology.

To refer to Christ as cosmic immediately suggests that he has a wider significance than God who becomes man in order to reveal himself to and to save human persons. 'Cosmic' implies that Christ is involved in some kind of universe. But without further specification it does not say how he is involved. Nor does it say what universe is being spoken about: whether, for example, the universe is the totality of human persons and, if they exist, of other rational creatures as well; or whether the universe includes sub-rational nature together with or apart from rational creatures. The meaning of 'cosmic Christ' depends both on Christ's relation to the cosmos and on the kind of cosmos to which he is related.

The term 'cosmic Christ' is recent. Its first occurrences date from the opening decades of the twentieth century; and its antecedents (such expressions as 'the cosmic significance of Christ' or 'Christ as a cosmic principle') appear to go back no further than the 1830s. This terminology embodies a peculiarly modern conception of Christ. In some of its manifestations, it has been employed to relate Christ to the universe as understood by natural science. More generally, it has worked as an integrating factor, bringing together – more and more during the course of its development – various doctrinal themes which in the past have not necessarily been linked with one another. When the epithet 'cosmic' is used of Christ, he is said to be the instrument in God's creative activity, the source and goal of all things, the bond and sustaining power of the whole creation; he is called the head and ruler of the universe; and his redemptive influence and his body are considered to extend to the limits of the created order. The application of 'cosmic Christ' to these doctrinal themes leaves open whether they are capable of systematic interconnection or whether their grouping is merely verbal.

Despite its modern origin and orientation, cosmic-Christ language has also been applied to teachings in the New Testament[1] and in the writings of patristic, medieval and other pre-nineteenth-century theologians.[2] It could be argued that the application is justified, at least with regard to the New Testament and to the writings of the Greek patristic theologians, on the grounds that 'cosmos' and 'cosmic' come from Greek and are to be found in those places. Certainly it is true that some more recent authors have taken into account the New Testament meanings of 'cosmos', above all as they occur in the Pauline epistles. The fact remains, however, that cosmic-Christ language has arisen without attention being too closely paid to the usage of 'cosmos' either in the Bible or in any other past work. What has happened during the last 150 years is that a new kind of Christological terminology has gradually come into existence. And the use of this terminology has caused some theologians not merely to ask certain questions about Christological doctrine but to claim that these questions have also been asked in the past. The forging of new theological terminology has led to new theological insights.

The modernity of cosmic-Christ language and its application to past theology give rise to a further problem: whether this language calls for a reshaping of Christology. T. S. Eliot once wrote:

> The existing monuments form an ideal order among themselves, which is modified by the introduction of the new (the really new) work of art among them. The existing order is complete before the new work arrives; for order to

---

1. The following are the New Testament texts usually cited in connection with the theme of the cosmic Christ: 1 Cor. 3: 21–3; 8: 6; 15: 20–8; 2 Cor. 5: 19; Rom. 8: 19–23; Phil. 2: 9–11; 3: 21; Col. 1: 15–20; 2: 9–10, 15, 19; 3: 11; Eph. 1: 4, 9–10, 20–3; 3: 9–11; 4: 9–10, 12–13, 15–16; Heb. 1: 2–4, 10; 2: 5–9; John 1: 1–18; Rev. 1: 17; 2: 8; 3: 14; 22: 13.
2. Cosmic-Christ doctrine has been attributed to the following Greek patristic theologians: Justin, Irenaeus, Clement of Alexandria, Origen, Athanasius, Gregory Nazianzen, Gregory of Nyssa, Cyril of Alexandria, Maximus the Confessor. Among the Latin patristic theologians, it has been attributed to Ambrose. Among the medievals, it has been attributed above all to Duns Scotus, and also to Bonaventure, Aquinas, Hugh of St. Victor and Eckhart. It has been attributed as well to Jacob Boehme and Friedrich Christoph Oetinger.

persist after the supervention of novelty, the *whole* existing order must be, if ever so slightly, altered . . .[3]

This comment on Western European literature refers to but a particular instance of a more general process in human thought. The process has relevance to Christology. The growth of cosmic-Christ language not only admits new themes into Christology or recalls themes from the teachings of the past; it also suggests the possibility of seeing Christology from a different perspective.

From time to time the remark has been made that the long-neglected cosmic aspect of Christ either is being, or ought to be, recovered. This seems to indicate some awareness of a shift in Christological perspective. At first, however, the shift is minimal. For example, Christ's role in the creating and sustaining of the universe may be regarded as no more than an expression of his divine significance. His risen humanity may be invoked to account for his headship of all creation. Or the extension of his redemptive influence and his body to the total created order may be conceived in terms of the Church's mission to all men. But the moment comes when the accepted Christological categories seem to fail. They are being required to contain more than has gone into their formation.

Classical Christology, which gave rise to, and is summed up in, the Chalcedonian definition, bears witness to the Christian belief that God has entered and become part of human history in order to save men. Cosmic-Christ language eventually moves beyond this frame of reference. There is, however, no question of its repudiating classical Christology. Nor is its task expressly to articulate those issues of contemporary Christology which, as John Macquarrie has pointed out,[4] have resulted from what the modern mind considers to be the defects of classical Christology. That is to say, cosmic-Christ language does not commit one to a Christology from below rather than from above. Furthermore, while it naturally tends to become a species of muted metaphysical language (descriptive as opposed to deductive), its character is not determined by an attempt either to elaborate or to play down a metaphysical account of the union between the uncreated and the created in Christ. Again, it has no immediate bearing on the problem of mythology *versus* historicity in the Gospels. And though its subject-matter is clearly related to the

3. 'Tradition and the Individual Talent', in *Selected Essays*, 2nd ed., 1934, p. 15.
4. 'Some Problems of Modern Christology', in *The Indian Journal of Theology*, vol. 23, 1974, pp. 158–9.

theme of Christ's solidarity with the human race, it is not explicitly employed to compensate for the scanty treatment of that theme in classical Christology. The intention behind cosmic-Christ language lies elsewhere. Pressed to its limits, this language says that what God as Christ does for men he also does for the whole of creation; and it asks the question, if to be involved with humanity God becomes man, what does he become to be involved with the whole of creation? There is, however, a problem explored by contemporary Christology which does receive explicit attention within the context of cosmic-Christ language; namely, whether Christ is unique.[5] But even here there is a difference. Generally speaking, contemporary Christology enquires about the possibility of a plurality of incarnations within the human race. Cosmic-Christ language, on the contrary, looks to such a possibility beyond humanity.

Chapter One of the present study traces the history of cosmic-Christ language from its beginnings in Germany in the 1830s up to the 1970s. It is only through such a historical investigation that the range of issues involved in this language can be discerned; and because no previous attempt has been made to carry out the investigation, it is presented here in detail and at some length. Three features stand out in the history of cosmic-Christ language. First, with one exception, those who have used this language have not considered how it might affect the classical doctrine of the person of Christ. The exception is Pierre Teilhard de Chardin. Second, until the 1960s, when it received widespread attention, cosmic-Christ language seems to have been transmitted along narrow channels, apart from the period between 1889 and about 1920. During these years British authors employed cosmic-Christ language with some frequency; and from 1910 onwards French theological writers took it up. Among the French was Teilhard. The third notable feature of the history in Chapter One concerns Teilhard himself. His writings show the most extensive and developed use of cosmic-Christ language of any author. Posthumously, he became one of the major contributors to the discussion on the cosmic Christ during the 1960s and also one of the important influences in the application of the term 'cosmic Christ' to theological teachings of the past.

Although Teilhard created no finished theological system, his writings on Christology over almost forty years made, through their cumulative effect, the most impressive systematic contribution in

5. See John Macquarrie, op. cit., pp. 159, 174–5.

modern times to the idea of a cosmic Christ. His treatment of Christ's cosmic aspect ranged over most of the doctrinal themes associated with it and eventually led him to regard it as a topic equivalent in status to the topics of Christ's divinity and humanity. This methodological step was responsible for his proposing a revision to the doctrine of the person of Christ. In his assertion that Christ is not only divine and human but also cosmic, he assumed the Chalcedonian definition as a theological datum and tried to combine with it what can only be described as an Arian-type conception of Christ.

Teilhard believed that his task in Christology was to retrieve a long-neglected New Testament teaching which was essential for accommodating Christianity to the modern world. In carrying out this task, he considered himself to be at one with the Greek Fathers. He was endeavouring to understand Christ in relation to modern cosmology, just as they had attempted to understand Christ within the context of ancient cosmological views. From among the Greek Fathers Origen in particular has been compared with Teilhard. Teilhard himself seems to have had Origen in mind as he developed his conception of the cosmic Christ. The comparison of Origen with Teilhard is especially apt, inasmuch as Origen presented the Son not merely as a divine hypostasis but also as a subordinate cosmic principle and thereby helped sow the seeds of Arianism.

In Chapter Two of this study we shall examine the grounds for making a comparison between Origen's conception of the Son and Teilhard's cosmic Christ. The comparison is based partly on Teilhard's awareness of Origen, but more particularly on the similarity of Christological questions which they both tried to answer.

In the chapters of Parts Two and Three we shall discuss Origen and Teilhard in turn. The introductory chapter to the section on each author's position deals with the fundamental problem in cosmic Christology which he inherited from his background. For both Origen and Teilhard this problem concerned mediation between the absolute and the contingent, between Creator and creatures.

In Part Four, which concludes this study, a comparison is made between the positions of Origen and Teilhard, in order to consider the possibility of treating the cosmic Christ as an independent topic in systematic Christology.

# PART I
# THE PROBLEM OF THE COSMIC CHRIST

## 1. THE HISTORY OF COSMIC-CHRIST TERMINOLOGY

### I. LINGUISTIC BACKGROUND

COSMIC-Christ terminology is a product of the nineteenth and early twentieth centuries. It made its appearance in German during the 1830s and 1840s; and in 1849 it was taken up by a Danish theologian. It entered English in 1857. French theologians seem to have begun using it in 1910, though as early as 1840 there is an isolated instance in French by a non-theological writer. No evidence has come to light to suggest that the terminology was employed before the nineteenth century.

Its emergence and development appear to have been spontaneous rather than premeditated. They were probably due to the greater frequency and the expanding range of meanings with which 'cosmos' and its derivatives were used during the nineteenth century. That certainly was the case for these words in English. And, according to the lexical information available, a similar situation prevailed in French. For German only fragmentary information about these words exists; but what little there is agrees with the general picture presented by English and French.

In German, the adjective 'kosmisch' seems first to have been recorded in 1804, with the meanings 'worldly' and 'pertaining to the world'.[1] In 1817 it was given in the sense of 'universal' ('allweltlich').[2] Like 'kosmisch', 'Kosmologie' and 'kosmologisch' were in existence by 1804. The former had a scientific application; while the latter was employed in both science and natural theology and also meant 'pertaining to the universe'.[3] The root word 'Kosmos' appears to have gained currency only after the publication of Alexander von Humboldt's *Kosmos: Entwurf einer physischen Weltbeschreibung,* 1845–62. It is recorded as meaning 'universe' and 'the world considered as an ordered unity (as opposed to chaos)'.[4]

In French[5] the adjective 'cosmique', in the sense of 'pertaining to the cosmos or universe considered in its totality', had existed since the end of the fourteenth century. Further senses, however, were not added to the word until the nineteenth century. In 1862 it appeared with the meaning 'on the scale of the universe'; and in 1863 it was used with reference to interstellar space. Towards the end of the century it acquired the further meaning of 'immeasurable or vertiginous like the universe'. The noun 'cosmologie' and its adjective 'cosmologique' were present in the language by the late sixteenth century. But 'cosmos' did not enter it until 1821.[6] Its meaning is given as 'the universe considered as an organized totality'. Another meaning, 'interstellar space', was added in 1959.

In English[7] the oldest of these words is the adjective 'cosmical', dating from 1583 in the rare and obsolete sense of 'geographical' or 'belonging to the earth'. In the sense of 'pertaining to the universe as an ordered system or relating to the sum totality of things', 'cosmical'

1. See J. C. A. Heyse, *Allgemeines Wörterbuch zur Verdeutschung und Erklärung der in unserer Sprache gebräuchlichen fremden Wörter und Redensarten,* 1804, p. 181.
2. See F. E. Petri, *Gedrängtes Verdeutschungswörterbuch der in unserer Bücher–und Umgangssprache häufig oder selten vorkommenden fremden Ausdrücke,* 3. Auflage, 1817, p. 267.
3. See Heyse, op. cit., pp. 181–2.
4. See H. Schmidt, *Philosophisches Wörterbuch,* 1931, pp. 235–6.
5. See L. Guilbert *et al.* (ed.), *Grand Larousse de la langue française,* tome 2, 1972, pp. 1000–1; P. Imbs (ed.), *Trésor de la langue française: Dictionnaire de la langue du XIXe et du XXe siècle (1789–1960),* tome 6, 1978, pp. 251–5.
6. The *Grand Larousse* is incorrect in stating that 'cosmos' entered French in 1847. It had already been used in Joseph de Maistre, *Les Soirées de Saint-Pétersbourg, ou Entretiens sur le gouvernement temporel de la Providence, suivis d'un Traité sur les sacrifices,* Paris, 1821, tome 1, p. 118 (Bruxelles, 1837, tome 1, p. 101).
7. See J. A. H. Murray *et al.* (ed.), *A New English Dictionary on Historical Principles,* vol. 2, pp. 1031–3; R. W. Burchfield (ed.), *Supplement to the Oxford English Dictionary,* vol. 1, 1972, p. 648.

is recorded as having been used first in 1685 but not again until 1850.[8] Thereafter it recurred regularly. About the middle of the nineteenth century 'cosmical' acquired further meanings: 'relating to the cosmos', 'belonging to the material universe as distinguished from the earth', 'extraterrestrial' and 'characteristic of the vast scale of the universe'.

The adjective 'cosmic', which had previously meant 'this-worldly', now came to be employed as a synonym for 'cosmical'. And it took on the additional meanings of 'universal', 'infinite' and 'immense'.

The noun 'cosmology', in both a scientific and a philosophical sense, had existed in English well before the nineteenth century. But there is no known instance of its adjective 'cosmological' until 1825.

The root word 'cosmos', in the sense of 'the world or universe as an ordered system', is recorded as having been used first in 1650 but not again till 1848, after which it became common. During the latter half of the nineteenth century 'cosmos' came to be employed in two additional ways. It assumed the meaning of 'any kind of ordered system' (for example, the system of perceptions which constitutes the sum total of one's experience). And, in the abstract sense of 'order and harmony in general', it was explicitly contrasted with its antonym 'chaos'.

Finally, there is the word 'cosmosophical', which in its German form 'kosmosophisch' plays a part in the first instance of cosmic-Christ terminology. This we shall comment on, when we come to the author in whose work it is found.

The nineteenth-century usage of 'cosmos' and its derivatives parallels the usage of κόσμος and κοσμικός in Greek, whether classical, New Testament or patristic, on two points. In both usages, the words may refer to the world or universe as a well-ordered system or to the sum totality of things; and they may indicate that which lies beyond the earth – the firmament or heavens for the ancient usage, and extraterrestrial existence for the modern. In other respects, however, there are divergences.

Thus, according to the ancient usage, the meaning of κόσμος and κοσμικός may be related to the moral order or to human society. In particular, the New Testament frequently conceives the cosmos as the theatre of human history and of God's salvific work among men.

8. The absence of a quotation for 'cosmical' between 1685 and 1850 is indicative of the word's rarity during this period. Normally the editors of the *New English Dictionary* try to include at least one quotation per century for each sense of a word; see vol. 1, p. xxii.

Patristic Greek carries on this sense, when it takes the cosmos to be the inhabitants of the world who constitute the sphere of the Church's life and influence. The adjective in patristic Greek becomes further specialized with the meaning 'worldly or secular', as opposed to 'spiritual or clerical'. New Testament and patristic Greek may also understand the cosmos as this present world, which will pass away with the establishment of God's kingdom or the next life. The dualistic systems of Gnosticism supply a variant on this sense. For them the cosmos is the realm of the Demiurge which lies outside the pneumatic or divine realm of the Pleroma.

The modern usage, on the other hand, tends specifically to convey the immensity of the universe disclosed by the natural sciences. It is unlikely, unless some special context is signalled, to involve reference to the moral or the social or to connote the secular as opposed to the spiritual or this world as opposed to the next. In discussions on the Gnostic systems, however, the modern usage – particularly of the words 'cosmology' and 'cosmological' – normally implies the viewpoint of these systems.

To the extent that the modern and the ancient usages coincide, cosmic-Christ terminology reflects the usage of 'cosmos' in Greek. That is to say, it relates Christ to the sum totality of the created order and concludes by emphasizing that this relationship extends beyond the compass of earthly affairs. Some authors, especially those giving weight to the social dimension in the New Testament use of 'cosmos', seem to suggest that Christ's place in human history is his principal – possibly his sole – ontological link with the cosmos and not simply humanity's entrée to communion with the Christ who pervades the cosmos. Inevitably, however, cosmic-Christ terminology points beyond the narrow confines of human history. Having emerged against the background of the nineteenth century's expanding cosmic vocabulary, the outcome of its growing knowledge and consideration of the universe, this language is open to representing Christ as a person of scarcely imaginable magnitude and power, for whom involvement with terrestrial events is but an episode in his operations within a far wider world process.

It would be surprising if such a line of thinking did not set up a tension between conjecture and experience. Cosmic-Christ terminology seems to move in speculative regions outside of, and perhaps even at variance with, the Christian's actual experience of Christ. And yet, in its endeavour to relate Christ to the cosmos as a whole, it does no more than explicate certain aspects in the New

Testament experience of Christ. This, however, is not the only tension in cosmic-Christ terminology. A further tension is created by its expression of the cosmos itself. At one extreme, as we shall see in the earlier attempts by Germanic authors to situate Christ in the cosmos, the terminology may simply be a formulation based on *a priori* metaphysics or on mere biblicism. That way of putting the matter was necessarily superseded, with the expectation, fostered by scientific progress, that empirical observation should regulate the idea of the cosmos. But empirical observation has coherence and meaning for the observer only within the framework of theory, while theory for its part requires a return to the *a priori*. In the history of cosmic-Christ terminology that follows there is no neat resolution at the end. What does appear, however, is a broadening conception of who Christ is. It is a conception which has its roots in the New Testament; which eventually becomes accommodated to the modern world's view of the universe; which relies on philosophical reflection to achieve consistency; and which poses a new question for the history of Christology.

## II  GERMANIC BEGINNINGS

The starting-point for the history of cosmic-Christ terminology seems to be the Swiss schoolmaster, Leonhard Usteri the Younger. In his book on the development of Pauline doctrine (1824),[9] Usteri was the first author to reduce the theology of St. Paul to a system.[10] He conceived Pauline theology as a philosophy of history, comprising the time of ignorance and the fulness of time, with the coming of Christ marking their meeting-point. During the latter period the Christian community rapidly developed its notion of Christ. In the fourth edition of his work (1832), Usteri gave the following account of the situation. Jewish philosophical speculation, elaborated above all in Alexandria but based upon the Old Testament, so removed God as the ultimate ground of existence from the immediate reality of the world, that it became necessary to postulate a mediating divine

9. *Entwickelung des Paulinischen Lehrbegriffes in seinem Verhältnisse zur biblischen Dogmatik des neuen Testamentes.*
10. Cf. F. Prat, 'Paul (saint) et le paulinisme', in A. d'Alès (ed.), *Dictionnaire apologétique de la foi catholique*, 4e éd., tome 3, col. 1622–3; id., *La Théologie de saint Paul*, 2e partie, 6e éd., 1923, p. 568 (E. T., *The Theology of Saint Paul*, vol. 2, p. 478); W. G. Kümmel, *The New Testament: The History of the Investigation of Its Problems*, p. 95.

principle between God and the world. This principle was the λόγος προφορικός, the Word of God or the revelation of the Godhead. To the conception of a mediating divine principle was assimilated the title 'Son of God'. It had probably been applied to Jesus during his lifetime in a messianic sense, though within a tradition of philosophical and theological speculation. But with the spread of Christianity and the accompanying glorification of Jesus, it underwent development. 'To this expression υἱὸς τοῦ θεοῦ, which was understood not merely in an ethical but in an eminently metaphysical or cosmic sense, there were now attached theosophical and cosmosophical speculations.'[11].

The equating of 'metaphysical' and 'cosmic' in this quotation is characteristic of the earliest forms of cosmic-Christ terminology. We shall shortly meet further examples of conceiving 'cosmic' in this way. The peculiarity of the quotation consists in its use of 'theosophical' and 'cosmosophical'. The word 'theosophy' (with its derivations) was revived in the Western European languages during the seventeenth century to refer to doctrines based on divine wisdom, those of such mystics as Eckhart, Ruysbroek, and Boehme. On the analogy of 'theosophy', historians of philosophy appear to have coined 'cosmosophy' (and its derivatives) early in the nineteenth century to refer to doctrines based on worldly wisdom, those of such diverse authors as Paracelsus, Bruno, and Francis Bacon.[12] Clearly Usteri has not used 'theosophical' and 'cosmosophical' in the precise technical sense employed by the historians of philosophy. Nevertheless, by introducing this contrasting pair of terms, he appears to have had in mind the idea that, right from the beginning of the history of Christology, the understanding of Christ has been determined not merely by sources of divine revelation but also by man's conception of the cosmos. The idea that one's conception of the cosmos contributes to an understanding of Christ eventually came to play an important role in English-speaking theologians and in Teilhard.

After Usteri the cosmic aspect of Christ became for a while the province of systematic theology. During 1835 and 1836 I. A. Dorner

---

11. L. Usteri, op. cit., 4. Ausgabe, 1832, p. 303.
12. For the history of 'theosophy', see J. A. H. Murray et al. (ed.), A New English Dictionary on Historical Principles, vol. 9, part 2, [section 2], p. 279. The English word 'cosmosophy' is not recorded as having been used before 1848; see op. cit., vol. 2, p. 1031. Undoubtedly it was borrowed from the German 'Kosmosophie'. For the technical use of 'theosophy' and 'cosmosophy' in the history of philosophy, see J. E. Erdmann, Grundriss der Geschichte der Philosophie, 1866, 1. Bd., pp. 467–70, 502 (E. T., A History of Philosophy, 1890, vol. 1, pp. 546–7, 595).

published the preliminary sketch of his great work on the development of Christology.[13] At the end of this he asserted that Christianity requires us to go beyond the merely anthropological view of Christ which Schleiermacher had adopted. To deal with the unique and transcendent character of the God-man we need a metaphysical standpoint. Like the individual first Adam, Christ the second Adam sums up in himself as an individual the multiplicity of the natural creation. But Christ is also the head of the spiritual creation; and as such he 'points out away from and beyond humanity to a so to speak cosmic or, as we have termed it above, metaphysical significance of his person'.[14]

In so describing Christ, Dorner had anticipated a Christological theme that arose soon afterwards, in reaction to D. F. Strauss's *Life of Jesus*, published in 1835 and 1836, the same years that his own sketch in the history of Christology appeared. Strauss suggested[15] that the Incarnation is not confined to Jesus but extends to the whole of humanity. If Strauss's position were admitted, Jesus could not be maintained as the Christ, the unique incarnation of God's Word, in whom the human race finds its principle of unity. In a reply to Strauss in 1838, C. F. Göschel described Christ in terms of the 'central individual',[16] a notion which features in Hegel's *Science of Logic*. According to this notion, individuals belong to a class not because they possess some abstract property in common, but rather because they are all related to a concrete individual – the central member of their class – which is the exhaustive and the absolute embodiment of everything they are able to be.[17] Subsequently, the notion of central

13. 'Ueber die Entwicklungsgeschichte der Christologie, besonders in den neuern Zeiten: Eine historisch-kritische Abhandlung', in *Tübinger Zeitschrift für Theologie*, Jahrgang 1835, 4. Heft, pp. 81–204; Jahrgang 1836, 1. Heft, pp. 96–240.

14. Ibid., Jahrgang 1836, 1. Heft, pp. 238–9.

15. *The Life of Jesus Critically Examined*, E. T. by George Eliot, ed. by P. C. Hodgson, 1973, section 151, p. 780.

16. C. F. Göschel, *Beiträge zur spekulativen Philosophie von Gott und dem Menschen und von dem Gott-Menschen: Mit Rücksicht auf Dr. D. F. Strauss Christologie*, 1838, pp. 42–6, 60–7. Cf. I. A. Dorner, *Entwicklungsgeschichte der Lehre von der Person Christi*, 2. Aufl., 2. Theil, 2. Abtheilung, 1856, pp. 1143–53, 1151–2 n. 69 (E. T., *History of the Development of the Doctrine of the Person of Christ*, division 2, vol. 3, pp. 168–73, 299–300); E. Günther, *Die Entwicklung der Lehre von der Person Christi im XIX. Jahrhundert*, pp. 152–4; W. Pannenberg, *Jesus – God and Man*, pp. 388–9; G. Rupp, *Christologies and Cultures: Towards a Typology of Religious Worldviews*, pp. 140–4.

17. See G. W. F. Hegel, *Science of Logic*, vol. 2, section 2, ch. 1 C (a), E. T. by A. V. Miller, 1969, pp. 721–4.

individual played a part in systematic presentations of the cosmic aspect of Christ, above all by Richard Rothe, but also by the Danish theologian and friend of Dorner, H. L. Martensen, and then by Dorner himself.

Rothe dealt with this matter in the second volume of his *Theologische Ethik* (1845). According to his *assumptus-homo* Christology, it is only when the second Adam has transcended every material limitation that he becomes united absolutely with God. The union occurs at the moment of his death, which is also the moment of his resurrection. It is at this moment that the second Adam breaks through all barriers of physical existence, to be assumed into the superphysical (supermaterial) cosmic existence ('in das übersinnliche (übermaterielle) kosmische Sein') of God himself.[18] From his conception of the second Adam's union with God, Rothe drew several conclusions. The second Adam in his divine state of cosmic existence is not merely the central individual of humanity; he is also the head of all central individuals from every zone of spiritual creation.[19] And, as by degrees he assimilates the whole of humanity to himself, so too he assimilates it to the divinity. The consequence of this assimilation, Rothe inferred, is that the cosmic existence of the divinity is undergoing a process of expansion.[20]

Rothe took up again the cosmic aspect of Christ in his *Dogmatik*, published posthumously in 1870.[21] His representations of this theme remained essentially the same as his first treatment of it. Of more interest, as a further development in the application of cosmic-Christ terminology, is a work published in 1847, for which Rothe supplied an introduction. This was a book by C. A. Auberlen on the eighteenth-century theologian F. C. Oetinger,[22] 'the father of Swabian Christian theosophy'.[23] According to Auberlen, Oetinger and his school did not follow the general approach of Reformation theology by placing emphasis on the Epistle to the Romans; instead, they recognized the importance of Ephesians and Colossians, which gave prominence to the cosmic mode of interpreting Christianity.[24]

18. R. Rothe, *Theologische Ethik*, 2. Bd., 1845, pp. 291–4.
19. Ibid., p. 296.
20. Ibid., pp. 301–2.
21. 2. Theil, 1. Abtheilung, pp. 118–25, 172–5, 179.
22. *Die Theosophie Friedrich Christoph Oetinger's nach ihren Grundzügen.*
23. E. Benz, *Evolution and Christian Hope: Man's Concept of the Future from the Early Fathers to Teilhard de Chardin*, p. 168.
24. Auberlen, op. cit., p. 233 note. See F. C. Oetinger, *Theologia ex Idea Vitae Deducta in Sex Locos Redacta*, 1765, p. 322.

For Oetinger, the whole life of Jesus, from conception to death, expressed the cosmic significance of Christ; situated between the creation and the consummation of the world, its influence has pervaded all things.[25] But death did not bring Christ's work to an end; it was only after his death that it assumed its complete cosmic significance of imparting spiritual life to all creatures in heaven and on earth.[26] Auberlen's application of cosmic-Christ terminology to the doctrine of a theologian in the past was incidental; and no doubt it was made without any awareness that a new mode of theological expression was beginning to take shape. Before Auberlen, Usteri had used the terminology in biblical theology, while Dorner and Rothe had done so in systematic questions. By employing it in a historical discussion, Auberlen had completed the range of its application to the various fields of theology in which it would thenceforth be found.

In his *Christian Dogmatics* (1849) Martensen, like Dorner, rejected Schleiermacher's Christology. Besides a religious and ethical significance, Christ also has a cosmic significance, since he is the revelation of God's creative Word and the head not just of the Church but of the whole of creation.[27] As the head of creation, he is the centre of the human race, as well as the centre of all principalities and powers, of everything visible and invisible throughout the universe.[28] This is the doctrine of the Apostle Paul in Ephesians and Colossians; and it was appropriated by the earliest teachers of the Church, such as Irenaeus.[29] What this doctrine implies is that Christ's mediation between God and the world through the Incarnation does not depend upon the presence of sin in the world.[30] Thus, following the Scotist position on the motive for the Incarnation, which enjoyed a revival during the 1830s and 1840s,[31] Martensen conceived Christ's role as world-perfecter to be logically prior to his role as world-redeemer.

For Martensen, Christ's cosmic significance extends both to the Incarnation and to the Redemption. The Incarnation is the beginning

---

25. Auberlen, op. cit., p. 499 note. See Oetinger, op. cit., p. 360.
26. Auberlen, op. cit., p. 249. See F. C. Oetinger, op. cit., p. 198. See also E. Zinn, *Die Theologie des Friedrich Christoph Oetinger*, 1932, pp. 133–7.
27. H. L. Martensen, *Den Christelige Dogmatik*, 1849, p. 278 (E. T., *Christian Dogmatics*, pp. 272–3).
28. Ibid., pp. 266, 268 (pp. 261–3).
29. Ibid., p. 266 (p. 261). On the cosmic significance of Christ in the Gospels, see ibid., p. 247 (pp. 241–2).
30. Ibid., pp. 265–6 (pp. 260–1); also p. 174 (p. 171).
31. Cf. E. TeSelle, *Christ in Context*, p. 110.

of a spiritual dimension in the human race, a dimension beyond explanation in terms of natural law;[32] while the Redemption results from a struggle in which Christ pits his will against the cosmic principle, the principle of the world.[33] This is the principle to which the first Adam succumbed, instead of adhering to the principle of holiness (that is, to God),[34] and which thereby became the power of evil or the devil.[35] The cosmic principle is evil to the extent that it does not acknowledge its creaturely status; for the principle upon which the world ultimately depends is the Son.[36] The cosmic power of our Lord, however, does not fully appear during his earthly life; its complete manifestation occurs only after his death.[37] His descent into the kingdom of the dead indicates the universal efficacy of this power.[38] But only when he returns as judge of the world will his power become evident in every part of the spiritual creation.[39]

In a much later work, his study on the theosophy of Jacob Boehme (1881), Martensen returned briefly to the theme of Christ's cosmic significance.[40] According to Martensen, Boehme attributed to Christ not simply an ethical but also a cosmic significance, since for him Christ was the head and redeemer of the whole creation. By representing Christ primarily as the Redeemer, whose coming was occasioned by sin, Boehme reflected the outlook of the Reformation period, during which he lived. But, urged Martensen, Boehme's conception of the cosmic significance of Christ leads rather to the view that, even in the absence of sin, Christ would have come, not indeed as the saviour of creation, but as its consummator. In another respect, however, Boehme appreciated the import of Christ's cosmic significance, inasmuch as he saw no contradiction between the biblical idea of the world and the idea of the universe to which the Copernican revolution in astronomy has given rise.

Following in the steps of Rothe and Martensen, Dorner elaborated his treatment of Christ's cosmic significance in the second edition of

32. Martensen, op. cit., p. 21 (p. 18); also p. 281 (p. 276).
33. Ibid., p. 289 (p. 284).
34. Ibid., pp. 176–7 (p. 174).
35. Ibid., pp. 186–7, 194–7, 200, 202 (pp. 183–4, 190–3, 197–8).
36. Ibid., p. 194 (p. 190).
37. Ibid., pp. 321–2 (p. 315).
38. Ibid., p. 322 (p. 316).
39. Ibid., pp. 483–4 (p. 474).
40. *Jacob Bøhme: Theosophiske Studier*, pp. 221–2 (E. T. by T. Rhys Evans, *Jacob Boehme: His Life and Teaching, or Studies in Theosophy*, 1885, pp. 256–8; revised by S. Hobhouse, *Jacob Boehme (1575–1624): Studies in His life and Teaching*, 1949, p. 149).

his history of Christology. The relevant passages in this work occur in the final section, published in 1856.[41] Like Martensen, Dorner took up a Scotist position on the motive for the Incarnation. Without the Incarnation the world would have no principle of unity. The world is unified through its susceptibility to God ('Gottempfänglichkeit'), which God bestows on the world by his absolute self-revelation in the Incarnation and which the world in its turn centres upon the incarnate Logos. Thus, in the words of Irenaeus,[42] Christ recapitulates in himself the long narrative of men. They are words which shed light not only on the Old Testament but on extrabiblical history as well; and the more they do so, the more will Christ be recognized as the centre of history, both backwards and forwards. It is in his humanity that Christ is the central individual – the cosmic unifying principle – of the world. As this principle, he is no mere assemblage of the world's multiplicity. It is only by virtue of his divinity, by virtue of his being more than merely a cosmic principle, that he is able to act as this principle.[43]

Dorner's final contribution to the cosmic aspect of Christ, in the second volume of his long-awaited *System of Christian Doctrine* (1880), was largely a restatement of his earlier position.[44] One of his observations here, however, deserves mention.[45] If like Strauss we were to regard Christ as the *Homo generalis* – understood in a physical, not a nominalistic sense – we should be professing pan-Christism, which is but a species of pantheism. Such a doctrine would ultimately undermine the incarnation of the Logos in the human race; for, unless the incarnate Logos were an individual, he would lack the necessary *homoousia* with men. Pan-Christism in this sense, it should be noted, is quite different from the view which later on Blondel and

41. I. A. Dorner, *Entwicklungsgeschichte der Lehre von der Person Christi*, 2. Aufl., 2. Theil, 2. Abtheilung, pp. 1227–44; also pp. 1145–6 n. 61, 1229–35 n. 23, 1237–8 n. 23, 1245 n. 24 (E. T., *History of the Development of the Doctrine of the Person of Christ*, division 2, vol. 3, pp. 232–7; also pp. 298–9, 313–19, 321–3, 326).

42. *Adv. Haer.* 3: 19: 1, ed. Harvey, vol. 2, p. 95.

43. See also I. A. Dorner, 'Luther's Theology', in *The Contemporary Review*, vol. 3, 1866, p. 574. Here Dorner nuances his position. God, who is invisible and incapable of being apprehended by man in his present state, becomes 'visible, apprehensible, *cosmical*, so to speak . . . in the Incarnation. . . . The power and essence which belong to the inner Word in the Trinity, in the eternal self-determination of the Deity, dwell also in the temporal or cosmical self-determination of the Deity, viz., in the Word made flesh'.

44. I. A. Dorner, *System der christlichen Glaubenslehre*, 2. Bd., pp. 422–30 (E. T., *A System of Christian Doctrine*, vol. 3, pp. 319–27).

45. Ibid., pp. 423–4 (E. T., vol. 3, pp. 320–1).

Teilhard were to put forward. For them pan-Christism meant that Christ as the substantial bond of the universe (he in whom all things hold together, Col. 1:17) unites everything from above without in any way submerging either his own or any other being's individuality.[46]

With the aging of Dorner's generation, the reserve towards metaphysics that was centred on the Ritschlian school brought speculative theology into disfavour.[47] Looking back on the development of German theology during the previous hundred years, Otto Pfleiderer in 1890 expressed his inability to sympathize with Rothe's system and with the cosmic Christology of Dorner and Martensen.[48] At the turn of the century, Adolf von Harnack summed up the theological mood in Germany, when he referred to the identification which 'Greek philosophers' had made between Christ and the Logos:

> It gave metaphysical significance to an historical fact; it drew into the domain of cosmology and religious philosophy a person who had appeared in time and space. . . .
> Most of us regard this identification as inadmissible, because the way in which we conceive the world and ethics does not point to the existence of any logos at all.[49]

For German Protestants, Liberalism was in the ascendancy. Having abandoned the theme of Christ's cosmic significance, theologians left it to the biblical scholars as a matter for historical investigation. Prominent among these was Bernhard Weiss. His *Biblical Theology of the New Testament* (1866) provided a more thorough account of the relationship between creation and redemption – and hence of Christ's cosmic significance – than had

---

46. For Blondel's pan-Christism, see M. Blondel and J. Wehrlé *Correspondance (extraits)*, vol. 1, pp. 98–9; M. Blondel, *Lettres philosophiques*, p. 235; id., *Une Énigme historique: Le 'vinculum substantiale' d'après Leibniz et l'ébauche d'un réalisme superieur*, pp. 105–6, 143–5. For further texts and for comments, see M. Blondel and A. Valensin, *Correspondance (1899–1912)*, tome 1, pp. 43–8; id., *Correspondance*, tome 3, *Extraits de la correspondance de 1912 à 1947*, pp. 156–7, 170–1, 179; *BT*, pp. 20–1, 52–3 (E. T., pp. 22–3, 58–9); C. Troisfontaines (ed.), *Maurice Blondel, Le Lien substantiel et la substance composée d'après Leibniz: Texte latin (1893)*, pp. 128–31.
47. Cf. C. Welch, *Protestant Thought in the Nineteenth Century*, vol. 1, *1799–1870*, p. 273 n. 7.
48. See O. Pfleiderer, *The Development of Theology in Germany since Kant*, 1890, pp. 148–53, 163, 167.
49. A. von Harnack, *Das Wesen des Christentums*, 1900, p. 128 (E. T., *What is Christianity?*, pp. 204–5).

previous works in this field.[50] Dealing with Paul's captivity letters, Weiss discussed in turn the cosmic significance of Christ and the work of salvation in its cosmic relation. Like the systematic theologians before him, he placed Christ at the centre of the universe. But his notable contribution was a more fully developed presentation of cosmic redemption. Since the divine purpose of salvation for the whole created universe precedes creation and is thereby regulative for it, both salvation and creation must be grounded on the one mediator between God and creatures. Consequently, the scope of Christ's redemption is cosmic; it includes angels as well as men, and it dissolves the opposition, brought about by sin, between the heavenly and the earthly worlds.

For Weiss the cosmic aspect of Christ in the captivity letters was but a late development of Paul's theology.[51] Weiss's younger contemporaries, H. J. Holtzmann and Otto Pfleiderer, believed on the contrary that it was a post-Pauline doctrine. Holtzmann in his critique of Ephesians and Colossians (1872)[52] and Pfleiderer in his work on Paulinism (1873)[53] both pointed to the shift in Christology that occurs from 1 Cor. 8: 6 to Col. 1: 16 and 1: 20. In 1 Cor. 8: 6 Paul sees all things existing not only from the Father but also for him (εἰς αὐτόν); Christ simply mediates God's act of creation. In contrast, Col. 1: 16 and 1: 20 apply the εἰς αὐτόν to Christ himself; it is he who is now looked upon as the goal of creation. More generally, the conception of Christ in Ephesians and Colossians as the cosmic principle or centre of creation well accords with the Alexandrian Logos and clearly anticipates Johannine Christology, but it has little to do with Paul's idea of the heavenly man or the second Adam. As examples of Christ conceived as a cosmic principle, Pfleiderer cited Eph. 4: 10 (Christ is he who ascended to fill all things) and Col. 1: 17 (Christ is he in whom all things hold together).[54] In his later work on New Testament theology (1897), Holtzmann was prepared to admit that in 1 Cor. 8: 6 Paul assigns Christ a cosmic position ('eine

50. Cf. J. G. Gibbs, *Creation and Redemption: A Study in Pauline Theology*, pp. 9, 17.
51. B. Weiss, *Lehrbuch der Biblischen Theologie des neuen Testaments*, 1868, p. 431 (3 Aufl., 1880, p 413) (E. T., *Biblical Theology of the New Testament*, vol. 2, p. 75).
52. *Kritik der Epheser–und Kolosserbriefe*, pp. 227–35.
53. *Der Paulinismus*, pp. 372–4 (E. T., *Paulinism.*, vol. 2, pp. 101–3).
54. Op. cit., pp. 439–40 (E. T., vol. 2, pp. 170–1). See also id., *Lectures on the Influence of the Apostle Paul on the Development of Christianity*, 1885, p. 218. Here Pfleiderer discusses the cosmic position of Christ with reference to Col. 1: 15–19; 2: 9.

kosmische Stellung'),[55] but in other respects he retained his former opinion.

The search by Holtzmann and Pfleiderer for the authentic Pauline teaching was a product of the Tübingen school, stemming from F. C. Baur, which more and more called the single authorship of the Pauline corpus into question.[56] When the history of religions school arose near the beginning of the twentieth century, the search for the authentic Pauline teaching remained, though now it was less a question of distinguishing author from author than of going behind the mode of expression. Thus Rudolf Bultmann endeavoured to retrieve the purity of the Pauline message from its Hellenistic adaptation, expressed in terms of the cosmic mythology of Gnosticism, and then to reinterpret it for the modern age as a kind of existentialism.[57] On the other hand, Ernst Lohmeyer in his discussion of Phil. 2: 5–11 concluded that faith in Jesus Christ as agent of cosmic reconciliation was first proclaimed in the Jerusalem Church and that the manner of expressing this faith was inherited from Jewish sources, which had fused the Old Testament themes of Servant of Yahweh and Son of Man with an Iranian myth of the Primal Man.[58] Despite an often negative attitude towards the cosmic aspect of Christ in the Pauline writings, the German biblical theologians at least continued to draw attention to its presence there. We shall touch on their influence once again, when we examine the controversy about cosmic Christology among German Evangelicals during the 1960s.

Collectively, the nineteenth-century theologians of the Germanic world whom we have been considering created a climate for referring to Christ as cosmic. Their achievement was threefold. They introduced the theme of Christ's cosmic significance into the fields of biblical, systematic and historical theology, each of which was to play its part in shaping the idea of a cosmic Christ. They applied cosmic language to Christ's work as well as to his person, thereby opening up the broad issues associated with cosmic Christology. And with their various approaches to Christ's cosmic significance, they indicated

55. *Lehrbuch der neutestamentlichen Theologie*, 1897, 2. Bd., pp. 245–6; see p. 83.
56. Cf. Gibbs, op. cit., pp. 9, 15, 27.
57. See R. Bultmann, *Theologie des Neuen Testaments*, 1. Lieferung, 1948, pp. 130–3, 162–82, 186–8, 224–6, 299–300; also pp. 249–55 (E. T., *Theology of the New Testament*, vol. 1, pp. 132–3, 164–83, 190–1, 228–31, 304–5; also pp. 254–9).
58. See E. Lohmeyer, *Kyrios Jesus: Eine Untersuchung zur Phil. 2, 5–11*, 1928, pp. 13, 68–9, 73–5; id., *Der Brief an die Philipper*, 1928, pp. 97–8, 97 nn. 4 and 6.

some of the potentialities in the cosmic terminology that was to promote more ample conceptions of Christ. Thus, while Rothe saw Christ's cosmic aspect as pertaining to the divinity into which the second Adam is assumed, Martensen and Dorner, according to their understanding of Christ as central individual, related his cosmic aspect to the Incarnation, that is, to his created nature. The uncertainty as to whether the cosmic aspect of Christ should be viewed in connection with his divinity or with his humanity left the way open for extending the idea of Christ beyond the divine Logos incarnate in Jesus of Nazareth. Indeed, such an extension of the idea of Christ seems already to have been present for a fleeting moment when, in the preliminary sketch of his Christological history, Dorner located Christ's cosmic significance beyond humanity, in his headship of the spiritual creation. What Dorner had done was to foreshadow a distinction, to be drawn much later, between an anthropic and a cosmic dimension of the Incarnation. Likewise, in their attempt to separate Pauline from post-Pauline Christology, Holtzmann and Pfleiderer also pointed to such a distinction, by contrasting the conception of Christ as the heavenly man or the second Adam with the conception of him as a cosmic principle. The developments in Christological thinking to which cosmic language in the long run gave rise led in various directions, not all of them consistent with one another. On one point, however, the different ways of approaching the cosmic aspect of Christ do show consistency: none of them represents a revival of Strauss's theory that Christ is a generic idea rather than a particular individual.

A generation after Holtzmann and Pfleiderer, Albert Schweitzer in *Paul and His Interpreters* (1911) and again in *The Mysticism of Paul the Apostle* (1930) maintained that for Paul the redemptive death and resurrection of Jesus Christ is a cosmic, eschatological event. This event, universal in scope, terminates the natural world and ushers in the Messianic Kingdom, into which the believer through faith and baptism is incorporated.[59] Schweitzer took Holtzmann and Pfleiderer to task for not recognizing that Paul regards the redemption of the individual person as bound up with a cosmic, es-

---

59. See Schweitzer, *Geschichte der Paulinischen Forschung*, 1911, pp. 43, 76–7, 81–2, 131, 175, 190 (E. T., *Paul and His Interpreters*, pp. 57, 97, 103–4, 166, 224, 245); id., *Die Mystik des Apostels Paulus*, 1930, pp. 23, 56, 100–1, 116; index, p. 392 (E. T., *The Mysticism of Paul the Apostle*, pp. 23, 54, 100, 115; index, p. 409).

chatological event.[60] But he himself did not advance beyond the assumption of the theologians preceding him that between the present material world and the spiritual world to come the Christian religion places a radical disjunction.[61] It was an assumption determined by the scope of their theological reflection. Thus, with a conception of Christ's cosmic significance controlled by the *a priori* metaphysical idea of central individual, Dorner, Rothe, and Martensen saw that significance only in terms of Christ's relation to persons, angelic as well as human. A similar outlook resulted from Weiss's biblicism, which naturally enough turned on personalist categories of thought. What escaped the notice of these theologians was whether the material universe contributes to this relation and whether it too is transformed through the Redemption. The realization that these were questions to be considered first dawned, under the influence of the natural sciences, in the English-speaking world.

### III. DEVELOPMENTS IN THE ENGLISH-SPEAKING WORLD

Cosmic-Christ terminology in the English-speaking world made its appearance in 1857, with the publication of the final work by E. W. Grinfield, the founder of the Septuagint lecturership in the University of Oxford. The title of this work, *The Christian Cosmos*, is undoubtedly dependent on Humboldt's *Kosmos*.[62] In *The Christian Cosmos* Grinfield expounded the doctrine of Christ the Creator, a subject to which he had alluded twenty years earlier.[63] He dealt with the doctrine's Scriptural foundations, its development in Tradition and its relation to modern thought, above all, to science. He was the first of several English-speaking authors to complain that this doctrine had fallen into abeyance; only its shadow remained in the Nicene Creed.[64]

The neglect of this doctrine in modern theology may, perhaps, be traced to the disuse of an essential distinction which was universally maintained by the primitive Church. . . . they attributed the design to the Almighty Father, '*of*

---

60. *Geschichte der Paulinischen Forschung*, pp. 76–7, 81–2 (E. T., pp. 96–7, 103–4).
61. See, for example, *Die Mystik des Apostels Paulus*, p. 56 (E. T., p. 54).
62. See E. W. Grinfield, *The Christian Cosmos: The Son of God the Revealed Creator*, 1857, p. 15, where the author refers to 'Humboldt's Cosmos'. The English translation of Humboldt's work began appearing in 1848. See also p. 10 above.
63. See Grinfield, *A Scriptural Inquiry into the Nature and Import of the Image and Likeness of God in Man*, 1837, pp. 20–3.
64. *The Christian Cosmos*, p. 3.

whom are all things', and who, as αὐτοθεός, the fountain of Deity, was styled 'the maker of heaven and earth'. But, as an act relating to man and the external world, they attributed creation to the Son, '*by* whom are all things'. This they denominated 'the *Economy*', as referring to the incarnation of Christ, 'both God and man'.[65]

The doctrine of Christ the Creator, Grinfield believed , is the ultimate goal of the modern quest for knowledge: 'the world, the Cosmos, is now labouring to bring forth its Creator'.[66] If only this doctrine were proclaimed, 'Men of science would . . . be more disposed to inquire into the evidences of revelation'.[67] They would realize that it is only because 'the image of God', Christ, is impressed on the intellectual and the material creation, that 'man can in any degree interpret the laws of nature.'[68] In any case, ignorance does not undermine the reality of Christ the Creator's dominion over the world: 'The cosmical relations of the Creator are immutable and eternal; they exist *in rerum naturâ*'.[69]

Grinfield's work seems to have received little notice. Such was not the case with J. B. Lightfoot's commentary on Colossians (1875). Lightfoot set out to refute Holtzmann's theory of interpolation in Colossians. The epistle hangs together as a whole, with its context and language arising naturally out of the occasion of its composition, the stand taken by St. Paul against the heretical teachers at Colossae.[70] The cosmical speculations of these teachers express their yearning for some form of mediation between God's unapproachable majesty and man in his material world. But they are speculations lacking a foundation in history and making no appeal to experience. To the cosmical speculations of the Colossian teachers and to their religious yearnings alike St. Paul supplies the true answer, Jesus Christ.[71] Lightfoot conceded that St. Paul makes Christ's mediatorial function in the Church his principal theme. But, he insisted, St. Paul also teaches that this spiritual office flows from the work of Christ in the physical universe as the mediator of its creation, as its bond and as its goal.[72] Lightfoot had no hesitation in assigning

---

65. *The Christian Cosmos*, pp. 5–6.
66. Ibid., pp. 175–6.
67. Ibid., p. 194.
68. Ibid., p. 195.
69. Ibid., pp. 314–15.
70. J. B. Lightfoot, *Saint Paul's Epistles to the Colossians and to Philemon*, 1875, p. vi (9th ed., 1890, p. viii).
71. Ibid., pp. 180–1 (pp. 112–13).
72. Ibid., pp. 182–3 (pp. 114–15).

the doctrine in Col. 1: 17, on Christ's relation to the physical universe, to the apostolic teaching. It is no more than a development of St. Paul's earlier teachings; it stands in the forefront of the prologue to St. John's Gospel; and it is hardly less prominent in the opening of the Epistle to the Hebrews.[73] Like the doctrine of St. John's prologue, that of Col. 1: 17 is a Logos doctrine, though St. Paul does not use the term. Alexandrian writers, such as Philo, providentially prepared the way for this doctrine; but while their phraseology often illuminates its meaning, it does not define it.[74] Lightfoot's commentary on Colossians is remarkable for its continuing authority with conservative theologians. Among them we must include Alfred Durand, Jules Lebreton, Ferdinand Prat and Joseph Huby, who stand in the background to Teilhard.

Besides adopting a conservative approach to apostolic teaching on the cosmic aspect of Christ, Lightfoot was also prepared to interpret this teaching in realistic, physical terms. On Col. 1: 17 he wrote:

> He [Christ] is the principle of cohesion in the universe. He impresses upon creation that unity and solidarity which makes it a cosmos instead of a chaos. Thus (to take one instance) the action of gravitation, which keeps in their places things fixed and regulates the motions of things moving, is an expression of His mind.[75]

Lightfoot was possibly echoing Grinfield, when he regretted that the doctrine of Christ's mediatorial function in creation, despite its presence in the creed common to all the Churches, exercised so little influence on the religious consciousness of his day. If theologians attended to this doctrine, they would be more in sympathy with the findings of science. The result of such sympathy would not be an unveiling of the mystery of creation. Twenty-five centuries of metaphysical speculation have failed to do that; and the physical investigations of the age, busied as they are with the evolution of phenomena, scarcely touch the difficulty. Nevertheless, 'revelation has interposed and thrown out the idea, which, if it leaves many questions unsolved, gives a breadth and unity to our conceptions, at once satisfying our religious needs and linking our scientific instincts with our theological beliefs.'[76]

Lightfoot's reference to evolution reflected one of the major interests of his age. From the eighteenth-century Enlightenment

73. Ibid., pp. 182, 188–90 (pp. 114, 120–2).
74. Ibid., pp. 209–10 (pp. 141–2).
75. Ibid., p. 222 (p. 154).
76. Ibid., pp. 182–3 (pp. 114–15).

onwards, ideas about evolution – particularly in the fields of cosmology, geology and sociology – had begun to appear. But it was only after Charles Darwin had provided a secure basis for the idea of biological evolution in his *Origin of Species* (1859), that the theory of evolution became widely accepted. The acceptance set in train a series of reassessments in Christian doctrine, initially within the English-speaking world. Traditional conceptions about God's relation to the world and man's special place in nature were called into question, while further doubt was cast upon the inerrancy of Scripture. These were the commonly debated subjects; and, though the disputes surrounding them appeared to be eroding the foundations of Christian belief, such was the strength of late Victorian optimism, that attempts were eventually made to reconstruct dogma within the framework of a scientific world-view.

In the work of reconstruction, evolution was seen to alter the perspective of yet another doctrinal area, that of Christology.[77] Lightfoot, as we have noted, perceived the relevance of evolution to doctrines about Christ. But what he said was no more than a hint. For an extended statement during this period we must go to the evangelist and geologist Henry Drummond, whose widely read *Natural Law in the Spiritual World* appeared in 1883. Behind this work lies Calvin's teaching that God continually intervenes in creation to prepare for Christ and that the eschatological kingdom will not be complete until it fills the whole created order.[78] According to Drummond, nature evolves, unable to attain with its own resources the end towards which it strives. Only the intervention of the supernatural allows it to cross from non-life to life and from organic life to spiritual life and, through the process of redemption, to reach its goal, Jesus Christ the Son of God. He is the new type, to whose image men are predestined to be conformed in the divine kingdom that unites all the kingdoms – non-living, living and human – of the natural world.[79]

When *Lux Mundi* broke on the Anglican scene in 1889, doctrinal reconstruction had begun in earnest. The authors of this volume of essays were attempting 'to put the Catholic faith into its right relation to modern intellectual and moral problems'.[80] In one of the essays,

77. Cf. H. W. Clark, *Liberal Orthodoxy*, pp. 275–86; J. S. Lawton, *Conflict in Christology*, pp. 11–16.
78. For Calvin's doctrine, see J. Tonkin, *The Church and the Secular Order in Reformation Thought*, pp. 97–102, 114–20, 127–9.
79. H. Drummond, *Natural Law in the Spiritual World*, 1883, pp. 68, 71, 293, 313–14, 397–407, 411–14; see Rom. 8: 29.
80. C. Gore (ed.), *Lux Mundi*, p. vii.

'The Incarnation and Development', J. R. Illingworth took the view that theories of biological and social evolution serve only to bring into relief much of the traditional teaching about Christ, and that objections to religion derived from these theories can be countered with negative argument. For instance, however minutely science may resolve the complexities of life into its elementary forces, it knows no more about origins than did the Greeks of old. Theology, on the other hand, states that in the beginning was the Word and in him was life. He is the source of the energy that makes up all life.[81] Again, the accidents of natural selection have proved an insufficient explanation for the change we observe in the world. Science now discloses a universe like an organism, intelligently designed to pursue an internal end, its own perfection. What science discloses is in perfect harmony with the doctrine of the divine immanence, the indwelling of God's eternal Reason or Word in his creation.[82] Furthermore, since science knows nothing of beginnings, it cannot contradict the miraculous in Christian teaching, in particular the event of the Incarnation. The Incarnation is a new beginning, the fulfilment of the long expectations in pre-Christian religion and philosophy. With Christ there emerges a new species, 'a Divine man transcending past humanity, as humanity transcended the rest of the animal creation, and communicating His vital energy by a spiritual process to subsequent generations of men.'[83]

Thus the theory of evolution, involving a new way of looking at things, becomes the occasion for recovering what Illingworth called 'the cosmical significance of the Incarnation'. It is a teaching drawn from the words of St. John and St. Paul, expressed with increasing clearness by the Fathers from Justin to Athanasius and revived after the Dark Ages by the mediaeval theologians, such as Aquinas, Bonaventure, and Hugh of St. Victor, in answer to Arabic pantheism and the materialism of the medical schools. The Reformers, through their preoccupation with soteriology, lost sight of this teaching. It was otherwise with those who went before. Without in any way underestimating the Redemption, they saw it in its right relation, as the means to an end, the reconsecration of the whole universe of God. Their insight is now being restored, thanks to the new light which the theory of evolution throws on the meaning of the Incarnation.[84]

81. J. R. Illingworth, 'The Incarnation and Development', in C. Gore (ed.), op. cit., p. 188.
82. Ibid., pp. 188–95.          83. Ibid., pp. 201–8.
84. Ibid., pp. 182–7; also pp. 192, 201, 211.

In his *Divine Immanence* (1898) Illingworth referred once again to the cosmic significance of the Incarnation.[85] He now attributed the neglect of this view of the Incarnation to the negative criticism of the eighteenth century. But, he declared, 'with the revival of constructive thinking, it has of necessity revived.'[86] Illingworth's own constructive thinking owed something to the metaphysics of Hermann Lotze, who sought to combine immanentist idealism with a mechanical interpretation of nature. According to a passage which Illingworth quoted from Lotze,[87] the Absolute is not only the source of all laws and processes in the natural universe, but also their undivided, omnipresent operator. The Incarnation, said Illingworth, is the supreme instance of this action of the Absolute. Given a belief in the Incarnation, we find that it has a cosmic as well as a human significance:

> It is not merely an event in the history of man, but an event, at least as far as our earth is concerned, in the history of matter; analogous upon a higher plane to the origin of life, or the origin of personality; the appearance of a new order of being in the world.

Epistemologically, the Incarnation has modified our view of the universe, just as the Copernican astronomy and the theory of evolution have done. Against idealism the Incarnation emphasizes the value of matter, while against mere materialism it interprets matter as the agent through which God effects his spiritual purpose.[88]

No doubt Illingworth was over-confident in his conviction that, by associating the doctrine of the Incarnation with the theory of evolution, he could neutralize science's strictures on religious dogma. And in his presentation of Christ as a new species within an evolutionary world, he appears to have said no more than Drummond before him. But he went beyond Drummond's simple examination of evolution from a particular theological standpoint. In his endeavour to ground his own theological interpretation in a contemporary metaphysics and to see it in continuity with the Logos teachings of the early Church, Illingworth laid down the terms of reference for the constructive thinking through which, he believed,

85. J. R. Illingworth, *Divine Immanence*, pp. 114–17; also pp. 95–100.
86. Ibid., p. 117.
87. Ibid., pp. 114–15; Lotze, *Metaphysic in Three Books*, E. T. by Bernard Bosanquet, 2nd ed., 1887, vol. 2, pp. 183–4.
88. Ibid., pp. 115–17.

interest in the cosmic significance of the Incarnation was being revived. The full flowering of this constructive thinking was not achieved until the publication, thirty years later in 1928, of L. S. Thornton's *The Incarnate Lord*. In essentials, Thornton merely followed the scheme which Illingworth had conceived in a few dozen pages. With the aid of A. N. Whitehead's process philosophy, Thornton described the universe as an ascending cosmic series which requires for its completion God's intervention through the Incarnation. He offered his work not as a statement of new doctrine, but as a development, consonant with an evolutionary outlook, of the doctrine taught by the New Testament and elaborated by the Church Fathers.

Illingworth's treatment of the cosmic significance of the Incarnation is important not only for the framework of constructive thinking which it pioneered but also for its review of the successive ages of theology. Auberlen, Martensen, and Dorner had ascribed a cosmic doctrine of Christ to individual authors of the past; while Grinfield had introduced the word 'cosmical', not in his historical treatment of the doctrine of Christ the Creator, but rather in his systematic consideration of the subject, and then only incidentally. For the theme of Christ's relationship to creation it was Illingworth who produced the first historical sketch containing 'cosmical' as the operative term. How he and those who followed him came to use this term in Christological contexts is not clear. Grinfield may have influenced them. But in all probability some of the Germanic authors whom we have been considering were the real source. Martensen, Dorner and Bernhard Weiss, for instance, had all acquired a longlasting theological audience in the English-speaking world.

During the thirty-year period following the publication of *Lux Mundi*, cosmic-Christ terminology enjoyed a measure of popularity among English-speaking theologians. Generally, it took the form of such phrases as 'the cosmical significance of Christ', 'the cosmic function of the Logos' and 'a cosmological conception of Christ'. But it was at this time also that the terms 'cosmical (or cosmic) Christology' and 'cosmic Christ' became established. The importance of these precise terms is that they encouraged the emergence of a new topic in Christological discussion. As we shall see, the furthest development of this topic occurred in the work of Teilhard, with its proposal that in Christ there is a third nature which is neither divine nor human but cosmic.

The term 'cosmical Christology' was used, apparently for the first

time, by James Denney in his *Studies in Theology* (1894). A year
earlier A. M. Fairbairn, dealing with what he called 'the Christological Epistles' (that is, Ephesians and Colossians), had written,
'Christ occupies not simply an historical, but a cosmical place.'[89]
Denney made reference to this remark in a short discussion on the
development from Paul's earlier to his later epistles. He observed that
Paul 'advanced, to use Dr Fairbairn's terms, from the historical to the
cosmical Christology.'[90] 'Cosmical (or cosmic) Christology' was next
taken up by D.W. Forrest (1897) [91] and then by H.R. Mackintosh
(1912).[92]

The expression 'cosmic Christ' seems to have first emerged in the
United States, in *The Christian Doctrine of Salvation* (1905), the final
work by G. B. Stevens of the Yale Divinity School.[93] The following
year it appeared again in *Christ and the Eternal Order* by
J. W. Buckham of the Pacific Theological Seminary, Berkeley.[94] In
Britain, during the period under discussion, 'cosmic Christ' was used
in W. R. Inge's *Personal Idealism and Mysticism* (1907)[95] and
W. L. Walker's *Christ the Creative Ideal: Studies in Ephesians and
Colossians* (1913).[96]

More often than not, the English-speaking theologians of this
period employed cosmic-Christ terminology in discussions about
New Testament theology.[97] We find it so used by A.M. Fairbairn
(1893),[98] James Denney (1894),[99] A. B. Bruce (1894),[100] G. B.
Stevens (1894, 1897, 1905),[101] R. L. Ottley (1896),[102] D. W. Forrest

89. A. M. Fairbairn, *The Place of Christ in Modern Theology*, 1893, p. 318.
90. J. Denney, *Studies in Theology*, 1894, p. 55.
91. *The Christ of History and of Experience*, p. 182.
92. *The Doctrine of the Person of Jesus Christ*, pp. 435 n. 1, 448.
93. pp. 438, 440, 537.
94. pp. xi, 85, 88, 90–1.
95. p. viii (3rd ed., 1924, p. xiv).
96. pp. vii, 45–51, 232.
97. The most important New Testament texts which these theologians cited or
    alluded to are given in brackets after the references to their works.
98. *The Place of Christ in Modern Theology*, pp. 318–20; see pp. xviii, 304 (Col. 1: 13,
    15–17, 19–20; 2: 9–10, 15; Eph. 1: 4, 10, 21, 23; 3: 10; 4: 10; Phil. 2: 9–11; 3: 21).
99. *Studies in Theology*, pp. 53–5 (Col. 1: 15–18).
100. *St. Paul's Conception of Christianity*, pp. 335–6 (1 Cor. 8: 6; 15: 27; Col. 1: 15–16;
    also 1 Cor. 3: 22–3; Rom. 8: 22, 28).
101. *The Johannine Theology*, 1894, p. 93 (Col. 1: 16–17; John 1: 3, 10; Heb. 1: 2–3);
    *The Theology of the New Testament*, 1899, p. 393 (1 Cor. 8: 6; Col. 1: 13–17); *The
    Christian Doctrine of Salvation*, 1905, pp. 359, 438, 440–40 (Col. 1: 15–20; Eph. 3: 9–
    11).
102. *The Doctrine of the Incarnation*, vol. 1, p. 110 (3rd ed., 1904, p. 110) (Col. 1: 15–
    20; Eph. 1: 10).

(1897),[103] H. A. A. Kennedy (1904, 1919),[104] W. R. Inge (1907,1909,1915),[105] C. L. Nolloth (1908),[106] H. R. Mackintosh (1912),[107] and W. L. Walker (1913).[108] In using cosmic-Christ terminology in connection with New Testament theology, what these authors generally had in mind was the divinity of Christ.

The main exceptions – apart from Inge, whom we shall discuss later – were Denney and Bruce. They interpreted St. Paul's Christology as involving a threefold distinction in Christ. As St. Paul developed his thought on Christ, said Denney, he advanced from a historical to a cosmical Christology, in the sense not that he left the historical behind but that he came to appreciate the universal scope of Christ's redemptive work. Such work requires that he who performs it should be 'related to God, to man, and to all that is'.[109] According to Bruce, St. Paul believed Christ to be both man and God. Even if Christ's humanity is of universal significance, analogous to that of Adam, it is also that of an individual descended from David.[110] Again, although we cannot be sure that in Rom. 9: 5 St. Paul has called Christ Θεός, the Trinitarian benediction of 2 Cor. 13: 14 conceives of Christ as a being who possesses, in common with God and the Holy Spirit, a divine nature.[111] In addition, in the 'Christological Epistles' attributed to St. Paul, especially in Colossians, 'a very high cosmic place is assigned to Christ'; he is the First-born of all creation, its originator and its final cause. This

---

103. *The Christ of History and of Experience*, pp. 177 n. 3, 178–9, 182, 393 (1 Cor. 8: 5–6; Col. 1: 13–18; John 1: 1–18; Heb. 1: 2–3).
104. *St Paul's Conception of the Last Things*, 1904, pp. xvii, 354; see pp. 235–6 (Rom. 8: 29; 1 Cor. 15: 20; Col. 1: 15, 16, 18); *The Theology of the Epistles*, 1919, pp. 152–60 (1 Cor. 8: 6; Phil. 2: 6–11; Col. 1: 15–20; Eph. 1: 10).
105. *Personal Idealism and Mysticism*, 1907, pp. 47–9, 56, 147–8 (Rom. 8: 21; 1 Cor. 8: 6; 15: 24–28; Phil. 2: 6; Col. 1: 15–17; 3: 11; Eph. 1: 10; John 1: 1–18); 'The Theology of the Fourth Gospel', in H. B. Swete (ed.), *Essays on Some Biblical Questions of the Day* [Cambridge Biblical Essays], 1909, p. 267 (1 Cor. 15: 22, 45–47; Phil. 2: 6–7, 11; Col. 1: 15–18); 'Logos', in J. Hastings (ed.), *Encyclopaedia of Religion and Ethics*, vol. 8, 1915, p. 136 col. 1 (1 Cor. 15: 24–28, 45; 2 Cor. 3: 18; Phil. 2: 6; Col. 1: 15–17; 2: 9; Eph. 1: 10, 22–23; 4: 15–16).
106. *The Person of Our Lord and Recent Thought*, pp. 316–17; see p. 360 col. 2 (1 Cor. 8: 6; Col. 1: 15–17; John 1: 1–18; Heb. 1: 1–5).
107. *The Doctrine of the Person of Jesus Christ*, pp. 69–71, 116–18, 435 n. 1, 447–8 (1 Cor. 8: 6; Col. 1: 15–17; John 1: 1–18).
108. *Christ the Creative Ideal*, pp. 46–50, 53, 55–6, 58, 60, 66–7 (1 Cor. 8: 6; Phil. 2: 6–11; Col. 1: 15–18; 2: 9–10; Eph. 1: 19–20; 3: 9, 11; Heb. 1: 2–4; John 1: 1–18; Rev. 3: 14; 22: 13).
109. J. Denney, *Studies in Theology*, p. 55.
110. A. B. Bruce, *St. Paul's Conception of Christianity*, pp. 331–5.
111. Ibid., pp. 336–43.

doctrine on Christ's cosmic relations, while it goes beyond anything to be found in the principal Pauline Epistles, is nevertheless anticipated there. Rom. 8: 22 implies that Christ is the Mediator of God's activity in the world, while 1 Cor. 8: 6 makes this point explicitly.[112]

Systematic theology provided further scope for the use of cosmic-Christ terminology. Except for Illingworth and Inge, the tendency once again was to relate the terminology to the divinity of Christ. This was the case with P. T. Forsyth (who acknowledged his debt to Richard Rothe, among other German theologians).[113] In *The Person and Place of Jesus Christ* (1909) and *The Work of Christ* (1910), Forsyth discussed Christ's relation to the cosmos in the context of the Atonement, a theme which had become central to his theology. Christ is not simply the interpreter of life, as depicted by liberal theology; nor is he merely a cosmic principle, as philosophers have proposed.[114] Much more, he is the one in whose divine nature reconciliation between God and the world as a cosmic whole is effected.[115] What this means is that God's 'creation is much more than cosmic in range; it is redemptive in power.' The Creator is also the Redeemer; and his work is incomplete until it reaches its goal, which is the redeemed Kingdom.[116]

In *The Doctrine of the Person of Jesus Christ* (1912), H. R. Mackintosh, like Forsyth, saw redemption as the fulfilment of creation, when he employed cosmic language in connection with Christ's divinity. On the supposition of there being but one universe, Mackintosh argued that, if Christ is the organizing centre of the world of values by which faith lives, he must also be central to the world of facts. To put the matter another way, redemption and creation form a unity, with the one completing the other. Thus Christ's act of redeeming us discloses his cosmic function as the divine agent in creation and as the principle controlling the development of the world. Furthermore, Mackintosh indicated, since Christ's redemptive act is grounded in his divine filial response to the Father, we may say that his cosmic function is similarly grounded.[117]

---

112. Ibid., pp. 335–6.
113. P. T. Forsyth, *The Person and Place of Jesus Christ*, p. viii.
114. P. T. Forsyth, *The Work of Christ*, pp. 74–5 (new ed., 1965, p. 82).
115. Ibid., p. 77 (p. 84).
116. P. T. Forsyth, *The Person and Place of Jesus Christ*, pp. 325–6.
117. H. R. Mackintosh, *The Doctrine of the Person of Jesus Christ*, pp. 447–8; also p. 370.

Cosmic language associated with Christ's divinity was also incorporated into discussions on kenoticism. According to the classical form of kenoticism, the Son renounces the metaphysical attributes of God relative to the world – omnipotence, omniscience, and omnipresence – in order to become incarnate. We find these and similar attributes referred to as the cosmic functions of the Son by Charles Gore (1895),[118] D. W. Forrest (1897),[119] Frank Weston (1907),[120] and H. R. Mackintosh (1912).[121] For another application of cosmic-Christ terminology to kenoticism, we turn to W. L. Walker.

In his day Walker was known for his theory of the eternal kenosis. The eternal kenosis is God's interior self-sacrificing love, which manifests itself impersonally within the evolutionary movement of creation and culminates by personalizing itself in the Incarnation.[122] This theory lies behind Walker's account of the cosmic Chirst in his work *Christ the Creative Ideal: Studies in Colossians and Ephesians* (1913). In the Epistles to the Colossians and the Ephesians we are presented with Christ as divine, though not in the supreme or absolute sense in which the Father is divine. Such a qualification to Christ's divinity, however, does not admit of an Arian interpretation. Christ is no creature, since he is before all things and all things were created in him. Rather, he is divine by participation in the Godhead as the Son.[123] (Charles Gore made a similar point. What confronts us in St. Paul's letters is that the Son, while he is accorded strictly divine attributes, nevertheless exercises his cosmic and redemptive activities, as recipient to source, in subordination to the Father.[124]) Sonship, according to Walker, is both a reality within God and the ideal and goal of creation. In the created order it finds its complete expression in the humanity of Christ.[125] Originating in God, the ideal of sonship is expressed *ad extra*, when God in the mode of Son goes out of himself, lowers himself, in order to create beings capable of sharing in this sonship.[126] As the spectroscope has shown, the same elements

118. *Dissertations on Subjects Connected with the Incarnation*, pp. 91–3.
119. *The Christ of History and of Experience*, pp. 200–2.
120. *The One Christ*, pp. 107, 110, 115.
121. Op. cit., pp. 267–8, 270, 483–5.
122. W. L. Walker, *The Spirit and the Incarnation*, 1899, pp. 260–70; *The Gospel of Reconciliation*, 1909, p. 169.
123. W. L. Walker, *Christ the Creative Ideal*, pp. 46–9.
124. C. Gore, *The Reconstruction of Belief*, [vol. 2,] *Belief in Christ*, 1922, pp. 85–6.
125. W. L. Walker, *Christ the Creative Ideal*, pp. 58, 61–2.
126. Ibid., p. 61.

prevail throughout the material universe, so that, wherever life appears, it is probably of the same essential type. In any case, we cannot conceive of personal and ethical life other than that of which the ideal is the life of Christ. For in Christ the very ideal of sonship to God has been realized; and thus Christ is the goal of creation.[127] For this reason, the Apostle could also speak of him as the mediator of creation. Christ is he through whom all things were made.[128] The loss of this doctrine, as Bishop Lightfoot once said, has been serious; until it is revived, we shall be narrow in our theological conceptions and out of sympathy with science.[129]

Like Walker, J. W. Buckham in his *Christ and the Eternal Order* (1906) saw the cosmic aspect of Christology as the means of reconciling the interests of theology and science. The Logos doctrine of Paul, the Apologists, Origen, and Athanasius appears to be no more than an illusion in the light of modern science.[130] And yet this same science cannot in itself tell us why the evolution of the universe has proceeded from 'an indefinite incoherent homogeneity, to a definite coherent heterogeneity'. The universe is a cosmos, not a chaos. What a cosmos demands is a cosmic Christ; the presence, within the structure and process of creation, of a divine Mind, a Logos. Without it the very uniformity in nature, upon which the possibility of science depends, would not exist.[131] Our ability to behold the beauty of nature provides further reason for affirming the existence of a Logos or cosmic Christ. An object of beauty and its beholder have no bond uniting them, unless it is a Logos which inheres in them both.[132] For Buckham the cosmic Christ is one among several aspects which make up an enlarged conception of Christ, a conception which goes beyond the restricted phenomenal Christ of Ritschlianism but at the same time adapts the 'older Christology' to the concerns of the present day.[133] Buckham distinguished five aspects of Christ: the human, the historic, the eternal, the living, and the cosmic.[134] In terms of the older Christology, the first two aspects pertain to Christ's humanity, while the eternal and the cosmic aspects are related to his divinity. The

127. Ibid., pp. 63–6.
128. Ibid., pp. 53–6.
129. Ibid., pp. 54–5; also pp. 69–70.
130. J. W. Buckham, *Christ and the Eternal Order*, p. 87.
131. Ibid., pp. 86–8.
132. Ibid., pp. 89–90.
133. Ibid., pp. 3–9.
134. Ibid., pp. 57–94.

Living Christ is the 'completer Christ', the Christ whom we know in the blending together of all his aspects.

In the context of historical theology, there was no tendency to restrict cosmic language to the divinity of Christ. Mackintosh applied it in two ways. When discussing Origen's doctrine on the union between the Logos and the humanity of Jesus, he had in mind the divinity of Christ. Origen, he noted, refuses to confine the Logos to the human life of Jesus, on the ground that after the Incarnation the Logos continues to exercise his cosmic functions.[135] On the other hand, Mackintosh was also prepared to use the terminology in a sense involving neither the divinity nor the humanity of Christ. The Christologies of Justin and Arius, he pointed out, make Christ a cosmological principle, subordinate to God as one of his creatures.[136] Again, when Ottley spoke of 'the cosmic significance of the Atonement' as a distinctive feature of Origen's teaching, he was concerned with both the divinity and the humanity of Christ. 'The entire universe,' said Ottley, 'participates in the effect of the Divine work.' Then, summarizing a passage from Origen which focuses on Christ's humanity, he added that it is Christ as High Priest who brings about reconciliation between God and the universe.[137] In *Monophysitism Past and Present* (1920), A. A. Luce argued that Christology is linked to cosmic questions. When the Pauline and Johannine Christologies gave the person of Christ cosmic significance, they identified Jesus of Nazareth with the Neo-Pythagorean or Stoic Logos: 'He stands not only between God and man, but between Creator and creation. He is the embodiment of the cosmic relation.'[138] Similarly, cosmic questions helped to shape the fifth-century Christologies. Whereas Nestorianism and Monophysitism reflected the dualism of earlier Platonism and Neo-Platonic monism respectively, orthodoxy caught the spirit of Aristotle, who upheld both the distinction and the unity of God and the world. In ascribing to Christ both divine and human natures, Catholic Christology conceived him as 'the cosmic unity of opposites'.[139] Finally, in sketching the history of opinion about Christ's cosmic aspect, Illingworth and Inge alike suggested something over and above his

135. H. R. Mackintosh, op. cit., p. 168.
136. Ibid., pp. 143–4, 178; also pp. 185, 187.
137. R. L. Ottley, *The Doctrine of the Incarnation*, 1896, vol. 1, p. 252 (3rd ed., 1904, p. 252).
138. A. A. Luce, *Monophysitism Past and Present*, p. 7.
139. Ibid., pp. 8–24.

divinity and humanity. Illingworth, as we have seen, referred to the cosmical significance of the Incarnation; while Inge, to whom we shall now turn, made the point that, from the cosmological aspect of the Logos doctrine, we are made aware of an extension of the Incarnation beyond the historical Jesus.

In her work on mysticism (1911), Evelyn Underhill wrote:

> The Incarnation, which is for popular Christianity synonymous with the historical birth and earthly life of Christ, is for the mystic not only this but also a perpetual Cosmic and personal process. It is an everlasting bringing forth, in the universe and also in the individual ascending soul, of the divine and perfect Life, the pure character of God, of which the one historical life dramatized the essential constituents.[140]

This passage echoes a remark made by Inge in 1902 on the Christian Platonists of Alexandria, that their great aim was 'to bring the Incarnation into closest relation with the cosmic process.'[141] What it does not pick up is the ecclesial dimension in the cosmic aspect of the Incarnation, a point which Inge dealt with in *Personal Idealism and Mysticism* (1907). This was Inge's most developed account of the cosmic Christ and included biblical, historical, and systematic discussions of the topic. One aspect of the Logos doctrine in St. John's prologue, said Inge, presents Christ as a cosmic principle. St. Paul also has this doctrine, even though he does not employ the term 'Logos'. That was Lightfoot's view. But Inge went on to indicate the far greater prominence that the doctrine has in St. Paul's thought than it does in St. John's.[142] Echoing Lightfoot again, Inge considered it necessary to stress this doctrine, since it is 'almost entirely neglected in modern religious teaching.'[143] The cosmological aspect of the Logos doctrine – derived from St. John and St. Paul and developed by the Christian Platonists and the speculative mystics, Eckhart and Hugh of St. Victor – does not bypass the doctrine of a historical incarnation; but it does underline the continuance of the Incarnation in the life of the Church.[144] Moreover, it forms a bridge between Christian belief and the nineteenth-century discovery of the

140. E. Underhill, *Mysticism: A Study in the Nature and Development of Man's Spiritual Consciousness*, 1911, p. 141 (with slight changes in the text, 15th ed., 1945, p. 118).
141. W. R. Inge, 'The Person of Christ', in *Contentio Veritatis*, p. 74.
142. W. R. Inge, *Personal Idealism and Mysticism*, pp. 47, 56.
143. Ibid., pp. 50–1.
144. Ibid., pp. 83–92; also pp. 65–82.

interrelatedness of all life in the universe. Science bids us not to see the world as a collection of isolated individuals, but to take a 'cosmo-centric view of reality'. Even the distinction between living and dead matter, which Drummond has stressed in his Calvinist interpretation of biology, is now regarded as dubious. The doctrine of panpsychism, Inge believed, is destined to gain ground; and this can scarcely be reconciled, as Hermann Lotze has tried to do, with a theory of persons as self-contained monads. No doubt a cosmocentric view of reality commits us to holding that, besides mankind, Christ must redeem any other spiritual beings who may exist in the universe – and the probability that there are many is overwhelming. But it also reinforces St. Paul's hope that 'the creation may one day be delivered from the bondage of corruption into the glorious liberty of the sons of God' (Rom. 8: 21).[145]

To the extent that they exhibited a variety of usage in cosmic-Christ terminology, the English-speaking theologians whom we have been examining reflected the work of their Germanic counterparts. At the same time, several advances emerged from their work. One of these – the introduction of scientific questions into cosmic Christology – occurred at the outset with Grinfield. Another was a more developed awareness, best exemplified in the writings of Illingworth and Inge, that past authors had treated of Christ's cosmic significance. With Denney and Stevens the precise expressions 'cosmic Christology' and 'cosmic Christ' first appeared. At a later time these expressions were to assist in bringing discussions about the cosmic aspect of Christ into sharper focus. But perhaps the most notable advance made by the English-speaking theologians was the suggestion that, besides his divinity and his humanity, there is in Christ a further aspect, which is cosmic. We have previously mentioned that Dorner and then Holtzmann and Pfleiderer had foreshadowed the drawing of a distinction between an anthropic and a cosmic dimension of the Incarnation. Illingworth, with especial clarity in his *Divine Immanence*, made this distinction. He said there that the Incarnation has not merely a human but also a cosmic significance; that is, as well as being involved with man's history, the Incarnation marks the introduction of a new order of being into the world. Likewise Inge proposed some such distinction when present-ing the cosmological aspect of the Logos doctrine in his *Personal Idealism and Mysticism*. For him, this aspect of the doctrine indicated

145. Ibid., pp. 146–8; also pp. 103, 115–17, 138–9.

that the Incarnation extends beyond the human life of Jesus to include Christ's indwelling in the Church; and it also led to the affirmation, within a cosmocentric view of reality, of Christ's redemptive activity throughout the universe. Again, Evelyn Underhill spoke of the mystic's finding the incarnation of God above all in Christ but also in the individual ascending soul and in the cosmic process at large. Allied to these positions is Mackintosh's account of the Logos doctrine in Justin and Arius, inasmuch as, when describing the Logos as a cosmological principle, Mackintosh was referring neither to Christ's divinity in any strict sense nor to his humanity. A further variant appeared in Walker's notion of the cosmic Christ, which underlined the subordinate rank of Christ's divinity, without, however, reducing him to the creaturely status maintained in Arianism. According to this notion, that which defines Christ's subordinate place in the Godhead – namely, sonship – is also the ideal of the created order, an ideal which achieves its complete expression in Christ's humanity. In agreement with Walker, Gore observed that in Pauline theology the Son, though strictly divine, exercises his cosmic activities in subordination to the Father. Each of these positions has some feeling for a cosmic aspect in Christ which is beyond the merely human but is also not – or, in the opinion of Walker and Gore, not absolutely – divine. In them we may perceive some anticipation of Teilhard's concept that in Christ there are three natures: divine, human, and cosmic. Where, however, we find a truly striking anticipation is in the threefold distinction in Christ proposed by Denney and Bruce. Finally, Buckham's fivefold distinction, while it is reducible to a two-nature doctrine of Christ, seems nevertheless to be tending in the same direction.

## IV. TEILHARD'S COSMIC CHRIST

Writing in his journal on 13 March 1916, Teilhard considered the conflict that one may experience between a Christian desire to renounce the 'Kosmos' and an appreciation of its value. He continued: 'And the last position, surrender to the cosmic Christ, secures the life, the immortal persistence, of all that is truly good and lasting in the first two attitudes.[146] This quotation contains one of the earlier instances of the use of the term 'cosmic Christ'. With Teilhard we enter a new terminological world. The authors we have so far

146. *Journal*, tome 1, p. 57.

surveyed employ cosmic-Christ terminology very sparingly, at times as little more than a labelling device. But with Teilhard it multiplies in both frequency and form, to become a complex instrument for exploring, systematizing, and then generating further an expanding field of discourse, which involves not only his intellectual position but also his personal spiritual life. The term 'cosmic Christ' itself, with which his name more than any other is associated, is chronologically the original term he used in this field.[147] It appears over thirty times in his writings, especially from 1916 to the early 1920s, and then again during his last ten years or so, the final example occurring in the essay 'Le Christique', which he completed in March 1955, a few weeks before his death.[148]

Teilhard's notion of the cosmic Christ can best be summarized by looking at some of the other terms which it generated in his writings. In 1916, about a month after he had hit upon the term 'cosmic Christ', Teilhard wrote that, in coming to save mankind, Christ had to animate the whole universe which bears it; for mankind is not a group of isolated monads but, with the universe, makes up a single totality, consolidated by life and matter. Thus besides his mystical body, Christ also has a cosmic body spread throughout the universe. And just as the mystical Christ has still to attain his full growth, so too has the cosmic Christ.[149] Teilhard saw the evolutionary movement of the universe as directed towards the building up of Christ. The completed Christ is the goal of the universe. In 1918 Teilhard introduced the term 'Christ-Omega' to designate Christ as this goal.[150] Besides Christ, the universe has no other goal. Its goal belongs to the supernatural order.[151] Teilhard retained the term 'Christ-Omega' for the rest of his life, but after 1924 he ceased speaking about the

---

147. The only possible exceptions are the traditional terms 'Body of Christ' and 'mystical Body', which Teilhard began using, about a month before he adopted 'cosmic Christ', in his preparatory notes for the essay 'La Vie cosmique'. See *Journal*, tome 1, pp. 39–57.
148. Instances of 'cosmic Christ' in Teilhard's writings are listed in the Appendix. See pp. 220–1 below.
149. 'La Vie cosmique', 24.4.1916, *Oeuvres* 12, pp. 67–9 (*ETG*, pp. 47–9; *WTW*, pp. 57–9); see also 'L'Union créatrice', ibid., p. 223 (*ETG*, p. 196; *WTW*, p. 175): 'L'Élément universel', ibid., p. 440 (*ETG*, p. 408; *WTW*. p. 297).
150. *Journal*, tome 1, 7.3.1918, p. 288; 19.12.1918, pp. 382–3; 25.12.1918, p. 387; 'Note sur "l'Élément universel" du Monde', 22.12.1918, *Oeuvres* 12, p. 392 (*ETG*, p. 361; *WTW*, p. 274).
151. Lettre à Auguste Valensin, 29.12.1919, *LI*, pp. 43–4 (*BT*, pp. 45–6; E. T., pp. 49–50); 'Le Christ évoluteur', *Oeuvres* 10, p. 168 (*CE*, p. 143).

building-up of Christ's body.[152] The general idea, however, he did not abandon. From 1939 onwards, he re-expressed it much more sharply by means of the term 'Christogenesis', together with its correlative 'cosmogenesis'.[153] Cosmogenesis means that the cosmos or universe is evolving towards its full realization at Omega. But since Omega coincides with the fully realized Christ, Teilhard could say that cosmogenesis is being transformed into Christogenesis.[154] Teilhard's use of these two terms presupposes his doctrine that creation is a teleological process towards union with the Godhead, effected through the incarnation and redemption of Christ, 'in whom all things hold together' (Col. 1: 17).[155] Creation will not be complete until participated being is totally united with God through Christ in the Pleroma, when God will be 'all in all' (1 Cor. 15: 28).[156]

It would be contrary to Teilhard's intention to suppose that the linking of Christogenesis with cosmogenesis in any way implies an impersonal cosmic Christ. Between cosmogenesis and Christogenesis Teilhard placed a middle term – anthropogenesis or noogenesis. That is to say, the universe is oriented towards its goal through the human or reflectively thinking level of being which emerges from its evolutionary process.[157] Moreover, beginning in 1918, Teilhard often employed the term 'universal Christ',[158] which he regarded as a synonym for 'cosmic Christ',[159] but which for him had a strong

152. The last clear expression of this seems to be in 'Mon Univers', 1924, *Oeuvres* 9, p. 96 (*SC*, p. 67).

153. 'Christogenesis' first occurs in 'La Mystique de la Science', 20.3.1939, *Oeuvres* 6, p. 221 (*HE*, p. 179). It is first used with 'cosmogenesis' in *Le Phénomène humain*, juin 1938 – juin 1940, *Oeuvres* 1, p. 331 (*PM*, p. 297).

154. 'Note sur la Notion de Perfection chrétienne', *Oeuvres* 11, p. 116 (*TF*, p. 104); 'Christianisme et Évolution', *Oeuvres* 10, p. 214 (*CE*, p. 184).

155. *Le Milieu divin*, *Oeuvres* 4, pp. 148–9 (*MD*, pp. 111–12); 'Introduction à la Vie chrétienne', *Oeuvres* 10, p. 183 (*CE*, p. 155); 'Réflexions sur le Péché originel', ibid., pp. 229–30 (p. 198); 'Comment je vois', *Oeuvres* 11, p. 213 (*TF*, p. 198).

156. 'Mon Univers', 1924, *Oeuvres* 9, pp. 113–14 (*SC*, p. 85); 'Panthéisme et Christianisme', *Oeuvres* 10, p. 91 (*CE*, p. 75); 'Introduction à la Vie chrétienne', ibid., pp. 199–200 (p. 171); 'Un Sommaire de ma Perspective Phénoménologique du Monde', *Oeuvres* 11, p. 236 (*TF*, p. 215).

157. *Le Phénomène humain*, *Oeuvres* 1, p. 331 (*PM*, p. 297); 'Superhumanité, Super-Christ, Super-charité', *Oeuvres* 9, p. 213 (*SC*, p. 168); 'Trois Choses que je vois', *Oeuvres* 11, p. 170 note (*TF*, p. 156 note); 'Comment je vois', ibid., pp. 200, 218–19, 222 (pp. 184, 204, 207).

158. 'Le Prêtre', 8.7.1918, *Oeuvres* 12, p. 319 (*ETG*, p. 290; *WTW*, p. 210). For the frequency of this term, see P. L'Archevêque, *Teilhard de Chardin: Index analytique*, p. 22; id., *Teilhard de Chardin: Nouvel index analytique*, pp. 30–1.

159. See 'Introduction à la Vie chrétienne', *Oeuvres* 10, p. 186 (*CE*, p. 158); 'Christianisme et Évolution', ibid., p. 210 (p. 179).

personalistic nuance.[160] Christ is universal, not in the sense that he is
an abstract idea or a substratum of undifferentiated general energy,
but in the sense that he is a conscious and loving centre who attracts
all other persons into community with himself, thereby occasioning
each to activate to the utmost his own individuality.[161] This he does
as the supreme personality who, in controlling and directing the
evolutionary current, personalizes it.[162] Finally, the divine Logos
could not become the cosmic Christ, the Omega of evolution, except
by being born into the stream of its history as an individual, by
suffering death, the inevitable consequence of this birth, and then by
rising from the dead to assume his function as universal centre.[163] It
is only the Incarnation in Jesus of Nazareth that guarantees, as far as
our experience is concerned, the reality of the universal Christ.[164]

Though Teilhard never doubted that the divine Logos, Jesus of
Nazareth and the cosmic Christ are identically the one person, he
came more and more during the last twenty years of his life to
distinguish the cosmic aspect of Christ from Christ's divinity and
humanity.[165] Eventually, in 'Le Christique' (1955), he could say that
there is in Christ, besides his divine and human natures, a third aspect
or function or even, in a true sense, nature, which is cosmic.[166] One
reason why Teilhard drew such a distinction was to differentiate, on
the one hand, between Christ's human individuality and his universality as a cosmic principle[167] and, on the other hand, between the

160. 'Comment je crois', ibid., p. 117 (p. 96).
161. 'La Parole attendue', *Oeuvres* 11, pp. 107–8 (*TF*, pp. 98–9); also 'Introduction à
     la Vie chrétienne', *Oeuvres* 10, p. 186 (*CE*, p. 158). For Teilhard's notion of the
     'universal-personal', see 'Esquisse d'un Univers Personnel', *Oeuvres* 6, p. 103
     (*HE*, p. 83); 'L'Énergie Humaine', ibid., pp. 178–80 (pp. 143–5).
     Cf. H. de Lubac, *The Eternal Feminine: A Study on the Text of Teilhard de
     Chardin*, p. 122; M. Barthélemy-Madaule, *La Personne et le drame humain chez
     Teilhard de Chardin*, pp. 255–62.
162. 'Christianisme et Évolution', *Oeuvres* 10, pp. 214–15 (*CE*, pp. 184–5).
163. 'Mon Univers', 1924, *Oeuvres* 9, pp. 88–92 (*SC*, pp. 60–4); 'Introduction à la Vie
     Chrétienne', *Oeuvres* 10, pp. 186–7 (*CE*, pp. 158–9).
164. *Le Milieu divin*, *Oeuvres* 4, pp. 140–1 (*MD*, p. 105); Lettre à Édouard Le Roy,
     10.8.1929; Lettre à Pierre Lamare, 26.11.1929 (text, with incorrect date, in
     R. Speaight, *Teilhard de Chardin: A Biography*, p. 162); 'Christianisme et
     Évolution', *Oeuvres* 10, p. 211 (*CE*, p. 181).
165. The first clear statement of a triple distinction in Christ occurs in 'Quelques
     Réflexions sur la Conversion du Monde', 9.10.1936, *Ouevres* 9, p. 161 (*SC*,
     p. 122).
166. 'Le Christique', *Oeuvres* 13, p. 107 (*HM*, p. 93).
167. 'Quelques Réflexions sur la Conversion du Monde', *Oeuvres* 9, p. 161 (*SC*,
     p. 122); *Journal* XIII ( = 1), 8.7.1945, p. 133; 'Comment je vois', *Oeuvres* 11, p.

self-sufficiency of his divinity[168] and (according to the notion of Christogenesis) his process of formation as a cosmic principle. Another reason for the distinction is the possibility, in an immense universe, of extraterrestrial intelligent life. In 1918 Teilhard wondered whether we ought not to admit a 'polymorphic' manifestation of the cosmic Christ in various worlds; perhaps the human Christ is simply a 'face' of the cosmic Christ.[169] In his last years Teilhard, increasingly preoccupied with the idea of a plurality of inhabited worlds, linked it to his triple distinction in Christ.[170] Christ as divine and human is the classical Christological doctrine, while Christ as an emerging cosmic principle suggests a Christology with Arian tendencies. Several months before he died, Teilhard said that we appear to be living over again the great conflicts of Arianism, only this time the question is no longer how Christ is related to the Trinity but how he is related to a universe which now reveals itself to be of vast proportions, 'organic' in structure and probably 'polyhuman'. Our situation calls for a new Nicaea, to work out a subdistinction 'in the human nature of Christ, between a *terrestrial* nature and a *cosmic* nature'.[171] Whatever the complexities of Teilhard's three-nature terminology, it is at least clear that for him Christ's cosmic nature lies not on the side of divinity but on the side of creation. Teilhard seems to have sensed that the logic of his thought was leading him to attempt a fusion of classical and Arian Christologies.

Though Teilhard was a prolific inventor of terminology, there is one term which he said he did not coin – 'pan-Christism'. Late in life he attributed it to Blondel,[172] though there can be little doubt that

---

214 (*TF*, pp. 198–9); *Journal* XVI ( = 4), 11.6.1949, p. 64; Lettre à François Russo, 17.11.1953.
168. 'Comment je vois', *Oeuvres* 11, pp. 208, 210 (*TF*, pp. 193, 195); also 'Esquisse d'une Dialectique de l'Esprit', *Oeuvres* 7, p. 152 (*AE*, p. 146).
169. *Journal*, tome 1, 24.2.1918, p. 281.
170. The linking occurs in the following: *Journal* XIV ( = 2), 13.10.1946, p. 115; *Journal* XV ( = 3), 7.2.1948, p. 97; 'Une suite au Problème des Origines humaines', 5.6.1953, *Oeuvres* 10, pp. 281–2 (*CE*, pp. 235–6); Lettre à Claude Tresmontant, 7.4.1954; Lettre a Bruno de Solages, 2.1.1955, *LI*, p. 450; Lettre à André Ravier, 14.1.1955, ibid., p. 452; *Journal* XXI ( = 9), 5.2.1955, p. 26.
171. Lettre à André Ravier, 14.1.1955, *LI*, p. 452; see also Lettre à Claude Tresmontant, 7.4.1954; Lettre à Bruno de Solages, 2.1.1955, *LI*, p. 450; Lettre à Bruno de Solages, 16.2.1955, ibid., p. 459. Ten years previously, the beginnings of this line of thought were present in 'Christianisme et Évolution', 11.11.1945, *Oeuvres* 10, p. 207 (*CE*, pp. 176–7).
172. Lettre à Claude Cuénot, 15.2.1955 (relevant part quoted in C. Cuénot, *Pierre Teilhard de Chardin: Les grandes étapes de son évolution*, pp. 55–6); see also Lettre à Claude Tresmontant, 14.1.1954.

his immediate source for it was their common friend Auguste Valensin.[173] Is it also the case that he did not make up for himself the term 'cosmic Christ'? As we have seen, it had already appeared in works by Stevens, Buckham, Inge, and Walker some years before he came to use it. The evidence available does not provide a direct answer to the question. It does, however, tell us that between 1910 and 1916 a number of people in Teilhard's background introduced cosmic-Christ language into French theology, that much of the German and English literature so far examined either was known to them or was probably at hand to be consulted, and that a theosophical work, published in 1912 and employing the precise expression 'cosmic Christ', was reviewed by one of Teilhard's closest friends.

Before 1910 the only instance that has come to light of a French discussion on the cosmic aspect of Christ occurred outside the field of theology, in *De l'Humanité* (1840), the principal philosophical work of the Saint-Simonian, Pierre Leroux. According to Leroux's idiosyncratic interpretation of the Gospels, Christ is portrayed there in connection with the doctrine of palingenesy; that is, the doctrine concerning renewal, rebirth, resurrection, or new creation. Taken collectively, the Gospels manifest three forms of palingenesy: cosmic, political, and psychological.[174] Within the framework of cosmic palingenesy, which derives from astrology and is taught in its purest form by the Gospel of Matthew, Christ appears as a performer of miracles and a transformer of nature.[175] He is neither God nor the God-man; instead, he is a mystery, a person whose nature is human but whose power is divine.[176] In Leroux's cosmic idea of Christ – the idea of a figure more than merely human and less than fully divine –

173. This is suggested in Teilhard's mention of pan-Christism: 'Talks with V[alensin]. – I am discovering that my preoccupation with "pan-Christism" is widely held, and occupies all those whose thought is free and alive, today' (*Journal*, [tome 2], cahier 7, 10.8.1919, p. 18; quoted in H. de Lubac (ed.), *LI*, pp. 49–50).

   Blondel had been using the term, in private correspondence, from as early as 1903 (see M. Blondel and J. Wehrlé, *Correspondance (extraits)*, vol. 1, pp. 98, 175; also pp. 102–3). But he and Teilhard had no direct communication with one another, until the two first met in March 1920 (cf. R. Speaight, *Teilhard de Chardin: A Biography*, p. 108).

174. P. Leroux, *De l'Humanité*, 1840, tome 2, pp. 741–5, 754–5, 960 (2e éd., 1845, tome 2, pp. 212–15, 222, 379).

175. Ibid., tome 2, pp. 787–8, 819, 823–5, 878–9, 888–9 (2e éd., tome 2, pp. 246–7, 270–1, 274–5, 315–16, 323–4).

176. Ibid., tome 2, pp. 872–3, 878–9 (2e éd., tome 2, pp. 311–12, 315–16).

we encounter the earliest move, after Dorner, towards Teilhard's terminal position of a third nature in Christ.

It was during Teilhard's period of theological training, September 1908 to July 1912, that French theologians began using cosmic-Christ terminology. In 1910 Alfred Durand, one of Teilhard's Scripture professors, writing on Col. 1: 15–17, spoke of Christ as the 'cosmic mediator'.[177] It was also in 1910 that Jules Lebreton, who studied at the same theologate as Teilhard several years ahead of him, published his history on the doctrine of the Trinity. In it he said that the most explicit New Testament statement on the cosmological role of Christ comes in St. John's prologue;[178] in Col. 1: 17–18, on the other hand, St. Paul is more concerned with a religious than with a cosmological question about Christ.[179] C. C. Martindale, a fellow novice and friend of Teilhard's, suggested in a letter to Charles Raven that Teilhard had derived his appreciation of St. Paul from Ferdinand Prat's *The Theology of Saint Paul*.[180] In the second volume of this work (1912) Teilhard could have read, in a discussion by Prat on Col. 1: 19–20 and Eph. 1: 9–10, that even as man Christ has 'a kind of cosmic role', since he is head of the angels, lord of creation, and saviour of mankind.[181] Another person in Teilhard's background who used cosmic-Christ language was Adhemar d'Ales, the editor of the *Dictionnaire apologetique de la foi catholique*. During his theological training, Teilhard wrote a short article for the dictionary at the request of d'Alès.[182] In an essay published in 1916, d'Alès distinguished two senses in which Irenaeus used the notion of recapitulation in Christ, a logical and a cosmic sense.[183]

Although the various authors in Teilhard's background did not discuss the cosmic aspect of Christ in connection with the literature where the idea had developed (apart from Lightfoot's commentary on Colossians), they were, nevertheless, well acquainted with much of

177. 'Le Christ "Premier Né" ', in *Recherches de science religieuse*, 1re Année, 1910, p. 58.
178. J. Lebreton, *Les Origines du dogme de la Trinité*, 1910, p. 432 (5e éd., 1919, p. 498).
179. Ibid., p. 307 (p. 370).
180. Cf. C. E. Raven, *Teilhard de Chardin: Scientist and Seer*, p. 46.
181. F. Prat, op. cit., 2e partie, 1912, p. 152 (6e éd., 1923, p. 112) (E.T., vol. 2, pp. 93–4).
182. 'L'Homme devant les enseignements de l'Église et devant la philosophie spiritualiste', in A. d'Alès (ed.), *Dictionnaire apologétique de la foi catholique*, 4e éd., tome 2, 1911, col. 501–14.
183. A. d'Alès, 'La Doctrine de la récapitulation en saint Irenée', in *Recherches de science religieuse*, tome 6, 1911, p. 201.

this literature. Thus, besides referring to Lightfoot,[184] Lebreton referred as well to Dorner, Weiss, and Holtzmann,[185] and Prat to Usteri, Holtzmann, and Schweitzer.[186] Léonce de Grandmaison, a friend whom Teilhard much admired, cited Holtzmann, Mackintosh, Illingworth's *Divine Immanence*, and Gore's *Dissertations*;[187] while Marcel Chossat, one of Teilhard's professors in dogmatic theology, also cited Illingworth's *Divine Immanence*.[188] Some of this literature, moreover, was present in the houses where Teilhard studied philosophy and theology. In his philosophate there were copies of *Lux Mundi*, Illingworth's *Divine Immanence*, and Inge's *Personal Idealism*;[189] and in the professors' library of his theologate there were works relevant to the cosmic aspect of Christ by Martensen, Holtzmann, Inge, and Schweitzer.[190] There is no evidence that Teilhard ever read any of this literature. But there can be little doubt that he discussed Christological questions with those who would have had some acquaintance with it. Certainly he is reported as having discussed the Franciscan doctrine on the primacy of Christ – a doctrine closely related to cosmic Christology – with Lebreton, de Grandmaison and d'Alès.[191]

In 1912 the theosophist Édouard Schuré published *L'Évolution divine du Sphinx au Christ*, the concluding section of which is entitled 'Le Christ cosmique et le Jésus historique'. It is quite possible that Teilhard was acquainted with this work[192] through de Grandmaison,

184. J. Lebreton, op. cit. pp. 301–5, 309, 312–13, 500 (5e éd. pp. 364–8, 372, 376, 575). See p. 24 above.
185. Ibid., pp. 149, 199, 237, 239 (5e éd., pp. 153, 230, 270).
186. F. Prat, 'Paul (saint) et le paulinisme', in A. d'Alès (ed.), *Dictionnaire apologétique de la foi catholique*, 4e éd., tome 3, 1916, col. 1623, 1626–7, 1652, 1654.
187. L. de Grandmaison, 'Jésus Christ', in A. d'Alès (ed.), op. cit., 4e éd., tome 2, 1911, col. 1309, 1392–3, 1399, 1402.
188. M. Chossat, 'Dieu (connaissance naturelle de)', in A. Vacant et al. (ed.), *Dictionnaire de théologie catholique*, tome 4, 1911, col. 805.
189. The copy of *Lux Mundi* (1890) is now at the Centre Sèvres, Paris; only certain of its pages are cut, including those that contain Illingworth's 'The Incarnation and Development'. Illingworth's *Divine Immanence* (cheap ed., 1904) and Inge's *Personal Idealism* (1907) are now at Les Fontaines, Chantilly.
    Teilhard left the philosophate on Jersey in 1905; but he could have seen the copy of Inge's book, when he returned there during the late summer of 1913 (see *LHP*, pp. 406–15; *LP*, pp. 103–11).
190. Martensen (4th German ed., 1858), Holtzmann (1897), Inge (1909), Schweitzer (1911). These volumes are now at the Centre Sèvres, Paris.
191. See G. M. Allegra, *My Conversations with Teilhard de Chardin on the Primacy of Christ, Peking, 1942–1945*, p. 39.
192. In 1918 Teilhard was reading Schuré's earlier work, *Les Grands initiés* (1889), but

who had reviewed it (with less than sympathy).[193] But if Schuré were
Teilhard's source for the term 'cosmic Christ',[194] he certainly was not
the source of the doctrine which lay behind Teilhard's use of the
term.[195] Schuré's cosmic Christ is the solar deity, but one of many
Gods, from Archangels to Thrones, who manifest the Eternal. It is his
distinction, alone among the Gods, to have incarnated himself into
humanity.[196] His incarnation occurred at the baptism of Jesus. The
solar deity entered the body of Jesus and replaced his soul, which was
received back into the aura of the sun.[197] Through his incarnation the
cosmic Christ became the highest spiritual manifestation to mankind
and the axis of its evolution.[198] From the idea that the cosmic Christ
is the axis of mankind, a parallel between Schuré and Teilhard may
readily be established. In fact, on this point Schuré expresses himself
in Irenaean terms; and so too, on occasion, does Teilhard.[199] For the
rest, Schuré is completely at variance with the Catholic doctrines on
the Trinity and the Incarnation; while Teilhard, despite the audacity

he gives no hint that he had seen *L'Évolution divine*. See Lettre à Marguerite
Teillard-Chambon, 4.11.1918, *GP*, p. 323 (*MM*, p. 248); ditto, 20.11.1918, ibid.,
p. 334 (p. 256); ditto, 13.12.1918, ibid., pp. 349–50 (pp. 267–8); *Journal*, tome 1,
19.11.1918, p. 372; ibid., 5.12.1918, pp. 373–4; ibid., 10.12.1918, pp. 376–7; ibid.,
13.12.1918, p. 386.

193. See L. de Grandmaison, Review of É. Schuré, *L'Évolution divine du Sphinx au
Christ*, in *Études*, tome 132, 1912, pp. 571–2.

194. Another problem is Schuré's own source of 'cosmic Christ'. He may have coined
the term for himself; it does not seem to have occurred in theosophical literature
before his *L'Évolution divine*. He could have based the term on the phraseology of
his theosophical friend Steiner. See, for instance, Rudolf Steiner, *The Gospel of
St. John in Relation to the Other Gospels, Especially That of St. Luke*, London,
1933 [14 lectures first given in 1909], pp. 251–2: '. . . when the Cross was raised
on Golgotha and the blood ran from the wounds of Christ Jesus, a new cosmic
centre was created.'

195. According to J. Artur, 'À propos du P. Teilhard: En relisant Édouard Schuré', in
*La Pensée catholique*, no. 102, 1966, pp. 52–5, Teilhard derived more than the
term 'cosmic Christ' from Schuré; in his essay 'La Vie cosmique' he also presented
his doctrine on the cosmic Christ in a manner distinctly reminiscent of Schuré's
pantheism. Arthur's essay is a polemical piece which exhibits no understanding of
Teilhard's view on the relationship between Christ and the material universe.

196. É. Schuré, *L'Évolution divine du Sphinx au Christ*, pp. 349–50 (E.T., *From Sphinx
to Christ*, p. 229).

197. Ibid., pp. 372–3 (pp. 243–4).

198. Ibid., pp. 349, 417 (pp. 229, 271). The essentials of Schuré's doctrine on the
cosmic Christ reappear in V. Tweedale, *The Cosmic Christ*, [1930,] and in J. O.
Mackenzie, 'The Cosmic Christ', in E. J. Langford Garstin and Hugh J.
Schonfield (ed.), *Jesus Christ Nineteen Centuries After: The Search Symposium by
Leaders of the Great World Faiths*, 1933, pp. 179–90.

199. See p. 79 n. 33 below.

of his speculations in cosmic Christology, never for one moment betrays disagreement with the essentials of these doctrines.

Teilhard developed cosmic-Christ terminology as no other author has done. His initial use of it, however, seems to have depended not on his own inventiveness but on what he learnt from his background. Even his innovations in cosmic-Christ doctrine do not set him entirely apart. As this chapter is attempting to show, what he expressed was only a more complete version – a version taken to the logical extreme – of the tendencies, present in other expositions of the cosmic Christ, which the very use of 'cosmic' to qualify Christ appears to have generated.

### V. COMPARISONS WITH TEILHARD

On 1 May 1948 Teilhard transcribed the following passage into his journal:[200]

> . . . if we believe, as we may, with Professor B. Moore, that 'it was no fortuitous combination of chances and no cosmic dust which brought life to the bosom of our ancient mother earth . . . , but a well-regulated order of development, which comes to every mother earth in the universe in the maturity of its creation, when the conditions arrive within the suitable limits,'[201] it is not impossible that other worlds may know their Bethlehem, and their Calvary too. In a very real sense, the historic Jesus is for us the cosmic Christ.

The passage is from *Man and the Attainment of Immortality* (1922)[202] by James Young Simpson, Professor of Natural Science, New College, Edinburgh. Simpson was a colleague of H. R. Mackintosh and H. A. A. Kennedy, and he was a devoted disciple of Henry Drummond.[203] Like his master, Simpson held an interventionist position on creative development in the world.[204] Thus Christ's coming is 'no more, but no less, "a special intervention" than the appearance of life, or self-consciousness, or any of the other big lifts in the cosmic process.'[205] With his interventionism, Simpson com-

200. *Journal* XV ( = 3), pp. [119]–20.
201. B. Moore, *Biochemistry: A Study of the Origin, Reactions and Equilibria of Living Matter*, Edward Arnold, London, 1921, p. 34.
202. p. 315. The passage occurs in a chapter entitled 'The Historic Jesus and the Cosmic Christ', perhaps an echo of Schuré.
203. Cf. G. F. Barbour, 'Memoir', in J. Y. Simpson, *The Garment of the Living God*, 1934, pp. 16, 19–23, 32–4, 54, 59.
204. J. Y. Simpson, *Man and the Attainment of Immortality*, p. 314.
205. Ibid., pp. 311–12.

bined the view that evolution is a process of winning greater and greater degrees of freedom,[206] until in man there is the freedom to choose immortality through a steadfast love for God.[207] The way to immortality has been definitively established by Christ.[208] As the ultimate instance of the divine intervention,[209] the fulfilment of God's progressively incarnating himself in humanity, the Alpha and Omega of human history,[210] Christ provides the ideal for attracting the process, in the moral sphere, to its completion.[211] For Simpson, then, this is the cosmic significance of Christ. In the margin of his journal, Teilhard registered his dissent from Simpson. God's creativity is not fulfilled with the first coming of Christ but only at the Parousia. Simpson had underestimated both the role of Christ-Omega and the capacity of humanity for further development.[212]

A later work by Simpson, *Nature: Cosmic, Human and Divine* (1929), highlights more sharply the difference between his conception of the cosmic Christ and Teilhard's. Christ, according to Simpson, is the highest product of a single world-process[213] that moves from cosmic to human nature[214] and has God as the ground of its existence;[215] he is the ultimate manifestation of God's progressively incarnating himself in this process.[216] In other words, for the emergence of Christ cosmic nature acts as a substrate. According to Teilhard, on the other hand, cosmic nature, while contributing to Christ, becomes in turn dominated by Christ's formal causality. That is to say, cosmic nature is directed towards the building-up of Christ's cosmic body; or, to use Teilhard's later formulation, cosmogenesis is transformed into Christogenesis. In his final work, *The Garment of the Living God* (1934), Simpson stated his position this way: 'The most significant fact in the Universe is process, and the most

206. Ibid., pp. 236–9, 242–4, 260–2, 269.
207. Ibid., pp. 231–3, 284–301.
208. Ibid., pp. 284–90, 299–301.
209. Ibid., pp. 304, 311–12, 315.
210. Ibid., pp. 259–60, 311, 335–6.
211. Ibid., pp. 316–17.
212. See Teilhard, *Journal* XV ( = 3), p. [119]. Teilhard wrote in the margin: '[sous-estimat du χ-ω (d'*Hté*) Fulfil': à Parousie)'.
    He placed this comment beside the following sentence slightly adapted from Simpson (op. cit., p. 260): 'For in Jesus came to actuality for the first and only time that for which the whole process had been planned; and He is the fulfilment of all that was before.'
213. J. Y. Simpson, *Nature: Cosmic, Human and Divine*, pp. 136–8, 145–6.
214. Ibid., pp. 53, 112, 137.
215. Ibid., pp. 113, 117, 132.
216. Ibid., pp. 138, 145–6.

significant fact in the process is Jesus Christ. . . . '[217] In contrast, Teilhard would have said not that Jesus Christ is the most significant fact in the process, but that through his cosmic nature Christ controls and consummates the process.[218] Though Simpson entertained the possibility of extraterrestrial divine incarnations, his formulation of the cosmic Christ remained earth-bound. If the universal process is able to issue in a plurality of incarnations, then Jesus Christ on earth is not *the* most significant fact in this process.

Several passages in *The Unfinished Universe* (1935) by T. S. Gregory (at one time editor of *The Wiseman Review*), provide a further contrast with Teilhard's cosmic Christology. As we have noted, Teilhard originally referred to the cosmic Christ as the means for resolving the conflict he felt between a Christian desire to renounce the 'Kosmos' and an appreciation of its value. In his later writings, he worked out this theme in terms of what he called the Above and the Ahead ('L'En Haut' and 'L'En Avant'). The movement of the world towards its Omega is the resultant of two faiths – faith in the God above and faith in worldly progress ahead. And the possibility of synthesizing these two faiths rests on the transformation of cosmogenesis and anthropogenesis into Christogenesis.[219] Using terminology similar to Teilhard's, Gregory denied that the Ahead plays any part in the attainment of God. The universe moves 'not forward to the next stage of its own evolution but upward to the City of God'.[220] This, said Gregory, is the doctrine of St. Thomas Aquinas. The upward movement in no way implies that God capriciously irrupts into the world.[221] Rather, it means that in Christ, the God-man who is also the God-community, 'the whole natural process reaches its fruition and is superseded'.[222] For, according to Gregory, what constitutes Christ's cosmic incarnation is the incorporation of human life and the whole cosmos into a divine world.[223] Gregory's reading of St. Thomas needs to be clarified with

217. J. Y. Simpson, *The Garment of the Living God*, p. 259.
218. 'Quelques Réflexions sur la Conversion du Monde', *Oeuvres* 9, p. 161 (*SC*, p. 122); 'Christianisme et Évolution', *Oeuvres* 10, pp. 209–11 (*CE*, pp. 179–81); 'Comment je vois', *Oeuvres* 11, p. 214 (*TF*, pp. 198–9); 'Le Christique', *Oeuvres* 13, p. 107 (*HM*, pp. 92–3).
219. 'Trois Choses que je vois', *Oeuvres* 11, pp. 170–5 (*TF*, pp. 156–61); 'Réflexions sur la probabilité scientifique et les Conséquences religieuses d' un Ultra-Humain', *Oeuvres* 7, pp. 288–91 (*AE*, pp. 277–80).
220. T. S. Gregory, *The Unfinished Universe*, p. 307; also pp. 247–8.
221. Ibid., p. 246.
222. Ibid., p. 238.
223. Ibid., pp. 239, 244, 246.

the observation that St. Thomas envisages at the end of this life not an annihilation of the material world but its transformation into a fitting environment for man in his glorified state.[224] But even when this qualification is made, Teilhard's position remains contrasted with that of Gregory. In his attempt to combine the Upward with the Forward, Teilhard saw Christ's cosmic incarnation as occurring in such a way that the natural process, in its being supernaturally transformed by Christ, contributes at the same time to building him up.

Despite clear differences in their notions about the cosmic aspect of Christ, Simpson and Gregory were in agreement with each other and with Teilhard on one significant point. The cosmic aspect of Christ expresses neither his divinity nor simply the created humanity of Jesus of Nazareth. Thus, for Simpson, it is possible that the cosmic process, into which God progressively incarnates himself, gives rise in various parts of the universe to divine manifestations equivalent to that in the terrestrial Jesus; while, according to Gregory, the Incarnation in its cosmic dimension is Christ, the God-community into which human life and the whole cosmos are incorporated. Of these two positions, Gregory's is closer to the Teilhardian idea of a third nature in Christ. But both of them illustrate the tendency, which appears to result from the use of cosmic-Christ language, to find in Christ something else in addition to divinity and humanity.

## VI.  IN SEARCH OF THE COSMIC CHRIST

By about 1930 the impetus which cosmic Christology had received from the theory of evolution seems to have temporarily exhausted itself, except in the case of Teilhard's work, which remained generally unknown until the 1960s. Thornton's *The Incarnate Lord*, published in 1928, marked a turning to process theology, while Simpson's last work in 1934 was a throw-back to a previous way of thinking.

Cosmic Christology now began to take a new course. More thorough consideration was given to its New Testament foundations, to its fortunes during the course of theological history and to its place in the religious experience of Christians in the modern world. Eventually, at the beginning of the 1960s, what had hitherto been an obscure theological topic became an issue towards which world-wide

---

224. *Summa contra Gentiles*, 4: 97; *Summa Theologica*, 3 suppl.: 94: 1 ( = *Commentum in Librum IV Sententiarum*, 48: 2: 1).

attention was directed. Teilhard's writings, which were gradually being published from 1955 onwards, contributed in no small measure to the discussion. But there was another influence at work as well, an address given by Joseph Sittler at New Delhi in 1961. We shall now look at the line of development leading up to Sittler's address.

In 1929 there were posthumously published two works by H. T. Andrews, the son-in-law and a teaching colleague of P. T. Forsyth. In both of these works – an unfinished book, *The Christ of Apostolic Faith*, and an essay, 'The Christ of Apostolic Experience'[225] – Andrews proposed, in the same terms, an explanation for the cosmic conception of Christ in Col. 1: 15–17.[226] It was an explanation which to some extent echoed the opinions of H. R. Mackintosh and H. A. A. Kennedy. The fundamental question, said Andrews, is not what are the literary sources behind this conception, but why did Paul, using the categories of thought available to him, make Jesus Christ the centre of the cosmic system. So far the historico-critical school has failed to provide an adequate answer to this question. Paul's cosmic conception of Christ cannot be due simply to his reaction against the Christological heresy at Colossae. As 1 Cor. 8: 6 demonstrates, the conception had been developing in his mind for some years. The answer, then, must lie in Paul's inner experience of Christ, in his Christ-mysticism. Because Christ was the centre of Paul's own moral universe, Paul must have concluded that he was the centre of the whole universe. Logically the conclusion seems unwarranted. It may, however, be justified on the ground that, unless one is prepared to accept metaphysical dualism, the centre of moral reality and the centre of cosmic reality are but different aspects of the one ultimate fact.[227] Furthermore, it seems that Paul's cosmic conception of Christ was not merely a private conviction. If we are to judge from its repetition in Hebrews and the Gospel of John, the conception corresponded to what the Church at large experienced.[228]

Another author who dealt with the source of the cosmic conception of Christ was H. W. Clark. His account, however, was concerned less with the relation of this conception to Paul's religious psychology

225. Published in H. T. Andrews *et al.*, *The Lord of Life: A Fresh Approach to the Incarnation*.
226. *The Christ of Apostolic Faith*, pp. 133–9; see p. viii; 'The Christ of Apostolic Experience', in H. T. Andrews *et al.*, op. cit., pp. 108–10.
227. Compare H. R. Mackintosh, *The Doctrine of the Person of Jesus Christ*, 1912, p. 448; see also p. 370.
228. Compare H. A. A. Kennedy, *The Theology of the Epistles*, 1919, p. 157.

than with its original structure. On the basis of his account, he went on to examine the subsequent theological treatment of this structure. He discussed these matters in *The Cross and the Eternal Order: A Study of Atonement in Its Cosmic Significance* (1943). Like Andrews, Clark belonged to the same Free Church tradition as P. T. Forsyth. And in his use of cosmic-Christ language he made acknowledgement to Martensen.[229]

Clark suggested[230] that, in order to counter the heresies of his day, such as the Colossian heresy, Paul broadened his idea of Christ's redemption to cosmic proportions. And then, through some spiritual insight or through divine inspiration, he saw that, just as God in Christ redeems all, so too in Christ he has created all (Col. 1: 16) and continues to sustain all (Col. 1: 17). Thus arose Paul's cosmic conception of Christ. Clark outlined its structure in what he called the Pauline thought-series: Christ the creator, Christ the immanent sustainer and Christ the redeemer. The last member of the series implies that Christ has altered his relationship of immanence with the world, in order to overcome its sinful disruption and to bring it new life.

After the New Testament period Paul's thought-series went largely unappreciated. Greek theology overstressed Christ's immanence.[231] Latin theology was too legalistic to suggest 'a cosmic process to which Christ, from Creation to Redemption, belonged'.[232] In nineteenth-century European theology Dorner, Rothe, and Martensen, under the influence of Hegel's dialectic, reduced Christ to the individual who embodies the synthesis of God's self-maintaining and self-imparting; that is, they saw him principally as a revealer figure and passed over his functions of creator, sustainer, and cosmic redeemer.[233] Meanwhile in Britain S. T. Coleridge had to some extent regained the position of early Greek theology. Beginning with the idea of the Cambridge Platonists that between God and man there exists an intellectual correspondence, he maintained that, in the light

---

229. H. W. Clark, *The Cross and the Eternal Order*, p. 43.
230. Ibid., pp. 116–21.
231. Ibid., pp. 121–5.
232. Ibid., pp. 125–30.
233. Ibid., pp. 130–7. See I. A. Dorner, *Entwicklungsgeschichte der Lehre von der Person Christi*, 2. Aufl., 2. Theil, 2. Abtheilung, 1856, pp. 1227–44 (E.T., division 2, vol. 2, pp. 232–7); id., *System der christlichen Glaubenslehre*, 2. Bd., 1880, pp. 427–30 (E.T., vol. 3, pp. 324–7); R. Rothe, *Theologische Ethik*, 2. Bd., 1845, pp. 281–4; id., *Dogmatik*, 1870, 2. Theil, 1. Abtheilung, pp. 120–2; H. L. Martensen, *Den Christelige Dogmatik*, 1849, pp. 265–8, 278 (E.T., pp. 260–3, 272).

of the Redemption, we must also acknowledge a spiritual correspondence. Clark would appear to have been referring to Coleridge's doctrine that the indwelling of Christ's divinity in men is the fruit of the Redemption.[234] With Thomas Erskine of Linlathen, F. D. Maurice, and J. McLeod Campbell, the notion of Christ's indwelling was taken a step further. By virtue of his being head of the race, Christ dwells in every man; and salvation lies in recognizing this truth.[235] Such was Clark's historical survey of the doctrine on the cosmic aspect of Christ. He concluded it by noting with regret that the Pauline thought-series had not been recovered.[236]

Clark's conclusion was not unwarranted, considering the prevalence of restricted conceptions of the cosmic Christ. Some authors, such as J. Y. Simpson, equated Christ's cosmic significance with the incarnation in Jesus as the climax of divine purpose.[237] William Fairweather referred to the cosmic Christ simply as the underlying principle of the cosmos.[238] For J. M. Creed the cosmic Christ was merely God's agent in creation.[239] E. M. Root, in a poem entitled 'Cosmic Christ', and R. V. Sellers exhibited an awareness of the cosmic Christ only as sustainer of the universe.[240] A. S. Pringle-Pattinson and W. R. Inge, writing in his old age, saw somewhat further: the cosmic Christ is both organ of divine creativity and sustainer of the universe.[241] D. M. Edwards also acknowledged these two cosmic aspects of Christ but interpreted them as no more than

234. H. W. Clark, op. cit., pp. 137–8. See S. T. Coleridge, *Aids to Reflection*, 1825, pp. 307–9, 315–17, 398–9 (revised ed., 1884, pp. 211–13, 217–18, 272–3); id., 'Notes on the Book of Common Prayer', in *The Literary Remains of Samuel Taylor Coleridge*, ed. by H. N. Coleridge, vol. 3, 1838, pp. 7–8 (also in *Aids to Reflection*, revised ed., 1884, pp. 350–1).

235. H. W. Clark, op. cit., pp. 138–9. See T. Erskine, *The Brazen Serpent; Or Life Coming through Death*, 1831, pp. 43, 46, 51–5, 62–3, 66, 70–1, 100, 103, 166–7, 170; letters of F. D. Maurice (from 1833 to 1868), quoted in Frederick Maurice, *The Life of Frederick Denison Maurice Chiefly Told in His Own Letters*, 1884, vol. 1, pp. 155, 240, 376; vol. 2, pp. 138, 161, 376, 408, 581; F. D. Maurice, *Theological Essays* (first published 1853), 2nd ed., 1853, pp. 117, 144, 424 (2nd ed. reset, 1957, pp. 94, 112, 290); id., *The Doctrine of Sacrifice Deduced from the Scriptures*, 1854, pp. 282, 313; J. McLeod Campbell, *The Nature of the Atonement and Its Relation to Remission of Sins and Eternal Life*, 1856, pp. 159–60, 221–2.

236. H. W. Clark, op. cit., p. 139.

237. See pp. 46–7 above.

238. W. Fairweather, *The Background of the Epistles*, 1935, pp. 317, 320.

239. J. M. Creed, *The Divinity of Jesus Christ*, 1938, pp. 138–40.

240. E. M. Root, 'Cosmic Christ', in *Christian Century*, vol. 45, 1928, p. 876; R. V. Sellers, *Two Ancient Christologies*, 1940, p. 245.

241. A. S. Pringle-Pattinson, *Studies in the Philosophy of Religion*, 1930, pp. 193–4; W. R. Inge, *Mysticism in Religion* [1947], pp. 37–8.

values in the personal experience of Jesus. Edwards's interpretation resulted from his making Christ's divinity consist in a quality of will, conceived ethically rather than metaphysically, which is identical with the quality of God's will.[242] At the time when Clark was writing, only Teilhard, unknown to the public at large, had developed a doctrine about the cosmic Christ that covered the entire Pauline thought-series.

Unless Christians appropriate all the Pauline thought-series, said Clark, they cannot go beyond the partial viewpoints of secular philosophies to grasp the 'final fact' – that the world-process, originating with God through Christ, returns to God through Christ's cosmic redemption, which begins at the Cross.[243] But if the entire Pauline thought-series were to be upheld, might not some broadening of Christological categories be required? In this regard Clark made the following suggestion. Much more than a natural evolutionary movement, human development also consists in a movement towards a higher plane of existence, towards union with God. Thus Christ is immanent in men, not only as creator and sustainer of their constitutive elements and their faculties, but as the divine appeal, calling them to God. In this latter sense, Christ's immanence may be referred to as the Eternal Son's incarnation in the human race as a whole, as distinct from his incarnation in a historical personality, through which redemption is effected.[244]

Clark's observations raise, but leave unanswered, several questions. What difficulty do Christians of the modern world have to face in appropriating a cosmic doctrine about Christ? How may the difficulty be resolved? And why should anyone today even contemplate such a doctrine? We shall deal with the third of these questions shortly. The first two were considered by A. D. Galloway in *The Cosmic Christ* (1951), though his answers were related to only one part of Clark's Pauline thought-series. The original title of Galloway's work as a doctoral dissertation, *The Cosmic Significance of Christian Redemption*, conveys exactly the scope of the work.

The difficulty which the idea of cosmic redemption poses for the contemporary Christian had previously been formulated by H. Wheeler Robinson in his *Redemption and Revelation* (1942). Wheeler Robinson was the editor of H. T. Andrews's book *The Christ*

---

242. D. M. Edwards, 'The Doctrine of the Person of Christ', in *The Hibbert Journal*, vol. 23, 1924–25, pp. 462–5.
243. H. W. Clark, op. cit., pp. 144, 146, 156, 161–2, 235, 241–2, 251–4.
244. Ibid., pp. 150–1, 157–8.

*of Apostolic Faith*. As the starting-point for his work, Galloway[245] quoted Wheeler Robinson's formulation:

The modern emphasis tends to fall on salvation from the power of moral evil in present existence. The New Testament, without, of course, denying or excluding this element as an accompaniment or even a condition of salvation, finds its centre of gravity in a cosmic event.[246]

Galloway pointed out that the New Testament doctrine of cosmic redemption has its roots in a particular cultural experience, Jewish eschatological expectation. The Jews reacted to misfortune by building their hopes not on an other-worldly dualism but on a redemption that would transform their environment. Under the influence of its widening horizons, primitive Christianity pushed the expectation to its logical limit: the belief arose that Christ's redemptive act involves the whole of creation.[247] Subsequently, with the collapse of its cultural support, the doctrine of cosmic redemption became less relevant to immediate experience and eventually was lost. The Alexandrians failed to sustain a full doctrine of cosmic redemption, owing to their depreciation of matter;[248] while the Fathers of the West, though they reasserted the doctrine's biblical symbolism, were unable to relate it to a world in which Christ's presence in the Church had been substituted for his imminent return.[249] The doctrine of the resurrection forced mediaeval theologians to include the human body within the scope of redemption, but the dichotomy they maintained between nature and grace prevented them from extending it to the physical universe.[250] And for the Reformers there was no question of cosmic redemption, since their concern lay elsewhere, with inner personal experience.[251] As the history of theology makes clear, the New Testament doctrine of cosmic redemption was gradually stifled by a covert dualism.[252] In modern times dualism remains. The scientific revolution at the Renaissance established the physical world as an autonomous system, cut off from all experience of the personal, including religious experience.[253]

245. A. D. Galloway, *The Cosmic Christ*, p. vii.
246. H. Wheeler Robinson, *Redemption and Revelation in the Actuality Of History*, p. 233.
247. A. D. Galloway, op. cit., p. 55.
248. Ibid., p. 98.
249. Ibid., pp. 114–15.
250. Ibid., pp. 125–6.    251. Ibid., p. 130.
252. Ibid., p. 232.    253. Ibid., pp. 133–6, 232.

Mackintosh and Andrews had suggested that a doctrine on the cosmic Christ involves the repudiation of dualism.[254] Galloway developed this point. Faced with the contemporary dualism of scientific and religious experience, he argued, we must assert that, besides persons, Christ also redeems the cosmos; otherwise the cosmos stands condemned as intrinsically evil.[255] But here systematic thought poses a dilemma which it cannot overcome. Either we say that cosmic redemption is merely subjective (Christ changes the Christian's outlook towards the physical world), and then we scarcely do justice to New Testament teaching. Or we say that cosmic redemption is indeed objective (Christ transforms the physical world itself), in which case we find no generally accepted empirical evidence to support this claim. For example, the evidence of faith-healing is likely to be conclusive only for those who already believe that Christ is Lord of heaven and earth. We resolve the dilemma between the subjective and the objective only by discovering in an existential situation that they are correlative rather than strictly opposed. Thus to recognize that redemption is not only for ourselves but also for the cosmos to which we belong, we must rely on the existential situation of personal encounter with Christ.[256]

In *Christology and Myth in the New Testament* (1956) G. V. Jones suggested that Galloway had evaded instead of resolving the dilemma between the subjective and the objective. No matter what referent one attributes to it, an existential situation pertains entirely to subjective experience. As such, it does not come to terms with the intention, behind many New Testament passages, of affirming a doctrine on the cosmic Christ which has not simply mythological or existential significance but at least some minimal objectively cosmological meaning.[257] In reply, the existentialist would ask whether the cosmos has any meaning at all, apart from a relation to the subjects who know it. W. A. Whitehouse, in his essay 'Christ and Creation' (1956), adopted this kind of approach. We can only interpret Christ's instrumental creativity in terms of the new Creation, inaugurated through the Redemption, which brings men into existence as responsible partners of God for exercising dominion over the world. This interpretation is all the more necessary in view of the anthropo-

254. See p. 50 above.
255. Op. cit., p. 205.
256. Ibid., pp. 233–40.
257. G. V. Jones, *Christology and Myth in the New Testament*, pp. 161, 172–3, 177; also pp. 69, 151, 153.

centric character of Scripture, which makes it difficult for us to see Christ as a cosmic principle abstracted from his historical work for men.[258]

Existentialism, with its subordination of being to meaning, is perhaps less a solution to the problem of dualistic thinking than a reflection of the epistemological quandary into which the post-Enlightenment age has fallen. Nevertheless, Galloway's exposure of the problem was to have considerable influence in spreading discussion about the cosmic Christ. Such influence presupposes some general reason for the recovery of a cosmic conception of Christ in modern times. Illingworth, as we have seen,[259] ascribed the recovery to the revival of constructive thinking, which for him appears to have been a response to the alteration in perspective brought about by the theory of evolution. It was Teilhard, however, who suggested more forcibly that the recovery is due to the modern scientific world-view, even though he made the point with his own notion of convergent evolution in mind. The contemporary vision of a universe vast in size and evolving towards a personal goal has awakened Christians to the great cosmic attributes of Christ which St. Paul and St. John taught and upon which the Greek Fathers reflected.[260]

Illingworth and Teilhard wrote as though the recovery had virtually been accomplished. In fact, prior to the 1960s, little attention was given to the idea of a cosmic Christ. Recalling the circumstances in which he undertook his doctoral dissertation in the late 1940s, Galloway has said:

> I believe that the Board of Theological Studies in Cambridge were very hesitant about accepting it as a serious research project. The opinion was widely entertained that the notion of the cosmic significance of the person and work of Christ was merely an aspect of the mythological concomitants of the Gospel. It reflected only the cultural idiosyncrasies of New Testament times. . . . In the liberal theology, which still prevailed in this country in my youth, such notions were regarded as interesting curiosities for the historian of ideas, but of little or no contemporary theological or dogmatic significance.[261]

Thus, while a number of writers in the field of biblical theology had

258. W. A. Whitehouse, 'Christ and Creation', in T. H. L. Parker (ed.), *Essays in Christology for Karl Barth*, pp. 125–31.
259. pp. 27–8 above.
260. 'Christianisme et Évolution', *Oeuvres* 10, pp. 209–11 (*CE*, pp. 179–81); 'Catholicisme et Science', *Oeuvres* 9, pp. 238–40 (*SC*, pp. 188–90).
261. A. D. Galloway, *The Cosmic Christ* [unpublished paper], 1977, p. 1.

considered the theme of the cosmic Christ,[262] systematic attempts to appropriate it for present-day Christian belief were few and far between.[263] Apart from the authors so far discussed, only Karl Barth, E. L. Mascall, and the German Evangelicals O. A. Dilschneider and Adolf Köberle raised systematic questions about the cosmic Christ before Sittler's New Delhi address in 1961.

In one of the later sections of his *Church Dogmatics*, published in 1959, Barth asked in parenthesis, with reference to Col. 1: 15–20 and Eph. 1: 22, whether we do not have to declare a third form of existence in Christ, a third predicate of his being:

> Does He really exist only as the One He alone is with God, and then as the One He is with and in His community? Does He not already exist and act and achieve and work also as the *Pantocrator*, as the κεφαλὴ ὑπὲρ πάντα, as the One who alone has first and final power in the cosmos?[264]

These distinctions in Christ in no way imply that his person is divided. That was a point which Barth made five years later, when replying to questions on the cosmic Christ in an ecumenical seminar at the Château de Bossey.[265] The cosmic Christ, he said, is not 'another Christ but Christ crucified or risen'; 'the cosmic Christ is Christ's real presence and activity as the living Saviour, Lord, Creator in every element in nature and history'.[266] It should be noted that Barth used 'cosmic Christ' only in response to the seminar questions; the expression was not part of his normal theological language.

In the 1956 Bampton Lectures Mascall interpreted the cosmic Christ, with reference to Eph. 1: 20–1 and Heb. 2: 7–8, as the divine

262. For the situation in biblical theology, see J. G. Gibbs, *Creation and Redemption*, pp. 1–32; H. Riedlinger, 'How Universal is Christ's Kingship? – A Bibliographical Study', in *Concilium*, vol. 1, no 2, Jan. 1966, pp. 57–60; H. J. Gabathuler, *Jesus Christus, Haupt der Kirche – Haupt der Welt: Die Christushymnus Colosser 1, 15–20 in der theologische Forschung der letzten 130 Jahre*, pp. 150–2.

263. For a very brief historical sketch of the cosmic aspect of Christ treated systematically prior to the 1960s, see H. Berkhof, 'Christ and Cosmos', in *Nederlands Theologisch Tijdschrift*, vol. 22, 1967–68, pp. 423–4.

264. K. Barth, *Die kirchliche Dogmatik*, 4. Bd., *Die Lehre von der Versöhnung*, 3. Teil, 2 Hälfte, 1959, pp. 865–6 (E.T., *Church Dogmatics*, vol. 4, *The Doctrine of Reconciliation*, part 3, 2nd half, p. 756)

265. *Questions for the Seminar with Professor Karl Barth*, 18.1.1964, The Graduate School of Ecumenical Studies, Institut oecuménique, Château de Bossey, Céligny, 1.10.1963 – 15.2.1964.

266. Quoted in A. Szekeres, 'La pensée religieuse de Teilhard de Chardin et la signification théologique de son Christ cosmique', in id. (ed.), *Le Christ cosmique de Teilhard de Chardin*, p. 395.

Word who, through his incarnation in the human race, has acquired supremacy over the whole of creation and has enabled man, in fulfilment of God's promise, to dominate all things. The earth-centredness of this New Testament teaching, Mascall confessed, left him in a state of uncertainty, in view of the possibility that within the vast universe disclosed by modern astronomy there exist other races of corporeal rational creatures, in some of whom the Word of God may have become incarnate. Do we say that, for the restoration of right order in creation, the material universe must be subjected only to terrestrial man or to all other corporeal rational species as well?[267]

Despite the problems which scientific notions inevitably raise for religion, Mascall was confident that science had become during the twentieth century far more compatible with orthodox Christian theology than it had been in the past.[268] Quite a different view of the contemporary relationship between science and Christianity was taken by Dilschneider (1953) and Köberle (1957). Speaking within the tradition of the Lutheran Reformation, they charged that theology had retreated into a subjective world concerned only with individual salvation. In so doing, it discarded the New Testament doctrine of the cosmic Christ, the doctrine that Christ is Lord and Redeemer not just of persons but indeed of the whole universe.[269] This teaching, which persisted in the West to the end of the Middle Ages and still thrives in the Eastern Churches, cannot be rejected through an appeal to Luther. Though admittedly it remained only at the periphery of his attention, Luther himself did not exclude it.[270] And, as Köberle pointed out, it continued to be upheld by a number of Luther's own followers, among them Oetinger and the Swabian school.[271] Another reason for rejecting the doctrine of the cosmic Christ, whether in its New Testament or in some modern theological form of expression, has been its alleged surrender to Gnosticism.[272] In fact, the true

---

267. E. L. Mascall, *Christian Theology and Natural Science*, 1956, pp. x, 44–5; also pp. 36–44.
    Note: This discussion was originally an article, 'Is the Incarnation Unique?', in *Theology*, vol. 56, 1953, pp. 288–94. When the article reappeared in the published Bampton Lectures, the term 'cosmic Christ' was incorporated into the summary of contents.
268. E. L. Mascall, *Christian Theology and Natural Science*, p. 46.
269. O. A. Dilschneider, *Gefesselte Kirche, Not und Verheissung*, 1953, pp. 19, 137–46; A. Köberle, *Der Herr über alles*, 1957; 2. Aufl., 1958, pp, 101–6, 111–12.
270. O. A. Dilschneider, op. cit., pp. 19–21, 136.
271. A. Köberle, op. cit. p. 113.
272. O. A. Dilschneider, op. cit., p. 137; A. Köberle, op. cit., p. 104.

reason lies elsewhere. According to Dilschneider, when theology found itself confronted with the Copernican revolution and even more with the advent of the space age, both of which contributed to awakening mankind to the possibility of mastering an immense universe, it lost its nerve and abandoned the world to the forces of secularization.[273] Köberle, for his part, saw theology's retreat from the natural world, especially since the Enlightenment, as the logical outcome of the Cartesian split between the moral and the material spheres of existence.[274]

Thus for these two German Evangelicals the dualism to which Galloway had referred was very much a controlling influence in the theological attitudes of their Christian contemporaries. In such circumstances, the reason for recovering a cosmic conception of Christ could be interpreted as a moral imperative. This was the approach of Joseph Sittler, Lutheran professor in the University of Chicago Divinity School, when he addressed the Faith and Order Movement at New Delhi in 1961. With Col. 1: 15–20 for his text and Galloway's book as his guide, he announced that, for the Church seeking unity the more effectively to bring light to the world, the 'way forward is from Christology expanded to its cosmic dimensions', from Christology which takes account of the goodness that God saw in creation and of the command that men are to care for the earth.[275] From Augustine onwards, said Sittler, Western Christendom has been marked by an inability to connect the realm of grace with that of nature. Grace has been looked upon as operative only within personal morality and history. It is true that, at the very moment when vast changes in the relationship between man and nature were taking place, the Reformers attested to the sovereignty of grace over all nature. But in the post-Reformation period that insight of theirs was neglected. And at the Enlightenment a combination of Rationalism and Pietism narrowed down the idea of redemptive grace to an effect in the individual person.[276] We must now take our stand not with Augustine but with Irenaeus, for whom all goodness, whether in this world or at the final consummation, manifests the grace of God.[277] '... a doctrine of redemption is meaningful only when it

273. O. A. Dilschneider, op. cit., pp. 22, 139, 146.
274. A. Köberle, op. cit., pp. 101–3.
275. J. A. Sittler, 'Called to Unity', in *The Ecumenical Review*, vol. 14, 1961–62, pp. 184–6.
276. Ibid., pp. 179, 181, 183.
277. Ibid., pp. 179–81.

swings within the larger orbit of a doctrine of creation.'[278] Redemption conceived as 'an "angelic" escape from the cosmos of natural and historical fact' bespeaks a dualistic split between the spiritual and the temporal which is both inappropriate to the organic character of biblical language and unintelligible in the present state of man's knowledge and experience.[279] For an age that has known Hiroshima, damnation threatens not just individual men and societies, as has always been the case; it now threatens physical nature, the foundation of life itself. In such an age, besides its Christologies of the moral soul and of history, the Church also needs a life-affirming Christology of nature, a cosmic Christology.[280]

## VII. DISSEMINATING THE COSMIC CHRIST

Sittler's address evoked a response of near incomprehension from most of the delegates at the New Delhi assembly.[281] But among a wider audience it had considerable impact.[282] This was particularly so in German Evangelical circles, where, apart from the isolated considerations of Dilschneider and Köberle, the cosmic Christ as a topic in systematic theology had not in recent times been raised.[283] A number of commentators there [284] saw Sittler's address as the kind of pioneering vision which the Church so urgently needed to inspire its

278. Ibid., p. 178.
279. Ibid., p. 179.
280. Ibid., pp. 183–4, 187.
281. Cf. D. G. Moses, 'Jesus Our Contemporary: The Emmanuel and the Cosmic Christ', in *National Christian Council Review*, vol. 82, 1962, p. 460; C. Simonson, *The Christology of the Faith and Order Movement*, pp. 98–9.
282. Cf. C. Simonson, op. cit., pp. 94–5.
283. Cf. S. M. Daecke, *Teilhard de Chardin und die evangelische Theologie: Die Weltlichkeit Gottes und die Weltlichkeit der Welt*, p. 403. Daecke refers only to the systematic discussion by Dilschneider.
284. J. W. Winterhager, 'Neu-Delhi und die Anfänge einer ökumenischen Theologie', in *Theologia Viatorum*, 8. Jahrgang, 1961–2, p. 308; id., 'Ökumenischer Vorspruch', in O. A. Dilschneider, *Christus Pantokrator: Vom Kolosserbrief zur Ökumene*, 1962, pp. [11–12]; R. Scheffbuch, 'Die Herausforderung von New Delhi', in *Lutherische Monatshefte*, 1. Jahrgang, 1962, p. 6; H. Meyer, *Kirche für die Welt: Gedanken zur 3. Vollsammlung des ökumenischen Rates der Kirchen in Neu Delhi*, 1962, p. 13; H. Bürkle, 'Die Frage nach dem "kosmischen Christus" als Beispiel einer ökumenisch orientierten Theologie', in *Kerygma und Dogma*, 11. Jahrgang, 1965, pp. 103–4 (E.T., 'The Debate of the "Cosmic Christ" as Example of an Ecumenically Oriented Theology', in H. Bürkle and W. M. W. Roth (ed.), *Indian Voices in Today's Theological Debate*, 1972, pp. 198–200).

ecumenical task and its mission to the non-Christian world. Others, however, expressed reservations. According to Wilhelm Andersen, Sittler's cosmic Christology had undervalued the Atonement; it took less seriously than does Paul's teaching the power of evil in the world, and it oriented God's redemptive act back towards the Creation rather than forward to the coming Kingdom.[285] From Gerhard Rosenkranz came a twofold stricture. Sittler had neglected the findings of such exegetes as Ernst Käsemann that the Christological hymn in Colossians is affected by the very heresy of Gnostic cosmology which it means to repudiate;[286] consequently, he had failed to appreciate that the true Christian intention behind the hymn is not cosmological, but soteriological and eschatological.[287] Furthermore, he had left himself open to being interpreted in terms of Indian cosmology, which is ahistorical.[288] In the German Evangelical reaction to Sittler's address, the final word was had by Horst Bürkle. Generally sympathetic towards Sittler, he rejected the criticisms of Andersen and Rosenkranz, on the ground that they had resulted from the very dualistic thinking – creation set against redemption, situation in the world set against experience of salvation, ontology ('ontische Seinslehre') set against personal faith – which the discussion on Christ's oneness with all things had endeavoured to eliminate. Nevertheless, he charged that Sittler himself had fallen into a kind of dualism, admittedly more verbal than conceptual, by making too sharp a distinction between Irenaean nature theology and the theology of history and personal salvation in the Augustinian tradition of the West.[289]

During the 1960s the influence of Sittler and to some extent of Galloway combined with that of Teilhard to produce an upsurge of interest in the cosmic Christ. The long succession of commentary on Teilhard's cosmic-Christ doctrine had been under way in the French-speaking world since his death in 1955.[290] The two streams of

285. W. Andersen, 'Jesus Christus und der Kosmos: Missionstheologische Überlegungen zu Neu-Delhi', in *Evangelische Theologie*, 23. Jahrgang, 1963, pp. 483–6, 490, 492.
286. See. E. Käsemann, 'Eine urchristliche Taufliturgie', in *Exegetische Versuche und Besinnungen*, 1. Bd., p. 48 (E.T., 'A Primitive Christian Baptismal Liturgy', in *Essays on New Testament Themes*, pp. 164–5).
287. G. Rosenkranz, 'Die Rede vom kosmischen Christus angesichts der indischen Geisterwelt', in *Evangelische Missionszeitschrift*, Neue Folge, 20. Jahrgang, 1963, pp. 151–3, 159–60.
288. Ibid., pp. 156, 160.
289. H. Bürkle, op. cit., p. 108 (E.T., pp. 204–5).
290. For the earliest references to Teilhard's cosmic Christ, see C. Cuénot, 'Teilhard

influence were brought together in 1964 during the Faith and Order
Conference at Aarhus. In its discussions on the relationship between
creation and redemption, which were the direct outcome of Sittler's
New Delhi address,[291] Wilhelm Dantine from Vienna University
referred to the cosmic Christology of Teilhard. Dantine argued that
identification of the Prime Cause with God the Father confronts any
doctrine on Christ's lordship over creation with a dilemma. Either the
doctrine is an empty claim, or it requires Christ the Mediator to be
interpreted as a Gnostic-type being intermediate between the Creator
and creation.[292] A resolution to this dilemma is not forthcoming
from traditional dogmatic Christology, which seems unable, with its
concentration on the doctrine of the two natures, to integrate
statements in the New Testament about Christ's lordship.[293] What
resolves this dilemma is the kind of anthropology of which Teilhard
has been the most telling exponent. It presents man as the one who
shapes his own history, as one who by means of technology gradually
assumes dominion over all forms of life on earth, as the one who is
beginning to move out beyond the earth into the wider universe,
finally as the one who perhaps has responsibility for the future of the
cosmos itself.[294] Such an anthropology enables us to approach
Christology with new insight. It is precisely as man that Christ is
regarded by the New Testament as possessing the cosmic attributes of
creator, redeemer, and consummator of the world; and thus it is that
in Christ men are able to know themselves with respect to their origin,
their liberation from guilt, and their final goal. In Teilhard's Christ-
mysticism, said Dantine, we find these ideas in the form of scientific
theory; his expression of them is exemplary for our contemporary
situation, even though it exhibits a tendency towards determinism
and attends insufficiently to the power of evil.[295]

In India, where Sittler had delivered his address, there was evident
interest in the cosmic Christ. Speaking on the summing up of all

de Chardin et les philosophies', in *La Table ronde*, no 90, juin 1955, p. 36; N. M.
Wildiers, 'L'Expérience fondamentale du P. Teilhard de Chardin', ibid.,
pp. 53–4.

291. Cf. C. Simonson, op. cit., pp. 138, 140.
292. W. Dantine, 'Creation and Redemption: Attempt at a Theological Interpretation
     in the Light of the Contemporary Understanding of the World', in *Scottish
     Journal of Theology*, vol. 18, 1965, p. 130.
293. Ibid., pp. 136–7.
294. Ibid., pp. 134–6, 143–4.
295. Ibid., pp. 137–9. Dantine reversed his opinion about determinism in Teilhard in
     'Zur kosmischen Stellung des Menschen nach Teilhard de Chardin', in *Acta
     teilhardiana*, 5. Jahrgang, 1968, pp. 16–32.

things in Christ (Eph. 1: 9–10), in a lecture published in 1963, J. G. Bookless referred to Sittler's cosmic Christology as indicating how the dichotomy between nature and grace in much contemporary theological thinking might be overcome.[296] More important, however, was the contribution by A. F. Thompson to a group of six articles on the cosmic Christ in *The Indian Journal of Theology* for 1966.[297] Thompson developed his argument with both Sittler and Teilhard in mind.[298] If the doctrine of the cosmic Christ is to have any meaning, we must recognize that, as well as being cosmic, Christ is also 'supra-cosmic' or 'a-cosmic'; that is, he is 'of one substance with the Father as regards his Godhead'. If Christ were not divine, he would be no more than a small event within the cosmos.[299] The doctrine of the cosmic Christ, according to which the cosmos is rooted in Christ, eliminates not only the dualism between nature and grace, as Sittler and Teilhard have so clearly pointed out, but also the dichotomy between the Church and the world.[300] The development of a cosmic Christology is opportune. No longer is it possible to establish from ontology a unifying principle of reality. But from the Christological vision of Col. 1: 15–20 we may derive a unification of our understanding of the world around the man Jesus Christ. Such a unification has been attempted by Teilhard, not as an undertaking in ontology, but rather as a more limited endeavour to bring coherence to scientific phenomena.[301] A further reference to the Indian discussion on the cosmic Christ will be made below.

In his preface to André Feuillet's *Le Christ Sagesse de Dieu* (1966), Yves Congar spoke of Sittler and Teilhard as having been pre-eminently influential in bringing cosmic Christology to the attention of theologians. A study of cosmic Christology, said Congar, has become urgent in view of the contemporary understanding of the immense age and size of the universe. If Christ is the way, and constitutes the unity, of all created things, how can he have been

296. 'The Summing Up of All Things in Christ', in *The Indian Journal of Theology*, vol. 12, 1963, pp. 101, 113–14.
297. 'The Colossian Vision in Theology and Philosophy', ibid., vol. 15, 1966, pp. 121–9.
298. For further references to Sittler and Teilhard in this group of six articles, see: J. C. Hindley, 'The Christ of Creation in New Testament Theology', ibid., p. 96; A. Bruggeman, 'The Cosmic Christ: Some Recent Interpretations', ibid.,pp. 131–8, 141.
299. A. F. Thompson, op. cit., pp. 121–2.
300. Ibid., pp. 122–4.
301. Ibid., pp. 125–7.

present to creation during the long ages before the coming of Abraham and the People of God? And, even more enigmatic, how can he be present among the millions upon millions of stars where life has very likely found the conditions that make it possible?[302] In the body of the work Feuillet expressed reservations about Teilhard's understanding of Pauline cosmic Christology.[303] His main criticism rested on the premise that between the supernatural and the natural there is a radical disjunction. Because the Mystical Body and the Pleroma in St. Paul's theology are essentially supernatural realities, their growth does not coincide with the development of the cosmos. Furthermore, in magnifying Christ to cosmic proportions, the captivity letters do no more than teach the subjection of all things to his creative and reconciling activity; there are no grounds for supposing that the cosmos becomes Christ's physical body or that in Christ there is a third nature, which is cosmic.[304] Nevertheless, Feuillet acknowledged the importance of Teilhard for having aroused theologians' interest in Pauline cosmic Christology.[305]

Feuillet's objections to Teilhard involved adherence to the dualistic mentality which Galloway and Sittler had endeavoured to overcome. One way to eliminate dualism – the way adopted by Dantine and Thompson, as we have seen – would be to find in Christ's humanity that which unifies our understanding of the cosmos. The consequences for Christology of such a procedure were examined by J. P. Martin in the United States, in his essay 'Cosmic Christ and Cosmic Redemption' (1967). Martin took up Galloway's point that for biblical faith redemption is cosmic in scope and discussed it with reference to the thought of Teilhard.[306] According to Teilhard, the Incarnation and the Redemption, as much as the Creation, are not simply facts localized in time and space; they are dimensions of the world.[307] If we accept Teilhard's assertion, Martin argued, we find ourselves faced with a theological problem. Considered in relation

---

302. Y. M.-J. Congar, Préface, in A. Feuillet, Le Christ Sagesse de Dieu d'après les épîtres pauliniennes, 1966, pp. 8–11.

303. A. Feuillet, op. cit., pp. 376–85.

304. Ibid., p. 380.

305. Ibid., pp. 381–2. See also id., Christologie paulinienne et tradition biblique, 1973, p. 64.

306. J. P. Martin, 'Cosmic Christ and Cosmic Redemption: An Essay in Interpretation', in Affirmation, vol. 1, 1967, pp. 7–8; see A. D. Galloway, The Cosmic Christ, p. 9.

307. Martin, op. cit., p. 18; see Teilhard, 'Quelques Vues générales sur l'Essence du Christianisme', Oeuvres 10, p. 157 (CE, p. 135).

only to his life and death, Jesus Christ does not speak to us of the destiny and hence of the dimensions of the world. Life and death are ambiguous. In a world in which they are present there is always the risk that life will fail to maintain itself. Nor would the problem be settled, were man to colonize extraterrestrial bodies or to discover intelligent life elsewhere in the universe; it would merely be intensified. To see revealed in Christ the destiny of the world, we must include his resurrection, which provides us proleptically with the assurance that the cosmos has been redeemed from the ambiguities of life and death.[308] This view of Christ requires us to leave behind the Christological models of the past, those which represent a Platonically timeless or a historical and humanistic Christ. Our model now must be cosmic, assigning priority to Christ's resurrection rather than to his life or death.[309] No doubt such a model well accords with the broadened outlook of our present age; but its final justification lies in the priority which the New Testament itself gives to the Resurrection.[310] A Christological model in which the Resurrection takes priority relates Christ to the cosmos not in terms of causality and historical fact but of teleology and eschatology; for if his resurrection resolves the ambiguity inherent in life and death, it can be understood as doing so only at the goal of cosmic history. This, suggested Martin, 'is the *essential* truth in Teilhard's evolutionism to the Omega Point'.[311]

In 1967 S. M. Daecke of Stuttgart and Nikolaus Kehl of Innsbruck pointed out that Teilhard's eschatologically oriented Christology is to be clearly distinguished from Sittler's Christology of nature. In their opinion, Sittler relies on a static conception of creation. Creation for him seems to be an established framework in which the relationship between Christ and nature is simply given; it is scarcely a movement forward towards its fulfilment, through the Redemption, in the New Creation.[312] Daecke characterized Sittler's position as a species of traditional natural theology.[313] Kehl for his part asserted that it is in danger of becoming a Christ myth, since its way of presenting the relationship between Christ and nature is ontic rather than

308. Martin, op. cit., pp. 18–19, 22–3.
309. Ibid., p. 17.
310. Ibid., pp. 26–31.
311. Ibid., pp. 26–7.
312. S. M. Daecke, *Teilhard de Chardin und die evangelische Theologie*, pp. 403–7; N. Kehl. *Der Christushymnus im Kolosserbrief: Eine motivgeschichtiliche Untersuchung zu Kol 1, 12–20*, pp. 24–6; also p. 165.
313. Daecke, op. cit., pp. 405, 407.

ontological.[314] That is to say, it assumes that the created order merely discloses this relationship, independently of the believer's experiencing Christ in his work of salvation.

These criticisms recall the observation made by Bürkle that Sittler was inclined to separate nature from human history.[315] In his address 'Christ and Cosmos' (1968), Henrikus Berkhof from the Netherlands attributed this tendency to Sittler's having used the term 'creation' in the sense of subhuman nature.[316] To relate Christ directly to creation in this sense would be to forget that he is the historical redeemer of our sins and to turn him into a cosmic or even a Gnostic principle.[317] Because of this possibility, Berkhof interpreted the $\delta\iota$' $\alpha\dot{\upsilon}\tau o\hat{\upsilon}$ (and $\delta\iota$' $o\hat{\upsilon}$) in 1 Cor. 8: 6, Col. 1: 16, Heb. 1: 2 and John 1: 3 to mean not 'through him' but 'in view of him'. ($\Delta\iota\dot{\alpha}$ with the genitive does not necessarily signify 'through'; it often approximaes $\delta\iota\dot{\alpha}$ with the accusative.) Those passages are not concerned with the pre-existent Logos, through whom the creation of all things is mediated. They refer to the historical Jesus or, more specifically in Col. 1: 16, to Jesus as the risen redeemer; and they tell us that in view of his coming and exaltation, seen from the standpoint of his redeeming work, God created the world.[318] Such an interpretation, in eschatological terms, of Christ's mediating creation has clearly been influenced by Ritschl.[319] Berkhof, however, was prepared to admit a limited place for cosmology in Christian faith. Though soteriology is at the centre of Christian faith, theologians with existentialist convictions, such as Käsemann, do not correctly interpret Col. 1: 15–20, when they reject its cosmology as an intrusion from Gnosticism. On the contrary, there is in Christian faith a confession about the cosmos – about its creation, its future and its domination by Christ. Nevertheless, it must be recognized that these matters do not constitute the centre of Christian faith; they lie at the horizon of its concerns and are accessible to believers only through the recognition of Christ as redeemer.[320] When the New Testament speaks of creation ($\kappa\tau\dot{\iota}\sigma\iota\varsigma$), it has primarily in view the world of men. Subhuman nature is intended, only

314. Kehl, op. cit., pp. 25, 165.
315. See p. 61 above.
316. 'Christ and Cosmos', in Nederlands Theologisch Tijdschrift, vol. 22, 1967–68, pp. 424, 434.
317. Ibid., pp. 424–5.
318. Ibid., pp. 426–7, 431–3.
319. See A. Ritschl. The Christian Doctrine of Justification and Reconciliation, pp. 401–4; cf. J. M. Creed, The Divinity of Jesus Christ, p. 94.
320. H. Berkhof, op. cit., pp. 430–1, 433–5.

inasmuch as the New Testament does not dissociate it from human existence. There is, of course, no reference to the planets and the galaxies. 'They were beyond the world-view of the New Testament. They are also beyond the limits of faith in Christ as the Redeemer of this world.' If a cosmic Christology considers subhuman nature independently of mankind, it naturalizes the Christian faith and makes Christ simply 'the focus of a cosmic élan vital'. Sittler's position moves in the direction of such a cosmic Christology; so too, Berkhof believed, does Teilhard's.[321]

Although there is clearly no firm consensus about cosmic Christology among the various reactions to Sittler and Teilhard that we have reviewed, certain dominant trends of thought do nevertheless emerge. To a large extent there is acceptance of the premise that theological dualism – the split between nature and grace – must be overcome, lest faith should appear irrelevant in the world of human existence. Faith itself provides the remedy for theological dualism, when it sees Christ as man uniting the realms of nature and grace through the exercise of his cosmic function of lordship over all creation. However, because faith goes beyond present reality considered in itself and refers instead to present reality in connection with reality to come, it must necessarily speak about Christ's cosmic function from an eschatological point of view. From this point of view faith sees Christ as resurrected; for it is only in his risen state that Christ transcends present reality and anticipates the New Creation, which creation as present reality awaits.

If these trends of thought represent the central insights achieved in the discussions about Sittler and Teilhard, they are by no means assured results. At every point in the complex of ideas upon which cosmic Christology impinges, there remain contentious issues and open questions. Some of these were mentioned by Anselm Urban of Salzburg in his essay 'Kosmische Christologie' (1971). Discussing Teilhard's concept of a cosmic nature in Christ, as presented in 'Le Christique',[322] Urban spoke of its appropriateness for an age in which the fundamental influence on man's consciousness is not, as might be supposed, social change but scientific and technological development, especially in the fields of astronomy and space exploration. In this age of cosmic consciousness the cult of Jesus Christ is likely to have no more significance than consulting a

321. Ibid., pp. 434–5.
322. Urban quoted the passage in 'Le Christique' from 'Dans le Christ total' to 'se volatiliser? . . . '; see *Oeuvres* 13, pp. 107–8 (*HM*, p. 93).

psychotherapist or resorting to narcotics, unless his person has a cosmic dimension. Unfortunately, as Teilhard remarked at the end of a life spent trying to bridge the gap between science and Christian faith, the cosmic aspect of Christ is afforded scant recognition. A classic example of this situation, said Urban, was supplied by the cool reception which Sittler's New Delhi address received from European theologians.[323] The neglect of cosmic Christology undoubtedly results from the fact that we live in a period of Christological minimalism, when exegetes speak with extreme caution about the historical Jesus and are unable to reach any agreement on the relationship between the historical Jesus and the kerygmatic Christ. The *ipsissima verba* of Jesus offer no foundation for cosmic Christology; and even if the Church's post-Easter preaching is permitted to have the status of divine revelation, its cosmic Christology can still be dismissed as vague speculation of a metaphysical or a Gnostic variety. Hence, when Teilhard in 'Le Christique' appeals to Col. 1: 17 to substantiate his concept of a cosmic nature in Christ, many exegetes would regard its scriptural foundations as less than secure. In their judgement the Christological hymn in which that verse occurs is heterodox in origin, coming from either Gnostic or Stoic sources.[324] Urban himself considered it possible to support Teilhard's cosmic Christology by demonstrating that, whatever the literary background of the hymn, its doctrine is entirely Christian.[325] Nevertheless, without expressly saying so, he advanced a position at variance with Teilhard's. According to his reading of Col. 1: 15–20, it is Christ as man in whom all creation is grounded.[326]

## VIII.  EMERGING ISSUES IN COSMIC CHRISTOLOGY

Scriptural interpretation is perhaps the least of the problems connected with cosmic Christology. It presents a serious difficulty only if one concedes that certain parts of the New Testament contain the essential core of Christian belief, while other parts teach doctrines either marginal or even contrary to faith. If, on the other hand, the starting-point for theology is taken to be the Church's acceptance of such passages as the Colossians Christological hymn into the canon

323. A. Urban, 'Kosmische Christologie', in *Benediktinische Monatsschrift*, 47. Jahrgang, 1971, pp. 472–4.
324. Ibid., pp. 374–6.
325. Ibid., p. 485.
326. Ibid., p. 483.

of its scriptures, the theologian then has the task of seeking to
understand a faith whose authoritative expression involves pluralism.
A striking instance of pluralism in the New Testament is the variety of
its Christological models. Their diversity is such, that apparent
incompatibilities may invite us to play down or possibly to exclude
some of them. As to cosmic Christology, there are theologians who
draw back from the doctrine of Christ's mediating creation. Dantine,
we have seen, was not prepared to link it with the lordship of Christ
over creation, since it seems to make Christ a Gnostic-type being
intermediate between the Creator and creation. Likewise Berkhof was
unwilling to relate Christ directly to creation, for fear that the
relationship should undermine his office as historical redeemer and
turn him into a Gnostic principle; and because of this, he interpreted
$\delta\iota'$ $\alpha\dot{\upsilon}\tau o\hat{\upsilon}$ to mean 'in view of him' rather than 'through him'. Behind
the introduction of 'Gnostic' into these discussions lies a twofold
assumption: that certain aspects of Christology in the New Testament
are normative, to the exclusion of other aspects which may be found
there; and that if any doctrine in the New Testament bears some
resemblance to, or has points of contact with, Gnostic teaching, it
cannot be genuinely or at least purely Christian. Regarding the latter
part of the assumption, it may be that Christ's mediatorship in
creation recalls the work of the Gnostic Demiurge, in consequence of
a contribution from Gnosticism to the shaping of that New Testament doctrine. But there *is* a crucial difference. In its completed state
the New Testament doctrine offers no hint that Christ is like the fallen
Gnostic aeon who fashions a world alien to the supreme God.

A problem more fundamental than scriptural interpretation which
cosmic Christology has to face is the effect of the Copernican
revolution in dislodging mankind, together with the Saviour and his
work of cosmic salvation, from the mid point of creation to an
obscure corner in the universe. Urban indicated the relevance of
Teilhard's thought to this problem.[327] Teilhard had returned mankind to the mid point of creation by placing it, in his world-vision, at
the head of the central line in evolutionary development. However
attractive may be this view of mankind's place in nature, Urban
admitted that it left a further problem unsolved. The New Testament
sees salvation history as a way forward from creation to
consummation, both of which occur in Christ. Christ is Alpha and

---

327. Ibid., pp. 485–6.

Omega. But whether evolution has any bearing on salvation history must remain a question open to debate. It is, in fact, the old problem of the relationship between nature and grace in a new guise.

We shall examine these matters at a later stage in our study.[328] For the moment it needs only to be said that Teilhard did not, strictly speaking, return mankind to the mid point of creation. When he located it at the head of evolution, he had principally in mind the evolutionary process as it may be inferred from biological phenomena on the earth.[329] At the same time, he appreciated that, because pre-biological phenomena observable everywhere suggest an evolutionary movement throughout the universe, the possibility exists that other intelligent races besides mankind have emerged.[330] Mankind, then, stands at the mid point of creation, only in the sense that it is a segment of the evolutionary process open to direct union with Christ at the end of this process. But given the possibility of other such segments, it cannot be said to hold the mid-point position. After Copernicus – and even more so after Edwin P. Hubble's confirmation of the galaxies in 1924 – the question must be seriously asked whether the appearance of the absolute within the contingent, of the Creator within creation, is restricted to the terrestrial incarnation of the divine Logos. However, as Teilhard remarked in one of his earlier essays, the task of disengaging Christological doctrine from the matrix of geocentricism in which it developed seems almost hopeless.[331] Certainly it is a task to which theologians have not yet generally been prepared to address themselves. Without mentioning those for whom cosmic Christology does not figure as a theological question, we may instance the attitude of Berkhof. His declining to allow Christian faith any relevance to the world beyond the earth was a retreat into biblicism. Looking further, we find, for example, that Dantine, Martin, and Urban all recognized, if only cursorily, the need to take the universe at large into account. Nevertheless, they appeared to see the Christian faith more as a terrestrial affair than as a matter of universal significance, since for them it was simply Christ as man who exercises the cosmic functions

---

328. See pp. 208–10 below.
329. See *Le Phénomène humain, Oeuvres* 1, pp. 248–9 (*PM*, p. 224); 'Un problème majeur pour l'Anthropologie', *Oeuvres* 7, p. 331 (*AE*, p. 316).
330. See *Le Phénomène humain, Oeuvres* 1, pp. 333–4 (*PM*, pp. 300–1); 'La Centrologie', *Oeuvres* 7, pp. 133–4 (*AE*, pp. 126–7); 'Les singularités de l'Espèce Humaine', *Oeuvres* 2, pp. 318–21 (*AM*, pp. 228–30).
331. 'Chute, Rédemption et Géocentrie', 20.7.1920, *Oeuvres* 10, p. 57 (*CE*, p. 44).

of consolidating the universe and acting as its goal. Whatever may be argued in favour of their position, it has to be stated that they conveyed no sense of having felt the impact of the Copernican revolution. Teilhard, on the other hand, was disturbed by the Copernican revolution; and the implications which he detected in it helped to persuade him in his later years to formulate his doctrine on the cosmic nature in Christ.[332]

Astronomical discoveries were, of course, not the only influence behind Teilhard's idea of a cosmic nature in Christ. Undoubtedly the very use of the term 'cosmic' played a part, as seems also to have been the case with other authors who related the cosmic aspect of Christ neither to his divinity nor to his humanity. Most recently Galloway, in his latest reflections on the cosmic Christ, also appears to be moving in this direction:

> The doctrine of *illud extra calvinisticum* – that when the Word of God became man and made himself fully manifest to us as man he also continued to govern the universe in a manner not manifest in his incarnation – suggests that there is another relation of Christ to the universe not disclosed to us in his becoming man and to which we cannot become party.[333]

On Teilhard's thinking the term 'cosmic' had the greatest effect, the result of which was his triple distinction of natures in Christ. The force of this distinction becomes apparent, when we consider the contributions to cosmic Christology of two authors in India, P. V. Premasagar and J. M. Gibbs. Writing in 1975, both of them clearly distinguished within the one person of Christ the Jesus of history and the cosmic Christ.[334] At the same time, the divinity of Christ did not enter even into the background of their discussions. In his own work on cosmic Christology, Teilhard was not concerned with reflecting at length on the divinity of Christ. But with the aid of his triple distinction he was able to make what he regarded as a necessary move in Christology, without neglecting the insights of its classical position confirmed at Nicaea and Chalcedon.

During the 1960s Teilhard was recognized not merely for having contributed to the systematic aspect of cosmic Christology and its

---

332. The movement in Teilhard's thought towards this formulation is well illustrated by 'Une suite au Problème des Origines humaines: la Multiplicité des Mondes habités', 5.6.1953, ibid., pp. 273–82 (ibid., pp. 229–36).

333. A. D. Galloway, *The Cosmic Christ* [unpublished paper], 1977, p. 6.

334. P. V. Premasagar, 'Jesus: Cosmic Christ or a Man of History?', in *The Indian Journal of Theology*, vol. 24, 1975, pp. 104–7; J. M. Gibbs, 'Jesus as the Wisdom of God: The Normative Man of History Moving to the Cosmic Christ', ibid., pp. 108–25.

relation to biblical theology, but also for having drawn attention to the presence of cosmic Christology in the past. As we have noted, there has accompanied the development of cosmic-Christ language a certain awareness that many theologians of the past had given some account of Christ's cosmic dimension. The awareness led, however, to no comprehensive study of the matter, comparable, say, with Émile Mersch's history on a related topic, the Mystical Body of Christ.[335] The result of this hiatus has been inadequate judgement about the theological tradition on cosmic Christology. In particular, it has been suggested that Latin theology is deficient in cosmic Christology. Clark, Galloway, and Sittler leave one with that impression, and so at first sight does Teilhard. In his one reference to the Latin Fathers, Teilhard stressed the legalistic tendency in their theology,[336] whereas on a number of occasions he indicated that a cosmic view of Christ is to be found among the Greek Fathers.[337] His concern with the Greek Fathers is reflected in J. Dupuis's essay 'The Cosmic Christ in the Early Fathers' (1966)[338] and in G. A. Maloney's volume *The Cosmic Christ from Paul to Teilhard* (1968). Maloney said that after Maximus the Confessor in the seventh century 'There was an eclipse of the cosmic dimension in the study of christology'.[339] What his statement overlooks, no doubt among other things, is the rise of the Scotist doctrine on the primacy of Christ in creation. Teilhard was certainly aware of this doctrine and of its similarity with his own thought.[340] N. M. Wildiers (1960) pointed out this similarity;[341] and he was followed by Robert North (1967), who took the step of applying the term 'cosmic Christ' to the Scotist

---

335. *Le Corps mystique du Christ: Études de théologie historique*, 2 tomes, 2e éd., 1936.
336. 'Christologie et Évolution', *Oeuvres* 10, p. 107 (*CE*, p. 89).
337. See especially: 'Quelques Réflexions sur la Conversion du Monde', *Oeuvres* 9,p. 161 (*SC*, p. 122); 'L'Esprit nouveau, 1942', *Oeuvres* 5, p. 124 (*FM*, p. 94); 'Super-humanité–Super-Christ–Super-charité', *Oeuvres* 9, p. 210 (*SC*, p. 165).
338. In *The Indian Journal of Theology*, vol. 15, 1966, pp. 106–20. This is one of the group of six articles on the cosmic Christ referred to above, p. 63.
339. p. 15. The same judgement reappears in M. Day, 'Teilhard's Rediscovery of the Cosmic Christ', in *The Teilhard Review*, vol. 11, 1976, p. 111.
340. See 'Esquisse d'une Dialectique de l'Esprit', *Oeuvres* 7, p. 158 (*AE*, p. 150); *Journal* XVI ( =4), 24.10.1948, p. 14; also Gabriel M. Allegra, *My Conversations with Teilhard de Chardin on the Primacy of Christ*, pp. 37–40, 46–7, 69–71, 94–5, 104–7. Teilhard used the Scotist terminology 'primacy of Christ' in 'L'Esprit nouveau, 1942', *Oeuvres* 5, p. 123 (*FM*, p. 94); 'Le Christique', *Oeuvres* 13, p. 108 (*HM*, p. 93).
341. *Teilhard de Chardin*, Paris, 1960, pp. 92–5 (E.T.from the Flemish ed., 1963, *An Introduction to Teilhard de Chardin*, 1968, pp. 131–4, 145).

doctrine.[342] The doctrine of Christ's primacy in creation is usually associated with the Franciscan school of theology. Recently, however, T. R. Potvin (1973) has studied a version of this doctrine in Aquinas. Potvin wrote with the contemporary views about cosmic Christology in mind, including those of Sittler and Teilhard.[343] Among the Latin theologians before the Middle Ages, Ambrose has been named by François Szabó (1968) as having held a cosmic doctrine on Christ. Szabó compared Ambrose's doctrine with Teilhard's and noted that both authors had learnt from the Greek Fathers.[344] More strikingly, he suggested that it may have been from Ambrose that Teilhard derived his cosmic Christological formula 'Christus amictus mundo'.[345]

In the development of cosmic-Christ language the major figure to appear was Teilhard. He showed a way forward for Christology in a scientific age. But he also directed theologians to look back to Scripture and tradition and discover there, as he had done, the doctrine of the cosmic Christ. In our present study we shall look back to Origen. The Christological problem posed by his thought occurs once again in Teilhard's endeavour to advance Christology and make Christ relevant to the modern world.

342. *Teilhard and the Creation of the Soul*, pp. 119–20, 132.
343. T. R. Potvin, *The Theology of the Primacy of Christ According to St. Thomas and Its Scriptural Foundations*, 1973, pp. 1, 105–6, 106 n. 2.
344. F. Szabó, *Le Christ créateur chez saint Ambroise*, 1969, pp. 18, 151.
345. Ibid., p. 135 n. 75; also pp. 131–5.

## 2. TEILHARD AND ORIGEN IN RELATION TO THE COSMIC CHRIST

A number of writers have drawn attention to similarities between Teilhard and Origen. The earliest of these, Nicolas Corte, noted in 1957 that Teilhard had been likened to Thomas Aquinas and Duns Scotus. But the most appropriate comparison, he said, must surely be with Origen. Despite widespread controversy over their ideas, both Teilhard and Origen contributed to an enlargement of the Christian vision.[1] To these remarks of Corte's Kazimierz Klósak added the observation that, though Teilhard and Origen were stigmatized as heterodox thinkers, neither of them had any intention of deviating from Catholic orthodoxy.[2]

One point for which Teilhard has been criticized is eschatological optimism. According to Corte,[3] it is allied to Origen's notion of a 'final apotheosis', in which even Satan is united to God. Assessments like this of Teilhard's and Origen's eschatological doctrines are common enough. Less common are the qualifications that must be made.[4] As Teilhard saw the world's movement towards its term, damnation always remains a possibility. Underlying the aggregation of persons from which the New Earth is established, there is a segregating of evil elements.[5] It is a process that may include not only

---

1. N. Corte, *La Vie et l'âme de Teilhard de Chardin*, 1957, pp. 233–5 (E.T., *Pierre Teilhard de Chardin: His Life and Spirit*, pp. 114–15).
2. K. Klósak, 'Spór o Orygenesa naszych csasów' ['The Dispute about the Origen of Our Time'], in *Znak*, vol. 12, 1960, p. 256.
3. Op. cit., p. 235 (E.T., p. 115).
4. See E. Rideau, *Teilhard de Chardin: A Guide to His Thought*, pp. 188, 574 nn. 193–5.
5. See *Le Milieu divin, Oeuvres* 4, pp. 187–92 (*MD*, pp. 140–3); also 'Note sur quelques Représentations historiques possibles du Péché originel', *Oeuvres* 10, p. 69 (*CE*, p. 53); Lettre à Bruno de Solages, 8.2.1955, *LI*, p. 455. Cf. G.- H. Baudry, 'Les Grands axes de l'eschatologie teilhardienne (1946–1955)', in *Mélanges de science religieuse*, vol. 35, 1978, pp. 67–8.

individuals[6] but even man as a species.[7] Teilhard was aware, moreover, that his view about the world's evolutionary convergence, under the influence of Christ, towards final integration is in the nature of an intuition rather than of a strict deduction. He insisted merely that rejection of this view involves an attitude of despair scarcely in accord with Christian faith.[8] With regard to Origen, we do justice to his account of the Last Things, only if we bear in mind two principles which he kept together in tension. The first principle, that the end is like the beginning, signifies that the creation's final union with God is similar to its original state.[9] Witnesses hostile to Origen interpreted this principle to mean an apocatastasis or restoration of all moral agents to God.[10] But Origen also stressed the principle that moral agents remain perpetually free.[11] The test case is the devil. Origen spoke out against those who charged him with having taught that the devil is saved; while against the Valentinian Candidatus he argued that the devil is damned, not by nature certainly, but by having in fact willed to be so.[12] In the matter of eschatology Henri de Lubac

6. See 'Forma Christi', *Oeuvres* 12, pp. 381–2 (*ETG*, pp. 349–50; *WTW*, p. 265); 'Mon Univers', 1924, *Oeuvres* 9, p. 113 (*SC*, pp. 84–5); 'Introduction à la Vie chrétienne', *Oeuvres* 10, pp. 192–3 (*CE*, pp. 164–5). For further references, see *LI*, pp. 458–9; H. de Lubac, *Teilhard posthume: Réflexions et souvenirs*, pp. 80 n. 10, 86 n. 28.
7. See *La place de l'homme dans la nature, Oeuvres* 8, p. 172 (*MNP*, p. 120); also 'Note sur le Progrès', *Oeuvres* 5, p. 31 ad n. 1 (*FM*, p. 19 ad n. 1).
8. See 'Agitation ou Genèse?', *Oeuvres* 5, pp. 287–9 (*FM*, pp. 225–6). Cf. H. de Lubac, op. cit., p. 89; id., *Teilhard missionaire et apologiste*, pp. 93–107.
9. *De Princ.* 1: 6: 2 (*GCS* 5, p. 79, l. 19 to p. 80, l. 5); 2: 1: 1 (p. 107, ll. 6–10); 3: 5: 4 (p. 274, l. 12 to p. 275, l. 3); 3: 6: 3 (p. 284, ll. 3–10); 3: 6: 8 (p. 289, ll. 23–33); see also 1: 6: 4 (p. 84, ll. 22–7); 2: 1: 3 (p. 109, ll. 1–4).
10. See, for example, Jerome, *Epist. 84: Ad Pammachium et Oceanum* 7 (*PL* 22, col. 749, ll. 5–8); Justinian, *Lib. adv. Orig. ad Mennam* (Mansi, tomus 9, col. 517C-D); Theophilus Alex., *Epist. Pasch. 16 Frag.* (Diekamp, *Doctrina Patrum de Incarnatione Verbi*, p. 180, ll. 12–16). For these and other references, see Paul Koetschau (ed.), *Origenes Werke: De Principiis* (*GCS* 5), pp. 84, 182, 286.
   Origen employs the term ἀποκατάστασις in an eschatological sense in *Comm. in Joh.* 1: 91–2 (xvi, 16) (*GCS* 4, p. 20, ll. 11–18); 10: 291 (xlii, 26) (p. 219); *Comm. in Matt.* 13: 2 (*GCS* 10, p. 182, ll. 25–33); 15: 24 (p. 420, ll. 18–26). See also *De Princ.* 2: 3: 5 (*GCS* 5, p. 120, ll. 17–24); 3: 5: 7 (p. 278, ll. 21–3); 3: 6: 6 (p. 287, l. 21 to p. 288, l. 7); 3: 6: 9 (p. 290, ll. 14–18). Despite some of their strongly worded statements about the restoration of all things to God, all of these passages leave the question of universal salvation open.
11. *De Princ.* 1: Praef.: 5 (*GCS* 5, p. 12, l. 8 to p. 13, l. 6); 2: 1: 2 (p. 107, l. 28 to p. 108, l. 10); 2: 3: 3 (p. 118, ll. 14–15); 3: 1: 6 (p. 203, ll. 8–16; p. 204, ll. 1–6).
12. *Epist. Origenis ad Amicos Alexandriae* (in Rufinus, *Lib. de Adult. Lib. Orig.* (*PG* 17, col. 624A–625A); Jerome, *Apol. adv. Lib. Ruf.* 2:18 (*PL* 23, col. 442B-C)); *Dialogus Candidi Origenis* (in Jerome, op. cit. 2: 19 (op. cit., col. 443A)); see also

es a more illuminating comparison between Teilhard and
, when he indicates that both of them followed St. Paul's
........e on the world to come. The world to come is neither a
complete break with, nor simply a restoration of, this present world
but rather its unimaginable transformation.[13]

Further comparisons between Teilhard and Origen have been
made with regard to evil and original sin. Teilhard and Origen both
saw evil as a by-product of God's creative activity[14] and as a
correlative of multiplicity;[15] and both of them considered that the
transmission of original sin is due not just to heredity but more
broadly to the solidarity and general condition of the human race.[16]

But the subject in which Teilhard has most frequently been
compared with Origen is Christology. Teilhard's teaching on the
universal Christ, who by a 'mysterious Diaphany' shines through and
illuminates the world, has its counterpart in Origen. For Origen

---

*Comm. in Rom.* 8: 9 (*PG* 14, col. 1185 B); *De Princ.* 1: 6: 3 (*GCS* 5, p. 83, l. 9 to p. 84, l. 6).

Since Jerome was highly suspicious of Origen's orthodoxy and on other occasions (see n. 10 above) was prepared to condemn Origen for having taught the salvation of the devil, his witness must be regarded as compelling. Not only does he agree with his rival Rufinus that Origen rejected the charge of having taught the salvation of the devil; he also approves of the position which Origen upheld against Candidus.

Cf. G. Bardy, *Recherches sur l'histoire du texte et des versions latines du De Principiis d'Origène*, pp. 15–20, 95, 198; H. Crouzel, 'A Letter from Origen "To Friends in Alexandria" ', in D. Neiman and M. Schatkin (ed.), *The Heritage of the Early Church: Essays in Honor of the Very Reverend Georges Vasilievich Florovsky*, pp. 139–40, 143–4, 146–7. Crouzel (p. 146) makes the point that 'there is not a single text of Origen extant today that maintains expressly the salvation of the devil.'

13. H. de Lubac, *The Religion of Teilhard de Chardin*, pp. 141–2, 326–7 nn. 57–69.
   See Rom. 8: 19–23; Phil. 3: 20–21; Teilhard, 'Les Noms de la Matière', *Oeuvres* 12, pp. 460–4 (*ETG*, pp. 429–32; *HM*, pp. 234–8); id., Lettre à Auguste Valensin, 8.12.1919, *LI*. p. 29; id., 'Mon Univers', 1924, *Oeuvres* 9, p. 102 (*SC*, p. 73); Origen, *Frag. de Resurr.* (*PG* 11, col. 98C-D); id., *De Princ.* 1: 6: 4 (*GCS* 5, p. 85, ll. 4–24); id., *Comm. in Matt.* 17: 30 (*GCS* 10, p. 671, ll. 10–21).

14. See P. Smulders, *La Vision de Teilhard de Chardin*, 3e éd., 1965, p. 164.
   See Teilhard, 'Comment je vois', *Oeuvres* 11, p. 213 (*TF*, p. 198); Origen, *C. Cels.* 6: 55 (*GCS* 2, p. 126, ll. 25–31); also ibid., 6: 53 (p. 124, ll. 27–9).

15. See H. de Lubac, *The Eternal Feminine*, p. 206 n. 2.
   See Teilhard, 'La Lutte contre la multitude', *Oeuvres* 12, p. 143 (*ETG*, pp. 123–4; *WTW*, p. 105); Origen, *Hom. in Ezech.* 9:1 (*GCS* 8, p. 405, l. 26 to p. 406, l. 8).

16. See R. Leys, 'Teilhard de Chardin et le péché originel', in A. Szekeres (ed.), *Le Christ cosmique de Teilhard de Chardin*, pp. 195–6; also E. Rideau, op. cit., pp. 169–70, 540 n. 109, 542 n. 114; P. Smulders, op. cit., pp. 175, 193 n. 82.
   See Teilhard, 'Comment je vois', *Oeuvres* 11, p. 213 n. 1 (*TF*, p. 198 n. 37); Origen, *Comm. in Rom.* 5: 1 (*PG* 14, col. 1003D-1011A, 1018B-C).

Christ is present everywhere, diffused through all the universe, coextensive with the world and penetrating the whole of creation.[17]

Furthermore, Teilhard claimed that his understanding of Christ's body in relation to the world – the cosmic body of Christ, as he sometimes called it – is that of the Fathers.[18] Among the Fathers who teach such a doctrine we find Origen.[19] In the *De Principiis* Origen said that the world is like the one body with many members, held together by the power and reason of God as though by the one soul.[20] No doubt the background to this doctrine includes the Stoic theory of a world-soul. But in his simile of the one body with many members, Origen was also alluding to St. Paul's teaching on the body of Christ; and by the power and reason of God, he clearly intended Christ himself. More explicitly in one of his homilies on Psalm 36, Origen said that Christ's body is 'the whole human race, perhaps even the entire universality of creation'.[21] Elsewhere he conveyed the same idea with the expression 'total body of Christ'.[22]

In their concern with the universal or cosmic aspect of Christ, neither Teilhard nor Origen, de Lubac points out, passed over the incarnation of the Logos in Jesus of Nazareth.[23] Nevertheless, the characteristic of their Christology is to set, in L. W. Barnard's phrase, 'the Incarnation of the Divine Word against the widest background' and deliver theology from its ivory tower of compartmentalized disciplines.[24]

---

17. See H. de Lubac (ed.), *LI*, p. 50 n. 7,6; id., *The Religion of Teilhard de Chardin*, pp. 62–3, 294 n. 40, 295 n. 44; also G. A. Maloney, *The Cosmic Christ from Paul to Teilhard*, p. 14; R. Hale, *Christ and the Universe: Teilhard de Chardin and the Cosmos*, pp. 44, 112 n. 55.
    See Teilhard, Lettre à Leontine Zanta, 10.1.1927, *LLZ*, p. 81 (E.T., p. 74); Origen, *De Princ.* 2: 11: 6 (*GCS* 5, p. 190, l. 18 to p. 191, l. 4); 4: 4: 2 (p. 351, ll. 8–22); *Comm. in Joh.* 2:215 (xxxv, 29) (*GCS* 4, p. 94, ll. 12–14); 6: 154 (xxx, 15) (p. 140, ll. 9–12); 6: 188 (xxxviii, 22) (p. 146, ll. 15–16).
18. 'La Vie cosmique', *Oeuvres* 12, pp. 57–8 (*ETG*, p. 39; *WTW*, pp. 49–50).
19. See R. Hale, op. cit., pp. 41, 43–4, 112 n. 54, 112 n. 56; also H. de Lubac, *La Prière du Père Teilhard de Chardin*, 2e éd., 1968, p. 73 (E.T., *The Faith of Teilhard de Chardin*, p. 50); id., *Teilhard missionnaire et apologiste*, p. 105 n. 1.
20. *De Princ.* 2: 1: 3 (*GCS* 5, p. 108, ll. 11–16).
21. *Hom. in Ps.* 36: 2: 1 (*PG* 12, col. 1330A).
22. *Comm. in Joh.* 10:229 (xxxv, 20) (*GCS* 4, p. 209, l. 32).
    See H. de Lubac, *Teilhard missionnaire et apologiste*, p. 104.
23. H. de Lubac, *The Religion of Teilhard de Chardin*, p. 63; also id., *Teilhard missionnaire et apologiste*, p. 105.
24. L. W. Barnard, 'Origen's Christology and Eschatology', in *Anglican Theological Review*, vol. 46, 1964, pp. 318–19.

Indicative of their Christological thinking is the way in which they interpreted the doctrine of Rom. 8: 19–23 on redemption. A comparison between Teilhard and Origen in this context has been suggested by Paul Lebeau. The most common contemporary opinion holds that these verses, in speaking about the creation (ἡ κτίσις), refer not just to men alone or to non-human creatures alone but express 'an ontological solidarity between men and the rest of creation'; they affirm that all creation inclusive of men participates in Christ's redemptive benefits.[25] It is in accordance with this contemporary opinion, says Lebeau, that Teilhard cited Rom. 8: 22 in *Le Milieu divin*.[26] In contrast, Origen took ἡ κτίσις to be the heavenly bodies, which he regarded as rational beings.[27] Influenced as he was by Middle Platonism, he did not ask whether it also includes non-rational creatures in the sublunary world. In Origen's view, it is the heavenly bodies that have solidarity with the human race; they share in its destiny of redemption through Christ.[28] For Origen, then, as for Teilhard, redemption has a significance much wider than the personal salvation of human beings.

The comparisons that we have reviewed indicate some underlying affinity between Teilhard and Origen. As we have seen, a majority of the comparisons is concerned with Christology. It is in this connection that we find the affinity to exist. In their reflection on the person of Christ, neither Teilhard nor Origen was motivated by a detached intellectual interest in the subject. Henri de Lubac applies to Teilhard something that Origen wrote about St. Paul: 'Because of his deep love for Jesus, Paul spoke about him incessantly and, as it were, superfluously.'[29] These words could also be said most fittingly of their author. Origen's life and writing centred on Christ.[30] But more specific than personal devotion to Christ, what Teilhard and Origen had in common was a certain Christological perspective. Charles

25. P. Lebeau, 'L'Interprétation origénienne de Rm 8:19–22', in P. Granfield and J. A. Jungmann (ed.), *Kyriakon: Festschrift Johannes Quasten*, vol. 1, p. 336. See also R. North, *Teilhard and the Creation of the Soul*, p. 123.

26. *Oeuvres* 4, p. 50 (*MD*, p. 34).

27. On the heavenly bodies as rational beings, see Origen, *De Princ.* 1: 7: 3 (*GCS* 5, p. 87, l. 24 to p. 88, l. 11). But see also p. 133 below.

28. P. Lebeau, op. cit., pp. 336–40. See also R. North, loc. cit.
   See Origen , *De Princ.* 1: 7: 5 (*GCS* 5, pp. 91–4); *Comm. in Rom.* 7: 4 (*PG* 14, col. 1109B-1112C).

29. Origen, *Frag. in Eph.* 8, ll. 8–9 (*JTS*, vol. 3, 1901–2, p. 242). See H. de Lubac, *Teilhard missionnaire et apologiste*, p. 13.

30. Cf. J. Danielou, *Origen*, pp. 313–14; F. Bertrand, *Mystique de Jésus chez Origène*, pp. 9–10.

Raven points to that perspective when he says of Teilhard:

> . . . as his knowledge of cosmology, biology and anthropology spread and
> deepened, it merely expanded his sense of the universalism, personalism and
> consummation that is guaranteed by a full understanding of the cosmic
> Christ as St. Paul came to declare it in his three last great epistles Philippians,
> Colossians and Ephesians.[31]

In the history of the Church, Raven suggests, a response to the
'Christ-centred universalism' of those epistles, such as we find in
Teilhard, has rarely occurred. For a parallel we must look to Clement
and Origen of Alexandria.[32]

Undoubtedly the cosmic Christ has attracted more notice down
through the history of the Church than Raven allows. And, besides
the Pauline captivity letters, other parts of the New Testament have
also contributed to this Christological theme in Teilhard and Origen.
Especially in the work of Origen, the prologue to St. John's Gospel
plays a prominent role. Nevertheless, Raven's expression 'Christ-
centred universalism' well epitomizes Teilhard's affinity with Origen.
To describe this affinity, we shall turn to what Teilhard himself said
about Origen and the development of cosmic Christology. With
Clement, whom Raven also mentions, we are not concerned. In any
case, Teilhard betrays little consciousness of him. Origen, however,
he seems to have recognized as the Church Father closest to him in
dealing with Christ's relations to the cosmos.[33]

In 1952 Teilhard wrote to a friend:

> . . . I'm delighted to know you're at work. I imagine that Origen is a
> wonderful subject for tackling and discussing, under colour of history, the

---

31. C. E. Raven, *Teilhard de Chardin: Scientist and Seer*, p. 160.
32. Ibid., pp. 160–2.
33. The other Fathers whom Teilhard had in mind in connection with cosmic
    Christology are Justin, Irenaeus, Gregory of Nyssa and Augustine.
    For Justin, see 'La Route de l'Ouest', *Oeuvres* 11, p. 57 (*TF*, p. 51).
    For Irenaeus, see 'Réflexions sur la probabilité scientifique et les Conséquences
    religieuses d'un Ultra-Humain', *Oeuvres* 7, p. 290 n. 1 (*AE*, p. 279 n. 4); also 'La
    Mystique de la Science', *Oeuvres* 6, p. 208 n. 1 (*HE*, p. 167 n. 1). Cf. Dai Sil Kim,
    'Irenaeus of Lyons and Teilhard de Chardin: A Comparative Study of
    "Recapitulation" and "Omega" ', in *Journal of Ecumenical Studies*, vol. 13, 1976,
    pp. 69–93.
    For Gregory of Nyssa, see *Le Milieu divin*, *Oeuvres* 4, p. 128 (*MD*, p. 94); 'Mon
    Univers', 1924, *Oeuvres* 9, p. 104 (*SC*, p. 76).
    For Augustine, see 'Le Christ évoluteur', *Oeuvres* 10, p. 170 (*CE*, p. 145). Cf. K.
    Stern, 'Saint Augustine and Teilhard', in N. Braybrooke (ed.), *Teilhard de
    Chardin: Pilgrim of the Future*, p. 78.

hottest questions put to our modern religious thought by the need to rethink Christology within the dimensions of a 'new Universe'.[34]

Behind this remark lies Teilhard's view that Christianity involves a synthesis 'between faith in God and faith in the world' and that the heart of this synthesis contains an acknowledgement of Christ in his cosmic aspect.[35] A synthetic handling of doctrine has characterized Christianity from the beginning. 'In the first century of the Church', Teilhard wrote, 'Christianity made its definitive entry into human thought by boldly assimilating the Jesus of the Gospel to the Alexandrian Logos.'[36] As he told Claude Tresmontant, the New Testament Logos doctrine has 'nothing to do with Hebrew "metaphysics"'.[37] He confessed that he did not 'understand' the psychological leap from the Synoptics to the writings of St. Paul, where a Logos-type doctrine occurs. Perhaps there had been a new 'revelation'.[38] Whatever the case, it seemed to Teilhard that the development was necessary. In his journal he noted that 'The Apocalypse and St John and Paul "burst" the Synoptics' ceiling, which is too low (purely micro-terrestrial and human)'.[39] Again, according to another entry in his journal, 'It was inevitable and essential – and not only convenient, or "accidental" – that nascent Christianity was fused, was synthesized, with Hellenic thought (*Logos*, . . .) which was then the axis of human Thought: otherwise there would have been psychic dualism (bicephalism) in Humanity.'[40] After the first period of Christianity the process of doctrinal synthesis continued. 'Whatever you rediscover in Hebrew,' Teilhard said to Tresmontant, 'you will not change the expression that biblical thought has assumed in the Church through tradition, the Fathers and the Councils.'[41] He made the same point in a criticism of Loisy, whose fundamental mistake, he considered, was to

34. Lettre à Bruno de Solages, 2.2.1952, *LI*, pp. 404–5.
35. See 'Christianisme et Évolution', *Oeuvres* 10, pp. 210–11 (*CE*, p. 180); also 'Le Sens Humain', *Oeuvres* 11, pp. 43–4 (*TF*, pp. 37–9); Lettre à Auguste Valensin, 25.2.1929, *LI*, pp. 184–6.
36. 'Christianisme et Évolution', *Oeuvres* 10, p. 211 (*CE*, p. 180).
37. Lettre à Claude Tresmontant, 14.1.1954. In this remark Teilhard was referring to Tresmontant's *Essai sur la pensée hébraïque*, 1953, in which the author endeavoured to set out 'the organic structure of a metaphysics which is implicit, but really present in the biblical texts' (p. 11).
38. Lettre à Claude Tresmontant, 8.2.1954. See also *Journal* XIII ( =1), 11.6.1945, p. 125.
39. *Journal* XIII ( =1), 12.10.1944, p. 27.
40. Ibid., 15.10.1944, p. 30. The three points after 'Logos' occur in the original.
41. Lettre à Claude Tresmontant, 20.1.1954.

have imagined that 'revealed truth in Scripture can only be determined by exegesis.'[42]

Teilhard's concept of doctrinal synthesis undoubtedly depends on Newman's *Essay on the Development of Christian Doctrine*.[43] Concerning the assimilating power of dogmatic truth, Newman wrote:

> She [the Church] alone has succeeded in . . . rejecting evil without sacrificing the good, and in holding together in one things which in all other schools are incompatible. Gnostic or Platonic words are found in the inspired theology of St. John. . . .[44]

From this we may gather what Teilhard intended by the assimilation of Jesus to the Alexandrian Logos. He was interested not so much in summarizing the complex background to the New Testament's Logos-type doctrines, as in saying that these doctrines identify Jesus Christ as the principle of cosmic unity, which previously had been sought after through philosophical means in the Alexandrian Logos theories. Teilhard's choice of the epithet 'Alexandrian' was probably determined by the French theological literature current about the time of his training in theology (September 1908 to July 1912). One of his references to the Alexandrian Logos, where he parallelled it with the Stoic world-soul,[45] reflects the opinion of his contemporary Lebreton (1910)[46] and of P. Richard (1913)[47] that Philo's Logos derives partly from Logos conceptions in Alexandrian Stoicism. It is impossible to tell whether Teilhard believed that the Stoic influence on Philo indicates a similar influence on the New Testament. But certainly Lebreton, Prat (1904 and 1908), and Teilhard's contemporaries Rousselot and Huby (1912) were willing to concede that an undefined indirect connection exists between Philo's Logos and the Christologies of John, Colossians, and Hebrews.[48] Perhaps the

---

42. *Journal* XIII ( = 1), 1.1.1945, p. 67. See A. Loisy, *Mémoires pour servir à l'histoire religieuse de notre temps*, tome 1, 1930, p. 177.

43. For the influence of Newman's *Essay* on Teilhard, see Teilhard, *Journal*, tome 1, 23.2.1916, p. 41; H. de Lubac (ed.), *LI*, pp. 407–8.

44. J. H. Newman, *An Essay on the Development of Christian Doctrine*, 14th imp., 1909, p. 365.

45. 'Panthéisme et Christianisme', *Oeuvres* 10, pp. 76–7 (*CE*, p. 59).

46. *Les Origines du dogme de la Trinité*, p. 62 (5e éd., 1919, p. 62).

47. 'Fils de Dieu', in A. Vacant *et al.* (ed.), *Dictionnaire de théologie catholique*, tome 5, col. 2380–6.

48. J. Lebreton, op. cit., 1910, pp. 505, 515–23 (5e éd., 1919, pp. 580, 590–8); F. Prat, 'Logos', in F. Vigouroux (ed.), *Dictionnaire de la bible*, tome 4, 1904, col. 328; id., *La Théologie de saint Paul*, 1ère partie, 1908, p. 343n.2 (8e éd., 1920, p. 343 n. 2) (E.T., *The Theology of Saint Paul*, vol. 1, p. 288 n. 1); P. Rousselot and J. Huby, 'La

words of Richard[49] come as close as any to suggesting how Teilhard understood the relationship of the Alexandrian Logos to the New Testament:

... Greek philosophy seems to have evolved towards a theology and a cosmology preparing the way for the Christian dogma of the divine intermediary of creation, revelation and worship that the God-Word is; that happened above all after its contact with Judaism, a contact made at Alexandria.

In Teilhard's mind, the assimilation of Jesus to the Alexandrian Logos was only partly successful. The pantheism of the Alexandrian Logos was corrected in Pauline and Johannine theology by what Teilhard termed 'Christian pantheism'.[50] That is to say, whereas the Alexandrian Logos, in common with other philosophical conceptions ordinarily called pantheistic, tended to merge the beings it unified into an undifferentiated whole, the cosmic Christ was presented in the New Testament as holding all things together without undermining their individuality.[51] What the New Testament did not overcome, however, was the Greek cosmology of the Alexandrian Logos.[52] Teilhard depicted the Greek cosmos as a system whose measure had been taken and whose components were arbitrarily transposable in space and time without disturbance to its basic structure. It was a static system, offering no promise of an outcome to its operations.[53] In so describing the Greek cosmos, Teilhard seems to have been developing the point, made by others, that an ahistorical, cyclic concept of time dominated the whole of Greek thought.[54]

Religion chrétienne: Le Nouveau Testament', in J. Huby (ed.), *Christus: Manuel d'histoire des religions*, 1912, p. 742 n. 1 (1921, p. 1020 n. 1).
49. Op. cit., col. 2386.
50. Lettre à Marguerite Teillard-Chambon, 2.2.1916, *GP*, p. 117 (*MM*, p. 93); 'Panthéisme et Christianisme', *Oeuvres* 10, p. 91 (*CE*, p. 75); 'Introduction à la Vie chrétienne', ibid., p. 200 (p. 171).
51. See 'Panthéisme et Christianisme', ibid., pp. 73–4, 76–7, 86–9, 90–1 (ibid., pp. 56–7, 59, 69–72, 74–5).
52. See 'Christianisme et Évolution', ibid., p. 211 (ibid., pp. 180–1); 'Catholicisme et Science', *Oeuvres* 9, p. 238 (*SC*, p. 188).
53. See 'Catholicisme et Science', loc. cit.; 'La Mystique de la Science', *Oeuvres* 6, pp. 207–9 (*HE*, pp. 166–8); 'Un Seuil mental sous nos pas: du Cosmos à la Cosmogenèse', *Oeuvres* 7, p. 269 (*AE*, p. 261).
54. See P. Duhem, *Le Système du monde: Histoire des doctrines cosmologiques de Platon à Copernic*, tome 1, 1913, pp. 275–6; E. Bréhier, *Histoire de la philosophie*, tome 1, *L'Antiquité et le moyen âge*, 1928, p. 489.
Teilhard was acquainted with Duhem; see Lettre à Marguerite Teilhard-

Teilhard's own perception of the cosmos as evolving towards a decisive end led him to substitute for the Alexandrian Logos an evolutive principle – a neo-Logos, he called it. Just as Christ had once been assimilated to the Alexandrian Logos, so today we are able to take a corresponding step, thanks to the synthetic nature of doctrine, and assimilate him to the principle of a universe in evolution.[55] In Teilhard's world Christ in his cosmic aspect becomes the evolver who sustains the evolutionary process and, through the convergence of this process on him, completes himself.[56] Teilhard regarded his evolutionary neo-Logos, his cosmic Christ, less as an innovation in doctrinal construction than as the drawing-out of a tendency, already present in the Greek Fathers, 'to transpose the datum of Revelation into a mobilist-type Universe'.[57] This tendency he recognized in Origen, despite an important disagreement with his teachings.

In one of his essays Teilhard made what is evidently an allusion to Origen, when he turned to the 'Alexandrian School' for a theory about original sin comparable in scope with his own pan-cosmic conception.[58] According to Teilhard, original sin is equivalent to the imperfect state of a creation still in process towards completion.[59] This he proposed as an alternative to the doctrine of a pre-cosmic fall, which he attributed to the Alexandrian School.[60] Among the Alexandrians the doctrine is associated pre-eminently with Origen. One of Teilhard's objections against it was aimed at its reliance on an imaginary supramundane realm of existence.[61] It is an objection that also appears in his *Notes de lectures*, the exercise books containing

Chambon, 15.2.1917, *GP*, p. 238 (*MM*, p. 184). In his *Notes de lectures*, cahier 1, 1945, p. 79, Teilhard copied out Bréhier's words on the ahistorical and cyclic nature of the Greek cosmos.
55. 'Christianisme et Évolution', *Oeuvres* 10, p. 211 (*CE*, pp. 180–1); *Journal* XIII (= 1), 12.10.1944, p. 27; 13.10.1944, p. 28; 15.10.1944, p. 30.
56. 'Christologie et Évolution', *Oeuvres* 10, pp. 105–8 (*CE*, pp. 86–90); 'Christianisme et Évolution', ibid., pp. 207–11, 214 (pp. 176–81, 183–4).
57. 'Catholicisme et Science', *Oeuvres* 9, p. 239 (*SC*, p. 189).
Despite this explicit statement, Teilhard elsewhere seems to suggest that an evolutionary cosmic Christology is adumbrated in the New Testament. For example, on Rom. 8: 22 and Eph. 4: 9–10, see 'Panthéisme et Christianisme', *Oeuvres* 10, p. 88 (*CE*, pp. 71–2); on Col. 1: 15–20, see 'Christologie et Évolution', ibid., p. 107 (pp. 88–9); on 1 Cor. 15: 26–8, see *Le Phénomène humain*, *Oeuvres* 1, pp. 327–8 (*PM*, pp. 293–4).
For the term 'mobilist', see p. 85 below.
58. 'Réflexions sur le Péché originel', *Oeuvres* 10, p. 223 (*CE*, p. 191).
59. Ibid., pp. 226–7 (ibid., pp. 194–5).
60. Ibid., pp. 223–5 (ibid., pp. 191–3).
61. 'Réflexions sur le Péché originel', *Oeuvres* 10, p. 225 (*CE*, p. 193).

annotated transcriptions from his reading. Here, in connection with two works on the interaction between paganism and early Christianity – Pierre de Labriolle's *La Réaction païenne* (1934) and Louis Rougier's *Celse* (1925) – he explicitly criticized Origen for his concern with a supra-mundane realm, at the same time discerning in him a foreshadowing of his own transformist outlook.

From his reading of de Labriolle's book, Teilhard[62] observed a paradox in Origen's Christology. Origen had spoken of Christ as a composite being ($\sigma\upsilon\nu\vartheta\varepsilon\tau\acute{o}\nu$ $\tau\iota$),[63] human in body and soul and as the Logos divine,[64] thus admitting that Christ pertains partly to the material world. And yet in Christ he saw only 'the educator of wills, the illuminator of spirits'.[65] This latter aspect of Origen's Christology drew from Teilhard a comment on his 'Platonism'. Origen had been fascinated with 'a metaphysical Beyond beside which the realities here below appear too puny, too precarious to engage the best in human effort'. In contrast, the pagan philosopher Celsus, against whom Origen wrote, had seen the same realities here below as established ('fixées'), self-contained ('cerclées'), subjected to the interests of the Empire ('romanisées').[66] But, as Teilhard realized, there was more to Origen than other-worldliness, as opposed to the this-worldliness of Celsus. Returning to de Labriolle, he noted further paradoxes in Origen's thought. Origen was capable of producing concordist as well as spiritual solutions to exegetical problems. He may have interpreted the days of Creation symbolically,[67] but for the dimensions of Noah's ark he had tried to provide a realistic estimate.[68] Likewise, he was able to sum up the essential feature of Christianity with a word borrowed from Greek philosophy, $\varphi\iota\lambda\alpha\nu\vartheta\rho\omega\pi\acute{\iota}\alpha$.[69] A similar point, Teilhard recalled, could be made about the term $\lambda\acute{o}\gamma o\varsigma$.

What these paradoxes represented for Teilhard were not contradictions. Rather, as he indicated[70] in his notes on Rougier's *Celse*, they were signs that Origen thought synthetically. From

62. *Notes de lectures*, cahier 1, 1945, p. 80.
63. *C. Cels.* 1: 66 (*GCS* 1, p. 119, l. 21).
64. Ibid., 2: 9 (ibid., p. 135, ll. 14–28). See P. de Labriolle, *La Réaction païenne*, pp. 142–3.
65. Teilhard quoted these words from P. de Labriolle, op. cit., p. 143.
66. For Celsus the cosmos is static and humanity equals the Roman state, said Teilhard previously, op. cit., p. 79.
67. *De Princ.* 4:3:1 (*GCS* 5, p. 323, ll. 5–12, 17–26; p. 324 ll. 1–4, 16–20).
68. *C. Cels.* 4: 41 (*GCS* 1, p. 314, ll. 9–24).
69. See, for example, *C. Cels.* 1: 67 (*GCS* 1, p. 121, ll. 23–8).
70. Op. cit., pp. 82–3.

Rougier Teilhard took up the distinction, popularized by Heine, between Nazarenes and Hellenes.[71] To the former type belong ascetical iconoclastic and spiritualistic tendencies; to the latter realist tendencies tinged with pride. Each of us, said Rougier, should recognize in himself either the one or the other. Teilhard replied that the Nazarene and the Hellene alike are 'immobilists'; the Nazarene contemplates an unalterable spiritual order, while the Hellene remains agnostic about any finality to existence. In contrast with them, there is a third type, who has been feeling his way in an abscure manner from the beginning and whom we are now aware of. He is the 'mobilist', combining within himself the qualities of the other two types; he sees the world moving not in an aimless cycle but towards increasingly higher states of consciousness and spirit.[72] Origen was such a person. If he and Celsus were merely antitheses of one another, the Nazarene and the Hellene, it would be difficult to choose between them. The modern world has, in fact, sided with Celsus and the Hellenes. But what persists as a living force is the mobilist outlook, shared by Origen, through which the cosmos and the humanity that Celsus supposed stable have been recast.[73] The mobilist outlook, Teilhard perceived,[74] was beyond Rougier's ken. Agreeing with Tertullian that Athens and Jerusalem have nothing in common, Rougier looked upon Origen's attempt to synthesize Hellenism and Christianity as an impossibility.[75]

Teilhard's comments on Origen indicate the affinity between the two. Both of them stood in the tradition, established with the New Testament teachings on Christ as a Logos principle, of synthesizing Christian revelation and secular thought. Teilhard considered Origen's synthesis incomplete, inasmuch as Origen had proposed a supra-mundane sphere of being which arises independently of the material world's development. Nevertheless, the synthesis that he did achieve disclosed a mobilist outlook recognizable to Teilhard as anticipating his own. Origen's world was not caught up in endless recurrences or rigidly dichotomized into a material and a spiritual

71. See L. Rougier, *Celse ou le conflit de la civilisation antique et du christianisme primitif*, pp. xxxii–xxxiii; H. Heine, 'Ludwig Börne, Eine Denkschrift', in *Sämtliche Schriften*, ed. by K. Briegleb, 4. Bd., 1971, p. 18.
72. See Teilhard, 'Note sur le Progrès', *Oeuvres* 5, pp. 23–4 (*FM*, pp. 11–12); 'Action et Activation', *Oeuvres* 9, p. 225 (*SC*, p. 178); 'Comment je crois', *Oeuvres* 10, pp. 125–8 (*CE*, pp. 104–8).
73. Teilhard, *Notes de lectures*, cahier 1, pp. 82–3.
74. Op cit., p. 83.
75. L. Rougier, op. cit., pp. 60–1, 63.

order, but was on the move towards a higher mode of existence. Thus when Teilhard spoke of Origen as an appropriate figure to discuss in rethinking Christology within the dimensions of a 'new Universe',[76] he was undoubtedly touching upon something in his general view of the Greek Fathers. In their theology he had found 'striking agreement' with his own conception of a Christ whose cosmic attributes – in contradistinction to his human and divine attributes – make him the personal centre of an evolving universe.[77]

Christ's cosmic attributes are precisely what commentators have mentioned when remarking on the similarities between the Christologies of Teilhard and Origen. They have referred to the omnipresence of Christ, to his cosmic body and to his work of cosmic redemption – aspects of a Christological perspective that Charles Raven calls Christ-centred universalism. In Teilhard's terms Christ-centred universalism pertains to his doctrine of the cosmic nature in Christ. The synthetic character of this doctrine enables the Christ of the Synoptics to be identified with the organizing principle of the world seen from a mobilist point of view. It is here that Teilhard perceived his affinity with Origen, without, however, spelling out its implications.

As we have already noted, Teilhard became aware shortly before he died that his doctrine of a cosmic nature in Christ raises once again the question of Arianism. It was suggested that, in proposing three natures in Christ, he was attempting to combine a Chalcedonian with an Arian Christology. With Origen we find a similar situation. Some commentators read his doctrine on the Son in such a way that it does not conflict with Nicene orthodoxy.[78] Others, however, see it as looking forward to the subordinationism of Arius.[79] The seeming

76. See pp. 79–80 above.
77. 'Quelques Réflexions sur la Conversion du Monde', *Oeuvres* 9, p. 161 (*SC*, p. 122).
78. See W. Marcus, *Der Subordinatianismus als historiologisches Phänomen*, pp. 156–63; M. Simonetti, 'Sull'interpretazione di un passo del *De Principiis* di Origene (I,3,5–8)', in *Rivista di cultura classica e medioevale*, Anno 6, 1964, pp. 15–32; H. Crouzel, 'Les Personnes de la Trinité sont-elles de puissance inégale selon Origène, Peri Archon 1,3,5–8?', in *Gregorianum*, vol. 57, 1976, pp. 109–25.
   For other references, see P. Nemeshegyi, *La Paternité de Dieu chez Origène*, pp. 55–6.
79. See M. Wiles, 'In Defence of Arius', in id., *Working Papers in Doctrine*, pp. 30–4; G. C. Stead, 'The Platonism of Arius', in *JTS*, new series, vol. 15, 1964, pp. 20–2, 26–8, 30; F. Ricken, 'Nikaia als Krisis des altchristlichen Platonismus', in *Theologie und Philosophie*, 44. Jahrgang, 1969, pp. 327–9, 331–2; L. W. Barnard, 'The Antecedents of Arius', in *Vigiliae Christianae*, vol. 24, 1970, pp. 176, 180–2, 185–6.
   For other references, see P. Nemeshegyi, op. cit., pp. 56–9.

contradiction between these two interpretations can be resolved by arguing that Origen conceived the Son under two aspects, as both equal and subordinate to the Father. The subordinate aspect corresponds to Teilhard's notion of a third or cosmic nature in Christ.

Only in Part Four of this study shall we be in a position to compare Origen's subordinate aspect of the Son and Teilhard's cosmic nature in Christ with one another and to evaluate them. Before that, in Parts Two and Three, we shall deal in turn with the cosmic Christologies of Origen and Teilhard, introducing each of these parts with a background discussion on the question of mediation between the Creator and his creatures, between the absolute and the contingent. Mediation touches all aspects of cosmic Christology – Christ as exemplar, instrument, bond, redeemer, and goal of creation. It is the basic problem behind Origen's subordinate aspect of the Son and Teilhard's cosmic nature in Christ.

# PART II
# THE COSMIC CHRIST IN ORIGEN

## 3. THE PLATONIC AND GNOSTIC BACKGROUND TO ORIGEN'S COSMIC CONCEPTION OF CHRIST

ONE of the recurring debates about Origen concerns his debt to extra-Christian sources, in particular his debt to Platonism and Gnosticism. The debate is mainly over the kind of influence which these sources have exerted on Origen. There can be no question that they stand in the background to his thought. Like the Platonic and Gnostic authors about his time, Origen was faced with the problem of linking God with the world, the absolute with the contingent. The solution which he proposes to the problem pertains to his doctrine on Christ. In this doctrine he considers Christ not only as a divine being who manifests himself in creaturely form but also as the principle of cosmic unity.

The characteristics of Origen's solution will be best appreciated, if the problem is first reviewed in connection with Platonism and Gnosticism. Our treatment of Platonism extends from Plato himself to the Neo-Platonism of Plotinus; but we shall be chiefly interested in the writers of what is loosely called the Middle Platonic period, which covers the first and second centuries A.D. With Gnosticism, it will be sufficient if we confine our attention to Heracleon, whose work Origen confronts in his *Commentary on John*, and to the *Tractatus Tripartitus* from the Jung Codex, which has been attributed to Heracleon.

By way of anticipating the course of our discussion, we may indicate here that, though Origen's doctrine on the link between God and the world has something in common with both Platonism and Gnosticism, on certain fundamental points it is at variance with them. In what he teaches Origen is governed by a commitment to the communally professed faith of the Christian Church. Nevertheless, there remains the contentious issue whether Platonic and Gnostic influences have merely helped him to articulate that faith or whether they have distorted his representation of it. We shall deal with this matter in Part Four of our study.

## I. THE PLATONIC BACKGROUND

Among Greek speculations on cosmic unity there is a line of development, from the *Timaeus* of Plato to the *Enneads* of Plotinus, which includes the work of such Middle Platonic authors as Philo, Plutarch, Numenius of Apamea, and Albinus. The line of development is related to the tripartite cosmological scheme which attempts to link God with the world, the absolute with the contingent, by means of an ontological middle term. Whatever may be the sources of this scheme – be they mythological heritage, cultural presuppositions or mystical experience – the line of development itself is marked by a move towards increasing speculative coherence.

During the Middle Platonic period, which is of particular importance in relation to the thought of Origen, the *Timaeus* provided the background out of which discussion developed on the relationship between the absolute and the contingent. By this time there was widespread agreement that the world depends for its order on an absolute and transcendent divine principle.[1] Acceptance of this absolute and transcendent divine principle raised the question of mediation between it and the world. But here opinion became divided. It ranged between two general types of mediation. The first type presupposes some kind of distinction within, or some attribute of, the transcendent principle and is seen as an influx from this principle into the world. In contrast, the second type is conceived as occurring through an intermediate being, extrinsic to the transcendent principle. In the first type of mediation reality is understood almost as a continuum of being; while in the second type it is understood as a

---

1. Cf. H. Dörrie, 'Die Frage nach dem Transzendenten im Mittelplatonismus', in *Les Sources de Plotin, Entretiens Hardt*, tome 5, 1957, pp. 191–223; J. Zandee, *The Terminology of Plotinus and of Some Gnostic Writings* pp. 7–13.

hierarchy of beings. We may characterize these two types of mediation by calling the first emanationist and the second subordinationist. The first is exemplified in Monarchianism, the second in Arianism.[2] In the system of Plotinus the two types become fused together.

The doctrine of emanation ($\mathring{\alpha}\pi\acute{o}\rho\rho o\iota\alpha$) from the transcendent God, with which the first type of mediation is associated, occurs for the first time, as far as is known, in the Wisdom of Solomon (*c.* 50 B.C.).[3] Wisdom is an attribute of the Godhead, not a subordinate second deity.[4] She is 'a pure emanation of the glory of the Almighty'; 'and while remaining in herself, she renews all things' (7: 25, 27). Belonging to the same period as this work, the Pseudo-Aristotle's *De Mundo* provides the simplest example of the first type of mediation. It draws a distinction between God's essence ($o\mathring{v}\sigma\acute{\iota}\alpha$) and his power ($\delta\acute{v}\nu\alpha\mu\iota\varsigma$). In his essence God exists remote from the world, in the highest place; but through his power (the precise nature of which remains undefined) he interpenetrates the world, creating and preserving all things.[5]

The subordinationist type of mediation finds early expression in the second Platonic Epistle.[6] The author speaks of the King of all as the cause and end of everything and adds that there are besides a second and third order of things, each related to its own principle.[7] The same approach is clearly evident in the teaching of Albinus about the triad, God, World-soul, and World. God is all perfect[8] and transcends the world's divisibility and mutability.[9] Below God, underived from him and eternal,[10] stands the World-soul, the Demiurge within the triad.

2. The comparison is borrowed from Praechter, who says that Philo in his conception of the Logos wavers between doctrines analogous to Monarchianism and Arianism but would have found a doctrine analogous to that of Athanasius wholly foreign to his religious consciousness. See K. Praechter (ed.), *Friedrich Ueberwegs Grundriss der Geschichte der Philosophie*, 1. Teil, *Die Philosophie des Altertums*, p. 577.
3. Cf. E. R. Dodds (ed.), *Proclus, The Elements of Theology*, 2nd ed., 1963, p. 214.
4. Cf. C. Larcher, *Études sur le Livre de la Sagesse*, pp. 377–8, 384–8, 387 n. 3; J. M. Reese, *Hellenistic Influences on the Book of Wisdom and Its Consequences.*, p. 45.
5. *De Mundo* 397B: 17–398A: 1 (6).
6. 312E.
7. The identification of the members of this triad 'seems to me a problem incapable of solution': G. R. Morrow, *Plato's Epistles*, pp. 115–16. Cf. J. Harward, *The Platonic Epistles*, p. 172.
8. *Epitome*, ed. Louis, 10: 3 ('Alcinoi Didascalicus', in Hermann (ed.), *Platonis Dialogi*, vol. 6, p. 164, ll. 24–37).
9. Ibid. 10: 4 (Hermann, p. 165, ll. 4–14); 10: 7 (p. 165, l. 30 to p. 166 l. 7).
10. Ibid. 14: 3 (Hermann, p. 169, ll. 30–1).

In many authors the two approaches stand together, not always too comfortably combined. Thus Philo resembles the author of the *De Mundo* in regarding God both as transcendent and as influencing the World,[11] but differs from him in not restricting his description of God's influence on the world to the one model. His Jewish belief leads him uncompromisingly to assert divine transcendence.[12] God is not merely the One and the Monad,[13] beside whom all other things are wanting in coherence;[14] he is also purer than the One and more primordial than the Monad,[15] and it is he who is the measure of the Monad rather than *vice versa*.[16] But if God is the transcendent cause and mind of the universe,[17] he is also the immanent all-prevading presence within the universe,[18] as he imparts existence from himself to all creatures,[19] working to produce everything[20] and dividing one being from another.[21] Although Philo affirms that God acts directly on the created universe, more usually he says that God acts through the instrumentality of his Logos. It is through the Logos that God creates the world,[22] guides it,[23] and dispenses to it his gifts.[24] So central is the role of the Logos in God's action on the universe, that Philo calls the Logos the bond of the universe.[25] This much is clear. Less certain is the kind of mediating role that Philo assigns to the Logos. This depends upon whether he places it within or outside of the Godhead. He adopts the first type of mediation by including within the Godhead the Ideas according to which the Logos forms the

---

11. On the possible influence of the *De Mundo* on Philo with regard to expressing the notion of a transcendent God, see P. Boyancé, 'Le Dieu très haut chez Philon', in P. Lévy and É. Wolff (ed.), *Mélanges d'histoire des religions offerts a Henri-Charles Puech*, pp. 145–9.
12. Philo is 'unquestionably the first theologian to treat fully of the divine transcendence': J. Daniélou, *A History of Early Christian Doctrine before the Council of Nicaea*, vol. 2, *Gospel Message and Hellenistic Culture*, p. 326.
13. *Leg. Alleg.* 2: 1–3 (1); 3: 48 (15); *Quod Deus Immut.* 11 (3); *De Spec. Leg.* 2: 176 (30); *De Praem. et Poen.* 162 (28).
14. *Quis Heres* 187–8 (38).
15. *De Vita Contemp.* 2 (1); see also *De Praem. et Poen.* 40 (6); *Quaest. Exod.* 2: 37.
16. *Leg. Alleg.* 2: 3 (1).
17. *De Opif. Mundi* 8 (2).
18. *De Post. Caini* 30 (9).
19. *De Cherub.* 86 (25).
20. *Leg. Alleg.* 2: 9–13 (4).
21. *Quis Heres* 130–1 (26); *Quaest. Gen.* 3: 5.
22. *Leg. Alleg.* 3: 96 (31); *De Cherub.* 127 (35); *De Sacrif.* 8 (3); *De Spec. Leg.* 1: 81 (16).
23. *De Migr. Abr.* 6 (1); *De Agric.* 51 (12).
24. *Quod Deus Immut.* 57 (12).
25. *De Fuga et Invent.* 112 (20); *Quis Heres* 188 (38); *De Plant.* 9 (2); *Quaest. Exod.* 2: 89–90, 118.

world.[26] The Ideas are thoughts in God's mind, on the analogy of plans in the mind of an architect.[27] If the Ideas are in God, so too is the Logos. The Logos is the divine reason where the Ideas in God are specifically located;[28] and it comprehends within itself the Powers emanating from God,[29] which are no other than equivalents of those Ideas.[30] But Philo also expresses the mediating role of the Logos in subordinationist terms. In this second type of mediation the Logos stands midway between God and the world,[31] represented either as a second God,[32] as the first-born and most comprehensive of creation[33] or as an intermediate being, neither created nor uncreated.[34] The second type of mediation emphasizes the indirectness of God's relationship to the world; thus nothing mortal can be made in the likeness of the Father, only in the likeness of the second God, the Logos.[35] The subordinationist tendency in Philo cannot be wholly absorbed into his emanationism, except through too thorough a systematization of his thought.[36] On one point, however, Philo remains constant: the transcendent God is the sole source from which all other beings are derived. By taking up this position, he reduces to a unity the plurality of first principles that we find separated in the *Timaeus*.

With the *Enneads* of Plotinus the line of development from Plato's *Timaeus* reaches a synthesis. Though he retains a hierarchy of divinities, Plotinus reduces to one the plurality of first principles which his predecessors, with the exception of Philo, had maintained.

26. *De Confus. Ling.* 63 (14).
27. *De Opif. Mundi* 15–20 (4–5).
    'Philo is the first witness to the doctrine that the Ideas are God's thoughts': H. Chadwick, 'Philo and the Beginning of Christian Thought', in A. H. Armstrong (ed.), op. cit., p. 142. But there is evidence to suggest that the doctrine may have arisen earlier than Philo; see C. J. de Vogel, 'À la recherche des étapes précises entre Platon et le néoplatonisme', in *Mnemosyne*, ser. 4, vol. 7, 1954, pp. 118–21; id., *Greek Philosophy*, vol. 3, p. 401.
28. *De Opif. Mundi* 20 (5).
29. *De Cherub.* 27–8 (9).
30. *De Spec. Leg.* 1: 47–9 (8).
31. *De Somn.* 2: 188–9 (28); *Quaest. Exod.* 2: 68.
32. *Quaest. Gen.* 2: 62; Frag. apud Euseb., *Praep. Evang.* 7: 13: 1–2 (323A) (Mras, *GCS* 43: 1, p. 389, 11. 5–12).
33. *Leg. Alleg.* 3: 175 (61).
34. *Quis Heres* 205–6 (42).
35. *Quaest. Gen.* 2: 62; Frag. apud. Euseb., loc. cit.
36. As, for example, in C. Bigg, *The Christian Platonists of Alexandria*, rev. ed., 1913, pp. 40–6; E. R. Goodenough, *An Introduction to Philo Judaeus*, 2nd ed., 1962, pp. 99–111; H. A. Wolfson, *Philo*, rev. ed., 1948, vol. 1, pp. 269–71.

His sole first principle is the transcendent One. And, in contrast with Philo, he proposes a single model to describe the relationship between the absolute and the contingent. A hierarchy of divinities, together with the one first principle, enables Plotinus to employ a kind of mediation between the absolute and the contingent which is both subordinationist and emanationist. The three divine hypostases, which are Plotinus's interpretation of the divine triad in the second Platonic Epistle,[37] constitute the basic structure of his metaphysics.

The lowest divine hypostasis, Soul, is as much a cosmic as it is a psychic principle; it is Soul which endows not only living things but the whole universe as well with life and coherence.[38] Above Soul there is the second divine hypostasis, Intelligence ($voῦς$) which not only embraces Plato's world of intelligibles[39] but also unites the Model and the Demiurge of the *Timaeus*.[40] Since of its very nature Intelligence is a manifold, it is not the ultimate explanation of things.[41] Beyond Intelligence lies the source of everything, the One,[42] the first divine hypostasis, which is the transcendent centre of the whole circle of reality.[43] With reference to Plato's Idea of the Good, which is beyond being,[44] Plotinus emphasizes the transcendence of the One: the One is 'the Good which is both beyond Intelligence and beyond being' ($τἀγαϑὸν καὶ τὸ ἐπέκεινα voῦ καὶ ἐπέκεινα oὐσίας$).[45] Moreover, for Plotinus the One is the sole principle, notwithstanding his equation of Matter with the Receptacle in the *Timaeus*.[46] For Plato, the Receptacle is a first principle.[47] But Plotinus does not regard Matter as a first principle that either counterbalances or is coeternal with the One; he considers it to be simply the potentiality and the indefinable limit of that which proceeds from the One.[48] The emanation theory, by which Plotinus describes the generation of the

37. *Enn.* 5: 1: 8.
38. Ibid. 5: 1: 2; see also 2: 1: 5; 4: 3: 1–8; 4: 4: 10–13; 4: 8: 1.
39. Ibid. 5: 1: 4.
40. Ibid. 3: 9: 1; see also 4: 4: 10, 12; 5: 9: 9.
41. Ibid. 5: 1: 5.
42. Ibid. 5: 1: 6–7.
43. Ibid. 5: 1: 11.
44. *Republic* 509B.
45. *Enn.*5: 1: 8.
   On Plato's paradoxical conception of the Good and Plotinus's attention to only one side of the paradox, see J. M. Rist, *Eros and Psyche: Studies in Plato, Plotinus, and Origen*, pp. 50–5, 68–71.
46. *Enn.* 3: 6: 19.
47. *Timaeus* 49 A.
48. *Enn.* 1: 8: 7; 2: 5: 4–5; 3: 6: 7, 10, 11; 4: 8: 6.

total hierarchy and range of being from the One, links the contingent to the absolute in a single, all-encompassing scheme.[49] He uses such metaphors as light from the sun, heat from fire, or cold from snow not to exemplify literally but merely to illustrate what he understands by emanation; namely, that the One – and indeed all other existents down the scale of being that generate – produce without diminution of what they essentially are.[50] Equally important is his characterizing of emanation from the One as necessary,[51] eternal,[52] and productive of all possible modes of being.[53]

With his system comprising the three divine hypostases and emanation, Plotinus seems to be seeking a middle course between pantheism and theistic creationism, thereby avoiding, on the one hand, the elimination of all real distinction between the absolute and the contingent and, on the other hand, the conflict between God's immutability and his arbitrary production of participated being. The difficulty of such a compromise did not escape Plotinus's Neo-Platonic successors; one of their chief disputes was whether or not the three divine hypostases are really distinct from one another.[54] An implication of this difficulty is that Plotinus has not securely linked together the subordinationist and emanationist types of mediation. Nevertheless, his attempt to bring them together must be seen as the logical outcome of the reflection on cosmology which developed from the terms of reference established by the *Timaeus* and which absorbed on the way the notion of a transcendent God.

It is against this background in Greek thought that Origen discusses Christ, the divine Logos who mediates between God and the world. Resemblances between his teaching on Christ and the doctrines of various Middle Platonist writers are not difficult to find. But, as our subsequent chapters will show, his teaching does not

49. Ibid. 5: 2: 1–2.
50. Ibid. 5: 1: 6; 5: 3: 12; 5: 4: 1; see also 5: 3: 9; 6: 4: 7.
    Plotinus rarely uses the term ἀπόρροια (never in connection with the One) to express his emanation doctrine, apparently because it belongs more properly to contexts of physical rather than of metaphysical description and as such connotes a diminution of the giver; see H. Dörrie, 'Emanation: Ein unphilosophisches Wort im spätantiken Denken', in K. Flasch (ed.), *Parusia, Studien zur Philosophie Platons und zur Problemgeschichte des Platonismus: Festgabe für Johannes Hirschberger*, pp. 135–7.
51. *Enn.* 5: 1: 7; 5: 8: 7; see also 3: 2: 2–3.
52. Ibid. 5: 1: 6; see also 2: 4: 5; 2: 9: 3; 3: 2: 1; 4: 3: 9.
53. Ibid. 3: 2: 3, 14; 3: 3: 3; 4: 8: 6.
54. Cf. R. T. Wallis, *Neo-Platonism*, pp. 82, 92, 94, 110–19, 172; see also pp. 5–6, 72–3, 123, 129, 167.

correspond substantially to what any particular one of such writers holds. Like several of them he works with both emanationism and subordinationism, though for him they do not constitute two unrelated schemes for linking God with the world, as they do for Philo, and for others such as Plutarch and Numenius. Nevertheless, Origen does not have a single scheme organized in the manner of Plotinus. Whereas Plotinus uses the emanationist principle throughout the hierarchy of being, Origen applies it only to the generation of the Son from the Father. His creation doctrine lacks the distinguishing mark of emanation, an eternal procession of being; for, although he teaches the eternity of God's creative activity and of the divine ideas upon which creatures are modelled, he denies that the creatures themselves have existed from eternity.[55] Another difference between Origen and some of the Platonists concerns the distinction between the first and the mediating levels of divinity. For Origen the Father and the Son are unmistakably distinct.[56] In Plotinus, on the contrary, there is some doubt about a real distinction between the One and the lower divine hypostases, while in Philo's emanationist type of mediation the distinction between God and the Logos is only notional. On the other hand, Origen's teaching on the procession of the Son from the Father affords a striking parallel with the relationships of generation, participation, and imitation which Numenius sees between the first God and the Demiurge.[57] There is also a similarity between the Son in Origen and the world-soul of Albinus, inasmuch as both of them look in two directions, towards the absolute as well as towards the contingent.[58] But for Albinus there exists a plurality of first principles, whereas Origen sides with Philo and Plotinus in upholding the one source of all being.[59] The unitary doctrine of Plotinus, we have noted, can be construed as a version of pantheism; and with Origen's cosmic conception of Christ the question of pantheism must also be considered.[60] Origen's teaching, however, is not simply a development out of Middle Platonism as is that of Plotinus. It is above all an exposition of the Christian faith. In the light of this faith Origen is concerned with Christ not merely as the link between God and the world, but also as

55. See pp. 120–3 below.
56. See pp. 99, 107–8 below.
57. For generation in Origen, see pp. 98–9, 119–20 below. For participation in Origen, see p. 111 below. For imitation in Origen, see pp. 108, 127 below.
58. For Origen's doctrine, see pp. 107, 115–7 below.
59. For Origen's doctrine, see pp. 125–6 below.
60. See pp. 102 n. 104, 143–5 below.

the one who goes out from the Father and in bodily form sacrifices himself to restore all creation to God.[61] As we shall see, Christ in Origen's teaching has a threefold relationship – a relationship to God, to an individual created being and to the total created cosmos.[62] Similarities between aspects of Origen's teaching on Christ and Platonism illuminate that teaching but do not account for it as a whole.

## II. THE GNOSTIC BACKGROUND

Like Platonism, Gnosticism also provides parallels with Origen's teaching. Thus both Origen and the Gnostics are concerned with pre-cosmic events leading to a fall into a material world that was not from the beginning;[63] and both view 'the whole movement of reality in the categories of the loss and recovery of metaphysical Unity'.[64] Again, Origen appears in his exegetical methods to have much in common with Gnostic writers.[65] However, the similarities are outweighed by far more important differences. Origen certainly stresses that this present material world is only of secondary significance;[66] but he also recognizes that it is inherently good[67] and harmonious,[68] that it is an object worthy of some study[69] and that it manifests within itself the

---

61. See pp. 138–42 below.
62. See pp. 135–6 below.
63. Cf. E. von Ivánka, *Plato Christianus*, pp. 141, 143–4.
64. H. Jonas, *The Gnostic Religion*, 2nd. ed., 1963, p. 61.
65. Cf. J. Daniélou, *Origen*, p. 191; id., *A History of Early Christian Doctrine before the Council of Nicaea*, vol. 2, *Gospel Message and Hellenistic Culture*, pp. 496–500; R. McL. Wilson, *Gnosis and the New Testament*, p. 67.
66. See pp. 129–30 below.
67. (a) God is the beneficent creator and sustainer of all things, *De Princ.* 1: 4: 3 (*GCS* 5, p. 65, ll. 10–12); (b) the skilful construction and the beauty of the universe provide some insight into the nature of God, ibid. 1: 1: 6 (p. 21, ll. 5–9); (c) God's creative skill is displayed in both astronomical and terrestrial works, *Sel. in Ps.* 1: 4 (*PG* 12, col. 1081A-B); (d) the laws of nature derive from God, *Hom. in Jos.* 23: 3 (*GCS* 7, p. 444, ll. 5–15); *C. Cels.* 4: 57 (*GCS* 1, pp. 329–30); 8: 31 (*GCS* 2, p. 426, l. 23 to p. 427, l. 15); (e) creation is for the advantage of men and animals, *C. Cels.* 8: 52 (ibid., p. 267, ll. 18–25).
68. *De Princ.* 2: 1: 3 (*GCS* 5, p. 108, ll. 11–31); 2: 3: 6 (p. 122, ll. 13–21); 2: 9: 6 (p. 170, ll. 5–10); *C. Cels.* 1: 23 (*GCS* 1, p. 73, ll. 22–30).
69. (a) All knowledge, every talent and every art useful to man are gifts from God, *Hom. in Num.* 18: 3 (*GCS* 7, pp. 169–172); (b) philosophy, geometry, and astronomy serve as preparatory studies for theology, *Epist. ad Greg. Thaum.* 1 (*SCh* 148, pp. 186–9); (c) Origen used to introduce his pupils to the marvels of the universe and to the study of the natural sciences, Gregory Thaumaturgus, *Orat. Pan.* 8 (*SCh* 148, pp. 140–3).

all-prevading presence of God.[70] For the Gnostics, on the other hand, 'the world is really hell'.[71] In Origen's eyes the Gnostics have fallen away from the doctrines of God, the teaching of the Church and a true mind.[72]

Origen's vehement opposition to Gnosticism has not prevented a number of commentators from suggesting that he is closer to it than his express statements indicate. Quispel, in particular, takes this view of Origen. He points especially to Daniélou's suggestion that in his exegetical methods Origen has been influenced by Heracleon.[73] Quispel, for his part, believes that the relationship between Origen and Heracleon can be pressed still further. Just as Heracleon is the successor to Valentinus in a doctrinal development, so too is Origen a successor to Heracleon. This succession can be traced in a particularly interesting way if Quispel is right in seeing Heracleon as the author of the *Tractatus Tripartitus*, the fourth Treatise in the Jung Codex.[74] The relevance of the *Tractatus* to Origen lies especially in its doctrine on the eternal generation of the Son from the Father. The general assumption has been that this doctrine is Origen's special contribution to Trinitarian theology.[75] Origen's doctrine on the eternal generation includes the following three points: the only-begotten Son, who is without any conceivable beginning,[76] has his beginning in God alone;[77] the generation of the Son from the Father involves no division of the divine being;[78] and the Son proceeds from

---

70. *Comm. in Joh.* 6: 202–3 (xxxix, 23) (*GCS* 4, pp. 148–9); *Hom. in Luc.* 22: 9–10 (*GCS* 9, p. 138, ll. 13–20); *Comm. in. Rom.* 1: 17 (*PG* 14, col. 864C).

71. R. M. Grant, *Gnosticism and Early Christianity*, 2nd ed., 1966, p. 150.

72. *Comm. in Matt.* 12: 23 (*GCS* 10, p. 122, ll. 10–22).

73. G. Quispel, 'Origen and the Valentinian Gnosis', in *Vigiliae Christianae*, vol. 28, 1974, pp. 29–30. See also id., 'From Mythos to Logos', in id., *Gnostic Studies*, vol. 1, pp. 158–9.

74. Cf. R. Kasser *et al.* (ed.), *Tractatus Tripartitus*, Pars I, *De Supernis*, 1973.
    For the identification of the author of the *Tractatus* with Heracleon, see: H.-Ch. Puech and G. Quispel, 'Le Quatrième écrit gnostique du Codex Jung', in *Vigiliae Christianae*, vol. 9, 1955, pp. 83, 90 n. 43, 95 n. 57, 98 n. 61, 100–2; also G. Quispel, 'The Jung Codex and Its Significance', in F. L. Cross (ed.), *The Jung Codex*, 1955, p. 61; id., *Gnostic Studies*, vol. 1, 1974, pp. 166–7; id., 'Origen and the Valentinian Gnosis', in *Vigiliae Christianae*, vol. 28, 1974, p. 34.

75. Cf. J. F. Bethune-Baker, *An Introduction to the Early History of Christian Doctrine*, 8th ed., 1949, pp. 147–8; J. Daniélou, *A History of Early Christian Doctrine before the Council of Nicaea*, vol. 2, *Gospel Message and Hellenistic Culture*, p. 376.

76. *De Princ.* 1: 2: 2 (*GCS* 5, p. 29, ll 11–16).        77. Ibid. 1: 2: 9 (ibid., p. 41, ll. 3–6).

78. Ibid. 4: 4: 1 (ibid., p. 348, l. 15 to p. 349, l. 6); *Comm. in Joh.* 20: 157 (xviii, 16) (*GCS* 4, p. 351); *Frag. in Joh.* 108 (ibid., p. 562, ll. 17–20). Cf. A. Orbe, *Estudios*

the Father as an act of will proceeds from the mind.[79] These three points can be paralleled in the *Tractatus*: the only-begotten Son,[80] who exists from the beginning,[81] is without beginning;[82]he is engendered through the Father's bringing himself forth;[83] and he proceeds from the Father as the Father's complete self-knowledge.[84] Despite these parallels, it is not at all clear whether the author of the *Tractatus* understands the eternal generation in precisely the same way that Origen does. Origen insists on a real distinction between Father and Son.[85] The author of the *Tractatus*, on the other hand, is vague about such a distinction, and in one place at least he seems to be adopting a modalist conception of the relationship between Father and Son.[86] Nevertheless, the doctrine of the *Tractatus* on the eternal generation is certainly closer to that of Origen than are analogous doctrines found in Middle Platonism with which Origen's teaching has sometimes been compared.[87]

---

*valentinianos*, vol. 1: 2, *Hacia la prima teologia de la procesion del Verbo*, pp. 674–8.

79. *De Princ.* 1: 2: 6 (*GCS* 5, p. 35, ll. 1–7); 1: 2: 9 (p. 40, ll. 5–11); 4: 4: 1 (p. 349, ll. 7–10); *Frag. in Joh.* 108 (*GCS* 4; p. 562, ll. 17–18).
80. *Tract.* 56: 4; 57: 21, 39; 57: 40–58: 5.
81. Ibid. 57: 33–4; see also 57: 8–17.
82. Ibid. 58: 8, 17.          83. Ibid. 56: 1–4, 9, 16–17, 35.

> By so describing the generation of the Son, the author of the *Tractatus* stands opposed to the position commonly associated with Valentinianism; namely, that the divine being is divisible. On this point Origen disputed with the Valentinian Candidus, according to Jerome, *Apol. adv. Lib. Ruf.* 2: 19 (*PL* 23, col. 442D–443A).

84. *Tract.* 56: 1–6, 33–8.
85. Particularly (a) when he speaks of the Son as a second God, *C. Cels.* 5: 39 (*GCS* 2, p. 43, ll. 22–3); 6: 61 (p. 132, l. 2); (b) when he refers to the Father and the Son as two Gods, *Dial. cum Herac.* 2: 5, 24–31 (Scherer, p. 122, ll. 9–10; p. 124, ll. 3–9); (c) when he rejects the Valentinian view that the Logos is merely the Father's verbal utterance, *Comm. in Joh.* 1: 151 (xxiv, 23) (*GCS* 4, p. 29); (d) when he attacks the modalist Monarchians, ibid. 10: 246 (xxxvii, 21) (p. 212); *Frag. in Tit.* (*PG* 14, col. 1304D); *Dial. cum Herac.* 4: 1–7 (Scherer, p. 126, l. 14 to p. 128, l.1); *Comm. in Matt.* 17: 14 (*GCS* 10, p. 624, ll. 8–16).
86. *Tract.* 58: 23.

> 'The first and second persons of the Trinity have been, in them [the Father and the Son of the *Tractatus*], merged into a single being, under the name of "Father-and-Son". The expression υἱοπάτωρ is also found in Sabellius . . . ': Introduction théologique, in R. Kasser *et al.* (ed.), *Tractatus Tripartitus*, Pars I, *De Supernis*, p. 39. ' . . . the logos [the Son of the *Tractatus*] is not a separate hypostasis, but is a function of the Father . . . ': J. Zandee, *The Terminology of Plotinus and of Some Gnostic Writings*, p. 29. However, the Son seems at times to emerge as a hypostasis separate from the Father; for instance, when he thinks of himself as a son, *Tract.* 58: 12–14.

87. E.g by Hal Koch, *Pronoia und Paideusis*, pp. 260–1, and by J. N. D. Kelly, *Early Christian Doctrines*, 5th ed., 1977, p. 128.

If in his relationship with Gnosticism Origen has in some way developed his thought under its influence, he has most certainly also reacted against it. This reaction is evident in his Logos doctrine, which is partly shaped by a two-pronged attack on Heracleon. Against Heracleon Origen asserts that the Logos together with the Father is intimately present to the whole of creation. At the same time, also against Heracleon, he upholds a fundamental distinction between the Logos together with the Father and all that is created.

In the first part of his attack, Origen objects to Heracleon's view that the existence of the cosmos depends upon the double subordinate agency of the Logos and the Demiurge. According to Heracleon, the Logos belongs to the transcendent pneumatic world, called the Aeon or the Pleroma, the realm ruled by God, the Father of Truth.[88] Within this world the Logos is manifestly a subordinate being, though we are not told whether he is subordinate to the Father directly or through the mediation of other beings. It is the Logos who, acting as an intermediary, causes the Demiurge to make the cosmos; that is, the Demiurge in his turn is subordinate to the Logos.[89] Both the Demiurge and the cosmos which he makes pertain to an order of being inferior to that of the pneumatic; namely, to the psychic order.[90] But where the Demiurge originally comes from, Heracleon does not say.[91] A doctrine of double subordination, similar to that attributed by Origen to Heracleon, occurs in the *Tractatus*.[92]

Origen rejects Heracleon's distancing of God from the cosmos through the doctrine of double subordination, partly by appealing to the obvious sense of John 1: 3 and partly by reinterpreting the term 'Demiurge'.[93] According to John 1: 3, 'All things were made through him [the Logos], and without him nothing was made.'[94] As Origen

---

88. *Comm. in Joh.* 13: 97 (xvi, 16) (*GCS* 4, p. 240); 13: 147–50 (xxv, 25) (pp. 248–9).

89. Ibid. 2: 101–2 (xiv, 8) (ibid., p. 70).

90. Ibid. 13: 416–33 (lx, 59) (ibid., pp. 291–4).

91. According to Y. Janssens (ed.), op. cit., p. 279.

92. In the *Tractatus*, after Sophia-Logos has fallen, 75: 17–76: 4, it brings forth, according to the image of the Father, an appearance of which the Demiurge is the form; the Demiurge then becomes the instrument of Sophia-Logos in the creation of the world, 100: 21–35.

   Sophia-Logos is an aeon and should be distinguished from the Son, who is also called Logos, 66: 15–16.

93. *Comm. in Joh.* 2: 100–4 (xiv, 8) (*GCS* 4, pp. 70–1).

94. Like almost all witnesses before the fifth century, Origen terminates verse 3 (or, more accurately, places a stop) after ἕν and begins verse 4 (the next sentence) with ὃ γέγονεν. Cf. R. E. Brown, *The Gospel According to John (i–xii)*, p. 6; C. Blanc (ed.), *Origène, Commentaire sur saint Jean*, tome 1, *SCh* 120, p. 264 n. 3.

reads this verse, the Logos is the instrumental cause not merely of the cosmos but of all other created things as well, 'whether thrones or dominions or principalities or authorities' (Col. 1:16); that is to say, the Logos is subordinate to nothing created, not even to whatever realm of being may possibly correspond to the Gnostic Pleroma. He is subordinate only in the sense of being God's assistant (ὑπηρέτης)—or instrument—in the creation of all things. Even so, as Origen's use of the term 'Demiurge' indicates, there is a qualification to the sense in which the Logos is subordinate. The Demiurge, says Origen,[95] is not the assistant of the Logos; rather, the situation is the other way around. At the back of this assertion lies Origen's general anti-Marcionite position that the Demiurge, the Creator of the cosmos, is one and the same as the Father of the Logos, the more perfect God whom the Logos has announced to the world.[96] Origen, then, states categorically that God the Father is the Demiurge;[97] the Demiurge is not some mythical fabrication of the Gnostics.[98] But Origen further states that the Logos, Christ the Son of God, also is the Demiurge, inasmuch as he is Wisdom, the beginning of God's ways,[99] and inasmuch as he is the rational principle behind creation.[100] If the function of Demiurge belongs primarily (πρώτως) to the Father, it belongs immediately (προσεχῶς) with respect to the making of the world to the Logos.[101] In drawing this distinction, Origen undoubtedly introduces an element of subordinationism into his notion of the Logos.[102] Nevertheless, because the Father and the Logos in their capacity as Demiurge are, both of them, the source of creation, they are in some sense equal. Likewise, when he maintains against Heracleon that the Father and the Logos both penetrate the entire creation, Origen again sees their relationship to one another as involving subordinationism together with equality. What properly pertains to the Father—namely, filling the whole of creation—that

---

95. *Comm. in Joh.* 2: 104 (xiv, 8) (*GCS* 4, p. 71); see also 6: 200 (xxxix, 23) (p. 148).
96. Ibid. 2: 199 (xxxiv, 28) (ibid., p. 91); 6: 200 (xxxix, 23) (p. 148); 19: 12 (iii, 1) (p. 300); 20: 271 (xxx, 24) (p. 367).
97. See also *Comm. in Joh.* 1: 35 (vi, 8) (*GCS* 4, p. 11); 1: 102 (xvii, 17) (p. 22); 20: 271 (xxx, 24) (p. 367); also 2: 171 (xxviii, 23) (p. 85); 13: 117 (xix, 19) (p. 243).
98. Ibid. 13: 103 (xvii, 17) (ibid., p. 241).
99. Ibid. 1: 110–11 (xix, 22) (ibid., p. 23); see Prov. 8: 22.
100. *Frag. in Joh.* 1 (*GCS* 4, p. 483, ll. 1–8).
101. *C. Cels.* 6: 60 (*GCS* 2, p. 130, ll. 21–5).
102. See also *Comm. in Joh.* 1: 255 (xxxv, 40) (*GCS* 4, p. 45), where Origen says that the Father is greater than Christ acting in his role as Demiurge.

the Father grants to pertain also to the Logos.[103] If Origen has any agreement with Heracleon and the other Gnostics, it is the verbal agreement that he who is immediately present to the cosmos is the Demiurge. But Origen's Demiurge is none other than the Father himself together with his instrument, the Logos. Thus Origen repudiates the Gnostic teaching that some subordinate deity stands between the Father and a certain part of that which exists. Similarly, he corrects Heracleon's opinion that the Logos becomes present to the cosmos only with the Incarnation; the Logos has always been present there.[104]

Origen directs the second part of his attacks on Heracleon against the Gnostic teaching about the existence of a pneumatic class of men, who receive their initial formation and ultimate perfection directly from the Logos[105] and stand in sharp contrast to the psychics who belong entirely to the Demiurge and the cosmos.[106] In Origen's view, all distinction between pneumatic and psychic classes of men must be rejected. The pneumatic state is superior to being a man[107] and belongs by nature to God alone.[108] If it belonged by nature to a

---

103. Ibid. 6: 201–3 (xxxix, 23) (ibid., pp. 148–9); see also ibid. 6: 188–9 (xxxviii, 22) (p. 146); *C. Cels.* 6: 71 (*GCS* 2, p. 141).

    For further discussion, see R. Gögler, *Zur Theologie des biblischen Wortes bei Origenes*, p. 180 n. 71. Gögler recognizes Origen as teaching the essential equality of Father and Logos; but he also maintains (taking, it seems, too simplified a view of the evidence) that Origen's subordinationist expressions imply no more than personal and functional differences between Father and Logos.

104. *Comm. in Joh.* 6: 194–7 (xxxix, 23) (*GCS* 4, pp. 147–8).

    It should be noted that Origen does not substitute a Stoic doctrine of divine penetration of the cosmos for the Gnostic doctrine of divine remoteness from the cosmos. In *C. Cels.* 6: 71 (*GCS* 2, p. 141) he carefully distinguishes his position from that of the Stoics. According to Origen, the Stoics consider their first principles to be corporeal and hence as much subject to destruction as is the cosmos itself. For Origen, on the contrary, God and the Logos are incorporeal and thus not destructible. See also *C. Cels.* 5: 7 (*GCS* 2, pp. 6–8), where Origen again distinguishes his position from that of the Stoics.

    When Spanneut says, with reference to *C. Cels.* 6: 71, that Origen gives the doctrine of Providence a Stoic interpretation, he ignores the distinction which Origen draws between his own position and that of Stoicism; see M. Spanneut, *Permanence du stoïcisme*, p. 157.

105. *Comm. in Joh.* 2: 137 (xxi, 15) (*GCS* 4, p. 77, ll. 27–30).

106. Heracleon identifies the psychics with the Jews, ibid. 10: 210 (xxxiii, 19) (ibid., p. 206); 20: 168–70 (xx, 18) (p. 352). Subject to the law, they are akin to the Demiurge, ibid. 13: 416, 420, 424 (lx, 59) (pp. 291–2), and they worship him, ibid. 13: 96–7 (xvi, 16) (p. 240). More numerous than the pneumatics, the psychics belong to the cosmos, ibid. 13: 341 (li, 50) (pp. 279–80).

107. Ibid. 2: 138 (xxi, 15) (ibid., p. 77).

108. Ibid. 13: 123–30 (xxi, 21) (ibid., pp. 244–5); 13: 140–50 (xxiii–xxv, 23–5) (pp. 247–9); *De Princ.* 1: 1: 2–4 (*GCS* 5, pp. 17–20)

certain class of men as well, it would follow that God could sin, since according to Gnostic teaching pneumatic men have sinned.[109] It does not follow, however, that, because the pneumatic state belongs by nature to God alone, men cannot be raised to this state. All men, not just a privileged group of them, can be raised;[110] and in being raised they share in God's own divine life.[111] But they are raised only accidentally, since they fall from the pneumatic state, if through sin their souls are separated from God, from their Lord (that is, the Logos) and from the Holy Spirit.[112] Like his conception of pneumatic man, Heracleon's conception of psychic man is for Origen also misconceived. Heracleon believes that the essential element of the psychic, the soul ($\psi\upsilon\chi\dot\eta$) is mortal.[113] Origen admits that the soul is susceptible to death, but the death in question is that of sin, not of dissolution and annihilation; the soul is immortal.[114] And far from being that which distinguishes a man from the Logos, the soul contains the rational element in man which relates him to the Logos. All men are related in this way to the Logos; there is no element peculiar to the nature of some men only which constitutes between them and the Logos a special relationship not shared by other men.

Whatever Origen's Logos doctrine has in common with the teachings of Heracleon or any other Gnostic writer, it is not reducible to them, just as it does not correspond substantially to the teachings

109. *Comm. in Joh.* 13: 147–50 (xxv, 25) (*GCS* 4, pp. 248–9).

Elsewhere Origen says that man's rational soul ($\lambda o\gamma\iota\kappa\dot\eta\ \psi\upsilon\chi\dot\eta$) has by nature a certain relationship with God ($\tau\iota\ \sigma\upsilon\gamma\gamma\varepsilon\nu\grave\varepsilon\varsigma\ \vartheta\varepsilon\tilde\omega$), since both are intellectual ($\nu o\varepsilon\rho\acute o\varsigma$), invisible and incorporeal, *Exh. ad Mart.* 47 (*GCS* 1, p. 42, l. 29 to p. 43, l. 1); see also *C. Cels.* 1: 8 (ibid., p. 60, ll. 23–30). Jerome views this position of Origen's in an unfavourable light. He charges Origen with holding the consubstantiality of rational creatures and God, even though he admits that Origen qualifies his notion of their relationship with a 'quodammodo', *Epist. ad Avitum* 14 (*PL* 22, col. 1072). If Jerome were right, Origen would be adhering to the very doctrine which he condemns the Gnostics for teaching. Cf. H. Crouzel, *Théologie de l'image de Dieu chez Origène*, pp. 102, 106–10, 161.

110. *Comm. in Joh.* 2: 134–6 (xx, 14) (*GCS* 4, p. 77).

111. Ibid. 13: 140–3 (xxiii–xxiv, 23–4) (ibid., pp. 247–8).

For Origen's teaching on the pneumatic state in man, see J. Dupuis, '*L'Esprit de l'homme*', esp. pp. 76–83, 90–104.

112. *Comm. in Joh.* 13: 140 (xxiii, 23) (*GCS* 4, p. 247, ll. 18–27). See also *Comm. in Rom.* 2: 9 (*PG* 14, col. 892D–893D): conscience is the Spirit of God which is attached to the souls of the just and is separated from those in sin.

113. *Comm. in Joh.* 13: 417–18 (lx, 59) (*GCS* 4, pp. 291–2).

114. Ibid. 13: 427–9 (lxi, 59) (ibid., p. 293).

For further discussion on the immortality of the soul, see *De Princ.* 3: 1: 13 (*GCS* 5, p. 217, ll. 6–7); 3: 1: 23 (p. 242, l. 19); 4: 4: 9–10 (p. 362, ll. 9–10; p. 363, ll. 4–26); *Dial. cum Herac.* 24: 18–27: 8 (Scherer, p. 166, l. 23 to p. 172, l. 4); *Comm. in Matt.* 17: 29 (*GCS* 10, p. 665, l. 22 to p. 666, l. 31).

of any particular Platonist. If Origen owes his idea of the Son's eternal generation to the author of the *Tractatus*, he certainly does not share that author's tendency towards modalism. Again, although both Heracleon and Origen cast the Logos in a subordinate and mediating role, they conceive that role in quite different ways. With Heracleon it is consequent upon a dualistic doctrine of God's remoteness from the world, while with Origen it indicates the divine presence throughout creation. Furthermore, contrary to the Gnostics, Origen denies that there are classes of men by nature distinct from one another. For him, all men, because of their rationality, bear a special relationship to the Logos. However, as we shall see, Origen's Logos is related not just to men. He mediates between the Father and the whole of creation. As mediator he is subordinate to the Father. But as the Son he also possesses a certain equality with the Father. The paradoxical character of the Son in Origen's teaching is what we must now examine.

# 4. ORIGEN'S TWOFOLD DOCTRINE ON THE SON

A number of commentators have pointed out that Origen seems uncertain whether the Son stands closer to creatures or to the Father.[1] In Book 13 of his *Commentary on John* he expresses the former opinion:

> ... we say that the Saviour and the Holy Spirit transcend all creatures not by comparison but by surpassing pre-eminence, while he [the Saviour] is transcended by the Father as much as or even more than he himself and the Holy Spirit transcend all other beings, even those that are not inconsiderable.[2]

In his *Commentary on Matthew*, however, Origen places the Son closer to the Father than to creatures:

> It is more possible to see a close resemblance between God's goodness and the Saviour, who is the image of God's goodness, than between the Saviour and a good man, a good work or a good tree. For, inasmuch as he is the image of the goodness of God himself, the Saviour has more pre-eminence over lesser good things than even God for all his goodness has over the aforementioned Saviour.[3]

T. E. Pollard[4] has suggested that the contradiction may possibly be the result of a modification in Origen's opinion between the writing of the former passage (*c.* 234–8) and the writing of the latter (249).[5] However, it can be shown that Origen, both in his earlier and in his

---

1. See C. Bigg, *The Christian Platonists of Alexandria*, rev. ed., 1913, p. 223 n. 3; J. Daniélou, *Origen*, pp. 254–5; H. Crouzel, *Théologie de l'image de Dieu chez Origène*, pp. 116–17; M. F. Wiles, *The Spiritual Gospel*, p. 122; T. E. Pollard, *Johannine Christology and the Early Church*, p. 92.
2. *Comm. in Joh.* 13: 151 (xxv, 25) (*GCS* 4, p. 249, ll 19–22).
3. *Comm. in Matt.* 15: 10 (*GCS* 10, p. 375, l. 31 to p. 376, l.10).
4. loc. cit. See also R. Cadiou, *La Jeunesse d'Origène*, pp. 221–4.
5. The dates are those indicated in P. Nautin, *Origène*, tome 1, *Sa vie et son oeuvre*, pp. 376–8, 410–12. Pollard gives the dates as *c.* 235 and *c.* 244.

later works, takes a twofold view of the Son's relative distance from
the Father and from creatures. To support this contention two
examples running counter to those given above will suffice. At one
point in an early work, Book 2 of his *Commentary on John* (231),
Origen clearly places the Son closer to the Father than to creatures.
The Logos, says Origen, comes to men, who previously did not have
the capacity for his advent; but to the Father he does not come, since
he has never been separated from the Father.[6] On the other hand, in
his late work, the *Contra Celsum* (249), Origen can envisage the Son on
the side of creatures rather than of God. Whereas God gives a share in
being (οὐσία) to creatures and even to the Logos, who may be called
the being of beings (οὐσία οὐσιῶν), God himself, like the Good in
Plato, is simply beyond being (ἐπέκεινα οὐσίας).[7] It seems, then, that
Origen always looked upon the Son as existing on two levels.
However, instead of considering the matter in terms of distance, we
shall grasp his teaching more readily, if we attend to what he says
about the relationships of equality and subordination that the Son
has with the Father.

## I. THE SON AS EQUAL WITH THE
### FATHER

Equality between the Father and the Son derives from the divine
unity. They are one and exist in each other,[8] united not as one in flesh
or in spirit but as one God.[9] However, the divine unity does not imply
an undifferentiated Godhead. We worship, says Origen, one God, the
Father and the Son; but 'in no way do we defect to those who deny
that there are two subsistent entities (δύο ὑποστάσεις), the Father and
the Son'.[10] Something of Origen's thinking on the divine unity may be
gathered from a distinction that he draws in the *De Principiis*: God is
in every respect the Monad, and he may even be called the Henad.[11]

6. *Comm. in Joh.* 2: 8–9 (i, l) (*GCS* 4, p. 53).
7. *C. Cels.* 6: 64 (*GCS* 2, p. 135, ll. 4–6, 9–11). See Plato, *Republic* 509B.
8. *Hom. in Lev.* 13: 4 (*GCS* 6, p. 473, ll. 10–21); *C. Cels.* 8: 12 (*GCS* 2, p. 229, ll. 15–20);
see also *Comm. in Joh.* 6: 202 (xxxix, 23) (*GCS* 4, p. 148, l. 32 to p. 149, l. 4); *Dial. cum
Herac.* 4: 9–16 (Scherer, p. 128, ll. 2–7).
9. *Dial. cum Herac.* 3: 20–4: 2 (Scherer, p. 126, ll. 9–15); see also ibid. 2: 3–6, 24–31 (p.
122, ll. 8–10; p. 124, ll. 3–9); 4: 24–7 (p. 128, l. 13 to p. 130, l. 2).
10. *C. Cels.* 8: 12 (*GCS* 2, p. 229, ll. 21–5).
11. *De Princ.* 1: 1: 6 (*GCS* 5, p. 21, l. 14). Rufinus retains the Greek terms μονάς and ἑνάς
in his Latin translation.

The distinction appears to be Neo-Pythagorean.[12] If this is so, it indicates that God is not only the unity from which all multiplicity is derived (the Monad); he is also absolute unity (the Henad). In his 'more divine nature' ( θειοτέρα φύσις) Christ pertains to the Henad, since that nature is at one (ἡνωμένη) with the uncreated nature of the Father.[13] The unity (τὸ ἕν) does not apply to the God of the universe separated from Christ or to Christ separated from God.[14] But Christ also exhibits the monadic aspect of the divine unity: 'God is altogether one (ἕν) and simple, but because of the many things [in creation] our Saviour . . . has become many things . . . '[15] Thus if the divine unity is the root of equality between the Father and the Son, it is also paradoxically the point at which differences between them emerge. Further on we shall look at their differences, but for the moment we shall consider the various ways in which Origen expresses their equality.

His most characteristic way of doing so is in terms of the Son as the image of the Father. He applies to them the general observation that a father begets his son after his own image and that it is the image which preserves the unity of nature and being ('naturae ac substantiae unitatem') common to a father and his son.[16] However, because of God's incorporeity, Origen adds the qualification that the divine Son proceeds from his Father like an act of will from the mind; just as an act of will neither divides the mind from which it proceeds nor becomes separated from it, similarly there is no division of the Father

12. According to G. W. Butterworth, *Origen, On First Principles*, p. 10 n. 1.

On the Neo-Pythagorean distinction between the Monad and the One, see E. Zeller, *A History of Greek Philosophy from the Earliest Period to the Time of Socrates*, vol. 1, p. 391, especially n. 2.

13. *Comm. in Joh.* 19: 6 (ii, 1) (*GCS* 4, p. 299, ll. 14–16).

14. *Dial. cum Herac.* 4: 12–14 (Scherer, p. 128, ll. 4–6).

15. *Comm. in Joh.* 1: 119 (xx, 22) (*GCS* 4, p. 24).

In contrast with the Logos or Word of God, other words are neither the Monad nor that which is integrated (τὸ σύμφωνον) nor one (ἕν), ibid. 5: 5 (4) (p. 102, l. 29 to p. 103, l. 1).

16. *De Princ.* 1: 2: 6 (*GCS* 5, p. 34, l. 13 to p. 35, l. 3).

The phrase 'naturae ac substantiae unitatem' is said to betray the hand of Rufinus. See M. F. Wiles, *The Divine Apostle: The Interpretation of St Paul's Epistles in the Early Church*, p. 76 n. 2. Against this suggestion two points may be made: (a) The phrase fits easily into its context, where the relationship between the divine Son and his Father is contrasted with the relationship between man and his Creator. In the latter relationship there is no unity of nature and being; as the image of his Creator, man is like no more than a painted or carved object. Cf. H. Crouzel, *Théologie de l'image de Dieu chez Origène*, pp. 79, 101, 106–7. (b) The phrase has a parallel, ἐν οὐσίᾳ, in *Comm. in Joh.* 10: 246 (xxxvii, 21) (*GCS* 4, p. 212, l. 14).

and no separation of the Son from the Father.[17] As image, the Son shares in the Father's greatness; he is 'a beautiful image commensurate (σύμμετρον), so to speak, with the "invisible God" '.[18] The Father and his image, though two separate individuals (δύο τῇ ὑποστάσει πράγματα), are 'one in the agreement of their minds, in the concord of their utterance and in the identity of their wills'.[19] This identity means that the Son's will is the image of the first (that is, God's) will; that only the Son does the whole of the Father's will.[20] The Son is the image of the Father's goodness, such that there exists in him no other goodness.[21] Because he humbled himself to save men rather than consider his equality with God something to be held on to, his goodness paradoxically appears all the more in the Father's image.[22] Whatever the Father does, the Son as his image does in a similar fashion.[23] Their activities are the same in extent.[24] Indeed, because the Son as God's Wisdom is the 'spotless mirror of his activity' (Wis. 7: 26), their activities are identical.[25]

Besides referring to the Son as the image of the Father, Origen presents them in a number of other ways as equal. First of all, there are the essential divine attributes of incorporeity and goodness. Only God is incorporeal;[26] apart from him, everything else always possesses some kind of body.[27] Origen says that the members of the

17. *De Princ.* 1: 2: 6 (*GCS* 5, p. 35, l. 3 to p. 36, l. 3).
18. *C. Cels.* 6: 69 (*GCS* 2, p. 139, ll. 3–9).
19. Ibid. 8: 12 (ibid., p. 229, l. 31 to p. 230, l. 4). For the distinction between God and the Son as the image of God, see also *Comm. in Rom.* 7: 7 (*PG* 14, col. 1123C).
20. *Comm. in Joh.* 13: 228–34 (xxxvi, 36) (*GCS* 4, pp. 260–1).
21. *De Princ.* 1: 2: 13 (*GCS* 5, p. 46, ll. 11–13; p. 47, ll. 1–2, 9–16).
22. *Comm. in Joh.* 1: 231 (xxxii, 37) (*GCS* 4, p. 41); see also ibid. 6: 294–5 (lvii, 37) (p. 165, l. 33 to p. 166, l. 7); *Hom. in Gen.* 1: 13 (*GCS* 6, p. 16, l. 18 to p. 17. l. 16).
23. *Comm. in Joh.* 13: 233–4 (xxxvi, 36) (*GCS* 4, p. 261, ll. 20–5); see also ibid. 10: 247 (xxxvii, 21) (p. 212).
24. *De Princ.* 1: 3: 5 (*GCS* 5, p. 56, ll. 8–18); see also ibid. 1: 3: 7 (p. 59, ll. 4–6); *Frag. in Ps.* 9: 9 (Pitra 2, p. 462); 100: 2(1) (Pitra 3, p. 191); *Hom. in Lev.* 5: 2 (*GCS* 6, p. 337, ll. 6–21).
25. *De Princ.* 1: 2: 12 (*GCS* 5, pp. 45–6).
    Contrary to the data set out in this paragraph, there is also a subordinationist strain in Origen's doctrine on the Son as image. The most notable example is *Com. in Joh.* 13: 151–3 (xxv, 25) (*GCS* 4, pp. 249–50). But it is not as dominant a strain as is claimed by some writers, e.g. M. F. Wiles, *The Divine Apostle*, p. 76 n. 4.
26. Ibid. 1: 1: 1–7 (ibid., pp. 16–37); *Comm. in Joh.* 13: 123–31 (xxi–xxii, 21–2) (*GCS* 4, pp. 244–5); *C. Cels.* 7: 38 (*GCS* 2, p. 188, ll. 11–23).
27. *De Princ.* 2: 2: 1–2 (*GCS* 5, pp. 111–13); 2: 3: 2–3 (pp. 114–19); 4: 4: 8 (p. 360, l. 10 to p. 361, l. 9); see also ibid. 2: 9: 1 (p. 165, ll. 4–16).
    Although everything apart from God has a body, rational creatures are

Trinity are incorporeal;[28] and in particular, from the point of view of the present discussion, that the divine Son is incorporeal.[29] Incorporeity, Origen observes, is a Greek concept, and it is equivalent in scriptural terms to being invisible.[30] Thus he also speaks of God as invisible;[31] so too of the Trinitarian persons[32] and of Christ in his divinity.[33] With regard to goodness, only the Father, Son, and Holy Spirit are by nature good, unable to become evil; whatever else is good is capable of losing its goodness.[34]

For Origen both God and his Only-begotten Son possess a divinity that is transcendent ($\dot{\upsilon}\pi\epsilon\rho\acute{\epsilon}\chi o\upsilon\sigma\alpha$) with unutterable superiority.[35] The Son is 'a great power and a God like ($\kappa\alpha\tau\acute{\alpha}$) the God and Father of the universe'.[36] Not only is the Father uncreated ($\dot{\alpha}\gamma\acute{\epsilon}\nu\eta\tau o\varsigma$),[37] but so also is the Son.[38] And, as we have previously noted, Origen calls both of them the Creator ($\delta\eta\mu\iota o\upsilon\rho\gamma\acute{o}\varsigma$).[39] In the following passage a somewhat confused but nevertheless striking metaphor expresses the equality of the Trinitarian persons, without obliterating their distinction:

nevertheless incorporeal in respect of their proper nature, ibid. 1: 7: 1 (p. 86, ll. 5–24); 4: 3: 15 (p. 347, ll. 9–19). Cf. H. Cornélis, 'Les Fondements cosmologiques de l'eschatologie d'Origène', in *Revue des sciences philosophiques et théologiques*, vol. 43, 1959, pp. 58–63 (reprint, pp. 27–32).
28. *De Princ.* 1: 6: 4 (*GCS* 5, p. 85, ll. 17–20); 2: 2: 2 (p. 112, ll. 15–22); 4: 3: 15 (p. 347, ll. 19–22); 4: 4: 5 (p. 356, ll. 8–10); see also *C. Cels.* 6: 70 (*GCS* 2, p. 139, l. 29 to p. 140, l. 1); 6: 71 (p. 141, ll. 15–22).
29. *De Princ.* 1: 1: 8 (*GCS* 5, p. 26, ll. 2–14); 1: 2: 2 (p. 28, l. 17 to p. 29, l. 3); *Comm. in Joh.* 2: 195 (xxxii, 26) (*GCS* 4, p. 90, ll. 8–10).
30. *De Princ.* 2: 3: 6 (*GCS* 5, p. 124, ll. 19–25); 4: 3: 15 (p. 347, ll. 11–14); *Comm. in Joh.* 13: 132 (xxii, 22) (*GCS* 4, p. 246, ll. 4–5); see also ibid. 20: 158 (xviii, 16) (p. 351, ll. 10–11); *C. Cels.* 6: 64 (*GCS* 2, p. 135, ll. 8–9); 6: 69 (p. 139, ll. 10–11).
31. *De Princ.* 2: 4: 3 (*GCS* 5, pp. 130–1); *C. Cels.* 6: 64 (*GCS* 2, p. 135, ll. 6–8); see also *Hom. in Gen.* 3: 2 (*GCS* 6, p. 39, ll. 20–1).
32. *De Princ.* 2: 4: 3 (*GCS* 5, p. 131, ll. 16–18); *Hom. in Exod.* 6: 5 (*GCS* 6, p. 197, ll. 8–10; see also *Frag. in Joh.* 20 (*GCS* 4, p. 500, ll. 4–23; p. 501, ll. 18–21).
33. *De Princ.* 2: 6: 3 (*GCS* 5, p. 141, ll. 27–9); *Comm. in Joh.* 6: 154, 156 (xxx, 15) (*GCS* 4, p. 140, ll. 9–12, 17–22); *C. Cels.* 6: 69 (*GCS* 2, p. 139, ll. 14–25).
34. *De Princ.* 1: 6: 2 (*GCS* 5, p. 80, ll. 10–14); 1: 8: 3 (p. 100, ll. 11–21); see also ibid. 1: 5: 5 (p. 77, ll. 20–3).
35. *C. Cels.* 5: 11 (*GCS* 2, p. 12, ll. 9–10); see also *Hom. in 1 Reg.* 1: 13 (*GCS* 8, p. 21, ll. 26–30).
36. *C. Cels.* 2: 9 (*GCS* 1, p. 135, l. 29 to p. 136, l. 1).
37. *Comm. in Joh.* 2: 14 (ii, 2) (*GCS* 4, p. 54, l. 16); 2: 104 (xiv, 8) (p. 71, l. 7); 20: 184 (xxii, 20) (p. 354, l. 24); *Comm. in Rom.* 6:8 (Scherer, p. 226, l. 9); *Dial. cum. Herac.* 1: 21 (Scherer, p. 120, l. 8).
38. *Frag. in Joh.* 2 (*GCS* 4, p. 485, ll. 27–8); *C. Cels.* 6: 17 (*GCS* 2, p. 88, ll. 21–3).
39. See pp. 100–2 above.

God is entirely hand, since he scrutinizes all things; while the hands of God are the Son and the Holy Spirit, through whom he has created all things, especially man.[40]

When the Son is sent by the Father, it is the Almighty who is sent by the Almighty (Παντοκράτωρ ὑπὸ Παντοκράτορος).[41] Out of love and pity for men the Saviour suffered even before he assumed their flesh. But he was not alone in his suffering: 'God bears our ways, just as the Son of God carries our sufferings'.[42] The Father's love and the Son's love are the same; and because the Father and the Son do not differ in love, they differ in nothing else as well.[43]

According to the apostolic tradition within which Origen expounds his faith, 'the Holy Spirit is united ("sociatum") in honour and dignity with the Father and the Son.'[44] What we find, then, is that in many passages of his works Origen assigns the same attributes to both the Father and the Son – and at times to all three persons of the Trinity. Of these passages there is a sufficient number from Greek texts, for us to be confident that Rufinus's Latin version of the *De Principiis*, even though it tends to be a paraphrase rather than a literal translation, does not distort Origen's thought, when it says that 'nothing in the Trinity is to be called greater or less' and that 'the power of the Trinity is one and the same'.[45]

40. *Frag. in Ps.* 118: 73 (Waldis, p. 57); only partly represented in *Frag. in Ps.* 118: 73(3), (5) (Pitra 3, p. 279).
41. *Frag. in Ps.* 23: 10 (Pitra 2, p. 482); see also *De Princ.* 1: 2: 10 (*GCS* 5, p. 43, ll. 10–17).
42. *Hom. in Ez.* 6: 6 (*GCS* 8, p. 384, l. 21 to p. 385, l. 3); see also *Hom. in Num.* 23 : 2 (*GCS* 7, p. 212, l. 24 to p. 214, l. 3).
43. *Comm. in Cant.* Prol.: 2 (*GCS* 8, p. 69, ll. 24–6); see also *Comm. in Rom.* 4: 9 (*PG* 14, col. 997C).
44. *De Princ.* 1: Praef.: 4 (*GCS* 5, p. 11, ll. 3–4).
45. Ibid. 1: 3: 7 (ibid., p. 60, ll. 1–2, 13).
    Koetschau (note ad loc.) questions the authenticity of the former of these citations (that 'nothing in the Trinity is to be called greater or less'), on the ground that it is contradicted by a Greek fragment found in Justinian, *Lib. adv. Orig. ad Mennam* (Mansi, tomus 9, col. 524E–525A; inserted in *De Princ.* 1: 3: 5, *GCS* 5, p. 55, l. 4 to p. 56, l. 8). According to the fragment, 'The God and Father who sustains all things reaches out (φθάνει) to every being . . .' while the Son reaches out, to a lesser degree than the Father, only to rational beings (for he is second to the Father) . . .' Three points may be made against Koetschau:
    (a) Coming from a sixth-century text concerned with contemporary Origenist controversies, the fragment may not accurately represent what Origen wrote.
    (b) Even if it does accurately represent what Origen wrote, the fragment cannot be taken to contain the whole of his teaching on the Son's relations with creatures. This evident from a number of passages in Origen's works. See pp. 129–30, 136, 143–4 below.

## II THE SON AS SUBORDINATE TO THE FATHER

On the basis of the aspect of Origen's teaching that we have just reviewed Athanasius saw him as one who stood in the tradition preserved by Nicaea; yet Jerome became convinced that he was the source of Arianism, which assaulted that tradition.[46] Jerome's view has at least this justification, that Origen appears to hold a twofold doctrine on the Son. Although he can speak about the Son in terms of equality with the Father, he also draws a picture of the Son which is undeniably subordinationist and has something in common with the position of Arius.

The Father alone is unbegotten (ἀγέννητος).[47] He is the source of divinity;[48] and without qualification he is the beginning (ἀρχή) of all beings, of the Son as well as of created things (δημιουργήματα).[49] He is called *the* God (ὁ θεός),[50] the true God,[51] God-in-himself (αὐτό θεος).[52] The Son, on the contrary, like others beyond God-in-himself, becomes God by participation (μετοχῇ) in the divinity of God-in-himself.[53] Certainly he is the first beside God (πρὸς τὸν θεόν),[54] and indeed from all eternity he has been so placed.[55] But he continues to be God, only because he remains 'in uninterrupted contemplation of the Father's depths.'[56] Hence he is called simply

---

(c) The fragment is susceptible of a functionalist rather than a strictly subordinationist interpretation, in accord with the context of the citation referred to above. In this context (*GCS* 5, p. 59, l. 16 to p. 60, l. 21) the idea is opposed that differences in the functions of the Trinitarian persons require one of them to be elevated above the others. For this reason too the suggestion by Butterworth (*Origen, On First Principles*, p. 37 n. 6) that Origen in fact wrote some such phrase as 'there is no separation in the Trinity' is not convincing.

With the latter of the citations from *De Princ.* 1: 3: 7 (p. 60 l. 13), compare *Dial. cum Herac.* 2: 26–7 (Scherer, p. 124, ll. 5–6).

46. Jerome, *Epist. 84: Ad Pammachium et Oceanum* 4 (*PL* 22, col. 746, l. 47 to p. 747, l. 7).
47. *Comm. in Joh.* 1: 187 (xxvii, 26) (*GCS* 4, p. 34, l. 26); 2: 75 (x, 6) (p. 65, ll. 17–18); *C. Cels.* 8: 14 (*GCS* 2, p. 231, ll. 17–20).
48. *Comm. in Joh.* 2: 20 (iii, 3) (*GCS* 4, p. 55, ll. 20–1).
49. Ibid. 1: 102 (xvii, 17) (ibid., p. 22, l. 10).
50. Ibid. 2: 13–15, 17 (ii, 2) (ibid., p. 54, ll. 12–20, 29–30).
51. Ibid. 2: 17–20 (ii, 2) (ibid., p. 54, ll. 30–1; p. 55, ll. 3, 10, 18). See John 17: 3.
52. *Comm. in Joh.* 2: 17, 20 (ii–iii, 2–3) (GCS 4, p. 54, ll. 30, 32; p. 55, l. 18).
53. Ibid. 2: 17 (ii, 2) (ibid., p. 54, ll. 32–4).
54. loc. cit. (loc. cit., ll. 34–5).
55. Ibid. 2: 8–9 (i, 1) (ibid., p. 53).
56. Ibid. 2:18 (ii, 2) (ibid., p. 55, ll. 5–8); see also ibid. 2:11 (i, 1) (p. 54).

God (anarthrous θεός),[57] or the second God.[58]

Origen takes the distinction between ὁ θεός and θεός from John 1: 1. A further warrant for his subordinationist doctrine comes from John 14: 28, which according to his version of the text reads: 'The Father who sent me is greater than I.' The verse is perhaps more naturally understood in connection with the Incarnation; and this is how Origen on two occasions interprets it.[59] More often he sees it as an expression of the Son's relation to the Father. Christ is life, but the Father is greater than life.[60] The Saviour does not accept for himself the appellation 'good' in its absolute sense but refers it to the Father.[61] Contrary to the Gnostic view that he is more powerful than the Creator of all things, Origen asserts that the Son is subordinate (ὑποδεέστερος) to the Father.[62] He is transcended by the Father as much as or even more than he and the Holy Spirit transcend all other things; in no way is he comparable with the Father.[63]

Origen's subordinationism appears in a variety of contexts. As Wisdom and Truth the Son is inferior to the Father.[64] He is less than the Father in knowledge,[65] goodness,[66] and justice.[67] As agents of divine revelation, he and the Holy Spirit are represented by the two seraphim whom Isaiah saw attendant upon God[68] and by the two animals (or living beings) beside God in the song of Habakkuk.[69] It is not to the Son that we should pray but only to the Father through the

57. Ibid. 2: 14, 17 (ii, 2) (ibid., p. 54, ll. 15–17, 32–4).
58. *C. Cels.* 5: 39 (*GCS* 2, p. 43, ll. 17–26); 6: 61 (p. 132, ll. 1–3); 7: 57 (p. 206, ll. 24–7); *Comm. in Joh.* 6: 202 (xxxix, 28) (*GCS* 4, p. 148, l. 32 to p. 149, l. 4); see also *C. Cels.* 6: 47 (*GCS* 2, p. 118, l. 27 to p. 119, l. 3).
59. *Comm. in Joh.* 13: 237 (xxxvii, 37) (*GCS* 4, p. 262); 32: 363 (xxix, 18) (p. 475).
60. *Comm. in Joh.* 13: 19 (iii, 3) (*GCS* 4, p. 229).
61. *Comm. in Joh.* 13: 151 (xxv, 25) (*GCS* 4, p. 249, ll. 14–18).
62. *C. Cels.* 8: 15 (*GCS* 2, p. 233, ll. 1–9); see also ibid. 8: 14 (p. 232, ll. 3–8); *Comm. in Joh.* 6: 200 (xxxix, 23) (*GCS* 4, p. 148); *Ser. in Matt.* 45 (*GCS* 11, p. 92, ll. 24–7).
63. *Comm. in Joh.* 13: 151–2 (xxv, 25) (*GCS* 4, p. 249, ll. 14–22, 26–9).
64. Ibid. 2: 151 (xxiii, 18) (ibid., p. 80).
65. Ibid. 32: 350 (xxviii, 18) (ibid., p. 473, ll. 28–32).
66. Ibid. 1: 254 (xxxv, 40) (ibid., p. 45); *C. Cels.* 5: 11 (*GCS* 2, p. 12, ll. 17–23); see also *De Orat.* 15: 4 (ibid., p. 335, ll. 16–18); *Exhort. ad Mart.* 7 (*GCS* 1, p. 9, ll. 5–7). See Mark 10: 18; Luke 18: 19.
67. *Comm. in Joh.* 1: 252 (xxxiv, 40) (*GCS* 4, p. 44).
     Contrary to this text, Christ is justice-in-itself (αὐτοδικαιοσύνη), in ibid. 6: 40 (vi, 3) (p. 115, ll. 1–2).
68. *De Princ.* 1: 3: 4 (*GCS* 5, p. 53, ll. 4–8); 4: 3: 14 (p. 346, ll. 11–28); *Hom. in Is.* 1: 2 (*PG* 13, col. 221B–222A). See Is. 6: 1–3.
69. *De Princ.* 1: 3: 4 (*GCS* 5, p. 53, ll. 8–13). See Hab. 3: 2 (LXX).

Son,[70] since the Father is Lord of the Son, just as he is Lord of those who have through the Son become sons of God themselves.[71] The Son creates under the Father's direction;[72] and at the consummation of existence he is subjected to the Father.[73]

Like Arius, then, Origen conceives of a gulf separating the Father from the Son. On one side of the gulf stands the Father, who is God over all things (ὁ ἐπὶ πᾶσι θεός).[74] On the other side there is the Son, together with everything else; that is, with beings which are derived (γενητά).[75] Despite his unqualified pre-eminence, he shares with them a community of existence. This Origen expresses especially with the words κτίζειν and κτίσις,[76] which he finds in Prov. 8: 22 and Col. 1: 15 It has been observed that for Origen these words do not refer merely to creation but are able to indicate whatever proceeds from God.[77]

70. *De Orat.* 15: 1–4 (*GCS* 2, pp. 333–6).
71. Ibid. 16: 1 (ibid., p. 336, ll. 13–14).
    In *De Orat.* 15: 1–16: 1 Origen is apparently concerned with solemn liturgical prayer, in which it is the custom to address the Father through the Son. Elsewhere, however, he can speak of addressing the Father through the Son without resorting to an extreme subordinationist interpretation of the practice, as in *C. Cels.* 5: 4 (ibid., p. 4, ll. 23–8); 8: 26 (p. 242, ll. 24–9). He can also speak of addressing the Father and the Son together, as in *Hom. in Ez.* 12: 5 (*GCS* 8, p. 439, ll. 20–1); *Hom. in Luc.* 15: 5 (*GCS* 9, p. 94, ll. 25–6). Cf. F. Prat, *Origène: Le théologien et l'exégète*, pp. 60–1.
72. *Comm. in Joh.* 2: 72 (x, 6) (*GCS* 4, p. 64); *Hom. in Jer.* 20: 9 (*GCS* 3, p. 194, ll. 3–4); *C. Cels.* 2: 9 (*GCS* 1, p. 135, l. 29 to p. 136, l. 6); 2: 31 (p. 158, ll. 25–30); 6: 60 (*GCS* 2, p. 130, ll. 21–5); see also *Comm. in Joh.* 1: 255 (xxxv, 40) *GCS* 4, p. 45, ll. 11–13).
    See Heb. 1: 2; Gen. 1: 3, 6, 26; Ps. 32(33): 9; 148: 5.
73. *De Princ.* 3: 5: 6–7 (*GCS* 5, p. 277, l. 3 to p. 278, l. 23); *Comm. in Joh.* 6: 295–6 (lvii, 37) (*GCS* 4, p. 165, ll. 10–16).
    See 1 Cor. 15: 28.
74. *Comm. in Joh.* 2: 15 (ii, 2) (*GCS* 4, p. 54, ll. 19–20); *C. Cels.* 3: 39 (*GCS* 1, p. 231, l. 10); see also ibid. 3: 69 (p. 261, ll. 19, 26); 8: 13 (*GCS* 2, p. 230, ll. 20, 26).
75. *Comm. in Joh.* 2: 172 (xxviii, 23) (*GCS* 4, p. 85, ll. 6–7); *C. Cels.* 6: 17 (*GCS* 2, p. 88, ll. 21–2).
76. The word κτίσμα applied to the Son is not discussed. It occurs only in a suspect Greek fragment in Justinian, *Lib. adv. Orig. ad Mennam* (Mansi, tomus 9, col. 525C; inserted in *De Princ.* 4: 4: 1) (*GCS* 5, p. 349, l. 13). The source of κτίσμα seems to be a marginal note appended to the fragment. See G. Bardy, *Recherches sur l'histoire du texte et des versions latines du De Principiis d'Origène*, pp. 72–4, 148–9; F. Prat. *Origène: Le théologien et l'exégète*, pp. 57–8 n. 2.
    In *Schol. in Apoc.* 22, l. 11 (*TU* 38: 3, p. 30) and 26, ll. 8–9 (p. 32), it is denied that the Son is a κτίσμα. If κτίσμα in the fragment from Justinian is an interpolation and if the scholia are in fact from Origen, the various arguments attempting to reconcile the fragment and the scholia are undercut. For these arguments, see C. W. Lowry, 'Did Origen Style the Son a κτίσμα?' in *JTS*, vol. 39, 1938, pp. 39–42.
77. Cf. H. Crouzel, *Théologie de l'image de Dieu chez Origène*, p. 83 n. 50; also F. Prat, op. cit., p. 57.

Up to a point the observation is correct. However, the subordinationist overtone with which Origen endows the words in
various Christological contexts brings the Son into a sufficiently close
relationship with creatures to justify rendering them by the usual
terms, 'create' and 'creation'. Origen says that God created (κτίσας)
the Son in the beginning.[78] The Son is the radiance of all God's glory;
nevertheless, Origen can still think of him as grouped with the rest of
rational creation (ἡ λοιπὴ λογικὴ κτίσις), which receives from him
partial instances of that radiance.[79] Although as God's Wisdom the
Son is above all creation (κτίσις) God created (ἔκτισε) Wisdom to be
'the beginning of his ways' (Prov. 8: 22); that is, through this creative
act (κτίσις) all creation (κτίσις) is enabled to exist.[80] The Son is also
the First-born of all creation (πάσης κτίσεως). In his use of this title
Origen does not apply it to the incarnate Christ, unlike a number of
Fathers from Athanasius onwards, who do so in order to remove one
of Arianism's scriptural supports. He takes it as a reference to the
divine Son,[81] though for the most part he leaves open the question of
the Son's precise relationship with the Father. In several places,
however, he interprets the title in a subordinationist sense. The First-
born of all creation is being of beings, idea of ideas and beginning,
while the Father is beyond all of these.[82] The First-born is a world
(κόσμος) containing the principles (λόγοι) according to which all
things made by God have been created (γεγένηται).[83] It is through the
First-born that all things have been created (ἔκτισται) at God's
command.[84] With God as his beginning (ἀρχή), while he in turn is the
beginning of others, he is the image of the invisible God according to

---

Crouzel says that the proper term for 'create' is ποιεῖν. Origen, however, appears
to regard κτίζειν and ποιεῖν as equivalents in *Hom. in Jer.* 1: 10 (*GCS* 3, p. 9, ll. 5–9);
see also *Dial. cum Herac.* 15: 28–32 (Scherer, p. 154); *Schol. in Apoc.* 22 (*TU* 38: 3, p.
30, ll. 10–14); *Comm. in Joh.* 32: 187 (xvi, 9) (*GCS* 4, p. 451). What is true is that
Origen does not use ποιεῖν to express the generation of the Son from the Father.
78. *Comm. in Matt.* 14: 17 (*GCS* 10, p. 325, ll. 27–30).
79. *Comm. in Joh.* 32: 353 (xxviii, 18) (*GCS* 4, p. 474, ll. 7–10).
80. *Comm. in Joh.* 1: 244 (xxxiv, 39) (*GCS* 4, p. 43, ll. 22–4); see also ibid. 1: 115 (xix, 22)
   (p. 24).
81. For example, in the following explicit texts: *Comm. in Joh.* 1: 192, 195 (xxviii, 30)
   (*GCS* 4, pp. 35–6); 6: 35 (vi, 3) (p. 114); 19: 10 (ii, 1) (p. 300, ll. 10–14); *Comm. in Matt.*
   16: 8 (*GCS* 10, p. 500, l. 1 to p. 501, l. 4); *C. Cels.* 6: 69 (*GCS* 2, p. 139, ll. 3–9); 7: 65 (p.
   215, ll. 4–7).
82. *C. Cels.* 6: 64 (*GCS* 2, p. 135, ll. 9–11).
83. *Comm. in Joh.* 19: 147 (xxii, 5) (*GCS* 4, p. 324, ll. 4–8); see also *Frag. in Matt.* 506, ll.
   25–8 (*GCS* 12, p. 208).
84. *Comm. in Joh.* 2: 104 (xiv, 8) (*GCS* 4, p. 71, ll. 5–11).

which the others have been made.[85] As the one in whom all things visible and invisible are created and hold together, the First-born is a middle being ('medius') or mediator between God and creatures.[86] He is the 'eldest of all created things' ($\pi\rho\epsilon\sigma\beta\acute{\upsilon}\tau\alpha\tau o\varsigma$ $\pi\acute{\alpha}\nu\tau\omega\nu$ $\tau\tilde{\omega}\nu$ $\delta\eta\mu\iota o\upsilon\rho\gamma\eta\mu\acute{\alpha}\tau\omega\nu$) to whom God says, 'Let us make ($\pi o\iota\acute{\eta}\sigma\omega\mu\epsilon\nu$) man according to our image and likeness.'[87] The first to draw into himself the divinity of God, he is the means by which others become divinized.[88]

### III  THE SON AS DIVINE AND COSMIC

Our review of Origen's subordinationist doctrine indicates that it is centred on the Son's role of mediating between the Father and creation. The Son mediates, for example, in the ontological hierarchy of being, in the work of creating, in prayer to God, in the divinization of rational creatures. For Arius the Son is also a mediator, acting as God's instrument to bring the rest of creation into being.[89] In so conceiving the Son, Arius subordinates him to the Father not just in function but more particularly in essence. Because he does not distinguish between the personal attributes of the Father and the nature of divine being, Arius cannot concede that, though the Son is the instrument of creation under the Father, he is nevertheless essentially equal to the Father.[90] Origen, on the other hand, readily grants that the Son is essentially the Father's equal. But from the drift of his subordinationist language it is evident that, like Arius, he too can think of the Son as subordinate to the Father not only in function

85. *Comm. in Joh.* 1:104 (xvii, 19) (*GCS* 4, p. 22); see also *Hom. in Gen.* 1:1 (*GCS* 6, p. 1, ll. 2–10); 1: 13 (p. 16, l. 18 to p. 17, l. 9).
86. *De Princ.* 2: 6: 1 (*GCS* 5, p. 139, ll. 14–22).
 The idea that Christ is a middle being occurs also in *C. Cels.* 3: 34 (*GCS* 1, p. 231, ll. 7–10). Philo has a similar conception with regard to his Logos; see p. 93 above.
87. *C. Cels.* 5: 37 (*GCS* 2, p. 41, ll. 22–5).
 Origen can also say that the First-born of all created nature ($\gamma\epsilon\nu\eta\tau\tilde{\eta}\varsigma$ $\varphi\acute{\upsilon}\sigma\epsilon\omega\varsigma$) is uncreated ($\grave{\alpha}\gamma\acute{\epsilon}\nu\eta\tau o\varsigma$), ibid. 6: 17 (p. 88, ll. 21–2).
88. *Comm. in Joh.* 2: 17 (iii, 3) (*GCS* 4, p. 54, l. 34 to p. 55, l. 2).
89. Arius, *Thalia*, ap. Athanasius, *Orat.* 1 *contra Arianos* 5 (*PG* 26, col. 21A-B); id., *Thalia*, ap. Athanasius, *De Synodis* 15: 3 (Opitz 2: 1. p. 242, l. 14); id., *Confess. Fid. ad Alexandrum* (Opitz 3: 1, Urkunde 6: 2, p. 12, ll. 7–8); Arius and Euzoius, *Epist. ad Constantinum* (Opitz 3: 1, Urkunde 30: 2, p. 64, ll. 7–8); fragment attributed to Arius, Eusebius of Nicomedia and Asterius, ap. Athanasius, *Orat.* 2 *contra Arianos* 24 (*PG* 26, col. 200A); Alexander of Alexandria, *Epist. ad Episc.* (Opitz 3: 1, Urkunde 4b: 9, p. 8, ll. 6–7).
90. Cf. E. Boulerand, *L'Hérésie d'Arius et la 'foi' de Nicée*, 1ére partie, *L'Hérésie d'Arius*, p. 68.

but also in essence. The problem to be faced is how to deal with these opposing tendencies in his teaching on the Son.

To begin with, we need to recognize that, although Origen has been called the first systematic theologian,[91] he is in fact far from being systematic.[92] Rather, he is an explorer, whose writings lend themselves to being invoked in support of one side of a controversy as much as of the other. It was precisely because the exploratory character of his work was not appreciated that the ancient Christian world disputed whether he was a forerunner of the Catholic or of the Arian party at Nicaea. The argument has continued into modern times, in which the classic statement – a defence of Origen's orthodoxy against the criticisms of Pétau and Huet[93] – comes from Bishop Bull.[94]

If Bull was right to vindicate Origen from the charge of Arianism, he nevertheless provided an incomplete account of Origen's subordinationist teaching. For him it is to be summed up simply under the heads of the God-man's mediatorial office and the divine Son's procession from the Father.[95] Another approach, suggested by Crouzel, is that subordinationism in Origen is rooted in a failure to

---

91. Cf. H. T. Kerr, *The First Systematic Theologian: Origen of Alexandria*; C. W. Lowry, 'Origen as Trinitarian', in *JTS*, vol. 37, 1936, p. 239.

92. Cf. H. Crouzel, 'Origène est-il un systématique?', in id., *Origène et la philosophie*, pp. 179–215; B. Steidle, 'Neue Untersuchungen zur Origenes Περι ἀρχων', in *Zeitschrift für die neutestamentliche Wissenschaft und die Kunde der alteren Kirche*, 40. Bd., 1941, pp. 236–43.

   Crouzel points out (pp. 203–5) that, despite the title of his pamphlet, Kerr concludes that Origen is in fact no true systematic theologian.

   Westcott notes that the *De Principiis* 'is the earliest attempt to form a system of Christian doctrine', but that its 'composition is not strictly methodical'. More generally he says that Origen's 'writings represent an aspiration rather than a system, principles of research and hope rather than determined formulas.' See B. F. Westcott, 'Origenes', in W. Smith and H. Wace (ed.), *A Dictionary of Christian Biography, Literature, Sects and Doctrines; During the First Eight Centuries*, vol. 4, pp. 119, 138.

93. See D. Pétau (Dionysius Petavius), *De Trinitate* Praef.: 4: 2. (*Dogmata Theologica*, ed. nova, tomus 2, 1865, p. 272); 1: 4: 2–8 (pp. 301–6); 1: 14: 8–12 (pp. 372–5); P. D. Huet, *Origeniana* 2: 2: 9, 24–8 (*PG* 17, col. 751–2, 779–90).

   For a recent statement of Origen's subordinationism, see F. H. Kettler, *Der ursprüngliche Sinn der Dogmatik des Origenes*, p. 7 n 29; pp. 24–6 n. 110.

94. See G. Bull, *A Defence of the Nicene Creed*, 2: 9: 1–23 (E. T., 1851–52, vol. 1, pp. 217–85); 3: 3: 1–6 (vol. 2, pp. 411–20); 4: 1: 10 (vol. 2, pp. 568–71); 4: 2: 6 (vol. 2, pp. 582–5); 4: 4: 5 (vol. 2, pp. 632–5).

95. G. Bull, op. cit. 2: 9: 15 (vol. 1, pp. 256–9).

   See also P. Nemeshegyi, *La Paternité de Dieu chez Origène*, p. 99: 'His [Origen's] subordinationism does not, as a matter of fact, indicate a diversity of "nature" between the Father and the Son; it reduces itself to a "hierarchical conception of

distinguish the question of the Son's nature from that of his derivation.[96] Undoubtedly the positions of Bull and Crouzel are valid for some of Origen's subordinationist texts, but to press their conclusions everywhere would be to overlook one of Origen's insights into the nature of the Son.

Put briefly the insight is this: the Son possesses both divine and cosmic attributes. It is an insight which Arius's one-sided doctrine on the Son deformed and which Catholicism, when it asserted the Son's full divinity against Arian denials, perhaps began to minimize. Because Origen lacks an overall theological system, the insight cannot be related consistently with everything that he says about the Son. It does, nevertheless, emerge clearly from his endeavour to hold in balance the Son's equality with and his subordination to the Father.

---

the Trinity"; the Father is "superior" to the Son because of the unique dignity which he possesses inasmuch as he is the "Source of Divinity".'

96. See H. Crouzel, *Théologie de l'image de Dieu chez Origène*, pp. 105–6, 121, 127.
    G. L. Prestige, *God in Patristic Thought*, 2nd ed., 1952, p. 135, presents a similar point of view: ' . . . no satisfactory distinction had as yet been clearly drawn between derivation and creation.'

# 5. THE SON AND THE COSMOS IN ORIGEN

## I. MEDIATION IN ORIGEN

BECAUSE of its cosmic reference, Origen's teaching on the Son has been taken by some commentators to be derived, at least in part, from Platonist doctrines about mediation between God and the world. In Chapter Three[1] we have distinguished an emanationist type of mediation and a subordinationist type. It is largely in terms of the emanationist type of mediation that Eugène de Faye understands Origen's teaching on the Son. Between the Son's procession from the Father and the origin of rational creatures there is no fundamental difference.[2] The Son is the Platonic philosophers' cosmological Logos, not the Logos of the New Testament. Logos there has a mystical meaning and is used simply to enhance the divinity of Jesus Christ. From Origen's Logos 'emanates the life of beings, whether spirits, souls, or men. It draws this life from the bosom of God and transmits it to the beings in descending scales.'[3] Aloisius Lieske likewise sees the emanationist type of mediation in Origen's teaching on the Son:

If the world is regarded as a *necessary* emanation from God and if, at the same time, the Logos is conceived as its creative principle, undeniably there exists the greatest danger of attributing to the Son only that necessity and eternity which the world possesses. Origen's cosmological interpretation of the Logos is thus the gravest threat to the Trinitarian mystery of Sonship, the most decisive shift in his speculative thought towards Neo-Platonism, the most flagrant rationalization of the immanent Godhead's mystery that we encounter in him.[4]

1. See pp. 89–104 above.
2. E. de Faye, *Origène: Sa vie, son oeuvre, sa pensée*, vol. 3, *La Doctrine*, p. 121.
3. E. de Faye, *Origen and His Work*, pp. 103–4. See also C. W. Lowry, 'Origen as Trinitarian', in *JTS*, vol. 37, 1936, p. 233.
4. A. Lieske, *Die Theologie der Logosmystik bei Origenes*, p. 186.

In contrast to de Faye's and Lieske's discussion on Origen, that of R. A. Norris suggests the subordinationist type of mediation. As the unique transcendent source of all being, Origen's God recalls the supreme God in Middle Platonism, while below God the Logos occupies the position of first step down in the diffusion and diversification of being.[5] A similar view of Origen comes from J. N. D. Kelly. In his teaching on the Son Origen provides a striking parallel with the Middle Platonist Albinus, 'who believed in a supreme Father Who organized matter through a second God'.[6]

What these commentators – and many others – say seems to be an overstatement of the case. For, while it would be idle to disallow all resemblance between Origen and the Platonist philosophers, two points require making. First, Origen does not argue to his subordinationist position from metaphysical considerations, even though he is not loath to employ metaphysical notions for articulating what he holds.[7] The foundation on which he rests his position is the words of Scripture:[8] 'The Father is greater than I';[9] 'No one is good but God alone';[10] 'The Son will be subjected to him [God]';[11] and so on. The second point concerns the kind of mediation involved in Origen's teaching on the Son. It cannot be assimilated either to the emanationist or to the subordinationist type of mediation in the Platonic philosophers. We shall look at Origen's teaching in connection with each type of mediation and then with reference to its own special features.

It is not unreasonable to regard Origen's doctrine on the generation of the Son from the Father as a species of emanation. The first known use of ἀπόρροια to express emanation from God occurs in Wis. 7: 25;[12] and it is partly on this term and the verse in which it appears that Origen bases his doctrine.[13] If the Son emanates from the Father, the same cannot be said of creatures. Certainly they reflect God's nature,

---

5. R. A. Norris, *God and World in Early Christian Theology*, pp. 126–9. See also J. Daniélou, *Origen*, p. 252; id., *A History of Early Christian Doctrine before the Council of Nicaea*, vol. 2, *Gospel Message and Hellenistic Culture*, p. 381.
6. J. N. D. Kelly, *Early Christian Doctrines*, 5th ed., 1977, p. 128.
7. See p. 217 below.
8. See pp. 112–15 above.
9. John 14: 28.
10. Mark 10: 18; Luke 18: 19.
11. 1 Cor. 15: 28.
12. See p. 91 above.
13. *De Princ.* 1: 2: 4–5 (*GCS* 5, p. 32, l. 17 to p. 34, l. 1); 1: 2: 9 (pp. 39–41); *Comm. in Joh.* 13: 153 (*GCS* 4, pp. 249–50); *Frag. in Heb.* 3–4 (*PG* 14, col 1307D–1308C); *C. Cels.* 8: 14 (*GCS* 2, p. 231, ll. 11–20).

but they are not of his being ('substantia'),[14] as is the Son.[15] Whereas creatures are made out of nothing,[16] the Wisdom which emanates from God cannot be described as previously not having existed and then coming into being.[17] Furthermore, the doctrine of emanation entails the necessary production of created being and tends to obscure the freedom of creatures.[18] For Origen, on the other hand, creation takes place through the will of God;[19] events within the created sphere are not determined by God's foreknowledge[20] or will;[21] and all rational creatures are essentially free.[22]

Another consequence of emanationism is that the whole range of being, the world included, proceeds from God eternally.[23] Origen, as we have seen, teaches the eternal generation of the Son from the Father.[24] But whether he also holds the existence of creatures *ab aeterno* is a disputed point.[25] The assumption of not a few modern commentators that he does—especially in the case of discarnate rational creatures—has been occasioned by the discussion, in the *De Principiis*, of God's almightiness.[26] Just as it is not possible to be a

14. *De Princ.* 1: 1: 6 (*GCS* 5, p. 21, ll. 1–9).
15. Ibid. 1: 2: 6 (ibid., p. 34, l. 19 to p. 35, l. 1).
16. Ibid. 1: Praef.: 4 (ibid., p. 9, ll. 13–14); *Expos. in Prov.* 9: 1 (*PG* 17, col. 185B); 16: 17 (col. 196B); *Frag. in* 1 *Cor.* 84, ll. 31–2 (*JTS* 10, p. 46); *Comm. in Joh.* 32: 187 (xvi, 9) (*GCS* 4, p. 451).
    That which is created includes matter, *De Princ.* 2: 1: 4 (*GCS* 5, p. 110, l. 7 to p. 111, l. 12); 4: 4: 6 (p. 357, ll. 19–20); *Comm. in Gen.*, ad Gen. 1: 12 (*PG* 12, col. 48–9); see also *C. Cels.* 4: 60 (*GCS* 1, p. 332, ll. 8–15).
17. *De Princ.* 1: 2: 9 (*GCS* 5, p. 40, l. 12 to p. 41, l. 3).
18. See Plotinus on the necessary production of being, *Enn.* 5: 8: 12; 6: 7: 1; on whether there is free will in souls, ibid. 4: 3: 13; 6: 8: 1–7.
    Cf. R. T. Wallis, *Neo-Platonism*, pp. 63–4; J. M. Rist, *Plotinus: The Road to Reality*, pp. 66–83, 130–8.
19. *Comm. in Gen.*, ad Gen. 1: 12 (*PG* 12, col. 48A, 49A); *De Princ.* 2: 1: 4 (*GCS* 5, p. 110, ll. 7–13); *Hom. in* 1 *Reg.* 1: 11 (*GCS* 8, p. 20, ll. 22–3).
20. *Comm. in Gen.* 3: 6 (*PG* 12, col. 64B–65A); = *Philoc.* 23: 8 (Robinson, p. 195, ll. 5–11, 18–23); *Comm. in Rom.* 1 (*PG* 14, col. 841B, 842B); = *Frag. in Rom.* 1, ll. 1–8, 44–8 (*JTS* 13, pp. 210–11); = *Philoc.* 25: 1–2 (Robinson, p. 226, ll. 8–18; p. 228, ll. 8–14).
21. *Hom. in Gen.* 3: 2 (*GCS* 6, p. 40, ll. 1–4).
22. See p. 75 n. 11 above.
23. For Plotinus's doctrine, see *Enn.* 3: 2: 1; 5: 8: 12.
24. See pp. 98–9, above.
25. Cf. P. Nemeshegyi, *La Paternité de Dieu chez Origene*, pp. 113–26; Henri Crouzel, *Théologie de l'image de Dieu chez Origène*, p. 124 n. 251; id., *Origène et la 'connaissance mystique'*, p. 55 n. 6.
26. See, for example, J. Daniélou, *Origen*, pp. 255–6; id., *A History of Early Christian Doctrine Before the Council of Nicaea*, vol. 2, *Gospel Message and Hellenistic Culture*, pp. 384–5; H. Chadwick, *Early Christian Thought and the Classical Tradition*, p. 84; G. A. Maloney, *The Cosmic Christ from Paul to Teilhard*, p. 123; A.

father without having a son, so too God cannot be almighty unless he has creatures over which to exercise his power. Since, however, he does not undergo a transition from the non-exercise to the exercise of his power, it follows that creatures must always have existed.[27] What is more, the Son of God as Wisdom is 'an emanation of the glory of the Almighty' (Wis. 7: 25). This is interpreted to mean that the Father is almighty through the Son; that is, through the Son all things were made.[28] From these considerations the *De Principiis* does not go on to affirm, in Platonic fashion, that created being eternally emanates from God through the Son. Instead, what we find is a blunt assertion that creatures are neither unbegotten nor coeternal with God,[29] coupled with an attempt to resolve the paradox that has been raised.[30] The cosmic role of the Son as Wisdom provides the solution to this problem:

In this Wisdom, therefore, who was always with the Father, creation was always present in outline and form; and there never was a time when the prefiguration of the things that were about to be was not within Wisdom.[31]
... since Wisdom has always existed, in Wisdom there have always existed, in prefiguration and preformation, those things which afterwards were also made actual (quae protinus etiam substantialiter facta sunt).[32]

Along with God, then, what eternally exists is no more than the possibility of creation. The *De Principiis* clearly teaches that matter is

---

L. Townsley, 'Origen's ὁ θεός, Anaximander's τὸ θεῖον and a Series of Worlds: Some Remarks', in *Orientalia Christiana Periodica*, vol. 41, 1975, pp. 143–4, 148–9.

For further references, see P. Nemeshegyi, op. cit., p. 113 n. 2.

In the ancient world only Methodius and (in one passage) Justinian attributed to Origen the existence of creatures *ab aeterno*. See Methodius, *De Creatis* 2: 1–2 (Bonwetsch, *GCS* 27, p. 494, ll. 16–29; reproduced in Origen, *GCS* 5, p. 41 note ad l. 11); Justinian, *Epist. adv. Orig. ad Mennam* (Mansi, tomus 9, col. 528C–D; inserted in *De Princ.* 1: 2: 10, *GCS* 5, p. 42, ll. 11–14).

27. *De Princ.* 1: 2: 10 (*GCS* 5, p. 41, ll 11–12; p. 42, ll. 1–10, 15–20); 1: 4: 3 (pp. 65–6).

28. Ibid. 1: 2: 10 (ibid., p. 41, ll. 8–11; p. 42, l. 20 to p. 43, l. 4). See also 1: 2: 9 (p. 39, l. 12 to p. 40, l. 5).

29. Ibid. 1: 4: 5 (ibid., p. 67, ll. 17–18).

30. Ibid. 1: 4: 4 (ibid., p. 66, l. 15 to p. 67, l. 10).

31. Ibid. 1: 4: 4 (ibid., p. 67, ll. 12–15).

32. Ibid. 1: 4: 4 (ibid., p. 68, ll. 1–3).

The rendering of 'protinus' as 'afterwards' follows the common consent of translators: 'afterwards', in G. W. Butterworth, *Origen, On First Principles*, p. 42; 'successivamente', in M. Simonetti, *I Principii di Origene*, p. 185; 'par la suite', in M. Harl *et al.*, *Origène, Traité des principes (peri archôn)*, p. 58; 'später' in H. Görgemanns and H. Karpp, *Origenes vier Bücher von den Prinzipien*, p. 191.

See also *De Princ.* 1: 2: 2–3 (*GCS* 5, p. 30, ll. 2–14).

not coeternal with God[33] and that, as a pre-condition of their mutability, rational creatures have had a beginning.[34] Furthermore, the notion of creation *ab aeterno* suggests the existence of an unlimited number of creatures. The *De Principiis* teaches, however, that in order to comprehend and control creation, God made only a limited quantity of matter and a limited number of rational beings.[35] If souls are innumerable, they are so only *quoad nos*.[36] Again, creation *ab aeterno* finds no support in the idea, prompted by the doctrine of God's continuous creativity, that a succession of ages or worlds both precedes and follows this present one.[37] Though the ages are immeasurable,[38] they are not numerically infinite. Eventually they will be superseded by something more than an age, when 'God is all and in all'.[39] But whether or not the ages have had a beginning is a question which the *De Principiis* merely raises, without providing a direct answer.[40] Nevertheless, it does tell us, in general terms, that all of God's works have a beginning as well as an end.[41]

There can be little room for disputing that the *De Principiis* denies creation *ab aeterno*. That the denial comes from Origen and not from his translator Rufinus may be confirmed in a number of Greek texts. We learn from these texts that all things have been made according to the principles of things about to be, principles which are prefigured by God in the Son as Wisdom.[42] The Son is the eternal Logos in whom, through whom and for whom all created things, seen and unseen, are made; and as such he is their beginning, he is before ($\pi\rho\delta$) them all, he is in the bringing-into-being of all things.[43] The preposition $\pi\rho\delta$, as Origen uses it here, no doubt connotes a priority of importance; but predominantly it has the force of a temporal priority, just as it has in

---

33. Ibid. 1:3: 3 (ibid., p. 51, ll. 1–2); 2: 1: 4 (p. 110, l. 13 to p. 111, l. 1); see also *Hom. in Gen.* 14: 3 (*GCS* 6, p. 124, l. 6).

34. *De Princ.* 2: 9: 2 (*GCS* 5, p. 165, ll. 17–23); 4: 4: 8 (p. 360, ll. 12–20); see also ibid. 1: 3: 3 (p. 51, ll. 2–4); 2: 9: 6 (p. 169, ll. 20–8); *Hom. in 1 Reg.* 1: 11 (*GCS* 8, p. 20, ll. 21–6).

35. *De Princ.* 2: 9: 1 (*GCS* 5, p. 164, l. 10 to p. 165, l. 16); 4: 4: 8 (p. 358, ll. 26–33; p. 359, ll. 1–8, 14–15, 20; p. 360, ll. 1, 10–12).

36. Ibid. 3: 1: 14 (ibid., p. 220, l. 8).

37. Ibid. 3: 5: 3 (ibid., pp. 272–3).

38. Ibid. 3: 1: 23 (ibid., p. 242, l. 20).

39. Ibid. 2: 3: 5 (ibid., p. 120, ll. 10–29).

40. Ibid. 2: 3: 1 (ibid., p. 114, ll. 13–20).

41. Ibid. 3: 5: 2 (ibid., p. 272).

42. *Comm. in Joh.* 1: 114 (xix, 22) (*GCS* 4, p. 24, ll. 5–7).

43. *Frag. in Joh.* 1 (*GCS* 4, p. 483, l. 11 to p. 484, l. 27).

    See also *Comm. in Joh.* 2: 104 (xiv, 8) (*GCS* 4, p. 71); *Expos. in Prov.* 8: 22 (*PG* 17, col 185A).

Col. 1: 17,[44] from which he takes it. The temporal priority is underlined when Origen goes on to say that the Son as Wisdom 'resolved to assume a creative relationship towards those things which were about to be'.[45] The Greek texts further tell us that the Saviour is the beginning of creation, 'not as the first creature of creation, but as the cause of beginning it in the manner of a craftsman';[46] and the Logos is more ancient than those things made at the beginning, not only the firmament and the dry land but also heaven and earth.[47] By 'heaven' Origen understands rational or spiritual creatures in their pre-existent state.[48] Finally in the Greek texts, he rejects the opinion that the world is uncreated and hence without a beginning,[49] just as he will not allow that it is to be unending.[50]

For Origen, then, all created existence, whether mundane or pre-mundane, has a beginning, even though time begins only with the days of the present world's creation.[51] However duration outside the present world is to be regarded,[52] God alone is beyond the ages.[53] Nevertheless, while no creature has existed *ab aeterno*, Origen does admit an unending duration *in aeternum* for rational beings, inasmuch as they are immortal.[54]

Just as Origen's doctrine on the Son cannot be assimilated to the emanationist type of mediation in Platonism, likewise it does not belong to the subordinationist type. For Origen the Son is not subordinate to the Father *tout court*; he is also the Father's equal.[55] Hence the Son may not without qualification be called the first step down in the hierarchy of being; and for the same reason it cannot be claimed that, according to Origen, the Father is like the first God of

44. Cf. G. Kittel (ed.), *Theological Dictionary of the New Testament*, vol 6, p. 687. Compare Sir. 1: 4.
45. *Frag. in Joh.* 1 (*GCS* 4, p. 485, ll. 8–9).
46. *Schol. in Apoc.* 22, ll. 10–12 (*TU* 38: 3, p. 30).
47. *Comm. in Joh.* 2: 36 (iv, 4) (*GCS* 4, p. 58).
48. *De Princ.* 2: 9: 1 (*GCS* 5, p. 165, ll. 4–16); *Hom. in Gen.*1: 2 (*GCS* 6, p. 2, l. 23 to p. 3, l. 13).
49. *C. Cels.* 4: 79 (*GCS* 1, p. 349, ll. 9–16); see also ibid. 1: 19 (p. 70, ll. 19–27); 4: 60 (pp. 331–2).
50. *Comm. in Matt.* 13: 1 (*GCS* 10, p. 176, ll. 15–33).
51. *Hom. in Gen.* 1: 1 (*GCS* 6, p. 2, ll. 16–20); see also *De Princ.* 3: 5: 1 (*GCS* 5, p. 271, ll. 17–18, 21–2).
52. For an account of Origen's teaching on supra-mundane time, see J. Daniélou, *A History of Early Christian Doctrine before the Council of Nicaea*, vol. 2, *Gospel Message and Hellenistic Culture*, pp. 476–86.
53. *Hom. in Exod.* 6: 13 (*GCS* 6, p. 203).
54. See p. 103 n. 114 above.
55. See pp. 106–10 above.

124        *The Son and Cosmos in Origen*

Platonism, whose remoteness from creation constrains him to operate through the mediation of a second God.[56] Instead, what we find in Origen is that the Father and the Son, through a relationship of mutual interpenetration, are both totally present to creation. Without in any way relinquishing the distinction between Father and Son, he insists that they are one: the Father is in the Son and the Son in the Father.[57] To both of them alike, then, he is able to apply the words of Jer. 23: 24: 'Do I not fill heaven and earth? says the Lord.'[58] But for the way in which Father and Son are present to creation through their relationship to one another Origen in his *Commentary on John* offers a twofold account: either the Son as Logos and Wisdom pervades the whole cosmos, and the Father because he is in the Son does so too; or because the Son is in the Father, the Father who is encompassed by creation grants the Son as his Logos and as second after him to penetrate everywhere.[59] The former account may be seen as giving priority to the Son over the Father in their presence to creation. It may also be understood in an instrumentalist sense, equivalent to the application of Jer. 23: 24 in the *De Principiis*, which represents God as holding together the whole universe by means of his power and reason; that is, through the Son.[60] But unlike Platonist instrumentality which distances the first God from the world, the instrumentality in Origen's teaching keeps God and the world in direct contact with one another. Similarly with the latter account. Notwithstanding its more obvious subordinationism, it envisages the Father rather than the Son as the divine person more immediately present to the world.

What emerges in Origen's teaching is a type of mediation which is neither strictly emanationist nor entirely subordinationist. Rather, it is a kind of mediation which is co-operative, with an element of subordinationism. The twofold nature of this mediation corresponds to Origen's twofold doctrine on the Son. The co-operative aspect of the mediation appears in the interpretation which Origen puts on the words of the Psalmist: 'He commanded and they were created' (Ps. 148: 5). It is the Son who creates at God's command.[61] Hence Origen

56. See p. 119 above.
57. *C. Cels.* 8: 12 (*GCS* 2, pp. 229–30).
58. *Frag. in Jer.* 17 (*GCS* 3, p. 206). For Jer. 23: 24 applied to the Father, see *C. Cels.* 4: 5 (*GCS* 1, p. 277, ll. 17–25); applied to the Son, see ibid. 5: 12 (*GCS* 2, p. 13, ll. 1–19).
59. *Comm. in Joh.* 6: 202 (xxxix, 23) (*GCS* 4, pp. 148–9).
60. *De Princ.* 2: 1: 3 (*GCS* 5, p. 108, ll. 11–13).
61. *C. Cels.* 2: 9 (*GCS* 1, p. 136, ll. 1–14).

says that somehow Christ is the Creator.[62] And he clarifies this 'somehow', when he speaks of the Son as immediately (προσεχῶς) the Creator, in contradistinction to the Father, who is primarily (πρώτως) the Creator.[63] In their role as the Creator, the Father assumes priority over the Son. It is a priority of function rather than of nature, since not only is the Father he by whom (ὑφ' οὖ) things are made,[64] but so too is the Son.[65] In other words, both of them are the efficient cause of creation.

There is, however, another way in which Origen represents the Father and the Son as Creator. With this way there occurs a subordinationism not just of function but also of nature. Following 1 Cor. 8: 6, Origen distinguishes between the originative and instrumental causes of creation. The originative cause, he from whom (ἐξ οὖ) all things are made, is the Father; while the Son, the instrumental cause, is he through whom (δι' οὖ) all things are made.[66] Besides the originative cause, the underlying matter from which a new being is educed may also be indicated by ἐξ οὖ; but in creation, which is strictly *ex nihilo* and not from any matter coeternal with God, this further use of ἐξ οὖ finds no application.[67] Only God, the originative cause, is the ultimate source (ἀρχή) of being; as the Creator he is the source of creatures, and as the Father he is the source of the Son.[68] For this reason, he is greater than the Son, who is also said to be the Creator.[69] Specifically, the Father is greater than the Son as Logos.[70] The Logos, says Origen, became the servant (ὑπηρέτης) of the Creator;[71] that is, of the Father. However, the Son is called the Logos, because he too is the creator.[72] But here the sense of 'Creator' differs from that which is applied to the Father. In the case of the Logos the sense is instrumental, he through whom (δι' οὖ) things are made.[73]

62. *Comm. in Joh.* 1: 110 (xix, 22) (*GCS* 4, p. 23).
63. *C. Cels.* 6: 60 (*GCS* 2, p. 130, ll. 19–25).
64. *Comm. in Joh.* 2: 72 (x, 6) (*GCS* 4, p. 64, ll. 30–1); 2: 183 (xxx, 24) (p. 87, l. 21).
65. Ibid. 1: 110 (xix, 22) (ibid., p. 23).
66. *C. Cels.* 8: 4 (*GCS* 2, p. 223, ll. 26–8); see also *Frag. in Joh.* 9 (*GCS* 4, p. 490, ll. 21–2); *Comm. in Rom.* 3: 10 (*PG* 14, col. 956A–B); 7: 13 (col. 1140C-1141B); 8: 13 (col. 1202A–B).
67. *Comm. in Joh.* 1: 103 (xvii, 18) (*GCS* 4, p. 22).
68. Ibid. 1: 102 (xvii, 17) (ibid., p. 22, ll. 9–11).
69. Ibid. 1: 255 (xxxv, 40) (ibid., p. 45, ll. 11–13); see also *C. Cels.* 6: 47 (*GCS* 2, p. 118, l. 27 to p. 119, l. 3).
70. *Comm. in Joh.* 2: 72 (x, 6) (*GCS* 4, p. 64).
71. Ibid. 2: 104 (xiv, 8) (ibid., p. 71, ll. 2–5); see also *Frag. in Col.* 3 (*PG* 14, col. 1297C).
72. *Frag. in Joh.* 1 (*GCS* 4, p. 483, ll. 1–2).
73. *Comm. in Joh.* 2: 72 (x, 6) (*GCS* 4, p. 64, ll. 29–30); *Frag. in Joh.* 1 (ibid., p. 484, ll. 10–14).

For Origen, then, the instrumental cause of creation is subordinate to its originative cause.

The Son is the Creator in the further subordinationist sense that he is the exemplary cause of creation. Origen refers to the exemplary cause as that either in which (ἐν ᾧ) or according to which (καθ᾽ ὅ) something is made. Col. 1: 16 says that all things are created not only through Christ but also in him (ἐν αὐτῷ). Origen takes the 'in him' as equivalent to 'in Wisdom', following the words of Ps. 103(104): 24, 'In wisdom thou hast made them all'.[74] Wisdom is identical with the Logos; but whereas all things are made *through* the Logos, it is *in* Wisdom that they are made.[75] In other words, if the Logos represents the Son under the aspect of instrumental cause, Wisdom is regarded as the exemplary cause of creation. Wisdom is the archetypal universe containing the principles according to which (λόγους καθ᾽ οὕς) God creates all things.[76] As such, Wisdom is like the mind of a designer which gives rise to plans (τύποι) and calculations (λόγοι) for constructing a house or ship.[77] In his capacity as Wisdom Christ is the Creator, in the subordinationist sense that God created Wisdom 'the beginning of his ways for his works' (Prov. 8: 22).[78] That is to say, as Wisdom Christ the Creator is the active condition enabling creation to exist, as opposed to the first Creator, the Father, who creates in Wisdom.[79]

Together with the title 'Wisdom', another of the Son's titles, 'First-born of all creation', is also associated by Origen with the subordinate, exemplary cause of creation. The distinguishing feature of the latter title is that, according to Origen's usage, it sometimes makes explicit the Son's mediating role in creation. As Wisdom, the First-born is the

---

Rom. 11: 36 appropriates δι᾽ αὐτοῦ as well as ἐξ αὐτοῦ to God. In *C. Cels.* 6: 65 (*GCS* 2, p. 135, ll. 13–17) Origen interprets this δι᾽ αὐτοῦ as pertaining not to an instrumental cause but to God's conservation of creatures in being. Elsewhere in Origen Rom. 11: 36, represented by 'ex ipso, per ipsum, in ipso' and equivalent expressions, is applied to the threefold activity of the Trinity. See *De Princ.* 4: 3: 15 (*GCS* 5, p. 347, ll. 19–20); *Comm. in Cant.* Prol.: 2 (*GCS* 8, p. 71, ll. 4–6); *Comm. in Rom.* 8: 13 (*PG* 14, col. 1202A-B).

74. *De Princ.* 2: 9: 4 (*GCS* 5, p. 167, ll. 17–26).
75. *Comm. in Joh.* 6: 188 (xxxviii, 22) (*GCS* 4, p. 146), together with ibid. 2: 90 (xii, 6) (p. 68, ll. 7–9).
76. Ibid. 19: 147 (xxii, 5) (ibid., p. 324, ll. 4–8); see also ibid. 1: 244 (xxxiv, 39) (p. 43, ll. 20–3); p. 121 nn. 31–2 above.
77. *Comm. in Joh.* 1: 114 (xix, 22) (*GCS* 4, p. 24).
78. Ibid. 1: 111 (xix, 22) (ibid., p. 23); 1: 244 (xxxiv, 39) (p. 43, ll. 23–5); *Frag. in Joh.* 1 (ibid., p. 485, ll. 4–12).
79. *Comm. in Joh.* 2: 90 (xii, 6) (*GCS* 4, p. 68, l. 8); see also ibid. 1: 244 (xxxiv, 39) (p. 43, ll. 25–6); 1: 290 (xxxix, 42) (p. 51, ll. 15–16); *C. Cels.* 6: 69 (*GCS* 2, p. 139, ll. 16–17).

archetypal universe,[80] the exemplar of the forms from which the created universe is made.[81] The First-born is the one in whom all things are created;[82] and as such he is the middle being ('medius') or mediator between God and creatures.[83]

In his mediating role Christ the First-born of all creation is also said to be that according to which ($\kappa\alpha\vartheta'\,\ddot{o}$) men are made. The notion of exemplar remains, but it is now placed within a framework of what may be called an analogy of proportionality. That is, as God is to Christ, so Christ is to men. The analogy suggests itself to Origen from a combination of Col. 1: 15 and Gen. 1: 26–7: Christ the First-born of all creation is the image of God, while men are created according to in image of God. Origen interprets this combination of scriptural texts as follows: as God is the beginning ($\dot{\alpha}\rho\chi\dot{\eta}$) of Christ similarly Christ is the beginning of men; or, in exemplarist language, as God is that according to which ($\kappa\alpha\vartheta'\,\ddot{o}$) Christ exists, likewise Christ is that according to which men exist.[84] An analogy of proportionality involves four terms: the relationship of A to B is the same as or similar to the relationship of C to D; for instance, the relationship of corporeal vision to the eye is similar to the relationship of intellectual vision to the intelligence.[85] Origen's set of analogical relationships apparently contains only three terms: God, Christ, and men. In fact, however, there are four, since Christ does duty for two of the four requisite terms, B and C. He is both the sole reflection of God and the exemplary origin of men; or, if we employ language from the wider context considered in Chapter Four, he is of a divine as well as a cosmic constitution, being equal to God and subordinate to him, within the divine unity and the beginning of created multiplicity.

Origen presumes the twofold constitution of Christ, when he applies his set of analogical relationships to the notions of divinity ($\vartheta\varepsilon\dot{o}\tau\eta\varsigma$) and reason ($\lambda\dot{o}\gamma o\varsigma$).[86] Divinity applies principally to God the Father; with reference to creatures it means God's presence to them.[87] Likewise, reason is first and foremost a property of the Son,

80. *Comm. in Joh.* 19:47 (xxii, 5) (*GCS* 4, p. 324, ll. 4–8).
81. *Frag. in Matt.* 506 (*GCS* 12, p. 208, ll. 21–8).
82. *Comm. in Cant.* Prol.: 2 (*GCS* 8, p. 67, ll. 10–12).
83. *De Princ.* 2:6:1 (*GCS* 5, p. 139, ll. 14–21); see p. 115 n. 86 above.
84. *Comm. in Joh.* 1:104–5 (xvii, 19) (*GCS* 4, p. 22).
85. Cf. J. F. Anderson, *The Bond of Being: An Essay on Analogy and Existence*, pp. 231–2; J. H. Crehan, 'Analogy of Being', in H. F. Davis *et al.* (ed.), *A Catholic Dictionary of Theology*, vol. 1, p. 74A.
86. The present paragraph is concerned chiefly with supernatural relationships, in contrast with the previous paragraph, which deals with natural relationships.
87. *Sel. in Ps.* 4:6(2) (*PG* 12, col. 1161B).

the divine Logos; attributed to creatures, it indicates a relationship between them and the Logos.[88] In the matter of divinity, Origen says that the Father is the prototype, God-in-himself (αὐτόθεος), while everything else divine is so by participation (μετοχῇ). As the image of the Father, the Logos never ceases to be God, since he remains always with God the Father. And as the archetypal image or exemplar in relation to the many others who are his images, the Logos channels to them from the Father the divinity by virtue of which they too are called gods. Origen makes this point near the beginning of his *Commentary on John,* Book 2.[89] Elsewhere, using a variant terminology, he sharpens the distinction between the divinity of the Logos and that of creatures. The Saviour, he says, is God not by participation but in his very being (οὐ κατὰ μετουσίαν, ἀλλὰ κατ᾿ οὐσίαν), while those outside the Trinity who are called gods are so by participation in divinity (μετουσίᾳ θεότητος).[90] Reason (λόγος) involves a set of analogical relationships similar to those connected with divinity. The reason in rational creatures (λογικοί) bears the same relationship (λόγος) to the Reason in the beginning with God – that is, to God the Logos – as God the Logos does to God.[91] Through the application of his set of analogical relationships to divinity and reason, Origen points to a similarity between the Father and the Son. Each of them is a source (πηγή). The Father is the source of divinity, the Son as Logos the source of reason.[92] The similarity, however, is not a strict parallel; it is a further analogical relationship, since it entails predicating of them the concept 'source' partly in the same sense and partly in different senses. For while the Father as source is God-in-himself (αὐτόθεος), according to whose image creatures are called gods,[93] in contrast the Son as source is a manifold, the starting-point of multiple attributes applied to beings in the created cosmos. He is not only the Reason-in-itself (αὐτόλογος) but also the Truth-in-

88. *Comm. in Joh.* 2:21–2 (iii, 3) (*GCS* 4, p. 55).
   On the various levels of relationship between the Logos and creatures, see G. Gruber, *ΖΩΗ: Wesen, Stufen und Mitteilung des wahren Lebens bei Origenes,* pp. 307–22.
89. *Comm. in Joh.* 2:17–18 (ii, 2) (*GCS* 4, pp. 54–5).
90. *Sel. in Ps.* 135:2(2) (*PG* 12, col. 1656A).
   Creatures are gods not by nature but by grace, *Hom. in Exod.* 6:5 (*GCS* 6, p. 196, ll. 20–5); 8:2 (p. 220, ll. 14–16, 23–5); God differs from creatures called gods, just as the Only-begotten, who is the Son of God by nature, differs from the rest, who are sons of God by adoption, *Frag. in Joh.* 109 (*GCS* 4, p. 563, ll. 4–14).
91. *Comm. in Joh.* 2:20 (iii, 3) (*GCS* 4, p. 55, ll. 15–20).
92. Loc. cit. (loc. cit., ll. 20–1).
93. Ibid. 2:17–18, 20 (ii–iii, 2–3) (ibid., pp. 54–5).

itself (αὐτοαλήθεια) and the Righteousness-in-itself (αὐτοδικαιοσύνη) of which creatures may become images.[94] Origen's set of analogical relationships complements his anti-Gnostic doctrine that all men in some way possess a kinship of being with God.[95] In particular, it adds to this doctrine the refinement that the Son, who with his divine and cosmic constitution is partly the same as and partly different from the Father, mediates between God and creatures to secure their kinship.

But Origen's anti-Gnosticism is not confined to rational creatures, such as are men. We have already dealt with his assertions against Heracleon that the Logos mediates between God and the whole of creation.[96] To conclude our present discussion, we must note that for Origen the Son exercises his mediatorial function as instrument of creation and as exemplar with respect not only to rational creatures but also to those that are irrational. Behind this position lies a further aspect of Origen's doctrine on analogy. The sensible order (τὸ αἰσθητόν) is not a realm of existence completely other than the intelligible (τὸ νοητόν). Although it is not true as is the intelligible order, at the same time it is not false but bears a resemblance (ἀναλογία) to the intelligible.[97] For this reason, Origen can say, following Col. 1:16, that all things, visible as well as invisible, were

94. Αὐτόλογος, ibid. 2:20 (iii, 3) (ibid., p. 55, ll. 17–20); αὐτοαλήθεια, ibid. 6:38 (vi, 3) (p. 114, ll. 21–5); αὐτοδικαιοσύνη, ibid. 6: 40 (vi, 3) (p. 114, l. 34 to p. 115, l. 5).
Note: (1) The discussion on attributes with the prefix αὐτο- is restricted to contexts in which Origen is concerned with his doctrine on the image. It is in these contexts that the analogical relationship between Father and Son may be perceived.
(2) This analogical relationship finds support in Origen's general tendency to confine attributes with the prefix αὐτο- to the Son. Thus the Son is αὐτοσοφία, *Comm. in Joh.* 32:347 (xxviii, 18) (*GCS* 4, p. 473, l. 19); *Comm. in Matt.* 14:7 (*GCS* 10, p. 289, l. 18); *C. Cels.* 3:41 (*GCS* 1, p. 237, l. 6); 6:47 (*GCS* 2, p. 119, l. 13); αὐτοδύναμις, *Comm. in Joh.* 1:241 (xxxiii, 38) (*GCS* 4, p. 43, l. 9); αὐτουργός, *C. Cels.* 6:60 (*GCS* 2, p. 130, l. 23); αὐτοβασιλεία, *Comm. in Matt.* 14:7 (*GCS* 10, p. 289, l. 20); αὐτοαπολύτρωσις, *Comm. in Joh.* 1:59 (ix, ll) (*GCS* 4, p. 15, l. 14); αὐτοαγιασμός, *Comm. in Joh.* loc. cit.; *Hom. in Jer.* 17:4 (*GCS* 3, p. 147, l. 3); αὐτουπομονή, *Hom. in Jer.* loc. cit.
Contrary to this general tendency, God is αὐτοαγαθόν, frag. in Justinian, *Lib. adv. Orig. ad Mennam* (Mansi, tomus 9, col. 528A; inserted in *De Princ.* 1:2:13, *GCS* 5, p. 47, l. 4); αὐτοζωή, *Comm. in Matt.* 12:9 (*GCS* 10, p. 83, ll. 24–5); αὐτοισχύς and αὐτοστερέωμα, *Sel. in Ps.* 17:2–3(1) (*PG* 12, col. 1224C).
95. See pp. 102–4, especially n. 109, above.
96. pp. 100–2 above.
97. *Comm. in Joh.* 1:167 (xxvi, 24) (*GCS* 4, p. 31).
Origen also expresses the analogical relationship of one order of reality to another in the following ways: (a) The visible world is an image of the intelligible world, *Frag. in Ps.* 38:7(2) (Pitra 3, p. 3); see also *Hom. in Ps.* 38:2:2 (*PG* 12, col. 1402D–1403B); *Comm. in Cant.* 3:12 (*GCS* 8, p. 208, ll. 5–12).

created through and in Christ.[98] More specifically, he maintains that the teaching of John 1: 3 – all things were created through the Logos – applies not just to men but even to the least significant of things governed by nature.[99] He also tells us that in Wisdom 'there were contained every capacity and delineation of the future creation, whether of those things which exist in a primary fashion or of those things which come about in consequence of them'.[100] The distinction drawn here is between rational and irrational creatures.[101] More diversified and excellent than the sensible world, the First-born of all creation is the exemplary world in which, nevertheless, the world of matter participates.[102]

## II. ORIGEN'S COSMIC CHRIST

The doctrine on mediation, which we have been considering, forms the starting-point of Origen's conception of the cosmic Christ. A convenient summary of this conception is afforded by Rev. 22: 13: Christ is the Alpha and the Omega, the first and the last, the beginning and the end. Origen interprets the verse in this manner:

> ... God the Logos is the Alpha, the beginning and cause of all things, the one who is first not in time but in honour ... To him glory and honour are offered. Let it be said that, since he provides an end for the things created from him (παρ' αὐτοῦ), he is the Omega at the consummation of the ages. He is first and then he is last, not in relation to time, but because he provides a beginning

---

(b) The heaven and earth here below are named after those in a sphere beyond the fixed sphere, the heaven in which the names of the saints are written (Luke 10:20) and the earth promised to the meek and gentle (Matt. 5:5). See p. 132 n. 112 below.

(c) The Old Law is a shadow of Christ's first coming, which in turn is a shadow of his second coming, *De Princ.* 4:3:13 (*GCS* 5, p. 343, l. 17 to p. 344, l. 7); see also *Hom. in Jos.* 8:4 (*GCS* 7, p. 339, ll. 12–15, 18–20).

For further discussion, see J. Chênevert, *L'Église dans le commentaire d'Origène sur le Cantique des Cantiques*, pp. 83–7.

The analogy of one order of reality to another is the basis for Origen's doctrine on the goodness of the material creation.

See p. 97 nn. 67–9 above.

98. *De Princ.* 1:7:1–2 (*GCS* 5, p. 86, ll. 12–21, 31–2; p. 87, ll. 1–3); 2:6:1 (p. 139, ll. 14–22); 2:9:4 (p. 167, ll. 17–22); 4:4:3 (p. 352, ll. 4–8); *Frag. in Joh.* 1 (*GCS* 4, p. 484, ll. 19–22).

99. *C. Cels.* 6:71 (*GCS* 2, p. 141, ll. 22–5).

100. *De Princ.* 1:2:2 (*GCS* 5, p. 30, ll. 2–4).

101. *Comm. in Ps.* 1:3 (*PG* 12, col. 1089C); *C. Cels.* 4:74 (*GCS* 1, p. 343, l. 24 to p. 344, l. 5); see also ibid. 5:39 (*GCS* 2, p. 43, ll. 22–6); *De Orat.* 27:8 (*GCS* 2, pp. 367–8).

102. *Comm. in Joh.* 19:147 (xxii, 5) (*GCS* 4, p. 324, ll. 8–12).

and an end. Here are understood the extremities of the letters, which are the beginning and the end and include the others in between.[103]

For Origen, then, Christ's relation to the created cosmos is all-inclusive. But before we examine the precise nature of this relationship, Origen's usage of the term 'cosmos' and his conception of what the cosmos involves call for clarification.

In the *De Principiis* Origen enumerates the various ways in which he has found the word κόσμος to be understood. All of them reappear elsewhere in his writings. Apart from its being employed in the sense of ornament,[104] the word has the following meanings:

1. The earth and its inhabitants in subjection to sin.[105]
2. The universe consisting of heaven and earth.[106]
3. A world beyond the visible world from which the Saviour has come and to which the saints will go. It is not to be confused with the incorporeal world of imaginary forms which the Greeks call ideas. But whether it is located away from this present world or, as seems more likely, is a more excellent mode of existence within the confines of this present world remains uncertain.[107]
4. The entire universe of existing things, celestial and supercelestial, as well as terrestrial and infernal.[108]
5. Each of the spheres of the sun, moon and planets and the fixed sphere.[109]

---

103. *Schol. in Apoc.* 7 (*TU* 38:3, p. 23, ll. 1–8; corrected by Turner, *JTS* 13, p. 388); see also *Comm. in Joh.* 1:116 (xix, 22) (*GCS* 4, p. 24); 1:209, 219–25 (xxxi, 34) (pp. 38–40).
104. *De Princ.* 2:3:6 (*GCS* 5, p. 121, ll. 5–9); see also *Comm. in Matt.* 13:20 (*GCS* 10, p. 234, l. 26 to p. 235, l. 2).
105. *De Princ.* 2:3:6 (*GCS* 5, p. 121, ll. 11–19); see also *Comm. in Gen.* 3 (*PG* 12, col. 89A-C) = *Philoc.* 14:2 (Robinson, p. 62, ll. 6–28); *Comm. in Matt.* 13:21 (*GCS* 10, p. 238, ll. 13–23); *C. Cels.* 6:59 (*GCS* 2, p. 121, ll. 20–9).
    See John 1:29; 16:33; 17:14, 16; 2 Cor. 5:19; 1 John 5:19.
106. *De Princ.* 2:3:6 (*GCS* 5, p. 121, ll. 20–1); see also *Comm. in Matt.* 13:20 (*GCS* 10, p. 235, ll. 2–5, 24–5; p. 237 ll. 5–7); *C. Cels.* 6:59 (*GCS* 2, p. 129, ll. 18–20, 29–31; p. 130, ll. 1–6).
107. *De Princ.* 2:3:6 (*GCS* 5, p. 121, l. 21 to p. 122, l. 13).
    The world from which the Saviour has come is the intelligible world, identified with the First-born of all creation inasmuch as he is Wisdom. The Saviour is a citizen of this world by virtue of his human soul's union with the Logos. See *Comm. in Joh.* 19:146–8 (xxii, 5) (*GCS* 4, pp. 323–4). Origen rejects the theory of an independently existing world of ideas; in line with Middle Platonic tradition he places the world of ideas within the Godhead. See p. 93 n. 27 above.
108. *De Princ.* 2:3:6 (*GCS* 5, p. 122, ll. 13–21); see also ibid. 2:9:3 (p. 166, ll. 12–15); *Comm. in Joh.* 1:87 (xv, 15) (*GCS* 4, p. 19); *Hom. in Luc.* 6:10 (*GCS* 9, p. 39, l. 24 to p. 40. l. 4).
109. *De Princ.* 2:3:6 (*GCS* 5, p. 122, ll. 22–5); see also *Comm. in Matt.* 13:20 (*GCS* 10, p. 234, ll. 19–26).

6. Each of the seven heavens described in the Book of the Prophet Baruch.[110]

7. A sphere beyond the fixed sphere which is unseen, not in the sense that it is invisible and hence incorporeal,[111] but in the sense that it is not yet seen by those to whom it is promised. It contains the heaven in which the names of the saints are written and the earth promised to the meek and gentle; and it is from this heaven and earth that our own take their names.[112]

To complete the ways in which Origen uses κόσμος, we must add to the list from the *De Principiis* six more items:

8. Man, who is a lesser world or microcosm.[113]
9. The inhabited earth.[114]
10. Those who are in sin.[115]
11. Disciples of Christ unable to enlighten others but enlightened by those disciples who are the light of the world.[116]
12. The Church, which is the cosmos of the cosmos.[117]
13. The creation delivered from the bondage of corruption.[118]

This complex inventory brings together three distinct conceptions: the geocentric universe from Ptolemaic astronomy; the biblical doctrine that the present world is the stage of sin and redemption and that beyond it lies the world to come; the intelligible world of ideas, which, in accordance with Middle Platonic tradition, is held to exist not independently but within the Godhead. With these features we

---

110. *De Princ.* 2:3:6 (*GCS* 5, p. 122, l. 25 to p. 123, l. 1).

    The Book of the Prophet Baruch is believed to be a fuller version of the still extant *Greek Apocalypse of Baruch*, which describes five heavens. See R. H. Charles (ed.), *The Apocrypha and Pseudepigrapha of the Old Testament*, vol. 2, *Pseudepigrapha*, p. 527; G. W. Butterworth, *Origen, On First Principles*, p. 91 n. l.

    Origen refers to many heavens in *Comm. in Matt.* 13:31 (*GCS* 10, p. 270, l. 18 to p. 271, l. 3); *Ser. in Matt.* 51 (*GCS* 11, p. 115, ll. 3–29).

111. Only God is invisible and incorporeal. See pp. 108–9 above.

112. *De Princ.* 2:3:6 (*GCS* 5, p. 123, l. 1 to p. 124, l. 15); see also *Hom. in Gen.* 1:2 (*GCS* 6, pp. 2–5); *Hom. in Ps.* 36:2:4 (*PG* 12, col. 1332D–1333A); 36:5:4 (col. 1362C–1363A).

113. *Hom. in Gen.* 1:11 (*GCS* 6, p. 13. ll. 21–2); *Hom. in Lev.* 5:2 (*GCS* 6; p. 336, ll. 19–26).
    'Only man according to a certain proportion (ἀναλογία) is what the whole cosmos is', *Frag. in Jer.* 22 (*GCS* 3, p. 208, ll. 12–13). The idea of man the μικρὸς κόσμος, a commonplace in the ancient world, is first clearly recorded in Aristotle, *Physics* 252b:26–9 (8:2).

114. *Comm. in Joh.* 2:175 (xxix, 24) (*GCS* 4, p. 85, ll. 33–4); *Comm. in Matt.* 13:20 (*GCS* 10, p. 235, l. 3 to p. 237, l. 23).

115. *Comm. in Rom.* 5:1 (*PG* 14, col. 1012C–1013A).

116. *Comm. in Joh.* 1:162–3 (xxv, 24) (*GCS* 4, p. 31, ll. 8–17); see also ibid. 6:302–3 (lix, 38) (p. 167, ll. 28–32; p. 168, ll. 4–6).

117. See pp. 142–3 below.

118. *Comm. in Joh.* 1:170 (xxvi, 24) (*GCS* 4, p. 32).

must include several more to complete Origen's cosmological picture.

In common with the general outlook of his age, he accepts that the various components of the universe – the elements, plants and animals, human affairs – are administered by guardian spirits. These spirits are angels. He rejects the view that they are daemons; for him daemons are rather the cause of natural catastrophes and of harm to evil men who submit to them.[119] According to one of his texts, the heavenly bodies are also tended by angels,[120] but his usual teaching is that they are themselves rational beings.[121] Support for this comes from Job 25: 5: 'The stars are not clean in his (God's) sight.'[122] Even so, Origen has his doubts: the verse may simply be a hyperbolical expression;[123] the Church's tradition offers no firm guidance on the rationality of heavenly bodies;[124] and the truth of the matter will be discovered only in heaven.[125] The fact is that his teaching derives from Greek philosophy.[126]

In another area of cosmology Origen opposes Greek philosophy. The Stoic theory of endless world cycles is for him an absurdity,[127] though something of the theory does seem to lie behind his notion that the created order passes through a long series of ages or worlds both before and after the present one.[128] Biblical salvation history controls this notion, to the extent that the procession of ages sets out from a beginning and advances towards an end in which 'God is all and in all'.[129] Nevertheless, Origen provides his own version of salvation history, with especial explicitness in the *De Principiis*, where

119. *Hom. in Jer.* 10:6 (*GCS* 3, pp. 76–7); *Hom. in Jos.* 23:3 (*GCS* 7, p. 444, ll. 5–13); *C. Cels.* 8:31–6 (*GCS* 2, pp. 246–52).

120. *Hom. in Jer.* 10:6 (*GCS* 3, p. 76, ll. 21–4).

121. *De Princ.* 1:7:2–5 (*GCS* 5, pp. 86–94); *Comm. in Joh.* 1:257 (xxxv, 40) (*GCS* 4, p. 45); *Comm. in Matt.* 13:20 (*GCS* 10, p. 234, l. 4 to p. 235, l. 33); *C. Cels.* 5:10 (*GCS* 2, p. 10, l. 30 to p. 11, l. 18); 8:67 (p. 283, ll. 20–4).

122. *De Princ.* 1:7:2–3 (*GCS* 5, p. 87, ll. 16–17; p. 89, ll. 9–11).

123. *Comm. in Joh.* 1:257 (xxxv, 40) (*GCS* 4, p. 45, ll. 29–30).

124. *De Princ.* 1: Praef.: 10 (*GCS* 5, p. 16, ll. 7–8).

125. Ibid. 2:11:7 (ibid., p. 191, ll. 5–7).

126. See, for instance, Plato, *Timaeus* 40B; Ioannes ab Arnim, *Stoicorum Veterum Fragmenta*, vol. 2, *Chrysippi Fragmenta, Logica et Physica*, nos 684–7, pp. 200–1; Albinus, *Epitome* 14:7 (Hermann, p. 171, ll. 11–12).

127. See *De Princ.* 2:3:4 (*GCS* 5, p. 119); *C. Cels.* 4: 67–8 (*GCS* 1, pp. 337–8); ibid. 5: 20–1 (*GCS* 2, p. 21, l. 23 to p. 23, l. 8).

128. See *De Princ.* 3:5:3 (*GCS* 5, pp. 272–3); *Frag. in Ps.* 118: 96 (Cadiou, p. 114); *Com. in Joh.* 19:88 (xiv, 3) (*GCS* 4, p. 314, ll. 12–13).

129. See *C. Cels.* 4:8–9 (*GCS* 1, pp. 279–80); ibid. 8.75 (*GCS* 2, p. 292); *Comm. in Joh.* 13: 305–10 (xlvi–xlvii, 46) (*GCS* 4, pp. 272–4); *De Princ.* 2:3:6–7 (*GCS* 5, pp. 121–6); 3:6:8–9 (pp. 289–91).

he reiterates the dictum that the end is like the beginning. The history of the cosmos is a movement away from an original condition of equality among rational beings in union with God, through a phase of diversity in creation's present situation, and from here to a state of restoration (ἀποκατάστασις).[130] The mainspring of this movement is the freedom possessed by rational creatures.[131] In Origen's view, all of them except the soul of Jesus have rebelled against God, with the result that, according to their varying degrees of guilt, they have fallen into the state of either angels or men or devils.[132] His warrant for saying that there has been a fall from a previous mode of existence is the phrase καταβολὴ κόσμου in John 17: 24 and Eph. 1: 4. By recalling the etymological meaning of καταβολή, he is able to interpret the *laying down* or foundation of the present world, with its attendant inequalities and evil, as the *casting down* of the initial world in revolt against God.[133] Among the major patristic authors Origen stands alone in upholding the theory of the soul's pre-mundane existence. Because he finds no clear Scriptural or ecclesiastical commitment to either of its rivals, traducianism and creationism,[134] he supports this

130. For the dictum that the end is like the beginning, see p. 75 n. 9 above. For the restoration, see p. 75 n. 10 above. The restoration does not entail universal salvation, p. 75 n. 12 above.

　　Because rational creatures are perpetually free, Origen entertains the possibility of more than one fall and restoration during innumerable ages. See *De Princ.* 1:3:8 (*GCS* 5, p. 62, l. 20 to p. 63, l. 7); 2:3:3 (p. 118, l. 12 to p. 119, l. 3); 3:1:23 (p. 242, ll. 18–22); *Comm. in Joh.* 10:291–2 (xlii, 26) (*GCS* 4, p. 219); *C. Cels.* 4:69 (*GCS* 1, p. 338, l. 29 to p. 339, l. 4); 8:72 (*GCS* 2, p. 289, ll. 6–10). This suggestion does not rule out the prospect of a final return to the original state, when God's love will at last prevail. However, Origen appears not to have developed to any extent a way of reconciling God's overmastering love with the perpetual freedom of rational creatures. See H. Chadwick, 'Origen, Celsus and the Stoa', in *JTS*, vol. 48, 1947, pp. 41–2. The restoration poses but one aspect of a general problem inherent in Origen's theology: harmonizing God's consolidation of the cosmos with created freedom. See p. 145 below.

131. *De Princ.* 2:9:2 (*GCS* 5, pp. 165–6); 2:9:6 (pp. 169–70); 3:5:5 (p. 276).

132. Ibid. 1:6:2–3 (ibid., pp. 79–84); see also ibid. 1:8:4 (p. 101, l. 4 to p. 102, l. 10); 2:9:6 (p. 170, ll. 2–10).

133. *De Princ.* 3:5:4 (*GCS* 5, pp. 273–5); *Comm. in Joh.* 19:149 (xxii, 5) (*GCS* 4, p. 324); *Ser. in Matt.* 71 (*GCS* 11, pp. 167–8).

134. *De Princ.* 1:Praef.:5 (*GCS* 5, p. 13, ll. 7–11); *Comm. in Joh.* 6:86–7 (xiv, 7) (*GCS* 4, p. 124, ll. 8–12); see also *Comm. in Cant.* 2:5 (*GCS* 8, p. 146, l. 19 to p. 147, l. 9).

　　Whatever debt Origen may owe to Platonism for the doctrine of pre-existence, perhaps the decisive influence on him was the idea of a pre-mundane Church, which occurs in early Jewish Christianity and in Gnosticism close to Christianity. For this idea in early Christianity, see J. Daniélou, *A History of Early Christian Doctrine before the Council of Nicaea*, vol. 1, *The Theology of Jewish Christianity*, pp. 294, 297–313. In Gnostic literature the *Tractatus Tripartitus*, with which

theory as the best hypothesis[135] for reconciling humanity's in-equalities and deficiencies with the justice of God[136] and for refuting the Gnostic doctrine that there are fixed classes of men.[137] Inasmuch as he regards the process of fall and restoration as a cosmic principle, Origen concurs with the Gnostics. But so little does he share their deterministic outlook, that for him the world of free rational creatures possesses an autonomy of action which not even the foreknowledge of God cancels out.[138]

If Origen's cosmos consists principally in a complex of moral agents, it none the less displays an architecture as expansive as anything able to be imagined by the age of the Copernican revolution. Even its geocentric perspective is blurred by the spectacle of numerous ages and many heavens which Origen is able to evoke – without, however, committing himself to describing it with any precision. What gives this cosmos coherence is Origen's focusing of everything on Christ. As instrument and exemplar of creation, Christ, we have seen, mediates between God and the world. And just as this relationship gives expression to Christ's cosmic constitution, so too for Origen do others. Christ pervades the universe; he leads back to God a creation capable of falling away from him but powerless through its own resources to make the return; and in himself he holds together all things.

With reference to Christ's superior nature ($\pi\rho o\eta\gamma o\nu\mu\acute{e}\nu\eta$ $o\mathring{\nu}\sigma\acute{\iota}a$), Origen tells us that, although invisible in his divinity, Christ is coextensive with the entire cosmos.[139] He then goes on to remark that the invisible One who extends to the entire cosmos does not differ from him who became man and lived with men.[140] What Origen seems to have in mind is a threefold distinction in Christ. Christ's

Origen may have been familiar (see pp. 98–9 above), contains this idea; see *Tract.* 58:11–59:5.

For the pre-mundane Church in Origen, see pp. 136–7 below.

135. Origen clearly recognizes the hypothetical character of the doctrine on the soul's pre-mundane existence, *De Princ.* 2:8:4 (*GCS* 5, p. 162, ll. 7–10). Furthermore, he says that whoever raises questions about the soul's nature and origin is likely to be regarded as a heretic, *Frag. in Titum* (*PG* 14, col. 1306B–C). And in what is probably his last work he becomes extremely reticent about the soul's origin, *C. Cels.* 4:30 (*GCS* 1, p. 300, ll. 5–12); 4:40 (p. 313, l. 25 to p. 314, l. 2); 5:29 (*GCS* 2, p. 31, ll. 6–16); 8:53 (pp. 268–9).

136. *De Princ.* 1:7:4 (*GCS* 5, p. 90, ll. 7–21); 3:3:5 (pp. 261–2); see also ibid. 1:8:2 (p. 98, ll. 8–21).

137. Ibid. 2:9:5–6 (ibid., pp. 168–70); see also ibid. 1:8:2 (p. 98, ll. 8–21).

138. See p. 120 n. 20 above.

139. *Comm. in Joh.* 6:154 (xxx, 15) (*GCS* 4, p. 140, ll. 9–12).

140. Ibid. 6:156 (xxx, 15) (ibid., p. 140).

superior nature and his humanity are to be distinguished from one another. But there is also a subdistinction within Christ's superior nature between invisibility and extension to the entire cosmos. Invisibility is a strictly divine attribute; it is equivalent to incorporeity,[141] which not only pertains to the monadic unity of the manifold Son but goes beyond it to include the absolute henadic unity of the Godhead *in se*.[142] Extension to the entire cosmos, on the other hand, connotes involvement, through a multiplicity of relations *ad extra*, with the contingent history of creation. It is associated with the cosmic, subordinate aspect of the Son. Since the Son, says Origen, is the Logos through whom all things are made and Wisdom in whom they are made, he has penetrated the whole creation;[143] and it is as second after the Father that the Son has been granted by him the favour of doing so.[144]

Origen sees the Son's presence throughout the cosmos as including the non-rational creation. Thus the power which moves the heavens and their multitude of stars from east to west is none other than the Son together with the Father.[145] Such a conception of the divine presence in nature calls to mind the Stoic doctrine on divine penetration of the cosmos. There is, however, ample precedent for it in Scripture;[146] and, in any case, Origen's insistence on the incorporeity of God contradicts the Stoic supposition that ontological first principles are corporeal. But in what Origen teaches about the Son's extension to the entire cosmos, presence in nature is a secondary question; his chief concern lies with Christ's presence to rational creatures.[147] Initially Christ is united with them in the pre-mundane realm of existence, where they form his bride the Church.[148] The

---

141. See pp. 108–9 above.
142. *De Princ.* 1:1:6 (*GCS* 5, p. 21, ll. 10–14); see pp. 106–7 above.
143. *Comm. in Joh.* 6:188 (xxxvii, 22) (*GCS* 4, p. 146); 6:202 (xxxix, 23) (p. 148, ll. 32–4).
144. *Comm. in Joh.* 6:202 (xxxix, 23) (*GCS* 4, p. 149, ll. 1–4).
145. Ibid. 6:203 (xxxix, 23) (ibid., p. 149); see also *De Princ.* 1:2:9 (*GCS* 5, p. 40, ll. 2–8; p. 41, ll. 6–7); *Hom. in Luc.* 22:9–10 (*GCS* 9, p. 138, ll. 13–20).
146. See, for example, Job 38:1, Ps. 103(104):19; 135(136):7–9. Prov. 8:27; Is. 40:26; Amos 5:8; Wis. 13:1–9; Sir. 24:4–5; 43:1–10; Baruch 3:34–5.
147. Christ, says Origen, extends through the whole cosmos into rational souls, *Comm. in Joh.* 2:215 (xxxv, 29) (*GCS* 4, p. 94, ll. 12–15); see also ibid. 6:154, 156 (xxx, 15) (p. 140, ll. 11–12, 18–19).
148. *Comm. in Cant.* 2:8 (*GCS* 8, p. 157, ll. 11–19).
      For discussion on Origen's pre-mundane Church, see A. Lieske, *Die Theologie der Logosmystik bei Origenes*, pp. 33–6; J. Chênevert, *L'Eglise dans le commentaire d'Origène sur le Cantique des Cantiques*, pp. 13–43; H. J. Vogt, *Das Kirchenverstandnis des Origenes*, pp. 205–6, 211–13.

marital image here, drawn from Ephesians, expresses a cosmic relationship, one which concerns the whole world of rational creatures and on which their pre-mundane state depends. Established by the Father, the relationship involved the subordinate aspect of the Son:

And he [the Father] who at the beginning created (κτίσας) him 'Who is in the form of God' according to the image (κατ εἰκόνα) made (ἐποίησε) him male and the Church female and to both granted oneness according to the image.[149]

When the Church falls, Christ leaves the Jerusalem on high, the premundane realm, and enters the world to seek her out.[150] He begins his mission by coming in a spiritual manner to the patriarchs and prophets of Isreal,[151] among whom Adam is numbered.[152] The glory of God which, it is recorded, they have witnessed is the Son of God;[153] he is mediator between God and men even before his manifestation in the flesh.[154] Through the Incarnation the Son is totally present in the body of Jesus as well as being united to his soul; but at the same time he remains with the Father and exists everywhere else.[155] The Incarnation is the decisive event in the history of salvation. Before it occurs, God is known only in Israel; while afterwards his name is spread throughout the earth.[156] As the power of God, Christ is with his followers from Britain to Mauritania [the limits of the known world] and with everyone under the sun who has believed in him.[157]

149. *Comm. in Matt.* 14:17 (*GCS* 10, p. 325, ll. 27–32).
   For κτίσας and ἐποίησε, see pp. 113–14, especially n. 77, above.
150. *Comm. in Matt.* 14:17 (*GCS* 10, p. 325, l. 5 to p. 326, l. 13); *Hom in Jer.* 10:7 (*GCS* 3, p. 77).
151. *De Princ.* 1:Praef.:1 (*GCS* 5, p. 7, l. 13 to p. 8, l. 6); *Comm. in Joh.* 1:37 (vii, 9) (*GCS* 4, pp. 11–12); 6:15–26 (iii–iv, 2) (pp. 109–12); *Frag. in Ps.* 118:3 (Harl, p. 194, *a*, ll. 5–8); *Hom. in Is.* 1:5 (*GCS* 8, p. 247, l. 22 to p. 248, l. 6); 7:2 (p. 281, ll. 5–8); *Hom. in Jer.* 9:1 (*GCS* 3, p. 64, ll. 10–24); *Hom. in Luc.* 10:3 (*GCS* 9, p. 60, l. 10 to p. 61, l. 16); *Comm. in Cant.* 3:11 (*GCS* 8, p. 201, ll. 6–8); *C. Cels.* 6:5 (*GCS* 2, p. 74, l. 22 to p. 75, l. 15); 6:51 (p. 122, l. 21).
152. *De Princ.* 1:3:6 (*GCS* 5, p. 58, l. 5); *Comm. in Cant.* 2:8 (*GCS* 8, p. 157, ll. 23–5).
153. *Frag. in Eph.* 9, ll. 11–15 (*JTS* 3, p. 398).
   See Exod. 16:10; Ezek. 8:4.
154. *Frag. in Col.* 3 (*PG* 14, col. 1297C–1298C).
155. *De Princ.* 2:6:2 (*GCS* 5, p. 141, ll. 5–15); 4:4:3–4 (p. 352, l. 14 to p. 353, l. 13); *C. Cels.* 2:9 (*GCS* 1, p. 136, ll. 14–24); 4:5 (p. 277, l. 25 to p. 278, l. 1).
156. *Sel. in Ps.* 23:1(2) (*PG* 12, col. 1265A–B); 46:2(1) (col. 1436C); see also *Comm. in Joh.* 13:305–6 (xlvi, 46) (*GCS* 4, pp. 272–3).
157. *Hom. in Luc.* 6:9 (*GCS* 9, p. 38, l. 23 to p. 39, l. 14); *Hom. in Ezech.* 4:1 (*GCS* 8, p. 362, ll. 11–23); see also *Hom. in Cant.* 1:4 (ibid., p. 33, l. 27 to p. 34, l. 6); 2:6 (p. 49, l.

At his Second Coming he is everywhere, in the sight of all people, like lightning that comes from the east and flashes in the west.[158] As the souls of the departed receive progressive instruction in paradise and through a series of 'abodes', termed spheres by the Greeks and heavens by Scripture, they follow Christ, who 'is everywhere and runs through all things'.[159] Christ fills the heavenly places, since 'he has appeared to the angels' (1 Tim. 3: 16).[160] He is 'in the clouds [God's dwelling] and among the prophets and angels'.[161] His power 'has pervaded the world; that is, things celestial, terrestrial and infernal'.[162]

Origen's teaching on the ubiquity of Christ is associated with his attempt to discover in the doctrine of salvation a cosmic dimension, without which either salvation for the universe as a whole would appear inconceivably and perhaps impossibly dependent on a particular event in human history or else salvation would remain unduly confined to a narrow segment of creation. As we have noted, Origen regards the incarnation of the Son in Jesus as decisive for the work of salvation. Nevertheless, in his view this work of the Son's does not occur only through the human body of Jesus. He says that Christ varies his appearance according to the spiritual capacity and the merits of those who see him; in particular, at the Transfiguration[163] and the Resurrection,[164] when only certain disciples are privileged to behold the Son's glory.[165] But more than that, as the First and the Last, who transcends the sequential beginning and end of things, the Saviour becomes in a diviner way than Paul all things for all, in order

24 to p. 50, 1.4); *Comm. in Cant.* 1:4 (ibid., p. 101, ll. 13–16); *Ser. in Matt.* 65 (*GCS* 11. p. 152, ll. 17–24); *C. Cels.* 5: 12 (*GCS* 2, p. 13, ll. 1–19).

    The Son of Man sows the good seed not just in the Church but in the whole world, *Comm. in Matt.* 10:2 (*GCS* 10, p. 2, ll. 24–6).

158. *Ser. in Matt.* 70 (*GCS* 11, p. 165, l. 22 to p. 166, l. 9). See Matt. 24: 27.
159. *De Princ.* 2:11:6 (*GCS* 5, p. 190, l. 1 to p. 191, l. 1).
160. *Hom. in Luc.* 6:10 (*GCS* 9, p. 39, ll. 14–17); see also *Comm. in Matt.* 15:7 (*GCS* 10, p. 366, ll. 9–17).
161. *Frag. in Ps.* 88:7–8(4) (Pitra 3, p. 159).
162. *Hom. in Luc.* 6:10 (*GCS* 9, p. 39, l. 17 to p. 40, l. 5). See Phil. 2:10.
163. *Comm. in Matt.* 12:36–7 (*GCS* 10, p. 152, l. 4 to p. 153, l. 6); *Ser. in Matt.* 100 (*GCS* 11, p. 218, l. 18 to p. 219, l. 7); *C. Cels.* 2:64 (*GCS* 1, p. 185, l. 26 to p. 186, l. 6); 4:16 (pp. 285–6); 6:68 (*GCS* 2, p. 138, ll. 11–25); 6:77 (p. 146, ll. 14–19; p. 147, ll. 2–6).
164. *C. Cels.* 2:64–5 (*GCS* 1, p. 186, l. 22 to p. 187, l. 19); 2:66 (p. 188); see also *Frag. in Luc.* 255 (*GCS* 9, p. 335).
165. Origen also invokes the theory of changes in Jesus's appearance, in order to explain why Judas has to identify Jesus for the crowd which has come to apprehend him, *Ser. in Matt.* 100 (*GCS* 11, pp. 218–20); *C. Cels.* 2:64 (*GCS* 1, p. 186, ll. 17–22).

to win and perfect all.[166] Just as he becomes a man for men, likewise he becomes an angel for the angels.[167] Because Origen holds that angels and men have essentially the same nature[168] and are consequently transformable into one another,[169] his meaning is that the body of the soul united to the Logos acquires an angelic condition among the angels, just as among men it acquires a human condition.[170] The idea that Christ becomes an angel is to be found in the New Testament apocryphal literature,[171] though Origen claims to have deduced it from the appearance to the patriarchs and prophets of the Angel of the Lord,[172] whom Christian tradition once identified with the Logos.[173] Whatever the source of this idea, Origen's motive for adopting it clearly derives from a wish to give cosmic scope to the soteriological principle. What is not assumed is not healed.[174]

The suggestion has been made that Origen's teaching on the different appearances of Christ contains an incipient Docetism, attributable to Gnostic sources.[175] However, while it is true that Origen acknowledges the existence of a tradition behind his teaching,[176] the way he handles the tradition results in little more

166. See 1 Cor. 9:22.
167. *Comm. in Joh.* 1:209–10, 217, 219 (xxxi, 34) (*GCS* 4, pp. 38–9); see also *Hom. in Cant.* 2:3 (*GCS* 8, p. 45, ll. 9–11); *Comm. in Rom.* 1:4 (*PG* 14, col. 848A–B).
168. *Comm. in Joh.* 2:144 (xxiii, 17) (*GCS* 4, p. 79).
169. *De Princ.* 1:6:3 (*GCS* 5, p. 84, ll. 16–21); *Comm. in Joh.* 2:140 (xxii, 16) (*GCS* 4, p. 78); 10:187 (xxx, 18) (p. 203); *Comm. in Matt.* 15:27 (*GCS* 10, p. 429, 1. 27 to p. 430, 1. 6); 17:30 (p. 670, l. 31 to p. 671, l. 34).
170. In whatever state it exists the soul, in Origen's view, possesses a body. Moreover, the different bodies which a soul possesses from state to state are, in fact, transformations of the one perduring body.
    According to C. Blanc, *Origène, Commentaire sur saint Jean*, tome 1, p. 166 n. 2, 'To understand Origen's position, it is important to remember . . . that the soul of Christ has pre-existed in an angelic state.'
171. See *Epistula Apostolorum* 13–14 (Hennecke, *New Testament Apocrypha*, vol. 1, pp. 197–9).
172. *Comm. in Joh.* 1:218 (xxxi, 34) (*GCS* 4, pp. 38–9); *Hom. in Gen.* 8:8 (*GCS* 6, p. 83, ll. 10–14).
    Cf. G. Aeby, *Les Missions divines de saint Justin à Origène*, pp. 146–50.
173. Cf. J. Barbel, *Christos Angelos*, pp. 34–180.
174. For Origen's explicit use of this principle, see *Comm. in Joh.* 10:26 (vi, 4) (*GCS* 4, p. 176); *Dial. cum Herac.* 7:1–14 (Scherer, p. 136, l. 13 to p. 138, l. 2).
175. Origen's doctrine 'was perhaps well on the way to docetism', according to Henry Chadwick, 'Origen, Celsus, and the Resurrection of the Body', in *Harvard Theological Review*, vol. 41, 1948, p. 100. He considerably modifies this judgement in a later work, *Early Christian Thought and the Classical Tradition*, p. 77.
176. *Ser. in Matt.* 100 (*GCS* 11, p. 218, ll. 18–22).
    Witnesses to this tradition are: *Acts of John* 93 (Hennecke, *New Testament Apocrypha*, vol. 2, p. 227); *Acts of Peter* 20 (ibid., p. 302); *Excerpta ex Theodoto* 4: 1; 5: 3 (Casey, *Studies and Documents*, vol. 1, 1934, p. 42).

The Son and Cosmos in Origen

than providing some explanation for certain events narrated in the Gospels. Certainly, nowhere in his writings does he hesitate over the reality of Christ's human nature.[177] He is therefore categorical that any proclamation of Jesus as the Christ without reference to the cross must needs be defective.[178] It is by the folly of the cross that this world and the Prince of this world are conquered.[179] What is crucified is the sensible body ($\tau\grave{o}$ $\alpha\grave{\iota}\sigma\vartheta\eta\tau\grave{o}\nu$ $\sigma\hat{\omega}\mu\alpha$) of Jesus;[180] and only in our present age, the consummation of the ages, does Christ offer himself in sacrifice once for all.[181]

On the other hand, taking the view that redemption is operative throughout the cosmos, Origen tries to evade the restrictive geocentricism which a unique terrestrial sacrifice seems to impose, though from his extant writings it is not evident that he has done so in precisely the way alleged by Jerome. According to Jerome, Origen in the De Principiis taught that Christ will suffer again in the heavenly places to destroy the spiritual hosts of wickedness and that those whom he saves there are daemons. Such a doctrine, Jerome concludes, implies that, as Christ becomes a man to save men, he ought also to become a daemon to save daemons.[182] What Jerome maintains is almost confirmed by two of Origen's assertions: Christ must overcome the spiritual hosts of wickedness in the heavenly places to dwell there instead of them;[183] and he wins the angels by becoming as they are.[184] Undoubtedly Origen's doctrine on cosmic redemption includes an unresolved tension between Christ's taking on more than one created form and his offering a unique sacrifice. Despite this difficulty, it is possible to indicate the doctrine's essential feature: an

177. See H. de Lubac, 'Textes alexandrins et bouddhiques', in *Recherches de Science religieuse*, tome 27, 1937, pp. 339–42, 346–7; id., *Aspects of Buddhism*, pp. 86–130, especially pp. 96–8, 104, 113; H. Crouzel, *Origène et la 'connaissance mystique'*, pp. 470–4.
178. *Comm. in Matt.* 12:19 (*GCS* 10, pp. 111–13).
179. *Hom. in Exod.* 4:6 (*GCS* 6, p. 177, ll. 6–27).
    See 1 Cor. 1:18.
180. *Comm. in Joh.* 10:230 (xxxv, 20) (*GCS* 4, p. 210, l. 1).
181. *De Princ.* 2:3:5 (*GCS* 5, p. 120, ll. 1–10); see also *Comm. in Joh.* 1:255 (xxxv, 40 (*GCS* 4, p. 45, ll. 17–18).
182. See Jerome, *Epist.* 124: *Ad Avitum* 11–12 (*PL* 22, col. 1070–1); also Justinian, *Lib. adv. Orig. ad Mennam* (Mansi, tomus 9, col. 532D).
    Cf. J. Losada, 'El Sacrificio de Cristo en los cielos según Origenes', in *Miscelanea Comillas*, vol. 50, 1968, pp. 5–19; H. de Lubac, *Histoire et esprit*, pp. 291–4.
183. *Hom. in Num.* 7:5 (*GCS* 7, p. 46, ll. 7–9); see also *Comm. in Joh.* 10:182–3 (xxix, 18) (*GCS* 4, pp. 202–3); *De Orat.* 26:3, 5 (*GCS* 2, p. 360, ll. 14–17; p. 362).
184. See pp. 138–9 above.

omnipresent saving action which, in order to be efficacious, depends on its being expressed as a particular event in creation. Christ, says Origen, condescends to assume our flesh and endure the cross, because even before coming down to earth he has undergone for us the suffering of love.[185] There is a double aspect to Christ's sacrifice, symbolized by the two veils which as high priest he penetrates: the veil of his flesh and the veil of heaven.[186] It means that Christ makes peace with those on earth and those in heaven by the blood of his cross, which is poured out in Jerusalem but is also offered up spiritually in heaven.[187]

Origen's doctrine on cosmic redemption brings us once again to the cosmic and subordinate character of the Son. The connection occurs through the themes of Christ as king and Christ as light of the world. Kingship in relation to God denotes the rule of souls in the beatified state, but with Christ it is a function of his saving work.[188] Christ's exercise of kingship proceeds from his cosmic constitution; that is, from his superior nature ($\pi\rho o\eta\gamma o\upsilon\mu\acute{e}\nu\eta$ $\varphi\acute{\upsilon}\sigma\iota\varsigma$) of First-born of all creation[189] and from his multiple aspect, which is expressed by his titles (Logos, Wisdom, Justice, Truth, and so on).[190] Following 1 Cor. 15: 24–28, Origen sees Christ's saving work, accomplished on the cross, as taking effect everywhere only by degrees and the end of this process as entailing the subordination of the Son to the Father. When the Son has subjected all his enemies to himself and restored the Kingdom, he then hands it over to the Father, becoming in turn subject to him.[191] Subjection to the Father, however, does not involve Christ in loss of kingly status. He continues to hold sway over all creatures, invisible as well as visible and corporeal, but at the Father's right hand.[192] As soteriological themes, the kingship of Christ and Christ the light of the world stand in contrast with one another; whereas the former attends rather to the juridical action of redirecting creation back to its original state, the latter identifies more im-

185. *Hom. in Ezech.* 6:6 (*GCS* 8, p. 384, ll. 21–6).
186. See Heb. 9:3, 24; 10:20.
187. *Hom. in Lev.* 1:3 (*GCS* 6, p. 284, l. 21 to p. 285, l. 14); see also ibid. 2:3 (p. 294, ll. 9–14); *Hom. in Num.* 24:1 (*GCS* 7, p. 226, l. 29 to p. 227, l. 7); *Hom. in Luc.* 10:3 (*GCS* 9, p. 60, l. 10 to p. 61, l. 16); 13:3 (p. 78, ll. 11–27).
188. *De Orat.* 25:1–2 (*GCS* 2, p. 357, ll. 8–13; p. 358, ll. 12–21).
189. *Comm. in Joh.* 1:195 (xxviii, 30) (*GCS* 4, p. 36).
190. *Hom. in Luc.* 30:1 (*GCS* 9, p. 172, ll. 5–6).
191. *De Princ.* 3:5:6–8 (*GCS* 5, pp. 276–9); *Comm. in Joh.* 1:234–5 (xxxii, 37) (*GCS* 4, pp. 41–2); 6:295–6 (lvii, 37) (p. 166).
192. *Comm. in Matt.* 16:4–5 (*GCS* 10, p. 475, p. 29 to p. 476, l. 15; p. 477, ll. 19–21; p. 478, ll. 17–26; p. 479, ll. 23–7).

142 *The Son and Cosmos in Origen*

mediately Christ's essential connection with creatures. According to this latter theme, Christ's saving work is an enlightenment of rational beings (λογικοί) which enables them to perceive the object of vision proper to their minds[193] and to become divinely reasonable (ἐνθέως λογικοί), so that they do all for the glory of God.[194] Their enlightenment is a manifestation of Christ's relationship with the created cosmos. Not only does it result from their participation in Christ the Logos,[195] who as the source of reason (λόγος)[196] is the leading and essential element in their world.[197] It also follows from Christ's operation, in and through the Church, of constituting the cosmos an ordered totality. Distinguishing between Christ as first light of the world, which is taken to be the Church, and the Church as light of the world at large,[198] Origen calls Christ the cosmos of the Church and the Church the cosmos of the cosmos.[199] In this context the play on 'cosmos' – meaning in Greek adornment, order, or world – signifies that Christ is the initiator of order in the world and the Church its mediator; neither is presented merely as a passive embellishment.[200]

Origen's ecclesiology is clearly a facet of his cosmology. His idea of a church comprehends much more than a terrestrial assembly of Christ's followers. Besides the churches on earth, there exists as well the heavenly church of the first-born.[201] Beyond that, Christ's body the Church 'is every race of men, perhaps indeed the totality of all creation';[202] and throughout the cosmos – that is, the whole complex of heaven and earth – the Gospel has been announced.[203] The Church, however, is not simply coextensive with the cosmos; it is the

193. *Comm. in Joh.* 1:158–61 (xxv, 24) (*GCS* 4, pp. 30–1).
194. Ibid. 1:267–8 (xxxvii, 42) (ibid., p. 47).
195. Ibid. 1:268–9 (xxxvii, 42) (ibid., pp. 47–8).
196. Ibid. 2:15, 20–22 (ii–iii, 2–3) (ibid., pp. 54–5).
197. *Comm. in Joh.* 1:161 (xxv, 24) (*GCS* 4, pp. 30–1).
198. Origen derives the idea of the Church as light of the world from Matt. 5:14.
199. *Comm. in Joh.* 6:301–4 (lix, 38) (*GCS* 4, pp. 167–8); see also *Hom. in Gen.* 1:5 (*GCS* 6, p. 7, ll. 11–19).
200. On the Church as cosmos of the cosmos, cf. J. Losada, 'Una paradoja eclesiológica conservada por Orígenes', in *Miscelanea Comillas*, vol. 47–8, 1967, p. 72.
201. *De Princ* 4:3:8 (*GCS* 5, p. 334, ll. 5–10); *Hom. in Num.* 3:3 (*GCS* 7, p. 17, ll. 4–19); *Hom. in Luc.* 7:8 (*GCS* 9, p. 46, ll. 14–17); see also ibid. 23:8 (p. 146, ll. 15–19).
   See Heb. 12:22–23. The members of the church of the first-born are possibly those who occupy the highest place in heaven; but like Hebrews Origen is vague about their identity.
202. *Hom. in Ps.* 36:2:1 (*PG* 12, col. 1330A).
203. *Comm. in Joh.* 1:87–8 (xv, 15) (*GCS* 4, p. 19); see also *C. Cels.* 8:59 (*GCS* 2, p. 276, ll. 1–8).

internal regulative principle of the cosmos. It mediates Christ's work
of ordering the world, as we have seen, but also the world's extending
itself to Christ. Origen compares the world with the fig-tree in Christ's
parable and the Church with the fig-tree's branch that grows tender at
the approach of summer to put forth fruit. The fruit symbolizes
creation prepared for the *eschaton*. What produces the fruit is not so
much the branch as the fig-tree itself, which possesses living power
through the animation of Christ; but it is from the branch that Christ
plucks the fruit.[204] The Church affords the precondition for the final
state of the cosmos: until all the members of his body are subject to
him, Christ cannot bring creation to its perfection in his submission to
the Father, so that 'God may be all in all'.[205]

According to Origen, Christ bears the closest possible relation to
the Church and the cosmos. Christ's divinity is the soul of his body the
Church; without the Logos the members of the body can do
nothing.[206] So too, just as one soul holds together the 'many
members' of our 'one body', Christ the power and reason of God is
like a soul holding together that vast and enormous living being, the
universe.[207] The body concept from Pauline ecclesiology, contained
in both these instances, has been combined in the latter, perhaps also
in the former, with the Stoic *anima mundi*. The comparison, mentioned in the previous paragraph, in which the fig-tree represents the
world animated by Christ, has also been influenced by the Stoic
doctrine. With these ways in which Origen presents the bond between
Christ and creatures we must include the biblical image of the tree of
life. The Logos and Wisdom of God is the tree of life[208] whose fruit is
to its foliage as are things existing in a primary fashion to things
existing in consequence of them; the fruit, in other words, stands for
rational and the foliage for irrational creatures.[209]

Origen denies that either God or the Son of God is to be identified
with the world.[210] They are totally other than the corporeal first
principles of Stoicism;[211] nor is there from God, as opposed to within
the Godhead, any necessary and eternal emanation of being.[212]

---

204. *Ser. in Matt.* 53 (*GCS* 11, p. 118, ll. 15–32; p. 119, ll. 1–11, 22–30).
205. *Hom. in Lev.* 7:2 (*GCS* 6, p. 376, l. 28 to p. 377, l. 5).
206. *Frag. in Eph.* 9, ll. 113–20 (*JTS* 3, p. 401); *C. Cels.* 6:48 (*GCS* 2, p. 119, l. 26 to p. 120, l. 5).
207. *De Princ.* 2:1:3 (*GCS* 5, p. 108, ll. 11–16).
208. See Prov. 3:18.
209. *Comm. in Ps.* 1:3 (*PG* 12, col. 1089B–C).
210. *C. Cels.* 5:7 (*GCS* 2, pp. 6–8); 6:47 (p. 118, ll. 18–24).
211. See p. 102 n. 104 above.     212. See pp. 119–23 above.

Nevertheless, Origen's recourse to body-soul relationships and organic similes to express Christ's union with the Church and the world does suggest a kind of pantheism, confirmation for which in Christian teaching might be sought from several verses of the deutero-Pauline literature: Col. 1: 17b, Eph. 1: 10 and Eph. 1: 23. Origen's extant works cite Col. 1: 17b–'in him all things hold together'–though without significant comment.[213] But on Eph. 1: 10–'[God's purpose is] to sum up (ἀνακεφαλαιώσθαι) all things in Christ'–they furnish this passage:

> The term 'totalling-up' (ἀνακεφαλαίωσις) is used with reference to bankers and the like, when they reckon up accounts (λόγοι) and combine gifts and expenses or takings into the one total (κεφάλαιον). It is in the light of this, I think, that the Apostle has used the expression here. Thus in the management of all things in heaven and in the administration of all things on earth, there are many principles (λόγοι) which, seeing that they are parts of the one overall cosmos, co-operate and converge towards the one result (ἀποτέλεσμα). But the 'totalling-up' (ἀνακεφαλαίωσις) is in Christ. This is because, in the Logos and Wisdom of God, there are not only the subdivisions (κατακερματισμοί) of the things that are managed and the individual principles (λόγοι) of the things that are administered, but also the totalling-up (ἀνακεφαλαίωσις) and (as one might say) the totalling-together (συγκεφαλαίωσις) of all things.[214]

Origen has interpreted Eph. 1: 10 in terms of the exemplary world within the Logos. But since the logoi of that world constitute the principles which direct things in the created world towards the one end, it is not clear how close together or far apart the two worlds stand. The problem is intensified by Origen's affirmation, elsewhere in his works, that the logoi are present in sensible realities.[215] With reference to these realities, it is true, he avoids the expression λόγος σπερματικός associated with Stoic pantheism.[216] Nevertheless, he seems to be drawn, more by Scripture apparently than by philosophical theory, to finding a relationship between the Christian Logos and creation as intimate as any which the Stoics were able to conceive between their Logos and the world. On the other hand, in his remarks on Eph. 1: 23 – '[the Church] is his body, the fulness of him who is filled with all things everywhere'–Origen proposes a relationship between Christ and creatures described only through a juridical image. Christ's body is like a benevolent kingdom all of whose

213. *De Princ.* 3:5:6 (*GCS* 5, p. 277, ll. 17–18); *Frag. in Joh.* 1 (*GCS* 4, p. 484, ll. 23–4); see also *De Princ.* 2:6:1 (*GCS* 5, p. 139, l. 22); 4:4:3 (p. 352, l. 9).
214. *Frag. in Eph.* 6, 11. 2–11 (*JTS* 3, p. 241).
215. *Comm. in Joh.* 13:280–3 (xlii 42) (*GCS* 4, p. 268).
216. Cf. R. Gögler, *Zur Theologie des biblischen Wortes bei Origenes*, p. 256 n. 95.

subjects are loyal. The subjects cause the kingdom to be filled, but it is because of their presence in the kingdom that the king benefits and perfects them.[217] Such a comparison suggests a much looser relationship than do the organic body and tree similes used by Origen in other places.

The disparity between Origen's organic and juridical imagery is indicative of the dilemma which he faces. Though the one power, Christ, binds together the diversity of the world and directs all to the one end, nevertheless rational creatures may only be assisted, not compelled, towards that end, lest their freedom be nullified.[218] Organic images represent Christ's holding the diversified creation together, while juridical images portray a personal interaction between Christ and free created agents. The disaccord between these two types of relationship is rooted in a problem which is perennial for Christian belief, the conflict between divine omnipotence and created freedom. This problem Origen has well recognized. But, as the history of theology makes plain, it is a problem resistant to resolution. For Origen, however, created freedom is more than God's inscrutable work; it is the initiator of creation's diversity, a diversity which in turn is supposed to reflect the exemplary multiplicity within the Wisdom of God. To what extent, then, is Christ dependent on created freedom for exercising his cosmic role as exemplar, instrument of creation, and ubiquitous revealer and redeemer? Under the guidance of Scripture Origen has much to say about Christ's cosmic attributes and operations, while from the Church's teaching he affirms the freedom of rational souls.[219] But how these two matters are interconnected is a systematic question to which he does not address himself.

217. *Frag. in Eph.* 9, ll. 121–37 (*JTS* 3, pp. 401–2).
218. *De Princ.* 2:1:2 (*GCS* 5, pp. 107–8).
219. *Ibid.* 1: Praef.:5 (*ibid*, p. 12, l. 8 to p. 13, l. 6); *Comm. in Joh.* 32:189 (xvi, 9) (*GCS* 4, p. 451).

# PART III

# THE COSMIC CHRIST IN TEILHARD

## 6. THE THEOLOGICAL AND PHILOSOPHICAL BACKGROUND TO TEILHARD'S COSMIC CONCEPTION OF CHRIST

In discussing Origen we have had as one of our principal concerns the link between God and the world; in other words, mediation between the absolute and the contingent. Teilhard's treatment of the cosmic Christ raises this problem once again. For Teilhard the problem presented itself from two quarters, from his own personal awareness of things and from those who influenced him theologically and philosophically. We shall attend only in a marginal way to Teilhard's biographical details. The many issues that lie behind his understanding of the cosmic Christ emerge more readily from an examination of the authors who shaped his thinking.[1] Among these authors Pierre Rousselot and Maurice Blondel call for the most attention. To each of them we shall devote a section of the present chapter. However, the theological and philosophical background to Teilhard's consideration of the cosmic Christ extends well beyond the range of interests

1. For an attempt to show how Teilhard's personal development gave rise to the idea of 'Christ-Kosmos', which became the expression of his personal identity, see H. C. Cairns, *The Identity and Originality of Teilhard de Chardin*, Thesis presented for the Degree of Doctor of Philosophy, University of Edinburgh, 30 March 1971.

found in these two authors. A further section, dealing with the themes of cosmic sense and teleology, is needed to complete our appreciation of the climate in which Teilhard developed his reflections on the cosmic Christ.

I. TEILHARD AND ROUSSELOT

Teilhard's autobiographical essay 'Le Coeur de la Matière' (30.10.1950) tells of a quest, from childhood onwards, 'for the Necessary, the General, the "Natural", as opposed to the Contingent, the Particular and the Artificial'.[2] From his entry into boarding-school in 1892, when he was eleven years old, until he commenced his theological studies in 1908, Teilhard experienced the awakening and growth in himself of a feeling for coherence in the universe;[3] and together with this 'cosmic sense' there arose in him, as a result of his religious upbringing, a 'Christic sense'.[4] During the years prior to the First World War he began reflecting on a concern that was to occupy him for the rest of his life, the synthesis of what he came to call the Above and the Ahead ('l'En Haut et l'En Avant');[5] that is to say, the combining of two beliefs, Christian belief in the world's final union with God and secular belief in the world's progress to an eventual maturation point. But even before studying theology he had come to regard the Divine, symbolized by the Sacred Heart, as an energy irrupting into the cosmic order and through love transforming it.[6]

These autobiographical items suggest that Teilhard's years of theological education – at Ore Place, near Hastings (September 1908 to July 1912) – and the remaining pre-War period, which he spent in Paris, were a time when his early responses to the world, to human existence and to God received some kind of definitive shaping or direction. Among certain younger members of the Ore Place

2. *Oeuvres* 13, p. 26 (*HM*, pp. 18-19); see also 'Mon Univers', 1918, *Oeuvres* 12, pp. 296-7 (*ETG*, pp. 269-70; *HM*, pp. 197-8).
3. 'Le Coeur de la Matière', *Oeuvres* 13, pp. 27–32 (*HM*, pp. 20–4).
4. Ibid., p. 51 (p. 40).
5. Ibid., pp. 54–5 (p. 44). Teilhard regularly employed the terminology 'l'En Haut et L'En Avant' only from 1947 to his death in 1955. His earliest use of it, however, seems to be in Lettre à Marguerite Teillard-Chambon, 19. 1. 1929, *LV*, p. 118 (*LT*, p. 151); and the idea which it expresses can already be observed in his first writings.
6 'Le Coeur de la Matière', *Oeuvres* 13, p. 55 (*HM*, p. 44).

community there existed an intellectual atmosphere[7] from which Teilhard undoubtedly derived his attachment to Col. 1:17b (Christ is he 'in whom all things hold together'). This verse perhaps better than any other in Scripture epitomizes his cosmic Christology, and it is one of the two verses to which he most often referred.[8] Just over twelve months before Teilhard arrived at Ore Place, Yves de la Brière had crowned his long Jesuit training by being chosen to perform the 'Grand Act', a public defence before all comers of every thesis in Scholastic philosophy and theology, followed by a lecture.[9] The Grand Act was an infrequent event and would have formed a topic of conversation in the theologate for several years after its occurrence. Teilhard could not have failed to learn many of the particulars of that event. One of them has been recorded. In his lecture, on 'the union of Christ and the Church regarded as an extension of the hypostatic Union', de la Brière stated that 'the whole of theology is thus summed up in what St. Paul said of Christ: *Omnia in ipso constant.*'[10] Teilhard spoke in a similar manner. In 1920 he called Col. 1:17b the 'fundamental article' of belief;[11] and again in 1953 he said that it is the dogma in which all dogmas are summed up.[12] But he echoed de la Brière with a difference. Whereas de la Brière asserted the centrality of Col. 1:17b apparently within an ecclesiological context, Teilhard did so in response to a cosmological consideration; namely, whether the supreme place of Christ remains assured in a universe whose dimensions suggest the existence of a plurality of inhabited worlds. Whatever dogmatic adjustments the discovery of such worlds may

7. For this atmosphere, see R. d'Ouince, *Un Prophète en procès*, vol. 1, *Teilhard de Chardin dans l'Église de son temps*, pp. 51–8; also R. Speaight, *Teilhard de Chardin: A Biography*, pp. 37–8.

8. As far as can be judged, in Teilhard's writings Col. 1:17b appears 16 times alone and 3 times included in wider references to Col. 1. Somewhat more frequent is 1 Cor. 15:28c; see p. 171 n. 130 below.

    For Teilhard's references to Col. 1:17b, see p. 153 below.

    For Teilhard's wider references to Col. 1, see: 'Mon Univers', 1924, *Oeuvres* 9, 83 (*SC*, p. 54) (Col. 1:15ff.); Lettre [à Ida' Treat], 30. 10. 1926, *AH*, p. 62 (*LTF*, p. 48) (Col. 1:12–23); 'Le Sens Humain', *Oeuvres* 11, p. 35 n. 1 (*TF*, p. 28 n. 8) (Col. 1:15–19).

9. De la Brière's Grand Act took place on 21 May 1907. See H. C. de B., 'Un "grand acte" à Ore', in *Lettres d'Ore* [section 5 of *Lettres de Fourvière*, private publication of the Mediterranean French province of the Society of Jesus], vol. 1, 1907, supplément 2, avril, juillet, 1907, pp. 45–52.

10. Ibid., p. 46.

11. 'Chute, Rédemption et Géocentrie', *Oeuvres* 10, p. 57 (*CE*, p. 44).

12. 'Une suite au Problème des Origines humains: la Multiplicité des Mondes habités, ibid., p. 281 (ibid., p. 235).

force upon us, Teilhard concluded, the doctrine of Col. 1: 17b cannot, for the Christian, be altered.

In 1908, the year that Teilhard came to Ore Place, Ferdinand Prat published the first volume of his *La Théologie de saint Paul*. This was a work which helped Teilhard develop his conception of the cosmic Christ.[13] With reference to Col. 1: 16–17, Prat wrote:

> The [creatures] have been created through ('par') him [the Son] and 'they subsist in him'. Without him, without uncreated Wisdom, all creatures, unable to endure themselves, would be scattered, broken up and, in mutual conflict, plunged into nothing. He it is who preserves them in existence, cohesion and harmony. As the bond of the universe, Philo's Logos exercised the same role.[14]

Reproducing Prat's thought, Teilhard in one of his early essays put these words into the mouth of Christ:

> It is I who am the true bond of the World. Without me, even if they appear to make contact with one another, beings are separated by an abyss. In me they meet, despite the Chaos of the ages and of Space.[15]

Another work which appeared during Teilhard's period at Ore Place was the first volume of Jules Lebreton's history of the dogma on the Trinity (1910). Lebreton was among those with whom Teilhard discussed matters concerned with the cosmic Christ.[16] Commenting on Col. 1: 17b–18a, Lebreton wrote:

> 'And everything subsists in him, and he is the head of the body, the Church . . .' In this verse especially we catch St. Paul's unity of thought; he does not separate Christ's role in the Church from his role in the world: everywhere he is the first, everywhere he is the centre, everywhere he is the principle of life.[17]

Similarities to this passage occur in Teilhard's work. In particular, there is the linking of Col. 1: 17b to the theme of Christ as the centre of all things.[18] But there is also the close connection which Teilhard,

13. See p. 43 above.
14. F. Prat, *La Théologie de saint Paul*, 1ère partie, 1908, p. 348 (8e éd., 1920, p. 348) (E. T., *The Theology of Saint Paul*, vol. 1, p. 291).
15. 'Le Milieu mystique', 13.8.1917, *Oeuvres* 12, p. 184 (*ETG*, p. 160; *WTW*, p. 142).
16. See p. 43 above.
17. Lebreton, *Les Origines du dogme de la Trinité*, 1910, pp. 306–7 (5e éd., 1919, pp. 369–70).
18. 'Panthéisme et Christianisme', *Oeuvres* 10, p. 87 (*CE*, p. 71); *Le Milieu divin*, Oeuvres 4, p. 49 (*MD*, p. 33); 'Christologie et Évolution', *Oeuvres* 10, p. 107 (*CE*, p. 88).

prompted by St. Paul, sees between Christ's relation to the world and his relation to the Church. Adapting Col. 1: 18a, he calls Christ the '*caput creationis et ecclesiae*';[19] and he says that 'Christ has not only a mystical Body, but also a *cosmic Body* (whose principal attributes St. Paul above all (even though he does not use that term) describes for us).'[20]

Although de la Brière, Prat and Lebreton all made their contribution to Teilhard's appreciation of Col. 1: 17b for the development of his cosmic conception of Christ, the more immediate and important influence on him was Pierre Rousselot.[21] Teilhard and he were together at Ore Place during 1908–9 and then in Paris during 1913–14; the following year Rousselot was killed in the War. Rousselot is said to have been fond of citing Col. 1: 17b to summarize his theological thought.[22] Several surviving examples illustrate his use of this verse. Supporting a modified form of the dictation theory of revelation, Rousselot maintained that in Christ God has spoken to us with a human voice and that Christ's words disclose the transformation which his deeds have effected on earth:

The consolidation and consecration through Christ of the conceptual order, if one may put it like that, involves the more general scheme of reparation in Him of our terrestrial world and everything connected with it, which He has as it were stamped with his seal: *omnia in Ipso constant*, says St. Paul (*Col.*, 1, 17).[23]

The change wrought by Christ is not simply the restoration of a lapsed world but its elevation:

On the supposition that it has taken place, the Incarnation is the universal dispensation of salvation, in such a way that by becoming man Christ did not simply sustain what was fallen through human weakness but strengthened it and, so to speak, sealed it; for as Paul says, 'In him all things hold together' (Col. 1. 17.) Hence the so-called *sacramental* principle of our religion, that is, the assumption even of corporeal nature for the conferring of

19. 'Note sur l'Union physique entre l'Humanité du Christ et les Fidèles au cours de la sanctification', *Oeuvres* 10, p. 21 (*CE*, p. 15).
20. 'L'Union créatrice', *Oeuvres* 12, p. 223 (*ETG*, pp. 196–7; *WTW*, p. 175).
21. Cf. R. d'Ouince, op. cit., vol. 1, p. 55 n. 13; H. de Lubac, *La Prière du Père Teilhard de Chardin*, 2e éd., 1968, p. 49 n. 1 (E. T., *The Faith of Teilhard de Chardin*, p. 32 n. 10); id., *Teilhard posthume: Réflexions et souvenirs*, p. 56 n. 38.
22. Cf. H. de Lubac (ed.), *LI*, p. 51.
23. P. Rousselot, 'Intellectualisme', in A. d'Alès (ed.), *Dictionnaire apologétique de la foi catholique*, 4e éd., tome 2, 1911, col. 1075–6.

grace. . . . Hence against the gnostics it is taught that 'matter is susceptible to salvation' (cf. Irenaeus, Haer. I.6.1 etc.).[24]

Belief that God has elevated the world finds expression in the very form of the Christian religion (at least as the Catholic Church understands it). With its external social cult and its doctrine on Christ's real presence in the eucharist, this religion stresses the positive value of the visible world and of the flesh; and the connection between the two it finds 'in the one mystery of the incarnate Word . . . , in whom, as Paul teaches, "all things hold together".'[25]

Rousselot's disciple, Pierre Tiberghien,[26] placed Col. 1: 17b on the title-page of his essay of 1922 on the connection between the natural and the supernatural,[27] and in the essay itself he noted:

> To see the created world absolutely as God sees it, it would be necessary not only to see the natural order in relation to the supernatural order, but also to see the supernatural order in relation to Our Lord, who is its Chief and head. This is the viewpoint of St. Paul in his Epistles.[28]

Tiberghien presents a less direct relationship between Christ and the natural order than does his master Rousselot. But both are agreed that everything whatever is to be referred to Christ.

Tiberghien's use of Col. 1: 17b witnesses to the influence which Rousselot continued to exercise well after his death. Teilhard likewise reflects Rousselot's appreciation of Col. 1: 17b. We have seen that Rousselot cites this verse in support of his proposition that Christ in elevating the fallen world places his seal on it. Teilhard, in his turn, finds in the verse the idea of Christ as the one from whom all creation receives its stability ('consistance').[29] Whether or not, besides Rousselot's thought, Tiberghien's was also known to Teilhard,

24. P. Rousselot, *Quaestiones de Fide et Dogmatismo, Quas in Facultate theologica Parisiensi explicabat P. Rousselot*, MCMIX-MCMX [typescript, at Les Fontaines, Chantilly], p. 121.
25. P. Rousselot, 'De Christo rege gentibus in sacramento dominante', 25. 7. 1914, in *XXVe Congrès eucharistique international, tenu à Lourdes du 22 au 26 juillet 1914*, Secrétatiat Général, Paris, 1921.
26. Cf. M. Blondel and A. Valensin, *Correspondance*, tome 3, *Extraits de la correspondance de 1912 à 1947*, p. 91 n. 35, 2.
27. See P. Tiberghien, *La Question des rapports du naturel et du surnaturel dans sa relation avec quelques problèmes contemporains*, 2e tirage, post 1924 [mimeographed copy, at Les Fontaines, Chantilly].
28. Tiberghien, op. cit., p. 10 n. 7.
29. 'Panthéisme et Christianisme', *Oeuvres* 10, p. 87 (*CE*, p. 71); *Le Milieu divin*, *Oeuvres* 4, p. 149 (*MD*, p. 112); see also 'La Route de l'Ouest', *Oeuvres* 11, p. 60 (*TF*, p. 55).

certainly the above quotation from Tiberghien can, to some extent at least, be paralleled in the following words of Teilhard:' . . . a Christ whose supernatural domination . . . is matched by a physical power which rules the natural spheres of the world. "In quo omnia constant." '[30] These words illustrate the interest which, like Tiberghien and Rousselot before him, Teilhard had in the relationship between the natural and the supernatural.[31] But they further indicate that for Teilhard such an interest was but part of a more general concern with the cosmic aspect of Christ, a concern exceeding anything that Rousselot's influence might explain. That concern becomes evident whenever Teilhard refers to Col. 1: 17b. In relation to this verse he says that, thanks to the expansion of human consciousness brought about by scientific research, new ways of understanding Christ are now possible.[32] It is above all an evolutionary view of the universe which enables us to become aware of the cosmic properties which St. Paul attributes to Christ.[33] As the one who holds all things together, Christ exercises a supremacy over the universe which is physical, not simply juridical.[34] He is the unifying centre of the universe[35] and its goal.[36] The function of holding all things together indicates that Christ is not only man and God; he also possesses a third aspect – indeed, a third nature – which is cosmic.[37]

Teilhard's development of the cosmic-Christ theme, although outdistancing any account of it that Rousselot has left behind, was nevertheless in some measure anticipated by him. As Teilhard was to do after him, Rousselot turned to St. Paul and St. John for the Church's full teaching about Christ.[38] From St. Paul Rousselot and

30. 'Le Christ évoluteur', *Oeuvres* 10, p. 168 (*CE*, p. 143).
31. See pp. 166–7 below.
32. 'Barrière de la Morte et Co-Reflexion', *Oeuvres* 7, p. 428 (AE, p. 405).
33. 'Christologie et Évolution', *Oeuvres* 10, p. 107 (*CE*, pp. 88–9).
34. 'Mon Univers', 1924, *Oeuvres* 9, pp. 82–4 (*SC*, pp. 54–6); 'Réflexions sur le Péché originel', *Oeuvres* 10, p. 223 (*CE*, pp. 190–1).
    For Teilhard's distinction between 'physical' and 'juridical', see pp. 180–2 below.
35. *Le Milieu divin, Oeuvres* 4, p. 49 (*MD*, p. 33); see also 'Science et Christ', *Oeuvres* 9, p. 60 (*SC*, p. 34).
36. Lettre à Jean-Baptiste Janssens, 12.10.1951, *LI*, p. 399 (*LT*, p. 42); 'Un Sommaire de ma Perspective Phénoménologique du Monde', *Oeuvres* 11, p. 236 (*TF*, p. 215).
37. 'Christianisme et Évolution', *Oeuvres* 10, pp. 209–10 (*CE*, pp. 179–80); 'Le Christique', *Oeuvres* 13, p. 107 (*HM*, p. 93).
38. See P. Rousselot, 'Petite théorie du développement du dogme, fondée sur l'étude de la connaissance sympathique et la doctrine du Nouveau Testament', in *Recherches de science religieuse*, tome 53, 1965, p. 373.

Teilhard derive their conceptions of the Body of Christ; while in both those sacred authors they find the doctrine of a Christ who creates the world and through his redemptive activity transforms it.

In what they say about the Body of Christ Rousselot and Teilhard adopt virtually identical positions. The communal relationship expressed in St. Paul's teaching on the Body of Christ, Rousselot explains, is such that

> while Christ establishes us all together in the supernatural order, we too in our turn, according to the Apostle, in a manner establish Christ, causing his body to be and to grow: *ad aedificationem corporis Christi.*[39]

The Pauline doctrine is

> expanded in the Epistle to the Colossians and in the Johannine writings, even to affirming the 'recapitulation' of the absolutely entire creation in the Word of God made flesh.[40]

For Rousselot then the Body of Christ is constituted by means of a reciprocal relationship, and it extends beyond the confines of ecclesial fellowship to take in all things. Here Rousselot is without doubt foreshadowing Teilhard. If Teilhard sees Christ as the centre, natural as well as supernatural, which draws creation to itself,[41] he also considers that creatures through their works and achievements contribute to the formation of the Body of Christ:[42] 'All around us, Christ operates physically in order to regulate all things. . . . And, reciprocally, he physically profits from each one of them.'[43] In Teilhard's view, Christ's Body is not merely mystical; that is,

39. P. Rousselot, 'Le Verbe incarné', in *Revue de philosophie*, 12e année, no 6, 1912, p. 628.
40. P. Rousselot, 'La Grace d'après saint Jean et d'après saint Paul', in *Recherches de science religieuse*, tome 18, 1928, p. 95.
41. 'L'Union créatrice', *Oeuvres* 12, pp. 221–3 (*ETG*, pp. 195–6; *WTW*, pp. 173–5); Lettre à Auguste Valensin, 12.12.1919, *LI*, p. 35 (*BT*, pp. 33–4; E.T., p. 36); 'Panthéisme et Christianisme', *Oeuvres* 10, p. 88 (*CE*, p. 71); 'Super-humanité – Super-Christ – Super-charité', *Oeuvres* 9, pp. 209–10 (*SC*, p. 165).
42. 'Le Prêtre', *Oeuvres* 12, pp. 321–2, 329–30 (*ETG*, pp. 292–3, 299; *WTW*, pp. 213, 220); 'Note pour servir à l'évangélisation des temps nouveaux', ibid., p. 408 (*ETG*, pp. 375–6; *HM*, p. 217); 'Note sur l'Union physique entre l'Humanité du Christ et les Fidèles au cours de la sanctification', *Oeuvres* 10, p. 25 (*CE*, p. 19); *Le Milieu divin*, *Oeuvres* 4, p. 50 (*MD*, p. 34); see also Lettre à Marguerite Teillard-Chambon, 5.2.1917, *GP*, p. 234 (*MM.*, pp. 180–1).
43. 'Mon Univers', 1924, *Oeuvres* 9, pp. 87–8 (*SC*, p. 59). See also 'Le Prêtre', *Oeuvres* 12, p. 329 (*ETG*, p. 299; *WTW*, p. 220); 'Le Christique', *Oeuvres* 13, p. 107 (*HM*, p. 92).

ecclesial. It is also cosmic, extending throughout the universe[44] and comprising all things that attain their fulfilment in Christ.[45] Fundamentally, the Body of Christ is the one single thing that is being made in creation.[46] This was how Teilhard in his earlier writings stated the matter. Later on, he expressed more pointedly the developmental character of the cosmic building-up of Christ, by saying that cosmogenesis is being transformed into Christogenesis.[47]

Rousselot's presentation of Christ as creator and transformer is less integrated than that of Teilhard. In a well-known passage from the text-book *Christus*, Rousselot says that the Epistles to the Colossians and to the Hebrews in particular throw into relief the Son's creative and conserving activity and his role as unique mediator, while to this teaching St. John in the prologue of his Gospel brings the term 'Logos'. The Logos is no impersonal intermediary and no mere shadow of God, such as the Greeks postulated; he is the living and personal Christ, the unique and perfect mediator and revealer, the perfect image of God.[48] From other places in his writings, it is clear that Rousselot understands 'mediator' in a strictly soteriological sense.[49] In other words, he does not include the ideas of creator and mediator within a single conceptual field; he simply juxtaposes them. Thus what the passage from *Christus* indicates is not only a similarity of thought between Rousselot and Teilhard, but also a fundamental difference. Like Rousselot, Teilhard ascribes to Christ the creative activity of the Godhead. But for Teilhard Christ's work as redemptive mediator is not separate from his creativity; creation and redemption are linked as aspects of the one process. In the following quotation Rousselot draws very close to Teilhard's position, with the assertion that Christ transforms the visible order of

44. 'La Vie cosmique', *Oeuvres* 12, p. 67 (*ETG*, p. 47; *WTW*, p. 58); 'La Lutte contre la multitude', ibid., p. 148 (*ETG*, p. 128; *WTW*, p. 110); 'L'Union créatrice', ibid., p. 223 (*ETG*, pp. 196–7; *WTW*, p. 175); 'L'Élément universel', ibid., p. 440 (*ETG*, p. 408; *WTW*, p. 297); see also *Journal*, tome 1, 20.4.1916, p. 70; ibid., 14.11.1916, p. 144; ibid., 19.8.1917, pp. 215–16; ibid., 10.11.1917, p. 230.
45. 'L'Élément universel', *Oeuvres* 12, p. 440 (*ETG*, p. 408; *WTW*, p. 297).
46. 'Panthéisme et Christianisme', *Oeuvres* 10, p. 90 (*CE*, p. 74).
47. See p. 39 above.
48. See P. Rousselot and J. Huby, 'La Religion chrétienne: Le Nouveau Testament', in J. Huby (ed.), *Christus: Manuel d'histoire des religions*, 1912, pp. 739–42 (1921, pp. 1017–20).
49. See P. Rousselot, 'Petite théorie du développement du dogme', in *Recherches de science religieuse*, tome 53, 1965, p. 375; id., 'La Grace d'après saint Jean et d'après saint Paul', in ibid., tome 18, 1928, p. 95.

things; nevertheless, once again he perceives that function of Christ's only in juxtaposition to his creativity:

> The realities which are the object of our faith are not strangers to the sensible world. . . . Christ who contains them all is entirely above and here below. He sanctifies all our sensible world to which he belongs and which, having been created in him as the Word, has been renewed by him as Emmanuel.[50]

According to Teilhard, on the other hand, God cannot create without involving himself in his world through incarnation, nor can he become incarnate without engaging in the redemptive labour of raising the world up to himself. Creation, incarnation, and redemption constitute the one movement, which Teilhard calls 'pleromization'. It is a movement towards the 'pleroma', the fulness of being, in which God and his completed world exist united together.[51]

Rousselot, we have seen, uses the term 'mediator' in a strictly soteriological sense. That is not to say, however, that he lacks a notion of ontological mediation between God and the world. This more generally conceived idea of mediation occurs in his postulate of a 'metaphysical Adam'.[52] The postulate represents Rousselot's attempt to make more secure the idealist hypothesis that, in order to form a totality, the multiple world must be conceivable in a superior being's unity of consciousness. The plurality of conscious beings within the world cannot unite the world into a totality: in itself a plurality is not a principle of unity. Nor can the consciousness of God directly totalize the world. Consisting in part of material objects, the world is comprehended only within a consciousness which involves sensation as well as intellection. Such a consciousness belongs not to God but to a being who is both corporeal and spiritual; it is, in other

50. *La Renaissance de la raison*, draft work, *c.* 1913 (quoted in H. de Lubac (ed.), *LI*, p. 51).
51. Retraite, 20–28.10.1945, 8e jour [27.10.1945] *Carnet de retraites, 1944–1955*, p. 16 (quoted in H. de Lubac (ed.), *LI*, p. 22); *Journal* XIV (= 2), 26–27.10.1945, p. 2 (a summary of the previous reference); 'Christianisme et Évolution', *Oeuvres* 10, pp. 212–13 (*CE*, pp. 182–3); 'Réflexions sur le Péché originel', ibid., pp. 229–30 (pp. 197–8); 'Comment je vois', *Oeuvres* 11, p. 213 (*TF*, p. 198); see also Lettre à André Ravier, Vendredi-Saint 1955, *LI*, p. 465. It was not until 1945 that Teilhard subsumed creation, incarnation, and redemption under the general heading of pleromization. But already in 1918 he had stated that they are indissolubly linked together. See 'L'Âme du monde', *Oeuvres* 12, p. 258 (*ETG*, p. 231; *WTW*, pp. 189–90).
52. See P. Rousselot, 'Idéalisme et Thomisme', 1908, resumed 1911, in J. M. McDermott, 'Un Inédit de P. Rousselot: "Idéalisme et Thomisme"', in *Archives de philosophie*, tome 42, 1979, pp. 117–23; also pp. 103–6, 110–11.

words, the consciousness of a man. This man is the Adam who heads humanity and acts as ontological mediator between God and the world.

Rousselot notes that the role assigned to his metaphysical Adam is similar to that which the Scholastics conferred on the first man as educator of the human race,[53] the main difference being that the Scholastics would not allow the first man's comprehension of the world to include sense intuition. In a further observation Rousselot says that his doctrine on the metaphysical Adam does not presuppose the Incarnation. But given the Incarnation, we may follow the thought of Maurice Blondel and place the totalization of the world in Christ. Christ performs the totalizing function not precisely as Emmanuel (that is, as God among men) but as the second Adam.

Up to a point Teilhard is sympathetic to Rousselot's idealism, even though his own concern with thought as the basis of material existence moves in a different direction. What Teilhard develops is a version of panpsychism, according to which all entities in the world possess a 'within' ( 'dedans' ) of their being; at the upper levels of the evolutionary scale the 'within' becomes consciousness, while lower down it is a prefiguring of consciousness.[54] On occasion, however, he approaches Rousselot's position. Thus he once commented on the idealist strain in modern physics, whose theories not only interpret the phenomena investigated but also disclose the mind of the investigator, so that we are led to suspect that subatomic particles have as much reality outside of our thought as do colours independent of our eyes.[55] Even more in accord with Rousselot, he wrote in a letter that 'the World cannot exist other than founded on thought'.[56] Teilhard's early essay on original sin shows him yet again responsive to idealism. He refers to it when discussing that theory of original sin which represents mankind as having fallen, through the first Adam's disobedience, from a state of spiritual perfection and as now evolving towards spiritual reconstitution in Christ, the second

53. See Thomas Aquinas, *Summa Theologica* 1: 94: 3.
54. Lettre à Auguste Valensin, 17.12.1922, *LI*, p. 88; *Le Phénomène humain, Oeuvres* 1, pp. 49–64, 70–3 (*PM*, pp. 53–66, 71–4); 'Place de la Technique dans une biologie générale de l'Humanité', *Oeuvres* 7, pp. 161–3 (*AE*, pp. 155–6).
   Teilhard borrowed the concept of a 'within' of things from Blondel. See M. Blondel, *L'Action: Essai d'une critique de la vie et d'une science de la pratique*, 1893, pp. 87–102. Cf. C. d'Armagnac, 'De Blondel à Teilhard: Nature et intériorité', in *Archives de philosophie*, tome 21, 1958, pp. 302–6.
55. 'L'Énergie Humaine', *Oeuvres* 6, pp. 143–4 (*HE*, pp. 113–14).
56. Lettre à Auguste Valensin, 17.12.1922, loc. cit.

Adam. This theory, Teilhard says, is compatible with the idealist metaphysic which asserts the ontological dependence of non-spiritual beings on those that are spiritual.[57] Whether or not Teilhard is alluding here to Rousselot's notion of a metaphysical Adam, it is clear that what he rejects is not the idealist metaphysic but the possibility of an Adam other than Christ. There is no evidence for the world's having fallen from a more perfect state; rather, the sinful condition of the world is a consequence of the world's evolutionary struggle out of primordial nothingness towards ontological completion through union with Christ.[58]

By admitting the possibility of a metaphysical Adam, Rousselot at once diverges from Teilhard on the relationship between Christ and the world. Such a possibility entails the conclusion that Christ's function of totalizing the world is contingent. This way of conceiving the matter well accords with the simple juxtaposition of Christ's creative and transforming activities which, as we have noted, Rousselot makes. In other words, Rousselot does not regard Christ's multiform work as the necessary precondition for the existence and development of the world. For a while, during 1918, Teilhard considered an approach to Christ's link with the world similar to that of Rousselot's. Speaking in terms of finality, he distinguished between 'Omicron' and 'Omega', the natural and supernatural goals of creation.[59] However, he soon abandoned this position. The world has only one goal of creation, Omega, the supernatural goal, which is Christ.[60] For Teilhard, then, the world's very existence presupposes the operation of Christ. As we have seen above, Teilhard maintains that God cannot create without involving himself in his world through incarnation and he cannot become incarnate without undertaking its redemption. Nevertheless, despite their differences over the contingency or necessity of Christ's relation to the world, Rousselot and Teilhard are agreed that in fact the world holds

---

57. 'Note sur quelques Représentations historiques possibles du Péché originel', *Oeuvres* 10, pp. 66–7 (*CE*, pp. 49–51).
58. Ibid., pp. 67–9 (pp. 51–3).
59. 'Mon Univers', 1918, *Oeuvres* 12, pp. 301–2 (*ETG*, pp. 273–6; *HM*, pp. 202–4); *Journal*, tome 1, 14.5.1918, p. 325; ibid., 4.12.1918, pp. 374–5; ibid., 17.12.1918, p. 379. The development of the distinction between 'Omicron' and 'Omega' may be seen in ibid., 11.11.1916, p. 140; ibid., 17.1.1918, p. 258; ibid., 16.1.1918, pp. 260, 262–3.
60. 'Note sur "l'Élément universel" du Monde', 22.12.1918, *Oeuvres* 12, pp. 391–2 (*ETG*, p. 361; *WTW*, p. 274); Lettre à Auguste Valensin, 29.12.1919, *LI*, pp. 43–4 (*BT*, pp. 45–6; E.T., pp. 49–50).

together in Christ. For both of them Col. 1: 17b is a central dogmatic text. Furthermore, their agreement extends to affirming that everything is united through the reciprocal relationship between Christ and creatures which constitutes the Body of Christ.

## II. TEILHARD AND BLONDEL

When Rousselot suggested that the world is totalized in Christ, he acknowledged Maurice Blondel as the source of this idea.[61] Teilhard developed his own version of the idea, beginning with his account in 1916 of the cosmic Christ.[62] It is possible that, as early as 1900, Teilhard's contemporary Auguste Valensin had introduced to him the thought of Blondel.[63] Valensin was well qualified to do so; he had been a pupil of Blondel and with him kept up a lifelong correspondence.[64] In his earlier writings Teilhard reveals an acquaintance with some aspects of Blondel's work;[65] for instance, with the notion that everything holds together from on high.[66] But it was not until August 1919 that he became aware, in conversation with Valensin, of Blondel's 'pan-Christism' and of its similarity to his own view on the relation between Christ and the world.[67] He wrote to his cousin about the discovery that he had made:

> He [Valensin] told me that Blondel has such strong views on the stability ('consistance') of the the universe in Christo, that he doesn't dare follow him all the way, – although, he added, Rousselot didn't hesitate to do so. I didn't know that side of Blondel's thought, and I'm going to have it explained to me.[68]

The following month Teilhard made notes in his journal on Blondel's *L'Action* (1893). One of them reads: 'Necessity of a universal

61. See p. 157 above.
62. 'La Vie cosmique', *Oeuvres* 12, pp. 67–9 (*ETG*, pp. 47–9; *WTW*, pp. 57–9).
63. Valensin may have discussed Blondel's *L'Action* (1893) with Teilhard as early as 1900, according to C. d'Armagnac, 'De Blondel à Teilhard: Nature et intériorité', in *Archives de philosophie*, tome 21, 1958, p. 311 n. 53.
64. Cf. M. Blondel and A. Valensin, *Correspondance (1899–1912)*, tome 1, p. 7.
65. See *Journal*, tome 1, 15.9.1916, p. 114; ibid., 22.1.1917, p. 185; Lettre à Marguerite Teillard-Chambon, 28.12.1916, *GP*, p. 203 (*MM*, p. 158); ditto, 21.1.1917, ibid., p. 224 (p. 173); ditto, 29.1.1917, ibid., p. 228 (p. 176); ditto, 13.10.1917, ibid., p. 273 (p. 210); ditto, 2.8.1919, ibid., p. 390 (p. 298); 'Le Milieu mystique', 13.8.1917, *Oeuvres* 12, p. 175 ad n. 22 (*ETG*, p. 153 ad n. 22; *WTW*, p. 133 ad n. 22).
66. See p. 164 below.
67. See pp. 41–2 especially n. 173, above.
68. Lettre à Marguerite Teillard-Chambon, 8.8.1919, *GP*, p. 393 (*MM*, p. 300).

Centre of mediation, and of passion.'[69] This entry is based on the following passage from Blondel's work:

> It may be that man, destined to receive in himself the divine life, was able to play that role of universal bond and be equal to that creative mediation, because that immanence of God in us would be like the magnetic centre which connects all things, in the manner of a bundle of needles which are invisibly held together by a powerful magnet. But also, so that the mediation might nevertheless be total, permanent, voluntary – in a word, such that it might ensure the reality of everything which undoubtedly would be able not to be but which, being as it is, requires a divine witness – perhaps a Mediator was necessary to yield himself up to suffering for that entire reality and to be like the *Amen* of the universe, '*testis verus et fidelis qui est principium creaturae Dei*'.[70]

Reminiscent of the Hegelian central individual,[71] Blondel's Mediator provided the inspiration for the metaphysical Adam in Rousselot. What these conceptions of Blondel and Rousselot above all have in common is a contingent element. Both require that a central individual should exist, but they allow more than one possibility for who is to fulfil its function. Thus according to Blondel the work of cosmic mediation is voluntarily undertaken by the incarnate Word; it could have been carried out instead, albeit less perfectly, by man. In reading the passage from Blondel, Teilhard passed over the contingent element in the notion of Mediator. His summary accords with what we have remarked when relating him to Rousselot: for Teilhard the existence of the world necessarily presupposes the cosmic mediation of Christ.

Despite the fundamental difference that we have just noted, Blondel and Teilhard agree on the central place of Christ in creation. Blondel regarded his pan-Christism as a justification for the Franciscan theory that God has created the world in view of Christ and that the Incarnation is the climax of God's creative work. According to Blondel, 'the entire creation postulates Emmanuel with a consequent necessity'. That is to say, the world as it actually exists – not any possible world – presupposes the presence of God in the world and among men. Given this situation, Blondel believed that man exists only in relation to the incarnate Word, and that even 'the determinism of phenomena is suspended in the reality – infinitely gratuitous in its first creative initiative, infinitely obedient in the execution of the

---

69. *Journal* [tome 2] cahier 7, 30.9.1919, p. 32.
70. M. Blondel, *L'Action*, 1893, p. 461; see also pp. 463–4.
71. See pp. 13–14 above.

divine plan – of Christ, of the *Primogenitus omnis creaturae, in quo omnia constant*.[72] Among the lowest forms of matter 'one cannot fail to end at the α and the ω, the Word incarnate'. Thought and matter subsist only through Emmanuel, and reciprocally Emmanuel subsists only through his incorporating the universe into himself.[73] The Word incarnate is the *vinculum substantiale* of creation, the bond which gives unity to multiple created being.[74] He is the ontological Mediator through whom creatures are made and are united to the Father.[75]

In this account of Blondel's pan-Christism we should note the presence of Col. 1: 17b. As with Teilhard, the verse is a key text for Blondel.[76] Parallels between Teilhard and Blondel, then, will not come unexpectedly. Keeping in mind what we have so far presented from Blondel, we may take several excerpts from Teilhard's 'Mon Univers' (1924) to illustrate the resemblance:

Within the Cosmos all the elements are ontologically dependent on one another, in the ascending order of their true being (that is, of their consciousness); and the entire Cosmos, as a single whole is held up, 'informed', by the powerful energy of a superior and unique Monad which confers on everything below itself its definitive intelligibility and its definite power of action and reaction.[77]

Since Christ is omega, the Universe is physically impregnated, right to its material core, with the influence of his super-human nature.[78]

72. See Col 1: 15, 17b.
73. See M. Blondel, Lettre à Joannes Wehrlé, 14.1.1903, in id. and J. Wehrlé, *Correspondance (Extraits)*, vol. 1, pp. 116–17.
74. See M. Blondel, *Carnets intimes (1883–1894)*, 3.12.1887, pp. 113–14.
75. See M. Blondel, ibid., 23.1.1888, p. 125; id., Lettre à D. Sabatier, 12.3.1899, in id., *Lettres philosophiques*, pp. 175–6; id., *Carnets intimes*, tome 2, *(1894–1949)*, 2.11.1909, pp. 87–8.
76. For further instances of Blondel's use of Col. 1: 17b, see M. Blondel, 'Lettre sur les exigences de la pensée contemporaine en matière d'apologétique et sur la méthode de la philosophie dans l'étude du problème religieux', 1896, in *Les Premiers écrits de Maurice Blondel*, [vol. 2] 1956, p. 42 (E. T., *The Letter on Apologetics and History and Dogma*, p. 160); id., Lettre à Joannès Wehrlé, 6.1.1903, in id. and J. Wehrlé, *Correspondance (Extraits)*, vol. 1, p. 99; M. Blondel, Premier mémoire à Auguste Valensin, 5.12.1919, *BT*, p. 25 (E.T., p. 26); id., Lettre à Br, 31.1.1920 (quoted in id. and A. Valensin, *Correspondance (1899–1912)*, tome 1, p. 44); M. Blondel, Lettre à Auguste Valensin, 2.12.1930, in id. and A. Valensin, *Correspondance*, tome 3, *Extraits de la correspondance de 1912 à 1947*, p. 169; see also quotation, p. 163 below.
    It would not be too much to say that, in their use of Col. 1: 17b, de la Brière, Rousselot, Tiberghien and Teilhard are all to some extent dependent ultimately on Blondel. See, however, Le Roy, p. 176 below.
77. 'Mon Univers', 1924, *Oeuvres* 9, p. 85 (*SC*, p. 57).
78. Ibid., pp. 85–6 (p. 57).

All around us, Christ physically operates in order to control everything. From the lowest atomic stirring to the highest mystical contemplation, – from the lightest puff that blows through the air to the broadest currents of life and thought, he ceaselessly animates, without disturbing them, all the movements of the Earth. And, reciprocally, he physically benefits from each one of them.[79]

What immediately strikes us is that in these passages, especially in the first, Teilhard has put to use Blondel's concept of the *vinculum substantiale*.[80] We shall examine this concept further in a moment. But whatever the similarities between Blondel and Teilhard, we remain conscious of their differences. 'Mon Univers' (1924) is a case in point. When Blondel read the essay, he expressed reservations about it. Teilhard had not sufficiently recognized 'the heterogeneity of the scientific, metaphysical and mystical points of view'; he should appreciate that 'for the ontogeny of souls the spiritual domain is, in point of fact, beyond objects of scientific interest'.[81]

The reason for the disagreement between Blondel and Teilhard on Christ's relation to the cosmos is to be found in their respective starting-points. Blondel's initial philosophical interest lay with the notion of the *vinculum substantiale*, which Leibniz had developed as an explanation for transubstantiation.[82] The following passage shows Blondel extending the notion from a eucharistic context to a general ontological consideration:

The *Vinculum* is, as a matter of fact, not only a physical nature, a metaphysical essence, an immanent finality: it is also, without prejudice to all that, the supreme magnet, which attracts and unites from above, step by step, the total hierarchy of distinct and consolidated beings; it is that without which or rather He 'without whom everything that has been made would become

79. Ibid., pp. 87–8 (p. 59).
80. For a discussion of Blondel's *vinculum*, see J. Flamand, *L'Idée de médiation chez Maurice Blondel*, pp. 127–213.
81. M. Blondel, Lettre à Auguste Valensin, 12.9.1925, in id. and A. Valensin, *Correspondance*, tome 3, *Extraits de la correspondance de 1912 à 1947*, pp. 127–8.
82. Blondel's interest began in 1879, while he was still in high school, and reached fruition in his Latin thesis of 1893; in 1930 he produced a revised version of the Latin thesis in French. For the text of the Latin thesis, see C. Troisfontaines (ed.), *Maurice Blondel, Le lien substantiel et la substance composée d'après Leibniz: Texte latin (1893)*; for the notion of the *vinculum*, see especially pp. 268–79. For the revised version of the thesis, see M. Blondel, *Une Énigme historique: Le 'vinculum substantiale' d'après Leibniz et l'ébauche d'un réalisme supérieur*, 1930. For the history of Blondel's concern with the *vinculum*, see ibid., pp. v-xix. For Blondel's notes on the *vinculum* before 1893, see M. Blondel, *Carnets intimes (1883–1894)*, pp. 125, 222.

again as nothing'. . . . By substituting the *Vinculum ipsius Christi* for the natural being of bread and wine, Transubstantiation accordingly appears to us to act, under the veils of the mystery, as a prelude to the final assimilation, to the supreme incorporation of everything which belongs to the Incarnate Word: *Verbum caro factum ut caro et omnia assimilentur Deo per Incarnatum.* . . . For, if inferior nature admits of being transposed into a new earth and heaven where the Word, $\alpha$ and $\omega$, *primogenitus omnis creaturae*,[83] is the sole light, the unique aliment and the universal 'binding', *in quo omnia constant*,[84] the *Vinculum* is not a transnaturalizing clasp but an embrace which binds them while respecting their nature. . . . [85]

Here Blondel gives the impression of having perceived a pluralistic universe, whose unity he then tries to secure by means of the *vinculum*. A pluralist's view of reality lies behind his willingness to allow for possibilities other than the incarnate Word as the bond of creation. It comes to light again, when he registers disapproval at Teilhard's not having sharply distinguished the spiritual and the scientific from one another. Even the *vinculum*, as it is presented in the above quotation, appears detached from the beings which it unites. It is true that they are said to depend not just for their unity but for their very existence on the *vinculum*. The sacramental analogy, however, seems so to spiritualize the *vinculum*, that it leaves untouched the discernible and perhaps even the real nature of those beings.[86]

With Teilhard the opposite situation prevails. He sets out not from a consideration of sacramental metaphysics but, as we shall see below,[87] from a sense of cosmic unity. Eucharistic doctrine does not provide him with a point of departure for working out a conception of Christ's relationship to the cosmos; rather, in his hands the meaning of the doctrine is expanded to coincide with his vision of universal oneness. We meet this amplified meaning of the eucharist in his 'cosmic mass' celebrated in the Ordos Desert.[88] There he proclaims everything around him to be the body and blood of the Word.[89] His

83. Col. 1: 15.
84. Col. 1: 17b.
85. M. Blondel, *Une Énigme historique*, 1930, pp. 105–6; see also pp. 124, 143–5. In his Latin thesis of 1893 Blondel did not apply the concept of the *vinculum* to Christ's general relationship with creation. Already before 1893, however, such an application is to be found in his *Carnets intimes*.
86. See M. Blondel, Lettre à Auguste Valensin, 2.12.1930, in id. and A. Valensin, *Correspondance*, tome 3, *Extraits de la correspondance de 1912 à 1947*, pp. 169–70.
87. pp. 167–171, 177 below.
88. 'La Messe sur le Monde', *Oeuvres* 13, pp. 139–56 (*HM*, pp. 119–34).
89. Ibid., p. 149 ( p. 127).

utterance is not simply a rhapsodic devotional substitute for the liturgical rite which he was temporarily unable to perform. It indicates his true understanding of the eucharist, which is probably best summed up in the following remark:

> ... to adhere to Christ in the Eucharist is, inevitably and *ipso facto*, to incorporate ourselves, a little more each day, into a Christogenesis, which is none other ... than the universal Cosmogenesis.[90]

The dissimilarity of approach notwithstanding, Teilhard took over Blondel's concept of the *vinculum*. 'Everything here below holds together from on high', wrote Teilhard in 1918, echoing Blondel.[91] But it was only after 1919, when Valensin had given him a better acquaintance with Blondel's thought, that he made the concept truly his own. In 'Panthéisme et Christianisme' (1923), he likened Christ to the form of a vault which makes the individual stones contained in it a coherent whole without suppressing their individuality.[92] Again, in 'Mon Univers' (1924) he repudiated the Scholastic notion that in nature there are complete substances, asserting instead that the world consists of a hierarchy of incomplete substances which are ultimately held up by a supreme centre where everything converges.[93] Later still, he would say that, after sufficiently studying the complexities of the world's phenomena, we are led to affirm that things hold together from above.[94]

But it is only infrequently that Teilhard's work manifests the *vinculum* in its original Blondelian form. Rather, the *vinculum* becomes absorbed into, and persists as a guiding (though not dominating) influence behind, three of Teilhard's basic concepts – creative union, Omega and the proposition that 'union differentiates'. With creative union and Omega we shall be concerned below.[95] The formula 'union differentiates' does not receive its final concise shape until 1934,[96] but already in 1918 and early 1919 its emergence may be

---

90. 'Introduction à la Vie chrétienne', *Oeuvres* 10, p. 195 (*CE*, p. 166).
91. 'La Foi qui opère', *Oeuvres* 12, p. 353 (*ETG*, p. 322; *WTW*, p. 240). See also 'Mon Univers', 1924, *Oeuvres* 9, p. 78 (*SC*, p. 50); *Le Phénomène humain, Oeuvres* 1, p. 37 (*PM*, p. 43).
92. 'Panthéisme et Christianisme', *Oeuvres* 10, pp. 86–7 (*CE*, p. 70).
93. 'Mon Univers', 1924, *Oeuvres* 9, pp. 80–1 (*SC*, pp. 52–3).
94. *Le Phénomène humain, Oeuvres* 1, p. 37 (*PM*, p. 43); see also 'Sur l'existence probable, en avant de nous, d'un Ultrahumain', *Oeuvres* 5, p. 363 (*FM*, p. 278).
95. pp. 178–9 and 174–5 below.
96. 'Comment je crois', *Oeuvres* 10, p. 137 n. 1 (*CE*, p. 117 n. 5).

clearly observed.[97] Like Aristotle's notion of form and matter, Teilhard's formula represents an intuited solution to the problem of the One and the Many; and just as in Aristotle form is ontologically prior to matter, similarly in Teilhard union takes precedence over differentiation. The formula has general applicability, 'whether it be to the cells of a body or to the members of a society or to the elements of a spiritual synthesis'.[98] Principally, however, Teilhard uses it to express the strongest possible unity between Christ and created persons, though without capitulating to pantheism.[99] 'Panthéisme et Christianisme' provides the best instance of Teilhard's shifting from the concept of the *vinculum* to his formula 'union differentiates'. Having spoken of union with Christ in terms of the *vinculum*, Teilhard pursues the topic in this way:

> But let us imagine a unifying influence so powerful, so perfect, that it would accentuate the differentiation of assimilated elements all the more as that assimilation further proceeded (an attribute that seems entirely characteristic of true unification): Following this line, we arrive at a notion of Christ's mystical Body which certainly seems, at one and the same time, – fully to satisfy the legitimate 'pantheistic' aspirations of our minds and hearts, – and to afford both dogma and Christian mysticism the only open space where they can freely develop.
> . . . From the top to the bottom of things Christ is the principle of universal stability ('consistance'): 'In eo omnia constant'.[100]

For Teilhard and Blondel alike Col. 1: 17b is the scriptural justification for regarding Christ as the *vinculum* of created beings. But their ways of handling the verse move in opposite directions.

97. See *Journal*, tome 1, 26.1.1918, p. 266; ibid., 29.1.1918, p. 269; ibid., 8.3.1918, p. 290; ibid., 15.9.1918, p. 347; ibid., 3.10.1918, p. 355; ibid., 1.1.1919, p. 388; 'La Grande Monade', 15.1.1918, *Oeuvres* 12, p. 267 (*ETG*, p. 239; *HM*, p. 184); 'Mon Univers', 14.4.1918, ibid., p. 304 (*ETG*, p. 276; *HM*, p. 205); 'Forma Christi', 22.12.1918, ibid., p. 383 (*ETG*, p. 351; *WTW*, p. 266); 'Note sur "l'Élément universel" du Monde', 22.12.1918, ibid., p. 392 (*ETG*, p. 362; *WTW*, p. 275); 'L'Élément universel', 21.2.1919, ibid., p. 444 (*ETG*, p. 412; *WTW*, p. 301).
98. *Le Phénomène humain, Oeuvres* 1, p. 291 (*PM*, p. 262). See also 'La Grande Option', *Oeuvres* 5, p. 74 (*FM*, p. 53); 'La Centrologie', *Oeuvres* 7, pp. 122–3 (*AE*, p. 116); 'Le Coeur de la Matière', *Oeuvres* 13, p. 48 n. 1 (*HM*, p. 78 n. 15).
99. See 'La Route de l'Ouest', *Oeuvres* 11, p. 59 (*TF*, p. 54); 'Comment je crois', *Oeuvres* 10, p. 137 (*CE*, pp. 116–17); 'Esquisse d'un Univers Personnel', *Oeuvres* 6, p. 103 (*HE*, p. 83); 'Introduction á la vie chrétienne', *Oeuvres* 10, p. 200 (*CE*, p. 171); 'Action et Activation', *Oeuvres* 9, p. 232 (*SC*, p. 185); 'Pour y voir clair: Réflexions sur deux formes inverses d'esprit', *Oeuvres* 7, pp. 231–2 (*AE*, pp. 222–3).
100. 'Panthéisme et Christianisme', *Oeuvres* 10, p. 87 (*CE*, pp. 70–1). See Col. 1: 17b.

Teilhard is more attuned to the unity of things, and it is in unity that he finds the explanation for diversity. Blondel, on the other hand, having perceived the diversity of being, attempts to discover that element which accounts for its unity.

The difference between Teilhard and Blondel is well brought out in the letters which they exchanged through the good offices of Valensin. About a month after his conversations with Teilhard in August 1919, Valensin sent several of Teilhard's writings 'on the relations of the cosmos and Christ' to Blondel, requesting his comments.[101] Included among these writings, in all probability, was 'La Puissance spirituelle de la Matière',[102] in which Teilhard hails matter as the 'Clay moulded and quickened by the incarnate Word'.[103] Blondel, in reply, agreed that 'Christ is, in all things, an incarnate presence, a "real presence"'. But, he warned, we must not imagine that Christ plays the role of a diffuse pantheistic God. Otherwise we should have to admit that 'the natural order has a divine stability as natural order' and that through the Incarnation the world could become divinized without being supernaturalized, as if God were a demiurge and were also able physically to participate in the world.[104] Teilhard explained his position, first, by denying that the natural order possesses any divine stability and, second, by asserting 'that this order is characterized by a radical instability *in Christum*, with everything off balance, inclined, towards the *present* centre of the Pleroma'. It is because of that imbalance that Christ has something of a demiurge about him.[105] Blondel's reaction was to say that Teilhard divinized the universe, 'as if, naturally leaning off balance, this Universe naturally found in Christ its support and stability'. The end result of this position would be to make the supernatural an element among other elements in the world, an element that doubtless transfigures the others but does not transubstantiate them.[106] The term 'transubstantiate' is instructive. For Blondel the nature of Christ's presence in the world does not

---

101. A. Valensin, Lettre à Maurice Blondel, 18.9.1919, in M.R. and H.L. (ed.), *Auguste Valensin, Textes et documents inédits*, p. 133.

102. Cf. H. de Lubac (ed.), op. cit., pp. 11–12; also pp. 9–10 ( p. 12).

103. 'La Puissance spirituelle de la Matière', *Oeuvres* 12, p. 479 (*ETG*, p. 445; *HU*, p. 70).

104. M. Blondel, Premier mémoire à Auguste Valensin, 5.12.1919, *BT*, p. 23 (E.T., pp. 24–5).

105. Teilhard, Premier mémoire à Auguste Valensin, 12.12.1919, ibid., p. 33 (E.T., p. 36; *LI*, p. 35).

106. M. Blondel, Second mémoire à Auguste Valensin, 19.12.1919, ibid., p. 41 (E.T., p. 45).

outreach the eucharistic provenance of the *vinculum*. His presence remains entirely sacramental and supernatural, so that whatever transformation it may effect reveals itself to a faith enclosed within an ecclesial environment rather than to a faith open to movements among the general phenomena of the world. Teilhard was quite prepared to admit that Christ is an element – a super-element – in the world; this is what the Incarnation signifies.[107] As a consequence, he was able to say that Christ solidifies everything '*totaliter, etiam naturaliter*'. Nevertheless, everything holds together only through the final centre of cohesion – '$\omega$, Jesus Christ our Lord'. At any given moment we may prescind from the fact that the solidification of everything *in Christo* is still *in fieri*; hence it is possible to imagine that the world sustains itself '*naturaliter, extra Christum*'. The truth is, however, that the world's only stability is its destiny to enter the Pleroma.[108]

Commenting on Blondel's first communication to him, Teilhard summed up their respective emphases of thought. Whereas Blondel stressed the transcendence of the universal Christ, Teilhard put weight on his 'physicalness'.[109] We shall not pursue here the question whether Blondel's emphasis leads to a Christ who is a phantom mediator of creation. It only needs to be remarked that for Teilhard the reality of Christ's mediation depends not only on his physicalness but also on his transcendence. The combination of physicalness and transcendence is a function of the cosmic sense by means of which Teilhard perceives both the unity and the eschatological orientation of the created universe.

### III. COSMIC SENSE AND TELEOLOGY IN TEILHARD

Although much of Teilhard's doctrine on the cosmic Christ can be explained as a development of his intellectual heritage from Rousselot and, through Rousselot and Valensin, from Blondel, for one distinguishing feature of that doctrine – its monistic tendency – we must look elsewhere. The monistic tendency is apparent in Teilhard's

107. That is not to say, however, that Christ is 'a physical agent of the *same order* as organic life or the ether', as Teilhard was later to make clear; see Lettre à Auguste Valensin, 27.5.1923, *LI*, p. 105.
108. Teilhard, Second mémoire à Auguste Valensin, 29.12.1919, *BT*, p. 45 (E.T., p. 49; *LI*, pp. 43–4).
109. Teilhard, Premier mémoire à Auguste Valensin, 12.12.1919, ibid., p. 34 (E.T., p. 36: *LI*, p. 35).
    On the term 'physical', see pp. 180–2 below.

interpretation of Col. 1: 17b; more so than Rousselot and Blondel, Teilhard finds Christ involved within the cosmic process.[110] The tendency may also be seen in Teilhard's lacking any conception that in another order of things an alternative to Christ – that is, to God incarnate – might exist for uniting creation.[111]

This monistic tendency undoubtedly derives from the cosmic sense which Teilhard had discovered growing in him from his childhood onwards.[112] In his early writings of 1916 he speaks of a 'cosmic awakening', a sentiment which the following lines well evoke:

> No, no brutal shock, no gentle caress can compare with the vehemence and the envelopment of that first contact of our persons with the Universe, when, *beneath the ordinariness of our most familiar experiences*, suddenly, filled with religious horror, we observe that *the great Cosmos is rising to the surface in us.*
>
> This vision, once it has been seen, no one can forget; but, like the sailor whom the azure ecstasy of the South Seas has moved, he remains for ever – be he scientist, philosopher or humble worker –, confronted with his nostalgia for what is greatest, strongest, most lasting, for the Absolute whose presence and activity he has for an instant felt around him.[113]

Cosmic awakening is the recognition that one is united to the whole universe;[114] and in Teilhard it aroused the desire to find the heart and soul of the world.[115] His initial impulse was to search within, and to sink into, the world itself;[116] like a character in one of his short stories, he was naturally a pantheist.[117] Cosmic awakening had proved to be something of a pantheistic abduction ('rapt').[118] It could lead to a pagan attitude, in which conscious and personal life is regarded as secondary to inchoative and diffuse modes of being.[119]

In his early writing of 1916 it is clear that Teilhard had already rejected pantheism.[120] It was not, however, until February 1919, as

110. See pp. 150, 152–3, 161–4 above.
111. See pp. 157–61 above.
112. See p. 148 above.
113. 'La Vie cosmique', *Oeuvres* 12, pp. 32–3 (*ETG*, p. 17; *WTW*, p. 27).
114. *Journal*, tome 1, 5.3.1916, pp. 47–8; ibid., 6.3.1916, pp. 49–50; ibid., 9.3.1916, p. 53.
115. 'La Vie cosmique', *Oeuvres* 12, p. 36 (*ETG*, p. 21; *WTW*, p. 30).
116. 'Le Coeur de la Matière', *Oeuvres* 13, pp. 31–2 (*HM*, pp. 23–4).
117. 'La Custode', in 'Le Christ dans la Matière: Trois histoires comme Benson', *Oeuvres* 12, p. 125 (*ETG*, p. 105; *HU*, p. 53).
118. *Journal*, tome 1, 5.3.1916, p. 47.
119. 'La Vie cosmique', *Oeuvres* 12, pp. 34–5 (*ETG*, pp. 19–20; *WTW*, p. 29); *Journal*, tome 1, 5.3.1916, p. 48.
120. See 'La Vie cosmique', *Oeuvres* 12, pp. 34–5, 42, 52–3, 55–6, 75–6 (*ETG*, pp. 19–20, 26, 35, 37–8, 55; *WTW*, pp. 28–9, 35, 45, 47–8, 66).

his formula 'union differentiates' was emerging, that he worked out a systematic way of integrating his feeling for cosmic wholeness with the Christian's conviction that each person possesses an inalienable individuality. He was now designating that feeling 'cosmic consciousness', an expression which almost certainly he derived from R. M. Bucke through his reading of William James's *The Varieties of Religious Experience*.[121] The first author to provide an elaborated account of cosmic consciousness, Bucke described it as a species of illumination brought on by an awareness of life and order in the universe and elevating one so illuminated to a new plane of existence.[122] In contrast to Bucke, Teilhard regarded the essence of cosmic consciousness, not as a subjective state of exaltation, but as one's discovering the need for union with Another who embraces all things.[123] A pantheistic interpretation of cosmic consciousness, said Teilhard, is not possible, since 'union presupposes, right up to the limit of its perfection, *duality beneath the unification*'.[124] During the 1930s yet another expression for the intuition of universal wholeness – namely, 'cosmic sense' – appeared in Teilhard's writings. In many artistic and religious pantheisms, the experience of a cosmic sense has been understood as indicating that access to the great All signifies a dissolvent communion with nature. But on the supposition that we are striving towards union with the All who is supremely

121. Teilhard refers to James's work in 'L'Âme du monde', Épiphanie 1918, *Oeuvres* 12, p. 258 (*ETG*, p. 270; *WTW*, p. 187). Later, 'Conscience cosmique' appears in *Journal*, tome 1, 19.11.1918, p. 370 n. 1. Here no development of the term occurs. Next, Teilhard discusses James's work in Lettre à Marguerite Teillard-Chambon, 14.1.1919, *GP*, p. 362 (*MM*, p. 277). 'Conscience cosmique' then comes into use in *Journal*, [tome 2,] p. 432, 435–6 (*ETG*, pp. 402, 404–5; *WTW*, pp. 291, 293–4); *Journal*, [tome 2,] cahier 6, 3.3.1919, p. 27; ibid., cahier 7, 21.2.1920, p. 71.
     For James's reference to Bucke, see William James, *The Varieties of Religious Experience; A Study in Human Nature*, 1902, pp, 308–9.
122. See R. M. Bucke, *Cosmic Consciousness: A Study in the Evolution of the Human Mind*, 1901, p. 2. The term 'cosmic consciousness' seems rarely to have been used before Bucke. It occurred in W. Caldwell, *Schopenhauer's System in its Philosophical Significance*, 1896, p. 15. The phrase ' "cosmocentric" consciousness' was used by James in a letter to Oliver Wendell Holmes, Dresden, 15.5.1868; see R. B. Perry, *The Thought and Character of William James*, vol. 1, p. 514. In French the term 'sens cosmique' (which Teilhard was eventually to employ) appeared in J. Izoulet, *La Cité moderne: Métaphysique de la sociologie*, 1894, p. 294.
123. 'L'Élément universel', 21.2.1919, *Oeuvres* 12, pp. 432, 435 (*ETG*, pp. 402, 404; *WTW*, pp. 291, 293).
124. Ibid., pp. 435–6 (*ETG*, pp. 404–5; *WTW*, pp. 293–4).

personalized, this relationship must be personal, one that requires the differentiation of those entering into it.[125]

'Union differentiates' is not only Teilhard's answer to traditional pantheistic doctrines, which envisage the renunciation of self-consciousness and the 'dissolution of individuals into a diffuse immensity'.[126] It has the further function of summing up in a metaphysical formula his own 'Christian pantheism', which presents the union of created persons with God as being achieved not just without loss of their self-identity but indeed through its maximization.[127] The scriptural warrant for the differentiating union of Christian pantheism is 1 Cor. 15: 28c:[128] God does not become all; rather, he is to be all in all.[129] Teilhard cites 1 Cor. 15: 28c, either alone or together with the verses preceding it, somewhat more

125. 'Esquisse d'un Univers Personnel', 4.5.1936, *Oeuvres* 6, pp. 101–5 (*HE*, pp. 82–4).
126. Ibid., pp. 84–5, 103 (pp. 67, 83). See also 'La Route de l'Oeuest', *Oeuvres* 11, p. 59 (*TF*, p. 54).
    See 'Panthéisme de diffusion' and synonyms, in C. Cuénot, *Nouveau lexique Teilhard de Chardin*, pp. 146–55.
127. 'Introduction à la Vie chrétienne', *Oeuvres* 10, pp. 199–200 (*CE*, p. 171).
128. *Le Milieu divin*, *Oeuvres* 4, p. 139 (*MD*, p. 104); 'La Route de l'Ouest', *Oeuvres* 11, p. 59 (*TF*, p. 54); 'Esquisse d'un Univers Personnel', *Oeuvres* 6, p. 86 n. 2 (*HE*, p. 69 n. 1); *Le Phénomène humain*, *Oeuvres* 1, p. 344 (*PM*, pp. 309–10); 'Pour y voir clair: Réflexions sur deux formes inverses d'esprit', *Oeuvres* 7, p. 234 (*AE*, p. 225); Conversation avec F. Lafargue, 7.1954 (quoted in C. Cuénot, op. cit., p. 147).
129. *Le Phénomène humain*, *Oeuvres* 1, p. 344 (*PM*, pp. 309–10); Undated note (almost identical in wording with the previous reference), *Oeuvres* 12, p. 126 n. 18 (*ETG*, p. 105 n. 18; *HU*, p. 53 n. 1); 'Quelques Remarques pour y voir clair', *Oeuvres* 11, p. 228 (*TF*, p. 210); Lettre à Claude Tresmontant, 8.6.1953; see also 'Pour y voir clair: Réflexions sur deux formes inverses d'esprit', *Oeuvres* 7, pp. 231–2 (*AE*, p. 223).
    In these references, which belong to the late period 1948–53, Teilhard says that God is 'tout en tous'. During his earliest period, two years before he had begun to develop his principle that union differentiates, he was already thinking about Christian pantheism and, through the variant (and perhaps less satisfactory) formula 'tous en tout', connecting it with 1 Cor. 15: 28c. Writing to his cousin, he spoke of St. Paul as 'the surest theoretician of a sort of Christian pantheism', Lettre à Marguerite Teillard-Chambon, 2.2.1916, *GP*, p. 117 (*MM*, p. 93). Two days later he distinguished between 'naturalist pantheism' and 'the true pantheistic conception', associating the latter with 'the deep and passionate feeling of the Union of all in all ("Tous en Tout") and in One (Our Lord)', *Journal*, tome 1, 4.2.1916, pp. 27–8. Shortly afterwards, he wrote (without, however, making the above distinction), 'The pantheistic aspiration for the fusion of all in all ("tous en tout") is the *immanent side of our cosmic nature*', 'La Vie cosmique', 24.4.1916, *Oeuvres* 12, p. 20 (*ETG*, p. 6; *WTW*, p. 15).

frequently than Col. 1: 17b;[130] and like Col. 1: 17b the verses from 1 Corinthians are fundamental to his vision of Christ's relation to the cosmos. On the last page of his journal, written three days before his death, Teilhard set out a schematic synthesis of what he believed, incorporating into it 1 Cor. 15: 26–8 as his scriptural reference.[131]

The importance to Teilhard of 1 Cor. 15: 28 and the verses preceding it is threefold. First, there is the assertion that union with God is effected through the mediation of Christ. According to 1 Cor. 15: 28, when God has subjected all things to the Son, then the Son will be subjected to God, so that God may be all in all.[132] Next, from among the verses 1 Cor. 15: 28c provides Christian justification for an essentially monist view of reality,[133] a view to which Teilhard was drawn through his cosmic awakening and cosmic consciousness. But while cosmic consciousness is an awareness that all beings make up the one Whole, it is also a feeling that they are still on the way to becoming so;[134] it is a 'presentiment of and a need for *some* ω'.[135] Thus the third reason for the importance to Teilhard of 1 Cor. 15: 28 and the verses preceding it is that they are end-oriented; they afford a basis in Christian belief for his perception that the world is moving towards some ultimate state.

For Teilhard the world's movement is a process of evolution. What alerted him to the theory of evolution was his reading of Bergson's *L'Évolution créatrice* (1907) during his Ore Place period,[136] at the same time that he was beginning to be influenced by Rousselot. Through Bergson Teilhard came to realize that the cosmic Whole to

130. Teilhard cites or alludes to 1 Cor. 15: 28c 14 times alone and 7 times in connection with the verses preceding it. See p. 149 n. 8 above. For Teilhard's references to 1 Cor. 15: 28c alone, see n. 128 above, n. 132 below. For his references to this verse in connection with those preceding it, see n. 131 below.

131. *Journal* XXI (= 9), 7.4.1955, p. 35 (in *Oeuvres* 5, pp. 404–5; *FM*, p. 309; *Oeuvres* 13, p. 119; *HM*, p. 104).

132. 'L'Union créatrice', *Oeuvres* 12, p. 223 (*ETG*, p. 197; *WTW*, p. 175); 'Panthéisme et Christianisme', *Oeuvres* 10, p. 91 (*CE*, p. 75); 'Mon Univers', 1924, *Oeuvres* 9, pp. 113–14 (*SC*, p. 85); *Le Phénomène humain, Oeuvres* 1, p. 327 (*PM*, p. 294); 'Introduction à la Vie chrétienne', *Oeuvres* 10, pp. 179–80 (*CE*, p. 151); 'Un Seuil mental sous nos pas: du Cosmos à la Cosmogénèse', *Oeuvres* 7, p. 272 (*AE*. p. 264); *Journal* XXI (= 9), 7.4.1955, p. 35 (in *Oeuvres* 5, pp. 404–5; *FM*, p. 309); *Oeuvres* 13, p. 119; *HM*, p. 104.

133. 'Introduction à la Vie chrétienne', *Oeuvres* 10, pp. 199–200 (*CE*, p. 171); Lettre à Claude Tresmontant, 20.1.1954.

134. 'Panthéisme et Christianisme', *Oeuvres* 10, pp. 75–6 (*CE*, pp. 58–9); see also 'Mon Univers', 1924, *Oeuvres* 9, pp. 71–2 (*SC*, pp. 43–4).

135. *Journal*, [tome 2,] cahier 6, 3.3.1919, p. 27.

136. 'Le Coeur de la Matière', *Oeuvres* 13, pp. 33–7 (*HM*, pp. 25–9).

which he had awakened was in a state of development. His acceptance
of Bergson's position on evolution, however, was not unqualified.
Bergson had seen the evolutionary movement of the world as
divergent, the result of a driving force, a *vis a tergo*.[137] For Teilhard,
on the contrary, there existed a *vis ab ante* which gave rise to
convergent evolution. There had to be an attracting goal, a point to
which all things were drawn together for achieving their fulfilment.[138]
But in Bergson there was no such point, no Omega.[139]

The adopting by Teilhard of a teleological interpretation of
evolution needs explaining. Evolution is a scientific theory. But the
natural sciences do not normally operate within a teleological frame
of reference. Their concern is with antecedent rather than with final
causes.[140] By way of exception, a notable attempt to introduce final
causality into modern scientific discourse was the vitalism of Hans
Driesch.[141] This theory, together with its supporting experimental
research, commanded some attention during the first two decades of
the present century; that is, at the time when Teilhard was passing
through the various phases of his higher education. But since
Driesch's vitalism describes the internal finality of individual
organisms, it does not appear to be a forerunner of Teilhard's
position, which pertains rather to the external finality of the world at
large.[142] Teilhard himself tried to establish from scientific observation a teleological principle in evolution, by pointing out that
human reflective consciousness is the culmination of a development in
interiority or consciousness which has accompanied, through many
life forms over long ages, an increasing complexity in organisms,
above all, an increasing cerebral complexity.[143] But however valid this

137. See H. Bergson, L'Évolution créatrice, 1907, pp. 47–59, 95–106, 279–81, 286–94
    (E.T., *Creative Evolution*, pp. 46–58, 92–102, 271–2, 278–86).
138. 'L'Union créatrice', *Oeuvres* 12, pp. 203, 204 (*ETG*, pp. 179, 181; *WTW*, pp. 157,
    159); see also 'Comment je vois', *Oeuvres* 11, pp. 197–8 (*TF*, p. 182); 'Sur
    l'existence probable, en avant de nous, d'un Ultrahumain', *Oeuvres* 5, pp. 360–1
    (*FM*, pp. 276–7); 'Le Coeur de la Matière', *Oeuvres* 13, p. 33 n. 1 (*HM*,p.
    77 n. 5).
139. *Journal*, tome 1, 24.2.1918, p. 281; *Journal XIII* (= 1), 21.1.1945 p. [79].
140. Cf. B. Towers, 'Freedom and Causality in Biology', in id., *Concerning Teilhard
    and Other Writings on Science and Religion*, pp. 159–71.
141. Cf. W. H. Werkmeister, 'Driesch, Hans Adolf Eduard', in P. Edwards (ed.), *The
    Encyclopedia of Philosophy*, vol. 2, pp. 418–20; M. O. Beckner, 'Vitalism', in
    ibid., vol. 8, pp. 253–6.
142. On the various distinctions that may be made in the concept of finality, see
    B. Towers, 'Teleology and the Anatomist', in id., op. cit., pp. 84–5.
143. See, in particular, *Le Phénomène humain, Oeuvres* 1, pp. 88–92, 154–66, 195–7,
    333–8, 343–4 (*PM*, pp. 86–90, 142–52, 176–9, 300–4, 308–9). Teilhard's earliest

observation may be, he was unable to affirm, from empirical investigation alone, the existence of more than a local (that is, terrestrial) goal-directed tendency in the universe.[144] The fact is that his teleological outlook originated from a philosophical and religious background in which the world is seen to depend upon and to be oriented towards a transcendent God.

Certain aspects of Blondel's philosophy appear to have encouraged Teilhard to think teleologically. One of these is the principle of the *vinculum*, according to which everything holds together from on high.[145] Blondel also speaks, in a rudimentary way, of complexity-consciousness and convergence. The more complex a form is, the more its interiority becomes evident; while 'consciousness is the product, not of the final act alone, but of all the previous acts, conscious or unconscious, which converge and are summed up in it'.[146] Aristotelico-Thomistic Scholasticism, in which Teilhard was trained, left its mark on him as well. The First Unmoved Mover of Aristotle is a final cause which, in his famous phrase, 'produces motion as one that is loved' ($\kappa\iota\nu\epsilon\hat{\iota}\ \delta\grave{\epsilon}\ \dot{\omega}\varsigma\ \dot{\epsilon}\rho\dot{\omega}\mu\epsilon\nu o\nu$).[147] Teilhard, for his part, says that 'God chose the love of his incarnate Son as the *first mover of the restored Universe*'.[148] According to St. Thomas Aquinas, God is the ultimate end of all things without exception.[149] Since, then, every agent acts with some determined end in view,[150] God as the ultimate end or final cause must also be the first cause of all causes.[151] He is, moreover, the end of things, not as something put into effect, but as that which already exists[152] and which is extrinsic to (or, as we

attempts to state his cosmic law of complexity-consciousness occur in 1917; see 'La Lutte contre la multitude', *Oeuvres* 12, pp. 133–4 (*ETG*, pp. 114–15; *WTW*, pp. 96–7); 'L'Union créatrice', ibid., pp. 199–204 (*ETG*, pp. 176–80; *WTW*, pp. 154–8).

144. (a) Teilhard's law of complexity-consciousness is restricted to the earth; see *Le Phénomène humain*, *Oeuvres* 1, p. 334 (*PM*, p. 301). (b) Beyond the present level of human consciousness, the existence of a goal-directed tendency in the universe becomes speculative; see ibid., pp. 212, 322–3 (pp. 192, 290); also 'Le Christique', *Oeuvres* 13, p. 106 (*HM*, p. 91).

145. See p. 164 above.

146. M. Blondel, *L'Action*, 1893, p. 96.

147. Aristotle, *Metaphysics* 1072b: 1–4 (12.7.4).

148. 'La Lutte contre la multitude', *Oeuvres* 12, p. 144 (*ETG*, p. 124; *WTW*, p. 106); see also 'Le Christique', *Oeuvres* 13, p. 109 (*HM*, p. 94).

149. Thomas Aquinas, *Summa Theologica* 1: 2ae: 1: 8.

150. Ibid. 1: 2ae: 28: 6.

151. Ibid. 1: 2ae: 1: 2.

152. Thomas Aquinas, *Summa contra Gentiles* 3: 18.

should now say, transcends) the universe.[153] The spirit of St. Thomas is present when Teilhard remarks that God is 'the Source, the Movement and the End of the Universe';[154] or when he says that

> the principle which determines the shifting and ambiguous throng of contingencies is . . . providential Finality, the influence of the transcendent Centre whose faultless action is able infallibly to guide chance events towards their end.[155]

St. Thomas is also behind Teilhard's preference for referring to God as the final rather than the efficient cause of the evolving world, as the Prime Mover acting *ab ante* rather than *a retro*.[156]

In shaping his teleological view of evolution, Teilhard draws on Christian eschatology. He sees the evolving world as heading for an end-point, an Omega, where in the words of 1 Cor. 15: 28c God is all in all. The idea of an Omega, especially of Christ as Omega, pervades Teilhard's work,[157] though precisely how he arrived at this idea remains unclear. Whatever weight we give to the suggestion that his use of Omega owes something to the practice of marking points on geometrical diagrams with Greek letters,[158] undoubtedly for the identification of Omega with the world's end-point we must turn to the Book of Revelation, in which God and then Christ are called the Alpha and the Omega, the beginning and the end. Nevertheless, this source does not supply a complete answer to the problem. In comparison with the abundant presence of Omega in Teilhard's writings, Alpha and Omega together, as in the Book of Revelation, appear there but infrequently.[159] Perhaps a remark in Blondel

153. Thomas Aquinas, *Summa Theologica* 1: 103: 2; see further id., *In XII Libros Metaphysicorum* 12: 9.
154. 'La Maîtrise du monde et le règne de Dieu', *Oeuvres* 12, p. 94 (*ETG*, p. 73; *WTW*, p. 81).
155. 'L'Union créatrice', ibid., p. 216 (*ETG*, p. 191; *WTW*, p. 170).
156. 'Le Dieu de l'Évolution', Oeuvres 10, p. 288 (CE, p. 240); see also *Le Phénomène humain*, *Oeuvres* 1, p. 302 (PM, p. 271); *La Place de la nature*, *Oeuvres* 8, p. 173 (*MPN*, p. 121).
157. This idea first appears in *Journal*, tome 1, 11.12.1917, p. 241. It is not until 1918, however, that Teilhard clearly identifies Christ with Omega. See p. 38 n. 150 above.
158. The suggestion has been made by Roger Leys; see H. de Lubac, *The Religion of Teilhard de Chardin*, pp. 173, 342 n. 1.
   The suggestion would appear to be confirmed by Teilhard's first recorded use of Omega. It occurs on a quasi-geometrical diagram to indicate the supramundane world in which souls are united to Christ. See *Journal*, tome 1, 11.11.1916, p. 140.
159. Mentioning the thoughts that preoccupied him during one of his retreats, Teilhard wrote, 'Well, I tried to perceive more distinctly and practically a loving

indicated to Teilhard the possibility of concentrating one's attention on Omega. Not only did Blondel speak of Christ simply as Alpha and Omega.[160] Discussing the continual development of Christian life in its quest for Christ and the inadequacy of merely returning to primitive sources to find him more completely, Blondel also said (in 1904) that Tradition, whose concern lies less with conserving than with discovering, 'will only attain the α at the ω'.[161] This last phrase, with its forward-looking perspective, gives some hint of the way in which Teilhard was later on to elaborate the idea of Omega.

The origin of Teilhard's interest in 1 Cor. 15: 28c presents us with another puzzle. Rousselot and Blondel do not seem to have paid this verse any attention. Prat makes no mention of it in his *La Théologie de saint Paul*, nor does Lebreton in his history of the dogma on the Trinity. And certainly it was not taken up by Valensin, despite his study of pantheism[162] and the bearing which the verse has on that topic. Teilhard reproached Valensin for failing to recognize

that between the Spinozan 'Incarnation' according to which All is hypostatically divine, and the 'Incarnation' of the extrinsicist and timid Theologians for whom the Pleroma is only a social aggregate, there is room for an Incarnation

---

influence at the *alpha* and above all at the *omega* of our World and our lives in the making', Lettre à [Rhoda de Terra], 13.12.1939, *AH*, p. 165 (*LTF*, p. 138).

For Teilhard's other references to Alpha and Omega, see: 'La Lutte contre la multitude', *Oeuvres* 12, p. 135 (*ETG*, p. 116; *WTW*, p. 98); *Journal*, tome 1, 26.6.1918, p. 327; 'Note sur le Christ universel', *Oeuvres* 9, p. 39 (*SC*, p. 14); Note, 19.8.1920 (quoted in Henri de Lubac (ed.), *LI*, p. 50); 'Science et Christ', *Oeuvres* 9, p. 60 (*SC*, p. 34); Lettre à Henri Breuil, 25.3.1932 (quoted in Henri de Lubac (ed.), *LI*, p. (149); 'Esquisse d'un Univers Personnel', *Oeuvres* 6, p. 113 (*HE*, p. 91); 'Réflexions sur la Conversion du Monde', *Oeuvres* 9, p. 163 (*SC*, p. 124); *Le Phénomène humain*, *Oeuvres* 1, p. 286 (*PM*, p. 258). In these references it is generally Christ who is Alpha and Omega. In the second reference it is God, while in the last (which is describing the modern materialist outlook) it is the impersonal energy of the universe.

160. See M. Blondel, Premier mémoire à Auguste Valensin, 5.12.1919, *BT*, p. 25 (E.T., p. 26); id., Lettre à Auguste Valensin, 12.9.1925, in id. and A. Valensin, *Correspondance*, tome 3, *Extraits de la correspondance de 1912 à 1947*, p. 127; also pp. 161–3 above.

161. M. Blondel, 'Histoire et dogme: Les lacunes philosophiques de l'exégèse moderne', 1904, in *Les Premiers écrits de Maurice Blondel* [vol. 2], 1956, p. 214 (E.T., *The Letter on Apologetics and History and Dogma*, pp. 275–6).

162. See Teilhard, Lettre à Marguerite Teillard-Chambon, 2.8.1919, *GP*, p. 390 (*MM*, p. 298); ditto, 8.8.1919, ibid., p. 393 (p. 300); A. Valensin, 'Panthéisme', in A. d'Alès (ed.), *Dictionnaire apologétique de la foi catholique* [4e éd.], tome 3, 1916, col. 1303–33. (The fascicle containing Valensin's article did not appear until the end of 1919.)

that reaches completion with the building-up of an organic All, in which there are *degrees* of physical union with God.[163]

We have the right to speak like St. Paul, Teilhard added, alluding no doubt to 1 Cor. 15: 28c.

One writer who did cite this verse (together with Col. 1: 17b) was Édouard Le Roy, in his *Dogme et critique* (1906). Teilhard could scarcely have failed to be acquainted with the work. It was at the centre of a French theological controversy and in 1907 achieved the notoriety of being placed on the Index; while in articles published in 1911, during Teilhard's period of theological training, it was referred to by both Rousselot and Valensin.[164] Teilhard himself eventually met the author in 1921, after a long-standing wish to do so.[165] Several pages of *Dogme et critique*[166] sound almost Teilhardian in tone.[167] Here Le Roy deals with the resurrection as involving not only men but all the monads of the material world. The following quotations illustrate his approach:

> The glory appears in the final analysis as the fulfilment of all aspirations and desires, as the obscurely foreseen end towards which all nature is pregnant, which attracts it, shapes it and moves it, as the supreme communion in which all will be only in God.\*
>    \* Tradition rightly calls this terminal point the City of God, the heavenly Jerusalem: *Deus omnia in omnibus*.[168]

> Let us now consider universal destiny in relation to Christ. . . . He indeed it is *in quo omnia constant*, who in the absolute establishes and secures the conspiration of the monads.[169]

These passages anticipate Teilhard in several ways. One similarity between Le Roy and Teilhard is the employment of 'monad' in the

163. Lettre à Auguste Valensin, 17.12.1922, *LI*, p. 89. See also 'Panthéisme et Christianisme', *Oeuvres* 10, pp. 84–7 (*CE*, pp. 68–70).
164. See P. Rousselot, 'Intellectualisme', in A. d'Alès (ed.), *Dictionnaire apologétique de la foi catholique*, 4e éd., tome 2, 1911, col. 1079; A. Valensin, 'Immanence (Doctrine de l')', in ibid., col. 579. (Auguste Valensin collaborated with his elder brother Albert in the writing of 'Immanence'.) See also M. Blondel, Lettre à Auguste Valensin, 24.5.1907, in id. and A. Valensin, Lettre à Maurice Blondel, 27.6.1907, in ibid., pp. 327–9.
165. Teilhard, Letter to Édouard Le Roy, 19.10.1921 (quoted in C. Cuénot, *Teilhard de Chardin: A Bibliographical Study*, ed. R. Hague, pp. 33–4).
166. pp. 242–7.
167. Cf. J. Fitzer, 'Teilhard's Eucharist: A Reflection', in *Theological Studies*, vol. 34, 1973, p. 263 n. 25.
168. É. Le Roy, *Dogme et critique*, p. 243, including n. 2.
169. Ibid., pp. 243–4.

general sense of a unit of being, without commitment to the Leibnizian notion of a totally self-enclosed entity. Such a usage occurs in Teilhard as early as 1916.[170] Much more significantly, however, Le Roy like Teilhard after him views the world's process teleologically, in terms of what is to come attracting to itself what is now, though his idealist metaphysic goes well beyond the few concessions which Teilhard makes to that way of thinking. Again, like Teilhard he bases his understanding of the final unity on 1 Cor. 15: 28c and finds in Col. 1: 17b a declaration of Christ's effecting that unity.[171] Equally important for a comparison with Teilhard is Le Roy's monist tendency. For Le Roy as for Teilhard everything in the world, whether human or sub-human, is directed towards the final unity envisaged in 1 Cor. 15: 28c.

Le Roy's reference to Col. 1: 17b briefly acknowledges the central role that Christ exercises in mediating the final unity of all things. With Teilhard, in contrast, this role assumes predominance over all other considerations for a description of reality. In this regard the sentence from Teilhard's writings which perhaps more than any other elucidates the drift of his thought is one which we have already noted when comparing him with Rousselot:[172] 'Fundamentally, one single thing is always and for ever being made in Creation: the Body of Christ.'[173] To appreciate the full import of this sentence, we must recollect the main lines of our discussion in the present chapter. The sentence presupposes Teilhard's teleologically oriented cosmic sense, his monist view that the world is a totality directed towards a specific end. It implies also, in contradistinction to Rousselot's and Blondel's opinion, that creation is a process which reaches completion only as the establishing of a universal divine incarnation or, to employ

---

170. See, for instance, 'La Vie cosmique', 24.4.1916, *Oeuvres* 12, pp. 20, 24, 26–8, 35, 43, 48, 53, 67 (*ETG*, pp. 6, 10, 12–14, 20, 27, 31, 35, 47; *WTW*, pp. 15, 19, 22–3, 29, 36, 41, 45, 57).
171. For Teilhard's use of Col. 1:17b in this way, see *Le Milieu divin*, *Oeuvres* 4, p. 49 (*MD*, p. 33).
172. See p. 155 above.
173. 'Panthéisme et Christianisme', *Oeuvres* 10, p. 90 (*CE*, p. 74). See also *Journal*, tome 1, 26–27.8.1916, p. 101; ibid., 13.11.1916, p. 142; ibid., 26.6.1918, p. 326; 'La Vie cosmique', *Oeuvres* 12, pp. 72–3 (*ETG*, pp. 52–3; *WTW*, pp. 62–3); 'La Maîtrise du monde et le règne de Dieu', ibid., pp. 87, 94 (*ETG*, pp. 67, 73–4; *WTW*, pp. 75, 81); 'L'Union créatrice', ibid., p. 223 (*ETG*, pp. 196–7; *WTW*, p. 175); 'Note sur les Modes de l'Action divine dans l'Univers', *Oeuvres* 10, p. 43 (*CE*, p. 32); 'Note sur le Progrès', *Oeuvres* 5, p. 35 (*FM*, p. 23); 'Mon Univers', 1924, *Oeuvres* 9, p. 96, (*SC*, p. 67); *Le Milieu divin*, *Oeuvres* 4, p. 151 (*MD*, p. 113); 'Réflexions sur la Conversion du Monde', *Oeuvres* 9, p. 163 (*SC*, p. 124).

Teilhard's later way of expressing the matter, that cosmogenesis becomes transformed into Christogenesis.[174]

Teilhard's view of creation is correlated with a processive concept of being. Being is not 'to be' ('esse'), as in classical Scholastic metaphysics, but 'to unite' ('unire').[175] The difficulty with the classical concept of being, according to Teilhard, is that it does not take into account the condition upon which the possibility of participated being rests. For as soon as classical metaphysics has admitted the existence of the necessary and infinite being – that is, of God – it must go on to affirm that in him all possible modes of being are already exhausted. In his concept of being as union, on the other hand, Teilhard sees himself able to offer a reason for the existence of participated being alongside of God. Given that God is complete unity, we are still able to conceive of a further degree of unification; namely, the uniting with God of that which is reduced to a state of union from a state of pure multiplicity. At the exact opposite to God, pure multiplicity is Teilhard's notion of absolute nothing.[176]

In criticizing classical metaphysics, Teilhard neglects the provision which it makes, through its doctrine on analogy, for the possibility of participated being. The doctrine maintains that being may be predicated in a manner partly the same and partly diverse. Being does not have to be predicated univocally, while the suggestion that it could be predicated equivocally makes no sense. The analogous predication of being allows for the respective realities of both creatures and God, such that the participated being of creatures belongs to an order other than that of God's divine being and in no way adds to or subtracts from his infinite perfection. The doctrine on analogy is perhaps as much an assertion of, as it is an explanation for, the possibility of creatures alongside of God. Teilhard's conception of being as union, for its part, possesses no greater explanatory power, since the unity drawn from pure multiplicity cannot be regarded as of the same nature as the unity within God. If the two kinds of unity bear any relationship to each other, they must do so in analogous fashion.

174. See pp. 38–9 above.
175. 'Christianisme et Évolution', *Oeuvres* 10, p. 208 (*CE*, p. 178); see also 'L'Union créatrice', *Oeuvres* 12, pp. 200–1, 211 (*ETG*, pp. 177, 187; *WTW*, pp. 155, 165); 'Mon Univers', 1924, *Oeuvres* 9, p. 73 (*SC*, p. 45); 'Comment je vois', *Oeuvres* 11, pp. 207–8 (*TF*, pp. 192–3).
176. 'Christianisme et Évolution', *Oeuvres* 10, loc. cit. (*CE*, loc. cit.); see also 'Comment je vois', *Oeuvres* 11, pp. 208–11 (*TF*, pp. 193–6).

Teilhard's rejection of the classical concept of being seems, in fact, to be concerned less with that concept's alleged failure to account for participated being than with its indifference to an evolutionary type of creation. For Teilhard creation takes place as the reduction of pure multiplicity to unity in a single process. Thus the act of creating is not instantaneous, piecemeal, and recurrent but evolutive, universal, and once for all.[177] It is a work of 'creative Union', in which God the primordial unity draws to himself from pure multiplicity higher and higher unities of participated existence. [178] This view of creation is no variant on Neo-Platonic emanationism, according to which participated being necessarily proceeds from the One. Though Teilhard believes that, from the nature of reality, God is not free to create except evolutively (just as in classical metaphysics it is absurd to imagine that God could create something contradictory, such as a square circle),[179] nevertheless he readily admits that God is free either to create or not to create.[180]

Teilhard's theory of creative union is an inference based partly on the phenomenon of an evolving universe[181] and partly on the Christian belief that all things tend towards God through Christ.[182] It represents an attempt, not to derive either of these data from the other, but to discover within each the condition for their mutual illumination and their reconciliation.[183] Speaking in the light of his Christian faith, Teilhard posits the necessity for some kind of divine incarnation; it is the means by which God becomes united with his

177. 'Christianisme et Évolution', *Oeuvres* 10, p. 209 (*CE*, pp. 178–9); see also 'Note sur la Notion de Perfection chrétienne', *Oeuvres* 11, pp. 113–14 (*TF*, pp. 101–2); 'Le Dieu de l'Évolution', *Oeuvres* 10, p. 287 (*CE*, p. 239).
178. 'Comment je vois', *Oeuvres* 11, pp. 209–11 (*TF*, pp. 194–6); see also 'L'Union créatrice', *Oeuvres* 12, pp. 216–18 (*ETG*, pp. 191–3; *WTW*, pp. 169–71).
179. 'Note sur les Modes de l'Action divine dans l'Univers', *Oeuvres* 10, pp. 43–5 (*CE*, pp. 32–5); 'Contingence de l'Univers et Goût humain de survivre', ibid., pp. 268–70 (pp. 224–6).
180. 'L'Âme du monde', *Oeuvres* 12, p. 258 (*ETG*, p. 231; *WTW*, pp. 189–90); 'Mon Univers', 1924, *Oeuvres* 9, pp. 84, 114 (*SC*, pp. 56, 85); 'Christologie et Évolution', *Oeuvres* 10, p. 103 (*CE*, p. 84); 'Comment je vois', *Oeuvres* 11, p. 209, including n. 1 (*TF*, pp. 194–5, including n. 30).
181. 'L'Union créatrice', *Oeuvres* 12, p. 199 (*ETG*, p. 176; *WTW*, p. 154); 'Mon Univers', 1924, *Oeuvres* 9, pp. 74–5 (*SC*, pp. 46–7).
182. 'L'Union créatrice', *Oeuvres* 12, pp. 221–4 (*ETG*, pp. 195–7; *WTW*, pp. 173–6); 'Mon Univers', 1918, ibid., pp. 304–7 (*ETG*, pp. 276–9; *HM*, pp. 205–8); see also 'Mon Univers', 1924, *Oeuvres* 9, pp. 109–14 (*SC*, pp. 81–5); 'Comment je vois', *Oeuvres* 11, p. 222 (*TF*, p. 207).
183. 'Mon Univers', 1924, Oeuvres 9, pp. 81–2 (*SC*, pp. 53–4); 'Comment je vois', *Oeuvres* 11, p. 207 (TF, p. 192); see also 'Science et Christ', *Oeuvres* 9, pp. 59–60 (*SC*, pp. 33–4).

work of creation.[184] From the point of view of terrestrial experience, Christ, who is God incarnate, inserts himself into creation as the historical Jesus of Nazareth.[185] But Christ is not confined to earthly events. Through his resurrection he assumes the cosmic role of Omega.[186] As Omega, Christ is the supernatural goal of creation and the *vinculum* holding everything together from on high. These functions of Christ we have touched on when comparing Teilhard with Rousselot and Blondel.[187] They are concerned with mediation between the absolute and the contingent.

As the Omega that so mediates, Christ enters into the reciprocal relationship which we have discussed in connection with Rousselot.[188] Not only does Christ consummate the universe; the universe in its turn consummates Christ.[189] This reciprocal relationship involves the formation of the one thing which, according to Teilhard, is being made in creation; namely, the Body of Christ.[190] Understood in this way, the Body of Christ is not simply a juridical association, on the analogy of, for instance, a family or a nation.[191] A juridical conception of the Body of Christ is what Teilhard would have encountered in his student days;[192] and certainly he believed it to be the prevailing opinion among theologians.[193] But he rejected it

184. 'Christianisme et Évolution', *Oeuvres* 10, pp. 212–13 (*CE*, pp. 182–3); see also Retraite, 20–28.10.1945, 8e jour [27.10.1945], *Carnet de retraites, 1944–1955*, p. 16 (quoted in Henri de Lubac (ed.), *LI*, p. 22); 'Réflexions sur le Péché originel', *Oeuvres* 10, p. 229 (*CE*, p. 198); 'Comment je vois', *Oeuvres* 11, p. 213 (*TF*, p. 198).

185. 'Mon Univers', 1924, *Oeuvres* 9, pp. 88–92 (*SC*, pp. 60–3); 'Introduction à la Vie chrétienne', *Oeuvres* 10, pp. 186–7 (*CE*, pp. 158–9); 'Christianisme et Évolution', ibid., p. 211 (p. 181).

186. *Journal* XIII (= 1), 9.7.1945, p. [133]; 'Comment je vois', *Oeuvres* 11, p. 218 (*TF*, p. 203); see also *Journal* XVII (= 5), 28.8.1950, p. 141.

187. See pp. 158–9, 161–2 above.     188. See pp. 153–4, 158–9 above.

189. 'Le Christique', *Oeuvres* 13, pp. 105–9 (*HM*, pp. 90–4); see also 'Comment je crois', *Oeuvres* 10, p. 148 (*CE*, p. 128).

190. See pp. 155, 177 above.

191. 'La Vie cosmique', Oeuvres 12, pp. 57–61 (*ETG*, pp. 39–42; *WTW*, pp. 49–52); 'Note sur le Christ universel', *Oeuvres* 9, pp. 43–4 (*SC*, pp. 18–19); 'Panthéisme et Christianisme', *Oeuvres* 10, pp. 84–7 (*CE*, pp. 67–70); 'Mon Univers', 1924, *Oeuvres* 9, pp. 83–4 (*SC*, pp. 54–5); *Le Milieu divin*, *Oeuvres* 4, pp. 42–4 (*MD*, pp. 28–9).

192. Such a conception is to be found in [Stéphane] Harent, *De Ecclesiae divina Institutione, notis et proprietatibus ac membris, De Ecclesia Codex secundus*, Moldae, 1891–92 [polycopied manuscript, at Les Fontaines, Chantilly] p. 215: 'The Church of Christ is essentially one *through governmental unity* ("*unitate regiminis*")'. The author was one of Teilhard's professors in dogmatic theology; see A. Demoment and H. de Lubac (ed.), *LHP*, p. 103 n. 1 (*LH*, p. 70 n. 1).

193. *Le Milieu divin*, *Oeuvres* 4, loc. cit. (*MD*, loc. cit.); 'Super-humanité—Super-Christ—Super-charité', *Oeuvres* 9, p. 210 (*SC*, p. 165).

as an inadequate representation of the relationship between Christ and creatures. Instead, he regarded the Body of Christ as a physical entity, comparable to a natural organism. It is a view which, to some extent, is coloured by the modern biological doctrine of the cell as the primary organic entity. In all probability Teilhard picked up the idea of a cellular model for the Body of Christ from his reading of R. H. Benson.[194] He accepted this idea, with the reservations that the relationship between Christ and creatures is stronger than that which pertains among the cells of an organism and that, unlike the latter, it preserves the full individuality of the incorporated elements.[195] In other words, the cellular model expresses – but only up to a point – the hierarchy of incomplete substances and the differentiating union which, as we have seen, characterize for Teilhard Christ's relationship with creatures.[196] Equally important is the contrast which Teilhard makes between a physical and a juridical conception of the Body of Christ. It is insufficient to say, as does Christopher Mooney, that the term 'physical' is equivalent to 'ontological', 'which may be applied to whatever has existence in the concrete order of things'.[197] In this sense 'ontological' must also refer to juridical relationships; otherwise they would be either simply notional or indeed non-existent. By physical Teilhard clearly means constitutional, as opposed to declaratory, which is what juridical signifies for him. That is to say, Christ is related to all things, not because the Father has simply declared him to be universal ruler or controller, but because as Omega he is constitutionally the omnipresent organizing principle of a creation on its way to completion.[198]

194. See R. H. Benson, *Christ in the Church*, 1911, pp. 11–20. Teilhard's familiarity with this work is indicated in Lettre à Marguerite Teillard-Chambon, 14.1.1919, *GP*, p. 363 (*MM*, p. 278).
195. 'Mon Univers', 1924, *Oeuvres* 9, p. 84 (*SC*, p. 55).
196. See pp. 164–5 above.
197. See C. F. Mooney, *Teilhard de Chardin and the Mystery of Christ*, p. 85.
198. 'Super-humanité—Super-Christ—Super-charité', *Oeuvres* 9, pp. 210–12 (*SC*, pp. 165–7); see also 'Note sur le Progrès', *Oeuvres* 5, pp. 34–6 (*FM*, pp. 22–3); 'Panthéisme et Christianisme', *Oeuvres* 10, p. 90 (*CE*, p. 74); 'Mon Univers', 1924, *Oeuvres* 9, pp. 93–6 (*SC*, pp. 65–7); 'Comment je crois', *Oeuvres* 10, pp. 146–8 (*CE*, pp. 126–8).
Teilhard's distinction between physical and juridical appears to be of his own devising. But his way of using 'physical' has clear precedents in Rousselot. See P. Rousselot, *Pour l'histoire du problème de l'amour au Moyen Age*, 1908, p. 3: contrasting a physical with an ecstatic conception of love, he says '*Physical* signifies *natural* and serves here to designate the doctrine of those who base every real or possible love on the necessary propensity which beings have from nature to seek their own good.' See also id., 'Les Yeux de la Foi', in *Recherches de science*

In the following chapter we shall consider that aspect of Christ which, in Teilhard's opinion, expresses his physical relationship with creation; that is, his cosmic nature. Having examined that, we shall be in a position to deal, in the third and last chapter on Teilhard, with Christ in his cosmic function as Omega and supernatural goal of creation.

---

*religieuse*, tome, 1, 1910, p. 471:'. . . no one can deny . . . that there is, according to St. John, a difference that one may call *physical* between the sons of the devil and those who are born of God. . .'

# 7. TEILHARD'S NOTION OF A COSMIC NATURE IN CHRIST

ONE of the more controversial features of Teilhard's cosmic Christology is the notion that in Christ, besides a divine and a human nature, there is also a third nature, which is cosmic. We shall commence our study of this notion with a systematic exposition. Following that, we shall indicate that, despite his exploratory and apparently tentative handling of the notion, Teilhard nevertheless accords it a status comparable to the divinity and humanity of Christ. Finally, we shall examine, in connection with what commentators have had to say about this notion, its doctrinal importance for Teilhard.

## I. THE NOTION OF THE COSMIC NATURE IN CHRIST

Teilhard describes Christ's cosmic nature in the following manner:

> Between the Word on the one side and the Man-Jesus on the other, a kind of 'third Christic nature' (if I may dare to say so) emerges . . . : that of the total and totalizing Christ . . .[1]

This passage contains echoes of St. Augustine and Rousselot. The expression 'total Christ' ('totus Christus') comes from St. Augustine, for whom it signifies Christ not just as head of his Body the Church but as both head and members of the Body united together.[2]

However, whereas St. Augustine keeps the expression within an ecclesial frame of reference, Teilhard extends its application to the whole created cosmos, in accordance with the idea of his early period that Christ's Body is not merely mystical (that is, ecclesial) but also

---

1. 'Comment je vois', *Oeuvres* 11, p. 214 (*TF*, p. 98).
2. Cf. E. Mersch, *Le Corps mystique du Christ*, 2e éd., 1936, tome 2, pp. 87–90, 99 n. 1, 100, 106 n. 2, 118 n. 1, 128.

cosmic.[3] The concept of a totalizing Christ takes us a step further. According to Rousselot, Christ by reason of his Incarnation totalizes the world; that is, he is the principle which gives to the multiple world its unity.[4] Bringing together the notions of total Christ and totalizing Christ, Teilhard characterizes this Christ as him

> in whom the individual human element born of Mary is transferred, through the transforming effect of the Resurrection, to the state not only of cosmic Element (or Milieu, or Curvature) but of ultimate psychic centre of universal assembling.[5]

In this quotation Teilhard refers to two questions: the relationship between the human and the cosmic Christ and the cosmic function of Christ. For the moment we shall put aside the former question and examine the latter.

In the above account of the cosmic Christ Teilhard is presupposing his general cosmological view. We have already come across the essential elements of this view when considering Teilhard's background: a teleologically oriented universe, which evolves in the direction of increasing complexity accompanied by a rise in consciousness and whose theoretical natural goal is subsumed by one that is supernatural.[6] For Teilhard, the theoretical natural goal of the universe, the end-product of the law of complexity-consciousness, is what he calls 'a supreme focus of personalizing personality'. It is a goal which modern science is able to discern; but the problem with envisaging such a goal through natural enquiry is that it cannot be given a determinate form. This can only be done in the light of faith, which perceives the cosmic Christ as the goal of the world.[7] What Teilhard says is clear enough, except for his reference to modern science. As we have seen,[8] whether or not the universe has a goal is a question beyond the concerns of science. Two possible interpre-

---

3. See p. 155 n. 44 above; also 'Réflexions sur la Conversion du Monde', *Oeuvres* 9, p. 163 (*SC*, p. 124).

   Teilhard is not entirely consistent in his use of terminology. Elsewhere he equates the total Christ not simply with the third nature in Christ but rather with the complex of Christ's divine, human, and cosmic natures; see 'Le Christique', *Oeuvres* 13, p. 107 (*HM*, p. 93):
4. See pp. 156–7 above.
5. 'Comment je vois', *Oeuvres* 11, p. 214 (*TF*, pp. 98–99).
6. See pp. 158–9, 166–7, 171–5 above.
7. 'Christianisme et Évolution', *Oeuvres* 10, pp. 209–10 (*CE*, pp. 179–80); see also 'Réflexions sur la Conversion du Monde', *Oeuvres* 9, p. 161 (*SC*, p. 122); *Journal* XXI (–9), 14.11.1954, p. 8; 'Le Christique', *Oeuvres* 13, p. 109 (*HM*, p. 94).
8. pp. 172–3 above.

tations may be placed on Teilhard's reference. It may be simply a way of stating his own cosmological understanding of the scientific data of evolution. But it could also be an allusion to Marxism, which in the modern age has challenged Christianity with an alternative es-chatological view of the cosmos, supposedly based on scientific evidence. Among Teilhard's preoccupations was the endeavour to expose what he regarded as the weakness of that eschatology. The idea of a third nature in Christ (which, of course, contains an eschatological dimension) played its part here. It was one of 'the elements that should be taken up (in order to withstand a Marxist conflagration) by the theology of reputable priests, no longer among savages, but at the focus of modern Humanity'.[9]

Whatever Teilhard may be referring to when he speaks of modern science's discerning the goal of the universe, he leaves us in no doubt that his own view of the universe contains a Christological component. As we have seen in the previous chapter, this view presupposes a metaphysic of union rather than of being;[10] it involves an account of reality called Christian pantheism, in which the universe is presented as achieving its completed existence and fullest differentiation through union with God;[11] and it maintains that God effects the union of his creation with himself only by becoming incarnate within it.[12] Teilhard sums up his view by noting that 'In "Pantheism of unification" God becomes automatically "Christic" '. By 'Christic' he means here Christ's third nature.[13]

It is Christ in his third nature who is the organizing principle of the evolving universe.[14] As this principle, no longer can he be considered merely in terms of the Alexandrian Logos, with which the Church of the first century identified the Christ of the Gospel. Whereas the Alexandrian Logos was the organizing principle of the stable Greek cosmos, today we must identify Christ with a 'neo-Logos', the evolutive principle of a universe in movement.[15] To put the matter

9. Summary of [Lettre] à M[ar]g[uerite Teillard-Chambon], in *Journal* XX ( =8), 22.11.1953, p. 31.

10. See p. 178 above.

11. See pp. 168–71 above.

12. See pp. 156, 158–60, 180 above.

13. *Journal* XXI ( = 9), 29.12.1954, p. 16.
    To indicate that 'Christic' means Christ's third nature, Teilhard writes after it in parenthesis, 'Xristique³, "cosmique"'. This should be interpreted in the light of another entry which Teilhard made in his journal two days later: 'le X³ (3ᵉ nature)'. See ibid., 31.12.1954, p. 16.

14. *Journal* XIII ( = 1), 9.7.1945, p. [133].

15. 'Christianisme et Évolution', *Oeuvres* 10, p. 211 (*CE*, pp. 180–1).

another way, Christ in his third nature is the prime mover of the evolving universe.[16] And because Teilhard believes the universe to be teleologically oriented, he sees Christ in carrying out that function as the Omega point of evolutionary development.[17] Furthermore, it is precisely on account of Christ's being Omega that Teilhard attributes to him a third nature: 'Christ establishes himself as the cosmic face of Omega; and, in return, this face defines his cosmic "nature".'[18]

With the awareness in our present age that the universe is of vast proportions, we have been led to realize, Teilhard maintains, that Christ is far greater than we had once imagined.[19] What serve to express this magnified view of Christ are the characteristics of his third nature. The third nature involves the notion of the mystical Body pressed to its limits;[20] that is, according to Teilhard's early way of stating the case, the Body of Christ embraces the whole cosmos. The relationship between Christ and his Body the cosmos, as we have previously noted,[21] is reciprocal. Each contributes to the completion of the other: if Christ is like a centre seeking for itself a sphere, the cosmos is that sphere seeking a centre. In this relationship that aspect of Christ which comes to completion is his third nature.[22] Teilhard likewise has the third nature in mind when, employing his later manner of presenting the relationship between Christ and the cosmos, he says that cosmogenesis culminates in Christogenesis.[23] Again, the third nature signifies that Christ's kingly attributes have application not just to the social domain but to the cosmos at large;[24] and that in the exercise of his primacy over creation Christ must be conceived as related organically and not simply juridically to the whole cosmos.[25]

16. Ibid., p. 211 (ibid., p. 180); 'Le Christique', *Oeuvres* 13, p. 109 (*HM*, p. 94).
17. 'Christianisme et Évolution', *Oeuvres* 10, pp. 210–11 (*CE*, pp. 180–1); 'Le Christique', *Oeuvres* 13, pp. 108–9 (*HM*, p. 94); see also 'Réflexions sur la Conversion du Monde', *Oeuvres* 9, p. 163 (*SC*, p. 124); *Journal* XIII (= 1), 8.7.1945, p. [133]; *Journal* XX (= 8), 5.10.1953, p. 25.
18. *Journal* XIV (= 2), 24.10.1946, p. 117.
    From this reference we learn that the cosmic face of Omega is to be contrasted with the transcendence of Omega. For the complexity of Omega, see pp. 201–7 below.
19. 'Le Christique', *Oeuvres* 13, p. 108 (*HM*, p. 93).
20. 'Réflexions sur la Conversion du Monde', *Oeuvres* 9, p. 163 (*SC*, p. 124).
21. See pp. 154–5 above.     22. *Journal* XXI (= 9), 5.2.1955, p. 26.
23. 'Le Christique', *Oeuvres* 13, p. 109 (*HM*, p. 94).
24. 'Réflexions sur la Conversion du Monde', *Oeuvres* 9, p. 163 (*SC*, p. 124); *Journal* XXI (= 9), 14.11.1954, p. 8.
25. 'Le Christique', *Oeuvres* 13, p. 108 (*HM*, pp. 93–4); see also 'Christianisme et Évolution', *Oeuvres* 10, pp. 210–11 (*CE*, p. 180); 'Comment je vois', *Oeuvres* 11, pp. 213–14 (*TF*, p. 198).

A Christ on so universal a scale, Teilhard is ready to admit, could become absorbed into, and consequently be lost within, the immensities of the cosmos to which he is said to be intimately related. For this problem Teilhard offers a solution in terms of Christ's threefold nature:

> . . . he [Christ] dominates and assimilates it [the universe] by imposing on it the three characteristics of his traditional truth: the *personal* nature of the Divine; the manifestation of that supreme Personality in the Christ *of history*; the *supraterrestrial* nature of the world consummated in God.[26]

Having granted the threefold nature of Christ, we may concede the ontological correctness of this solution. Epistemologically, however, it is deficient, since, as presented, it gives no clear indication of how it might emerge from the realities of our empirical experience. That is perhaps why Teilhard puts forward another solution, ontologically less comprehensive but epistemologically adequate. According to this latter solution, the humanity of Christ is the empirical precondition of his cosmic nature:

> The more . . . we reflect on the profound laws of Evolution, the more we are convinced that the universal Christ could not appear at the end of time at the summit of the world, if he had not first entered there along the way, *by means of birth*, in the form of an *element*. If indeed it is through Christ-Omega that the universe in movement holds together, correspondingly it is from his concrete seed, the Man of Nazareth, that, as far as our experience is concerned, Christ-Omega (both theoretically and historically) derives his whole consistence.[27]

The precise link between Christ's human and cosmic natures Teilhard locates in the Resurrection.[28] Indeed, even when he is not speaking in terms of natures in Christ, it is a common theme of his that Christ assumes his cosmic role through the Resurrection.[29]

26. 'Réflexions sur la Conversion du Monde', *Oeuvres* 9, p. 163 (*SC*, pp. 123–4). See also 'Le Christique', *Oeuvres* 13, p. 13, p. 104 (*HM*, p. 89).
27. 'Christianisme et Évolution', *Oeuvres* 10, p. 211 (*CE*, p. 181). See also 'Introduction à la Vie chrétienne', ibid., pp. 186–7 (pp. 158–9).
28. 'Comment je vois', *Oeuvres* 11, p. 214 (*TF*, p. 199).
    See also: (a) Journal XIII ( = 1), 9.7.1945, p. [133], 'Truly, the great problem of theology is to determine the position and structure of the *Third Christ* (Christ-Omega), between the God-Word and the Man-Jesus. = the evolving/and evolutive/Christ, the resurrected Christ in whom the Kosmos is "corporeally" organized'; (b) Lettre à François Russo, 17.11.1953, '. . . we have reached the point (I think) where it is a question of making clear in Christ (resurrected and theandric) a *"third" nature*: the universal (or "cosmic") "nature" over and above the human nature and the divine nature'.
29. 'Chute, Rédemption et Géocentrie', *Oeuvres* 10, pp. 54–5 (*CE*, p. 41); 'La Messe

This latter solution may suggest that the cosmic nature of Christ is simply an extension or transformation of his human nature. But Teilhard's complex thought, continually exploring the implications of a cosmic Christ, does not allow us to make so simple a deduction. Writing in his journal towards the end of his life, Teilhard noted: 'The whole question: does Christ[3] (3rd nature) necessarily presuppose Christ[2] (of evolutive, psycho-organic necessity)?'[30] Although, in the light of what Teilhard says on many occasions elsewhere, we should not press the query of this entry too far, nevertheless it does indicate that for Teilhard the relationship between Christ's human and cosmic natures is not straightforward. What the relationship might be will best emerge from examining the status of Teilhard's three-nature terminology.

## II.  THE STATUS OF THE COSMIC NATURE

Teilhard's triple distinction in Christ – a distinction of the divine, the human, and the cosmic – provides us with an example of his genetic or developmental mode of thinking. His first unambiguous use of the distinction does not occur until 1936. But during the twenty preceding years we find it hinted at in his writings. For instance, in his journal in 1916 and 1918 he made the following notes:

> . . . one could do a complete study on the extremes that meet in Our Lord: Divine-Human, Personal-Cosmic . . .[31]

> In Christo, distinguish the esse humanum and the *Esse cosmicum.*[32]

An entry in Teilhard's journal in 1920 affords the most striking anticipation of the triple distinction:

> . . . in Christ there are only man and God. There are 1) Man -2) the Logos (centre of universal consistence) -3) God (Word).[33]

---

sur le Monde', *Oeuvres* 13, p. 153 (*HM*, p. 131); 'Mon Univers', 1924, *Oeuvres* 9, p. 92 (*SC*, pp. 63–4); 'Introduction à la Vie chrétienne', *Oeuvres* 10, p. 190 (*CE*, p. 162); 'Comment je vois', *Oeuvres* 11, p. 218 (*TF*, p. 203); *Journal* XV ( = 3), 8.9.1948, p. 154; Summary of [Lettre] à M[ar]g[uerite Teillard-Chambon], in *Journal* XVII ( = 5) [25.8.], 1950, p. 141; *Journal* XVII ( = 5), 28.8.1950, p. 141; 'Le Coeur de la Matière', *Oeuvres* 13, p. 68 (*HM*, p. 56); Lettre à Jean-Baptiste Janssens, 12.10.1951, *LI*, p. 400 (*LT*, pp. 42–3); 'Le Christique', *Oeuvres* 13, p. 104 (*HM*, p. 89).
30.  *Journal* XXI ( = 9), 31.12.1954, p. 16.
31.  *Journal*, tome 1, 20.3.1916, p. 64.
32.  Ibid., tome 1, 15.10.1918, p. 365.
33.  Ibid. [tome 2], cahier 8, 18.10.1920, p. 56.

Teilhard's thought here is more akin to that of Origen than to his own later on in his life, since he goes on to say that historically the Word is 'defined by his *function of forming the Kosmos*, rather than by his *generation ad intra*'. What Teilhard appears to have in mind is a distinction in Christ between the Word as Trinitarian person (equal to the Father) and the Word as divine instrument of creation rather than, as he eventually proposed, between God and cosmic principle in formation through the process of creation.[34] One further example will suffice to illustrate Teilhard's looking ahead to his triple distinction in Christ.

In 1933 he spoke of the need for Christ to be reincarnated in our present world. Although Christ cannot reappear tangibly among us, he can, nevertheless, reveal to our minds a new and triumphant aspect of his former countenance; that is, the universal Christ, the Christ of evolution.[35]

With his essay 'Réflexions sur la Conversion du Monde' (1936) Teilhard introduced his triple distinction:

. . . besides his strictly human and divine attributes (those with which theologians have hitherto been principally concerned), Christ possesses, in virtue of the mechanism of the Incarnation, 'universal' or 'cosmic' attributes . . .[36]

In the same essay Teilhard also spoke of the three characteristics of Christ's traditional truth (to which we have already referred):[37]

the *personal* nature of the Divine; the manifestation of that supreme Personality in the Christ *of history*; the *supraterrestrial* nature of the world consummated in God.[38]

It was not until nine years later that Teilhard again employed his triple distinction in one of his essays. In 'Christianisme et Évolution' (11.11.1945) he wrote:

Hitherto the thought of the faithful explicitly *distinguished* in practice hardly more than two aspects of Christ: the Man-Jesus and the Word-God.

---

34. For Origen's position, see pp. 115–7 above.
35. 'Christologie et Évolution', *Oeuvres* 10, p. 113 (*CE*, p. 95).
    For further examples, see: 'Le Prêtre, *Oeuvres* 12, pp. 318–20 (*ETG*, pp. 290–1; *WTW*, pp. 210–11); *Journal*, tome 1, 1.10.1918, p. 315; ibid., tome 1, 16.11.1918, p. 369; 'Forma Christi', *Oeuvres* 12, p. 372 (*ETG*, p. 342; *WTW*, p. 256); 'Mon Univers', 1924, *Oeuvres* 9, pp. 82–3 (*SC*, pp. 54–5).
36. 'Réflexions sur la Conversion du Monde', *Oeuvres* 9, p. 161 (*SC*, p. 122).
37. See p. 187 above.
38. 'Réflexions sur la Conversion du Monde', *Oeuvres* 9, p. 163 (*SC*, pp. 123–4).

Now it is evident that a third face of the theandric complex remained in the background; I mean the mysterious super-human person everywhere underlying the most fundamental institutions and the most solemn dogmatic affirmations of the Church; the One in whom all things have been created, – the One 'in quo omnia constant', – the One who, by his birth and his blood, restores every creature to his Father; the Christ of the Eucharist and the Parousia, the consummating and cosmic Christ of St. Paul.[39]

In contrast with the previous essay, suggesting as it does three aspects of equal status in Christ, this essay leaves unclear the precise relationship of the cosmic to the human and the divine in Christ. The cosmic seems to be either an amalgam derived from the divine and the human (from the 'theandric complex') or possibly a magnification of the human. What we find in these two essays, then, are the limits within which Teilhard explored the status of Christ's cosmic nature. Sometimes he was ready to place the cosmic nature on the same footing as the divine and the human natures; on other occasions, however, he was inclined to subsume it under one or both of the others.

Several months before he composed 'Christianisme et Évolution', Teilhard was already using, with reference to his triple distinction, the term which brings his cosmic Christology into relationship with the mainstream of Christological discussion; that is to say, the term 'nature'.[40] In his journal he made the following note:

Go deeply into the *Omega*- (consequently cosmic) *nature* of Christ, as distinguished from his individual human nature (o) and from his divine nature (Δ): This area has hitherto been left in the background and becomes the great modern theological problem:
Christ in his relations (no longer with the Trinity, but) with the Universe.[41]

In this note it is clear that Teilhard sees the cosmic nature of Christ not as subordinate to the human and divine natures but rather in parallel to them. After 1950 Teilhard often referred to the cosmic nature or the third nature of Christ without any suggestion that it is

---

39. 'Christianisme et Évolution', *Oeuvres* 10, pp. 209–10 (*CE*, p. 179).
40. With one exception, there is no reference to the triple distinction in Christ (with or without use of the term 'nature') in Teilhard's extant writings between 1936 and 1945. The exception occurs in *Journal* XIII ( = 1), 1.9.1944, p. 16 [bis]; and it reads simply: 'The 3rd Christ (human, Cosmic, Divine)'. It is not improbable, however, that Teilhard considered the question of a triple distinction in Christ in that portion of his journal which covers the years 1936 to 1944 and which he left behind in China.
41. *Journal* XIII ( = 1), 8.7.1945, p. [133].

subordinate to, or derived from, either of the other natures.[42] The same approach is probably implied in two further ways which Teilhard employed to express the cosmic aspect of Christ: 'the *Third Christ* (Christ-Omega), between the God-Word and the Man-Jesus';[43] and the Christic levels (individual, cosmic, and transcendent).[44]

Against this manner of presentation, Teilhard could also propose other relationships of the cosmic to the divine and the human in Christ. Shortly after he had finished 'Christianisme et Évolution', he made the following entry in his journal:

Analysis of the universal-Christ.
    The 3rd Christ is not a 3rd nature, but the interference fringe between the Word and the cosmic zone of *every* human nature . . . .[45]

In this note Teilhard not only rejects outright the use of the term 'nature'; he also reduces the cosmic aspect of Christ to an effect of the operation of the divine Logos. On both counts, the position adopted here is unique in Teilhard's work.[46] Nevertheless, there are other moments when Teilhard does approach the same position. Thus he uses the term 'nature' with some hesitation, when he says that in Christ there is a sort of third nature.[47] Or he can think of Christ's cosmic nature as a conjunction of the human and the divine:

The (Human + Divine) 3rd Nature (Omega) of Christ.[48]

Another suggestion which Teilhard makes is to place the three

42. (a) Cosmic nature: *Journal* XVIII ( = 6), 20.12.1950, p. [14]; Lettre à Jeanne Mortier, 11.11.1953.
    (b) Third nature: 'Une suite au Problème des Origines humaines: la Multiplicité des Mondes habités', *Oeuvres* 10, p. 282 (*CE*, p. 236); Summary of [Lettre] à M[ar]g[uerite Teillard-Chambon], in *Journal* XX ( = 8), 22.11.1953, p. 31; *Journal* XXI ( = 9), 14.11.1954, p. 8; ibid., 5.2.1955, p. 19 ('the 3rd Christic nature').
    (c) Cosmic nature and third nature together: *Journal* XX ( = 8), 15.11.1953 p. 30; Lettre à François Russo, 17.11.1953.
43. *Journal* XIII ( = 1), 9.7.1945, p. [133]. For the full text of the entry see p. 187 n. 28 above.
    See also *Journal* XIII ( = 1), 1.9.1944, p. 16 [bis]: 'The 3rd Christ (human, Cosmic, Divine)'.
44. *Journal* XVI ( = 4), 11.6.1949, p. [64].
45. *Journal* XIV ( = 2), 24.11.1945, p. [9].
46. In 'Mon Univers', 1924, *Oeuvres* 9, p. 83 (*SC*, p. 54), Teilhard insists that the cosmic attributes of Christ do not belong to the Godhead alone.
47. 'Comment je vois', *Oeuvres* 11, p. 214 (*TF*, p. 198); Lettre à Claude Tresmontant, 7.4.1954.
48. *Journal* XX ( = 8), 5.10.1953, p. 25.

natures or aspects of Christ in an ascending hierarchical sequence:

Neo-Christianity saves and exalts the *3 Christs*:
(1) *historical* (nuclear seed)
(2) *cosmic* (Hominizing)
(3) *transcendent* (irreversible)[49]

We have already come across the idea of the historical Christ as a seed of the cosmic Christ.[50] In the above quotation Teilhard takes one further step, indicating that the cosmic Christ is the means through which creation achieves its final union with the transcendent Christ, Christ as divine Person. The cosmic Christ is said to be hominizing; that is, he raises up creation, through the evolutionary process,[51] to a state in which it is able to form a personal union with the divine. Beyond that, Teilhard introduces the word 'irreversible'. From what he says about irreversibility in many places in his writings,[52] he probably intends the word to refer not to the transcendent or divine Christ himself, but rather to creation in its completed state of union with the divine.

In determining relationships among the natures of Christ, Teilhard's chief interest lies with the connection between the human and the cosmic. We have already seen that he considers the Resurrection as the link between the human and cosmic natures of Christ.[53] Apparently in line with this position is an idea which he put forward in two letters at the beginning of 1955; namely, that within Christ's human nature one may draw a subdistinction between a terrestrial and a cosmic nature.[54] On both the occasions that Teilhard made this suggestion, however, he was concerned not with relating the earthly and risen states of Christ to one another but with finding a suitable way of conceiving Christ in a universe which most probably (he believed) contains a plurality of inhabited worlds. How Christ with his cosmic and terrestrial natures fits into such a universe Teilhard did not at all make clear.

Nevertheless, from a number of passages elsewhere in his writings,

---

49. *Journal* XX ( = 8), 30.8.1946, p. [106] (quoted in J. Laberge, *Pierre Teilhard de Chardin et Ignace de Loyola: Les notes de retraite (1919–1955)*, p. 137).
50. See p. 187 above.
51. Christ the hominizer is equivalent to Christ the evolver, according to *Journal* XV ( = 3), 30.8.1947, p. 32.
52. See in particular 'Ma Position intellectuelle', *Oeuvres* 13, pp. 173–4 (*HM*, pp. 143–4).
53. See p. 187 above.
54. Lettre à Bruno de Solages, 2.1.1955, *LI*, p. 450; Lettre à André Ravier, 14.1.1955, ibid., p. 452.

it is possible to gather the drift of his thought on this subject. In 1918 he first became aware of the need to reconcile his notion of the cosmic Christ with that of a plurality of inhabited worlds:

Given that the Cosmos is *certainly* inseparable, and that Christianity is not smaller than the Cosmos, we have to admit a certain 'polymorphic' manifestation of the cosmic Christ to the various worlds to be integrated into the celestial Universe. The human-Christ would then be only a *face* of the cosmic Christ.[55]

A short time after writing this passage Teilhard developed his position; there is but a single incarnation which has, through its several faces, repercussions on all life, such that, without any knowledge of the Earth's existence, another inhabited world could take the incarnation as belonging to itself.[56] In 1920 Teilhard amplified his consideration of this matter. Confronted with the doctrine of the uniqueness of the Redemption, but unable to accept either that the earth had been singled out as the only place for its enactment or that the redemptive event on earth would be made known by special revelation in other parts of the universe, Teilhard postulated that the one Redemption is multiplied throughout the universe, just as the same sacrifice of the mass is multiplied at all times and in all places. The consequence of this postulate is that Christ becomes incarnate not only on earth but in other localities as well. The fact remains, however, that Christian dogma has been fashioned within a geocentric framework, which makes it almost impossible to deal satisfactorily with Christ in relation to the idea of a plurality of inhabited worlds, especially in view of St. Paul's teaching that once Christ has been raised from the dead he will never die again.[57] The most that Teilhard could do was to reiterate his opinion by suggesting that Christ's incarnation in each inhabited world is only the secondary, ulterior, or particular form of his general 'incosmization' as the universal centre of creation.[58]

This early concern of Teilhard's reappeared during his later years.[59] We cannot adequately conceive of Christ, he maintained,

55. *Journal*, tome 1, 24.2.1918, p. 281.
56. *Journal*, tome 1, 10.3.1918, p. 294.
57. 'Chute, Rédemption et Géocentrie', 20.7.1920, *Oeuvres* 10, p. 57 (*CE*, p. 44); see also *Journal* [ tome 2], cahier 8, 8.7.1920, p. 41. See Rom. 6:9.
58. *Journal* [tome 2], cahier 8, 18.10.1920, p. 56.
    For further references to Christ in relation to the plurality of inhabited worlds, see *Journal* [tome 2], cahier 7, 21.2.1920, p. 71; ibid., cahier 9, 30.12.1922, p. 31; ibid., cahier 9, 11.11.1924, p. 70.
59. Between the mid 1920s and the mid 1940s Teilhard appears not to have been interested in the theme of Christ in relation to the plurality of inhabited worlds.

without taking into account a plurality of inhabited worlds.[60] In an essay of 1953 he expanded on the subject.[61] Although there is no question of theologizing about such worlds, we must at least leave our classical theology open to the real possibility of their existence. From this consideration two points emerge. First, whatever the nature of the universe, the fundamental Christian position remains: Christ is the centre of all things. Second, owing to the vastness of the universe, it is impossible that Christ's influence should spread out from the earth to every other place. Even by electromagnetic means the distances involved are unbridgeable; and, in any case, long before our own galaxy had come into existence, others were already extinct. We must therefore conceive Christ the centre of the universe as having a third nature. Why Christ should be so conceived, Teilhard did not specify in the essay.[62] To discover his answer to this question we have to look elsewhere. Writing to his brother Joseph about the time of the essay's composition, he asserted, as he had done in 1920, that the earth is not the only region of the universe where Christ may become incarnate:

> . . . we must reject as absurd the idea of a Universe . . . with an exclusively terrestrial Incarnation about which millions of planets dispersed in Time and Space would be informed.[63]

For Teilhard's view on the relationship between the multi-incarnation and the cosmic nature of Christ, we must turn to his journal. One of his notes there recasts his speculation of 1918 in terms of his threefold division in Christ:

> Distinguish in Christ the 'three natures': divine, human, and cosmico-(*leader*): it is from this last one that He is able 'to be subdivided' on the 'n' living-thinking planets of the Universe.[64]

---

For a proposal as to why this should have been so, see Appendix, E, Additional note p. 221 below.

60. *Journal* XVI ( = 4), 10.2.1949, p. 39; *Journal* XVII ( = 5), 23.3.1950, p. 85; ibid., 20.4.1950, p. [92]; Summary of [Lettre] à Joseph [Teilhard de Chardin], in *Journal* XIX ( = 7), 31.5.1953, p. 71; *Journal* XXI ( = 9), 12.2.1955, p. 19.

61. 'Une suite au Problème des Origines humaines: la Multiplicité des Mondes habités, *Oeuvres* 10, pp. 280–2 (*CE*, pp. 233–6).

62. Nor did he on several other occasions when he adduced the prospect of a plurality of inhabited worlds as a reason for proposing a third nature in Christ. See Lettre à Claude Tresmontant, 7.4.1954; *Journal* XXI ( = 9), 5.2.1955, p. 26; also *Journal* XVIII ( = 6), 20.12.1950, p. [14].

63. Summary of [Lettre] à Joseph [Teilhard de Chardin], in *Journal* XIX ( = 7), 31.5.1953, p. 71.
    See also Lettre à Pierre Leroy, 31.5.1953, *LF*, p. 196.

64. *Journal* XV ( = 3), 7.2.1948, p. 97. See also *Journal* XIV ( = 2), 13.10.1946, p. 115.

For Teilhard, then, Christ is centre of the universe by virtue of his cosmic nature; but, in order to draw to himself as centre the segments of creation capable of personal union with him, he must manifest his cosmic presence through an incarnation wherever those segments arise.

It is not evident that Teilhard's subdistinction between a terrestrial nature and a cosmic nature within the human nature of Christ can be entirely harmonized with his notion of a multi-incarnate Christ made possible through a subdivision of his cosmic nature. Indeed, when we bring together all of Teilhard's statements on the third aspect or nature of Christ, what we find is circuitous exploration rather than a systematic working-out of the concept. Nevertheless, on this matter Teilhard's thought does manifest several firm features. First, Christ's cosmic nature does not fall within the ambit of his divinity but, together with his human nature, stands on the side of created being. The cosmic nature is intimately connected with the human nature on earth (through the Resurrection) and with any other incarnate nature that Christ may have assumed elswhere in the universe. Second, despite this intimate connection, the weight of Teilhard's thought seems to be in favour of affirming that the cosmic nature exists in its own right and not merely as an extension of the human nature. Third, though at times he hesitated over the term 'nature', Teilhard eventually decided that its application to the cosmic in Christ was appropriate. The latter two of these points are clearly expressed in 'Le Christique', which contains Teilhard's final declaration concerning a third nature in Christ:

> In the total Christ (on this point Christian tradition is unanimous) there are not only Man and God. There is also He who, in his 'theandric' being, gathers together the whole of Creation: '*in quo omnia constant*'.
> Hitherto, and despite the dominant place that St Paul gives it in his vision of the World, this third aspect or function – or even, in a true sense, this third 'nature' of Christ (a nature that is neither human, nor divine, but 'cosmic') – has not yet very much attracted the explicit attention of the faithful and of theologians.[65]

In this passage we observe Teilhard quite deliberately choosing the term 'nature'. The cosmic in Christ is not simply an aspect or function of his. It is of equivalent status to his humanity and divinity; and like these latter it merits being referred to as a nature. Not even the presence of 'theandric' is able to compromise that equivalent status,

---

65. 'Le Christique', *Oeuvres* 13, p. 107 (*HM*, p. 93).

as it does in the earlier essay 'Christianisme et Évolution'.[66]
Nevertheless, the qualification 'in a true sense' warns us that 'nature'
may not have exactly the same significance in all instances of its use.[67]
In classical theology 'nature' with respect to Christ's divinity means
that he is *homoousios* with the Father, and with respect to his
humanity that he is *homoousios* with mankind. Each case, however,
presents us with a different situation. Christ's relation to the Father
involves a numerical identity of being (at least according to later
Catholic theology). But in his relation to mankind the identity is
generic; Christ becomes only one among men, not all of them. When
we turn to Teilhard's cosmic Christology, we find that 'nature'
indicates yet another kind of relationship. Christ is identical with the
cosmos, in the sense that, through their reciprocal relationship to one
another, each of them completes the other in a final differentiating
union.

### III JUDGEMENTS ON THE COSMIC NATURE

Commentators on Teilhard who have discussed his idea of a cosmic
nature in Christ have been unanimous in disapproving of it. For some
of them, the disapproval has been mixed with an attempt to exonerate
Teilhard by claiming that, when he speaks of a cosmic nature, he is
using the term 'nature' loosely and is really referring to Christ's
humanity.[68] Strictly understood, the idea of a cosmic nature in Christ
cannot be justified from Scripture,[69] and it is at variance with

66. See pp. 189–90 above.
67. Opinions differ over the force of the phrase 'in a true sense'. According to
C. F. Mooney, *Teilhard de Chardin and the Mystery of Christ*, p. 179, it means 'that
the expression being used is poor but the idea is correct'. On the other hand,
according to Philippe de la Trinité, *Teilhard de Chardin: Étude critique*, vol. 2,
*Vision cosmique et christique*, p. 260, 'No author ever presents his argument "in a
false sense"', that is obvious, and clearly Teilhard wants to insist on the term *nature*
in a true sense, that is to say, in the sense of a proper and not a metaphorical
analogy'. It is the latter opinion which is followed here.
68. See R. Leys, 'Teilhard dangereux?', in *Revue Teilhard de Chardin*, no 14, mars
1963, p. 29; H. de Lubac, *La Prière du Père Teilhard de Chardin*, 2e éd., 1968
pp. 52–62 (E.T., *The Faith of Teilhard de Chardin*, pp. 40–2); C. F. Mooney, op.
cit., pp. 178–9; R. L. Faricy, *Teilhard de Chardin's Theology of The Christian in the
World*, p. 122 n. 51; É. Rideau, *Teilhard de Chardin: A Guide to his Thought*, pp.
535–6; G. A. Maloney, *The Cosmic Christ from Paul to Teilhard*, pp. 201–3;
P. Schellenbaum, *Le Christ dans l'énergétique teilhardienne: Étude génétique*, pp.
275–7.
69. A. Feuillet, *Le Christ Sagesse de Dieu d'après les épitres pauliniennes*, p. 380; C. F.
Mooney, loc. cit.; P. Schellenbaum, loc. cit.

Christian dogma.[70] The most that can be said for it is that, not contradicting the Chalcedonian definition, it is not heretical.[71] Possibly Teilhard developed the hypothesis of a cosmic nature in Christ, because he was unaware of the theological tradition (from the Church Fathers to J. M. Scheeben in the nineteenth century), which places within Christ's humanity, made perfect by its union with the divinity, the exercise of his cosmic function of ruling all creation.[72]

In view of its novelty, the commentators' reactions to the idea of a third nature in Christ are understandable. But against what they say several points must be made. From our examination of the third-nature texts in Teilhard (an examination a great deal more comprehensive than any carried out by the commentators), it is clear that, despite hesitations, Teilhard by and large and certainly in his final consideration of the matter was only too willing to affirm the existence in Christ of a cosmic nature over and above his divine and human natures. With this affirmation, Teilhard believed that he was simply restating a doctrine taught by St. Paul (particularly in Col. 1: 17b) and by the Greek Fathers.[73] We might also add that, if the notion of a cosmic nature in Christ is no more than a challengeable inference from scriptural sources, so too is the Chalcedonian teaching on the divine and human natures of Christ. With regard to the long theological tradition, referred to by some of the commentators, which ascribes the cosmic function of Christ to his humanity, it may be that Teilhard was not well informed about it. He appreciated, nevertheless, that through the Resurrection Christ's humanity is directly related to his cosmic aspect. His desire to place a sharp distinction between the human and cosmic aspects of Christ sprang not from ignorance of any theological tradition but from a conviction that the Christological developments of the first five centuries represent an unfinished task.[74] With Newman Teilhard understood

70. P. Smulders, *La Vision de Teilhard de Chardin: Essai de réflexion théologique*, 3e éd., 1965, pp. 249–50 n. 8; É. Rideau, loc. cit.; Philippe de la Trinité, op. cit., pp. 258–64; A. Haas, *Teilhard de Chardin-Lexikon: Grundbegriffe—Erläuterungen—Texte*, A-H, p. 166.
71. P. Bilaniuk, 'The Christology of Teilhard de Chardin', in *Proceedings of the Teilhard Conference 1964*, pp. 126–7.
72. P. Smulders, loc. cit.: Petro Bilaniuk, op. cit., pp. 125–6; see also M. Pontet, *Pascal et Teilhard: Témoins de Jésus-Christ*, pp. 156–7.
73. 'Réflexions sur la Conversion du Monde', *Oeuvres*, 9, p. 161 (*SC*, p. 122); 'Christianisme et Évolution', *Oeuvres* 10, p. 210 (*CE*, p. 179); 'Comment je vois', *Oeuvres* 11, p. 214 (*TF*, p. 198); 'Le Christique', *Oeuvres* 13, p. 107 (*HM*, p. 93).
74. *Journal* XVIII (= 6), 20.12.1950, p. 14; Lettre à Claude Tresmontant, 7.4.1954; Lettre à Bruno de Solages, 2.1.1955, *LI*, p. 450.

doctrine to be not a fixed statement of belief but a process of ever deepening religious insight. It is a process whose development depends on its power to assimilate whatever truths man may discover and to synthesize them with those truths which from divine sources it already possesses.[75] Such a view of doctrine leaves the course of its development completely open; and it prompted Teilhard, in connection with his notion of a third nature in Christ, to remark: 'The word ('parole') of God cannot be *exceeded*. . . . But precisely what are *the limits* of the Revealed!!!'[76] Certainly past formulations of the revealed have to be reconsidered in the light of recent discoveries. In calling for a new Nicaea to determine the relationship no longer between Christ and the Trinity but between Christ and the universe, Teilhard was moved by the universe disclosed by modern astronomy, a universe whose vastness seriously opens up the possibility of a plurality of inhabited worlds.[77] It hardly makes sense, in the face of such a universe, to attribute the cosmic function of Christ to the humanity through which he has manifested himself on earth. Something over and above that humanity – on the side of creation, not divinity, to be sure – is required. That is what Teilhard called the cosmic nature of Christ. He saw this question as raising once again the conflicts of Arianism.[78] What precisely he meant by that he did not say. We have suggested that he implicitly perceived an equivalence between his notion of a cosmic nature in Christ and the Christ of Arius.[79] Both are the instrument of creation; and both of them are less than divine but more than human. The heretical nature of Arianism lies not in its various affirmations but in its denial of Christ's full divinity. At no time did Teilhard make such a denial. He affirmed, together with the full divinity, the full humanity and cosmic dimension of Christ, unlike the Fathers of Nicaea, who under pressure from Arianism to uphold Christ's full divinity, allowed his cosmic dimension to fall into abeyance.

75. See pp. 79–83 above.
76. *Journal* XXI ( = 9), 12.2.1955, p. 19.
77. Lettre à André Ravier, 14.1.1955, *LI*, p. 452; Lettre à Bruno de Solages, 16.2.1955, *LI*, p. 459. See also *Journal* XIII ( = 1), 8.7.1945, p. (133); 'Christianisme et Évolution', *Oeuvres* 10, p. 207 (*CE*, pp. 176–7); Lettre à Bruno de Solages, 2.1.1955, *LI*, p. 450.
78. Lettre à André Ravier, 14.1.1955, *LI*, p. 452.
79. See p. 41 above.

# 8.  CHRIST AND THE COSMOS IN TEILHARD

## I. MEDIATION IN TEILHARD

OUR discussion of the background to Teilhard's cosmic Christ in Chapter 6 touched on the importance of mediation. In creation Christ acts as mediator between the Creator and creatures, between God and the world. According to Teilhard, Christ's mediatorial function is bound up with the nature of creation. Fundamentally but one thing is being made in creation, the Body of Christ; or, to use Teilhard's later mode of expression, cosmogenesis is being transformed into Christogenesis. The final outcome of creation, the completed Christ, is achieved through Christ's assuming the role of Omega, the goal towards which the created universe is attracted. In his operation as Omega, what we immediately encounter in Christ is not his divinity or his humanity but rather his cosmic nature, through which he holds together the whole creation.

Teilhard's reflections on the notion of Omega extend from the time of the first World War until his death in 1955.[1] Despite their complexity, they may be divided simply into religious considerations, on the one hand, and those of a phenomenological and metaphysical nature on the other. Having derived the notion of Omega in all probability from the Book of Revelation, Teilhard went on to employ it in elaborating his phenomenological and metaphysical view of the world. Teilhard's phenomenology is a description of reality as it presents itself to him. He sets down what he sees, 'a coherent order between consequences and antecedents'.[2] This kind of phenomenology is to be distinguished from that of Husserl, in which the

---

1. Teilhard's first recorded use of Omega occurs in *Journal*, tome 1, 11.11.1916, p. 140.
2. *Le Phénomène humain*, *Oeuvres* 1, p. 21 (*PM*, p. 29).

investigator reduces the field of enquiry to his own consciousness and prescinds from the real existence of the investigated phenomena. In other words, Teilhard's phenomenology takes for granted a realist and objectivist solution to the epistemological problem of our knowledge of the world. Another characteristic of this phenomenology is its tendency to develop into metaphysical discourse.[3] The tendency becomes especially apparent when the topic of Omega is being dealt with. In his examination of Omega Teilhard is quite prepared to raise the sort of questions which classical theism is concerned with.

Through his phenomenology Teilhard tries to discern the total pattern of the universe. To a large extent the pattern which emerges depends on the findings of science. But particularly where the future is concerned phenomenology moves beyond what science is competent to discuss. The predictions of science presuppose that the properties and activities of things in the future are uniform with those observable in the present. Whatever it may say about the dynamic development of the universe from less organized to more organized structures during past ages, science lacks the means to establish that the universe will proceed to still higher levels of organization in the future. It is left to phenomenology to determine whether the universe will continue its dynamic development into the future. In doing so, it has recourse to extrapolation from past events to future possibilities. Above all, Teilhard's vision of a universe converging towards an ultimate point, Omega, rests on extrapolation. Of its nature, the notion of Omega is a conjecture and a postulate.[4] Although extrapolation is to be understood not as an imaginary picture of the future but simply as the recognition of the conditions without which the future would be impossible,[5] nevertheless, Teilhard admits, there is a danger in extrapolation.[6] The only Omega that we are thus able to anticipate is vague and hazy in form; in it 'the Collective and the Virtual are dangerously mingled with the Personal and the Real'.[7] In

3. Despite Teilhard's disclaimer in *Le Phénomène humain*, *Oeuvres* 1, pp. 21–2 (*PM*, pp. 29–30), the tendency is also present in that work, especially when the attributes of Omega are dealt with. See op. cit., pp. 298–303 (pp. 268–72).
4. 'Le Christique', *Oeuvres* 13, p. 106 (*HM*, p. 91).
5. 'Un Sommaire de ma Perspective Phénoménologique', *Oeuvres* 11, p. 235 (*TF*, p. 214); 'Les singularités de l'Espèce Humaine', *Oeuvres* 2, pp. 338–41 (*AM*, pp. 244–7). See also *Le Phénomène humain*, *Oeuvres* 1, pp. 287–8 (*PM*, pp. 258–9); 'La Centrologie', *Oeuvres* 7, p. 117 (*AE*, p. 111); *La Place de l'homme dans la nature*, *Oeuvres* 8, pp. 166–7 (*MPN*, p. 116).
6. 'Le Dieu de l'Évolution', *Oeuvres* 10, p. 290 (*CE*, p. 242).
7. 'Le Christique', *Oeuvres* 13, p. 106 (*HM*, p. 92).

order to support this phenomenological projection and give it concrete substance, we must in the long run go beyond phenomenology to Christian revelation, which presents Christ as the goal towards which the universe is moving.[8]

As Teilhard perceives the universe, Omega, the point at which evolutionary events terminate, completes the pattern disclosed by phenomenology. The pattern is twofold. First, there is an automatically growing complexity of a material arrangement, which gives rise to conscious 'particles' as a function of that arrangement. Second, having become reflective (with the arrival of man, as far as the earth is concerned), the conscious particles increase in individuality and to a large extent assume control of the process of material complexification (by the play of invention), until such time as they achieve autonomy, freeing themselves of their material matrix. In this ultimate state of autonomy, the reflectively conscious particles form an integrated totality around Omega.[9]

But what, phenomenologically speaking, is Omega? Is it simply the terminal phase of evolution, in which the multiplicity of matter achieves complete unity? Teilhard's answer to this question is a clear negative. Phenomenology indicates an Omega which takes us beyond phenomenology:

> Seen as we ascend, from our side of things, the apex of the evolutionary cone (point Omega) stands out at first on the horizon as a focus of merely immanent convergence: Mankind totally reflected on itself. But, on examination, it turns out that, in order to hold together, this focus presupposes behind it, deeper than it, a transcendent — a divine — nucleus.[10]

The phenomenological Omega is only the apparent, not the real, end of evolutionary development. It is:

> the *meeting-point* between the Universe arrived at the limit of centration and *another Centre* that is deeper still, — a self-subsistent Centre and absolutely ultimate Principle of irreversibility and personalization: the only true Omega.[11]

8. 'Christianisme et Évolution', *Oeuvres* 10, p. 210 (*CE*, p. 180); 'Le Dieu de l'Évolution', ibid., pp. 290–1 (pp. 242–3); 'Le Christique', *Oeuvres* 13, p. 106 (*HM*, pp. 91–2).
9. 'Note-Mémento sur la structure biologique de l'Humanite', *Oeuvres* 9, pp. 267–9 (*SC*, pp. 206–8). See also *Le Phénomène humain*, *Oeuvres* 1, pp. 343–4 (*PM*, p. 309); 'La Centrologie', *Oeuvres* 7, pp. 127–9 (*AE*, pp. 120–2); *La Place de l'homme dans la nature*, *Oeuvres* 8, pp. 165–7 (*MPN*, pp. 115–16).
10. 'Esquisse d'une Dialectique de l'Esprit', *Oeuvres* 7, p. 152 (*AE*, p. 145).
11. *La Place de l'homme dans la nature*, *Oeuvres* 8, pp. 172–3 (*MPN*, p. 121). See also *Le Phénomène humain*, *Oeuvres* 1, p. 341 (*PM*, p. 307).

202     *Christ and the Cosmos in Teilhard*

With such statements as these phenomenology gives way to metaphysical reflection, by means of which Teilhard suggests what some of Omega's properties might be. Among them are personality, transcendence, and the role of prime mover of the universe.

Teilhard rejects the reductionist view that the universe can be analysed until it appears to consist of nothing more than impersonal particles. Reductionism is simply unable to account for the phenomenon of emergent and converging personality.[12] From this phenomenon Teilhard argues that Omega, the point towards which particles endowed with personality converge in order to receive their final integration, must be proportionate to that which it integrates. It must itself be personal; indeed, it must be supremely so.[13] In other words, although we arrive at the notion of Omega through the phenomenon of convergent personal particles, Omega is not this collective sum. A collectivity is not in itself personal. Thus Omega, which influences each of the personal particles, is distinct from each of them and from their collectivity; it is not a something but a Someone.[14]

Not only is Omega supremely personal; it is also transcendent. 'While it is the last term of the series, it is at the same time *outside the series*.'[15] It transcends evolution as the autonomous and actual centre of attraction, towards which the universe converges. If there were no such centre, the universe would not be convergent.[16] Phenomenologically we can say that the pattern of convergence observable in the universe is incomplete, unless we postulate a transcendent centre of attraction. But to do so is to enter the field of metaphysics.

The third characteristic of Omega that we are considering is its role as prime mover of the universe. One of the attributes of the universe is multiplicity. In an evolving universe, Teilhard argues, the very presence of multiplicity presupposes an Omega[17] which unifies by eliminating separateness but not distinction.[18] If there were no Omega acting in this way, there could be only pure multiplicity, that

12. *Le Phénomène humain*, *Oeuvres* 1, pp. 286-7 (*PM*, pp. 257-8).
13. Ibid., pp. 287-9 (ibid., pp. 258-60). See also 'L'Énergie Humaine', *Oeuvres* 6, p. 178 (*HE*, p. 143); 'La Centrologie', *Oeuvres* 7, p. 117 (*AE*, p. 111).
14. 'L'Énergie Humaine', *Oeuvres* 6, pp. 186-8 (*HE*, pp. 150-2); 'L'Atomisme de l'Esprit', *Oeuvres* 7, pp. 53-5 (*AE*, pp. 47-8).
15. *Le Phénomène humain*, *Oeuvres* 1, p. 301 (*PM*, p. 270).
16. Ibid., pp. 300-2 (ibid., pp. 270-1); 'La Centrologie', *Oeuvres* 7, pp. 118-19 (*AE*, pp. 112-13).
17. 'La Centrologie', *Oeuvres* 7, pp. 131-2 (*AE*, p. 125).
18. Ibid., p. 123 n. 1 (ibid., p. 117 n. 9).

is, complete disunity, which is nothing.[19] This account of the One and the Many, of unity in diversity, implies that Omega exercises causality. When dealing with Omega, Teilhard is inclined to speak in terms of final rather than efficient causality. Referring to Omega as God, he calls him the 'Mover, Gatherer and Consolidator, lying ahead of Evolution'.[20] Everything holds together from ahead, cantilevered ('en porte-à-faux') on Omega,[21] since Omega exercises its causality as the universal self-subsisting centre that attracts unity out of multiplicity, that is, being out of nothing.[22] Omega's power of attraction is love;[23] and this implies some degree of psychism throughout the whole range of evolutionary development (from matter through life to thought).[24] On this point, however, Teilhard is prepared to make a qualification. He proposes that if, in the case of pre-living elements in the universe, psychism is absent, Omega acts upon them externally and *a retro* (that is, as an efficient cause), not internally and *ab ante* (that is, as a final cause).[25] According to this qualification, then, Omega is not merely the focal point of unity; it is also 'ultimately the impulse that drives the initial cosmic dust in the improbable and upward direction of higher complexes'.[26]

Teilhard's metaphysical view of Omega as a transcendent person and the prime mover of the universe is very much a theistic conception. As such, it is incompatible with a merely collectivist interpretation of Omega. Teilhard does not exclude collectivism in itself from the notion of Omega; indeed, it is one of the conditions for unity.[27] But collectivism must be directed towards greater personalization, culminating in loving union with a transcendent person. Otherwise the ensuing unity would be little better than that of a termite colony.[28] Teilhard employs the image of a termite colony to

19. Ibid., p. 122 (ibid., p. 116).
20. *La Place de l'homme dans la nature*, Oeuvres 8, p. 173 (*MPN*, p. 121). See also *Le Phénomène humain*, Oeuvres 1, p. 302 (PM, p. 271); 'Esquisse d'une Dialectique de l'Esprit', *Oeuvres* 7, p. 153 (*AE*, p. 147); 'Le Dieu de l'Évolution, *Oeuvres* 10, p. 288 (*CE*, p. 240).
21. 'La Centrologie', *Oeuvres* 7, p. 110 (*AE*, p. 105).
22. 'Comment je vois', *Oeuvres* 11, pp. 207–9 (*TF*, pp. 192–5).
23. 'L'Énergie Humaine', *Oeuvres* 6, pp. 180–91 (*HE*, pp. 145–54); *Le Phénomène humain*, *Oeuvres* 1, p. 299 (*PM*, p. 269); 'La Centrologie', *Oeuvres* 7, pp. 125–6 (*AE*, pp. 118–20).
24. 'La Centrologie', *Oeuvres* 7, pp. 111, 127 n. 1, 132–3 (*AE*, pp. 105–6, 121 n. 10, 125–6).
25. Ibid., p. 127 (ibid., p. 121).
26. 'L'Analyse de la Vie', *Oeuvres* 7, p. 144 (*AE*, p. 138).
27. 'Esquisse d'un Univers Personnel', *Oeuvres* 6, p. 101 (*HE*, p. 81).
28. Loc. cit.; 'L'Atomisme de l'Esprit', *Oeuvres* 7, p. 58 (*AE*, p. 51).

characterize collectivism as an end in itself. This kind of collectivism represents a tendency in mature living species to strive towards the formation of a super-organism in which the totality overrides the individual.[29] In Teilhard's judgement, Marxism – Christianity's modern rival in proclaiming a goal for the world – has succumbed to this tendency. Because it directs its attention to the tangible forces of the world rather than to a spiritual transformation of the universe, to infra-structure instead of to super-structure, Marxism reduces men to the status of members of a termite colony.[30] Furthermore, seeing no ultimate centre of personal union and no prospect for individual immortality, Marxism is faced with the prospect that the very collectivity to which it looks forward can never be realized. Without an ultimate centre the universe lacks stability. And without individual irreversibility there is finally no collective irreversibility either; the universe has no purpose, it has no incentive to go anywhere.[31]

Teilhard's phenomenological investigation of Omega is not intended to be a study for its own sake. Rather, its purpose is apologetical. It is meant to show that, once the idea of Omega is raised, once an Omega of some kind is seen to belong to the pattern of the universe, there is no stopping our investigations until the Christian view of the world's end is taken into account. The phenomenological Omega is perceived as the meeting-point between the universe arrived at its limit of centration and another Centre that is deeper still – a self-subsistent Centre. Thus phenomenology gives way to metaphysics, which enables us, as we have seen, to discuss various properties of Omega, and above all establish that Omega is a person. But it cannot identify who the person is. The identification must be left to the person himself. It occurs in Christian revelation, where first of all God and then Jesus Christ his Son are called Omega.[32]

## II. CHRIST AS OMEGA

Set against this broad background, how is the specific role of Christ to be understood? Teilhard speaks of the one faith that is adequate to

29. 'L'Énergie Humaine', *Oeuvres*, 6, pp. 186–7 (*HE*, pp. 150–1); 'La Montée de l'Autre', *Oeuvres* 7, pp. 71–2 (*AE*, p. 65).
30. 'Sauvons l'Humanité', *Oeuvres* 9, pp. 180–1 (*SC*, pp. 139–40); 'Pour y voir clair', *Oeuvres* 7, pp. 233–4 (*AE*, p. 225).
31. 'Le coeur du Problème', *Oeuvres* 5, pp. 343–4 (*FM*, pp. 264–5).
32. The Lord God is called Omega: Rev. 1: 8; 21: 6. Then the Lord Jesus is called Omega: Rev. 22:19.

such a task as faith in a 'pleromizing' and 'parousiac' Christ, *in quo omnia constant.*[33] The two terms 'pleroma' and 'parousia' may serve to point us in turn to Christ's cosmic function and to the historical outworking of the process.

The term 'Omega' itself can be understood from several points of view. In the first place it indicates that final collectivity towards which the whole evolutionary process of creation is moving. The identification of this Omega with Christ is what contrasts it most sharply with Marxism, the only serious rival eschatology of the contemporary world. For it provides a point of cohesion which holds the collectivity together, and it is on this score, as we have seen, that the Marxist hope is particularly deficient.

This process of unification is being effected in the body of Christ in its cosmic dimension. It can also be described as the emergence of spiritual existence. The spiritual is not to be understood as an attenuation of the material from which the unification arises. Rather it is a transformation of the material, material carried beyond itself, super-material.[34] The spiritual (or intelligent) particles which are the products of the creative process are taken into the body of Christ and go to form the completed Christ. So the Pleroma which they constitute can be spoken of as a 'supernatural organism.'[35]

The possibility for such a union is grounded in Teilhard's understanding of the nature of the created order, and of personal being in particular. Every particle in the universe, even the smallest electron, is coextensive with the whole of space and time.[36] Each person reaches out, albeit unconsciously, to the limits of the universe. Unless persons were potentially coextensive with the universe, there would be no explanation for their interaction with one another.[37] Teilhard acknowledges a similarity between his view and Leibniz's monads. But there is also a fundamental difference. Leibniz's monads are isolated from one another in the static world to which they belong; Teilhard's persons exist in an evolving and convergent

---

33. 'Un Sommaire de ma Perspective Phénoménologique', *Oeuvres* 11, p. 236 (*TF*, p. 215).
34. 'Panthéisme et Christianisme', *Oeuvres* 10, p. 85 (*CE*, p. 68).
35. 'Note sur l'Union Physique entre l'Humanité du Christ et les Fidèles au cours de la Sanctification', *Oeuvres* 10, p. 22 (*CE* p. 16). See also 'L'Union Créatrice', *Oeuvres* 12, p. 223 (*WTW*, pp. 175–6); H. de Lubac (ed.), *LI*, p. 89; *Oeuvres* 10, p. 86 (CE, p. 69).
36. 'Comment je vois', *Oeuvres* 11, p. 186 n. 1 (*TF*, p. 169 n. 4).
37. 'Forma Christi', *Oeuvres* 12, pp. 368–9 (*ETG*, pp. 338–9; *WTW*, pp. 252–3); 'L'Élément universel', *Oeuvres* 12, pp. 438–9 (*WTW*, pp. 296–7).

universe in a solidarity with one another which includes their movement towards a single goal, the Omega.[38] For persons so conceived their final incorporation into the supernatural organism of the Pleroma will not be a destruction of their individuality, or of their distinctive natures. Rather it will be their completion.[39] For that final union is a further exemplification of the principle that union differentiates.

What is not so clear in this account of the Pleroma with its talk of material carried beyond itself is the ultimate destiny of the material matrix itself. Teilhard does not always distinguish clearly between that and the intelligent particles that arise out of it. In its transformation does the material matrix itself come to an end, or is the material environment itself to be thought of as continuing? This issue is left unresolved.

But Omega, as we have seen, can be applied more directly both to the person of Christ and to God himself. Its application to the person of Christ provides the link between the final collectivity towards which creation is moving and God himself. For Christ mediates between the multiplicity of creation and the ultimate mysterious unity of the triune God.

God is the controlling factor in the whole process of pleromization. For it is he who provides creatures with the capacity to unite with him. But Teilhard is faced with a difficulty in his desire to speak both of God himself and also of the final collectivity as Omega. The first implies that God is complete in himself; the second implies that in the Pleroma he finds fulfilment in his union with the universe.[40] The paradoxical character of the affirmations to which these convictions give rise can be vividly illustrated by two examples:

It is the mysterious Pleroma in which the substantial *one* and the created *many* fuse without confusion in a *whole* which, without adding anything essential to God, will nevertheless be a sort of triumph and generalisation of being.[41]

The second example is even more explicit:

38. 'La Centrologie', *Oeuvres* 7, p. 110 (*AE*, pp. 104–5).
39. 'Note sur "l'Élément universel" du Monde', *Oeuvres* 12, pp. 391–2 (*ETG*, p. 361; *WTW*, pp. 274–5); 'Forma Christi', *Oeuvres* 12, p. 383 (*WTW*, p. 266).
40. Letter to J. M. Le Blond, April 1953, quoted in 'Christianisme et Évolution', *Oeuvres* 10, p. 213 n. 1 (*CE*, p. 183 n. 6); 'Mon Univers', *Oeuvres* 9, p. 114 (*SC*, p. 85).
41. *Le Milieu Divin*, *Oeuvres* 4, p. 149 (*MD*, p. 122).

God is entirely self sufficient, and yet the universe contributes *something that is vitally necessary to him.*[42]

Two of the factors that lie behind this paradox in Teilhard's thought need to be noted. The first is the importance of 1 Cor. 15: 28 for Teilhard's eschatology.[43] It contributes to his vision that 'God is not alone in the Christianized universe (in the pleroma, to use St. Paul's word); but he is all in all of us (*'en pasi panta theos'*); unity in plurality'.[44] The second factor is Teilhard's understanding of being in terms of *unire* rather than *esse.*[45] In a metaphysics of *unire* created and uncreated complement one another. Each needs not merely to exist in itself but to be combined with the other 'so that the absolute maximum of possible union may be effected *in rerum natura.*'[46] But this metaphysics of *unire* is not in itself the final point at which Teilhard locates the paradox of existence. He pushes it back into the nature of the Creator himself. Even before one takes created being into account, there already exists in God a drive towards unification, which is the result of his trinitarian nature. The unity that stems from self-sufficient being as it reflects itself is further extended to include, through evolutive unification, the pure multiple ('positive non-being'), which originates in antithesis to the trinitarian unity of self-sufficient being.[47]

In this whole process Christ fulfils the essential mediatorial role of bringing the created beings out of pure multiplicity into the perfect unity of the Pleroma. And to draw something out of pure multiplicity is for Teilhard, as we have seen, the same as to bring something into being out of nothing.[48] Christ's mediatorial role is therefore a fully creative one. And he is able to fulfil it because he is a divine person. He does not stand ontologically midway between created and uncreated being. He is an uncreated, and therefore creative, person.

But Christ's role is not to be viewed solely in these broad cosmic terms. We need to see it also in terms of the known history of the process. And here it becomes natural to speak of the goal in terms of 'parousia' rather than 'pleroma'.

---

42. 'Christianisme et Évolution', *Oeuvres* 10, p. 208 (*CE*, p. 177).
43. See p. 171 above.
44. 'Introduction à la Vie chrétienne', *Oeuvres* 10, pp. 199–200 (*CE*, p. 171).
45. See p. 178 above.
46. 'Contingence de l'Univers', *Oeuvres* 10, pp. 271–2 (*CE*, p. 227).
47. 'Christianisme et Évolution', *Oeuvres* 10, p. 208 n. 1 (*CE*, p. 178 n. 4), 'Comment je vois', *Oeuvres* 11, pp. 210–11 (*TF*, pp. 195–6).
48. See pp. 178, 202–3 above.

In the work of creation, Teilhard can envisage the Word as drawing the world on historically until it was ready for the Incarnation. Christ's saving work in his life, death, and resurrection were a further continuation of that process. After that came the Christian Church. It (and specifically the Roman Catholic Church)[49] is that part of human existence which brings into focus the whole saving work of Christ, by which he is drawing on the whole world to its final state of existence.[50] Thus the Church can appropriately be designated the central axis of evolution.[51]

Evolution is not a matter of continuous, steady development. It is characterized by critical points, such as the transition from consciousness to self-consciousness, from unreflective to reflective intelligence. The Incarnation can be seen as one such critical point in the evolution of the universe.[52] So too may the Parousia. It is, indeed, the final critical point, at which humanity leaps from one plane of existence to another.

The New Testament, together with popular and traditional opinion, stresses the suddenness of the Parousia. Teilhard can do the same, referring to it as a flash[53] or as a spark.[54] But despite this acceptance of the idea of its suddenness, he is strongly opposed to the popular understanding of it as a catastrophic event, as if it were liable to come about at any moment in history, irrespective of any definite state of mankind.[55] Such an attitude is no mere theoretical error, but one that dangerously undermines contemporary Christian witness in the face of Marxism.[56] The whole concept of a critical point presupposes a logical development that leads up to a change, albeit sudden, in the mode of something's existence. Consequently the Parousia should not be seen as a catastrophic event, but as the moment coincident with human maturation. Just as the Incarnation did not take place until humanity had undergone a certain natural

49. 'Introduction à la Vie chrétienne', *Oeuvres* 10, pp. 195–7 (*CE*, pp. 167–8), 'Le Phénomène chrétien', *Oeuvres* 10, p. 234 (*CE*, p. 203).
50. 'Esquisse d'une Dialectique de l'Esprit', *Oeuvres* 7, pp. 155–8 (*AE*, pp. 147–51); 'Trois Choses que je vois', *Oeuvres* 11, p. 175 n. 1 (*TF*, p. 161 n. 9).
51. *Le Phénomène humain*, *Oeuvres* 1, p. 332 (*PM*, p. 298); Henri de Lubac (ed.) *LI*, p. 256 n. 2; 'Comment je vois', *Oeuvres* 11, p. 206 (*TF*, p. 192); 'Le Goût de Vivre', *Oeuvres* 7, p. 249 n. 1 (*AE*, p. 241 n. 1); *Hymne de l'Univers*, p. 107 (*HU*, p. 100).
52. 'La Vie cosmique', *Oeuvres* 12, p. 69 (*ETG*, p. 49; WTW, p. 59).
53. 'Mon Univers', *Oeuvres* 9, p. 113 (*SC*, p. 84); *Le Milieu Divin*, *Oeuvres* 4, p. 196 (*MD*, p. 150); 'Trois Choses que je vois', *Oeuvres* 11, p. 175 n. 1 (*TF*, p. 161 n. 9).
54. 'Le coeur du Problème', *Oeuvres* 5, p. 347 (*FM*, p. 267).
55. Ibid. See also 'Trois Choses que je vois', *Oeuvres* 11, p. 168 (*TF*, pp. 153–4).
56. Lettre à Claude Tresmontant, 8.2.1954.

evolution of anatomical constitution and social organization, so too the Parousia requires that humanity shall have reached the summit of its natural potentialities.[57]

The nature of this human maturation is not defined, though Teilhard uses such terms as the 'ultra-human' and 'superhumanity'. The strongly positive and all-embracing character of his eschatology has sometimes given the impression that he held a universalist position. But attempts to present him in that light are based on a selective handling of the evidence. He accepts that aspect of the traditional teaching on the Parousia which sees it 'as a dawn that will rise over a supreme onslaught of error'.[58] The fact that the spiritual universe is grounded in freedom allows that a portion of created being refuses to submit to Christ.[59] The end time may well be marked by an intensification of the splits between good and evil. The Parousia will see not only the limitless fulfilment of some of the spiritual particles that make up the universe as spiritualized matter, but also the endless decomposition of others as materialized spirit.[60]

Moreover while the human maturation is most frequently described in terms of the final state of natural human development, it can also be expressed in more explicitly religious terms as the climax of man's capacity for union.[61] Mankind progresses towards final unification in God 'by incorporation in the collective organism ("the mystic body") whose maturation will only be complete at the end of Time, through the Parousia'.[62]

These two ways of viewing human maturation correspond to the distinction between the Omega of science and the Omega of Christian revelation. Strictly speaking the Parousia belongs only to the latter context. But the two are inextricably related. The natural completion of humanity is the necessary, though not the sufficient and determining condition for the Parousia.[63]

Concern with human maturation is no rival or alternative to faith in God. Christians who regard the idea of earthly progress as a temptation of the devil are as mistaken as humanists who see the

57. 'Trois Choses que je vois', *Oeuvres* 11, p. 169 (*TF*, pp. 154–5).
58. 'La Maîtrise du monde et le règne de Dieu', *Oeuvres* 12, p. 105 (*ETG*, p. 83; *WTW*, p. 91).
59. 'Forma Christi', *Oeuvres* 12, pp. 381–2 (*ETG*, pp. 349–50; *WTW*, p. 265).
60. 'Mon Univers', *Oeuvres* 9, p. 113 (*SC*, p. 85).
61. 'Mon Univers', *Oeuvres* 9, p. 113 (*SC*, p. 84).
62. 'Agitation ou Genèse', *Oeuvres* 5, p. 285 n. 1 (*FM*, p. 223 n. 1).
63. 'Trois Choses que je vois', *Oeuvres* 11, p. 169 (*TF*, pp. 154–5).

Christian gospel as a dangerous form of opium.[64] Natural human completion and Parousia coincide and their concurrence is no fortuitous happening.[65] In his Journal Teilhard puzzles over how a revelation which does not alter the course of evolution can still be a free, supernatural revelation.[66] But that it is so, he is convinced. The problem with which the theological analysis of grace is concerned is a theoretical problem, the overcoming of an apparent opposition between human action and the power of God. That they do go together is inherent in a proper understanding of creation, incarnation, and redemption.[67] And to it too belongs the gratuitous character that marks all God does.[68] The Parousia is a two way process. In it is to be seen both the world as evolved and matured by God and also God's gratuitous receiving of the world through Christ.

64. 'Trois Choses que je vois', *Oeuvres* 11, pp. 172–3 (*TF*, p. 158). See also 'Réflexions sur la probabilité scientifique et les Conséquences religieuses d'un Ultra-humain', *Oeuvres* 7, pp. 288–9 (*AE*, pp. 277–9).
65. 'Trois Choses que je vois', *Oeuvres* 11, p. 175 (*TF*, p. 161).
66. *Journal* XIII (= 1), 5.11.1944, p. 48.
67. 'L'Âme du Monde', *Oeuvres* 12, pp. 258–9, especially footnote 4 (*ETG*, pp. 231–2 n. 4: *WTW*, pp. 189–90 n. 4). See also p. 156 n. 51 above.
68. 'Débat entre le Père Teilhard de Chardin et Gabriel Marcel', 21.1.1947, p. 4.

# PART IV

# CONCLUSION

## 9. THE QUESTION OF THE COSMIC CHRIST

O ur exposition of the cosmic Christ in Origen and Teilhard may appear, at first sight, to reveal more differences than likenesses between these two authors. But even when we indicate the differences, we must immediately qualify our statements. The qualifications may perhaps lead us to conclude that there is an even more significant underlying similarity of theological concern that unites them.

An obvious difference between Origen and Teilhard is the point of view which each adopts. Origen looks downwards from on high, from the realm of divine transcendence. In Platonic fashion he sees a multifarious creation of spirit and matter, of duration and location reflecting the eternal archetypal world which exists in Christ the Wisdom of God. Teilhard, on the other hand, looks forwards and upwards from a universe in evolutionary formation. What he discerns from this position is the emergence for creation of a state which transcends its present condition and in which it is to be transformed into the Body of Christ. With this contrast in mind, we could say that, whereas Origen proposes to us a cosmic Christology from above, Teilhard does so from below.

In one important respect this characterization of Origen's cosmic Christology requires modification. Like Teilhard's view of the cosmic Christ, Origen's appears to involve an element of extrapolation from mundane realities upwards to the transcendent world. In Teilhard the Omega point from which the cosmic Christ acts on creation is a concept derived partly from Scripture; but it is also the product of extrapolating from the trend of convergence towards a final goal which Teilhard perceives in the evolutionary universe. With Origen the multiplicity of the archetypal world in God's Wisdom is, to some extent, expressed through the titles of Christ found in Scripture. But it is not unreasonable to suppose that behind the very postulate of an archetypal world lies an implicit extrapolation back from the variety of the world of immediate experience. In other words, the archetypal world, which is the realm of the Platonic intelligibles, is an inference from sense data.

Our description of Teilhard's cosmic Christology also calls for modification. Although its main thrust is from below, it is not without a component from above. It does not proceed simply from the historical Jesus to the cosmic Christ. Rather, what Teilhard says is that, in order to undertake his cosmic role, Christ must insert himself into the history of creation as a particular (personal) element within its ongoing evolutionary development. In other words, Teilhard like Origen accepts the New Testament doctrine on Christ as the pre-existent Son or Logos of the Father.

Scripture also brings Origen and Teilhard together in another aspect of cosmic Christology. A distinguishing feature of Teilhard's teaching is its forward-looking perspective: creation is on the way to union with Christ at Omega, the end-point of its development. With Origen the apokatastasis, or restoration of a transformed creation to God through Christ, is an equivalent conception. In this matter Teilhard recognized an affinity between himself and Origen, when he noted that Origen possessed a 'mobilist' outlook.[1] What he did not mention, however, was the reason for their affinity: namely, that the thinking of both of them was controlled by a dominant theme in New Testament eschatology.

New Testament eschatology has the added importance of narrowing the gap between Origen and Teilhard with respect to the ontological bases of their cosmic Christologies. In general terms Origen presupposes an ontology of being; while Teilhard, with his assertion that existence means to unite rather than to be, professes an ontology of becoming. That one who sees things from above should work within an ontology of being comes as no surprise, while Teilhard's

1. See p. 85 above.

forward and upward outlook appears to necessitate an ontology of becoming. But although this broad distinction between the ontologies of Origen and Teilhard is undoubtedly correct, it is not exhaustive. There is a sense in which Origen is concerned with becoming too. Quite clearly he assumes that created souls are complete substances. And yet by reason of their fall they lack the perfections which they have been created to possess – ethereal bodies and the divine life of spirit. In their upward return to God they are in a state of becoming their perfect selves once more. Likewise Teilhard's ontology of becoming must be qualified. He is no Heraclitus or Hegel, finding in reality a perpetual flux. For him creation's evolutionary movement towards higher and higher states of union terminates in the Parousia. At the end of the uniting process there exists only what is united, which has to be described as the equivalent of being.

Another ontological question which divides Origen and Teilhard is the kind of causality which Christ exercises in creation. Origen presents Christ's role here principally in terms of exemplary and instrumental causality, while for Teilhard Christ is predominantly a final cause. The divergence between Origen and Teilhard in this matter seems to be rooted in their different viewpoints and ontological emphases. A viewpoint from above, coupled with an ontology of being, tends more naturally to raise questions about exemplarity and efficient causality (of which Origen's instrumental causality is a subdivision). In contrast, a viewpoint forwards and upwards, accompanied by an ontology of becoming of the kind that Teilhard propounds, is more readily developed in terms of finality. Whatever the validity of our reasoning, certainly the New Testament, with its attribution to Christ of all three types of causality with which we have been concerned, provides no explanation for the distinct approaches of Origen and Teilhard. Despite their dissimilarity, however, these approaches have one overriding concern in common. Each is a presentation of Christ in his function as creating mediator between the absolute and the contingent. In accord with this likeness, we may press further and say that as the mediator Teilhard's cosmic Christ, like Origen's, is also an instrumental cause. Whereas for Origen Christ is the instrument of creation in the line of efficient causality, for Teilhard he carries out this task in the line of final causality. We can make this assertion in the light of Teilhard's complete doctrine on Omega, which includes a distinction between Omega as the cosmic Christ and Omega as God. Omega in the former sense is the instrument of Omega in the latter.

Contrasting viewpoints condition the ways in which Origen and Teilhard deal with the question of cosmic redemption. Origen presents Christ's redemptive work as a transcendent action which gradually through time takes effect in every realm of creation but which, nevertheless, needs to find corporeal expression in a particular place on a particular occasion (that is, on Calvary). Teilhard, on the other hand, looks at the Redemption from within the creative process. It is like a feedback control, supplying a compensating correction to the process in order to bring it to a successful conclusion. Christ's redemption is but a single activity; nevertheless, on the supposition that the universe contains a plurality of inhabited worlds, its presence must be multiplied throughout those worlds (in a manner analogous to the multiplication of Christ's presence in the eucharist, Teilhard suggests). Such a multiplied presence presupposes a multiplicity of incarnations on the part of Christ. A similar notion is to be found in the thought of Origen. Christ, he says, becomes an angel to save the angels, just as he becomes a man to save men. But there is nothing in Origen's experience to prompt him to propose the idea of a multiplication of corporeal manifestations. But for Teilhard Christ's redemption must be known to be effective. And since it is physically impossible that knowledge of an event on the planet earth could be propagated through the immensities of the universe that astronomy has now declared to us, Christ must be incarnationally present wherever the need for redemption arises. New knowledge about the physical cosmos leads to new suggestions about what a fully cosmic redemption entails.

To conclude our discussion of the different viewpoints taken by Origen and Teilhard, we shall examine the contrasting estimates of Christ's cosmic status to which those viewpoints give rise. Looking at reality from above, Origen equates the cosmic aspect of Christ with God's Wisdom and Logos. Here plainly we are dealing with Christ on the side of divinity. Furthermore, even the title First-born of all creation expresses for Origen something about the divinity of Christ. Teilhard, for his part, takes a forward and upwards view of things; and what he sees is a cosmic Christ in the making, the building-up through evolving creation of the Body of Christ or, to use his later expression, cosmogenesis becoming Christogenesis. From Teilhard's point of view, then, it is clear that the cosmic nature of Christ is on the side of creation rather than of divinity. This is confirmed when he proposes only a subdistinction between human and cosmic natures of

Christ. Broadly speaking, the contrast that we have drawn between Origen's understanding of the cosmic Christ and Teilhard's holds good for most of what they say. But several anomalies in their doctrines must be taken into consideration. Like Teilhard Origen teaches that the whole universe of creation is perhaps the Body of Christ. But whether he regards the relationship between Christ and creation in precisely the same way as Teilhard cannot be definitively answered. Teilhard asserts that the relationship is physical and organic; he is opposed to conceiving it as a mere juridical association. Origen, for his part, can express Christ's relationship to creation in organic terms. But he does so juridically as well. In as much as he presents the relationship as organic, he seems like Teilhard to be placing the cosmic aspect of Christ on the side of creation. Similarly we find Teilhard apparently placing Christ's cosmic aspect on the side of divinity, when he speaks of Christ as the supernatural goal of creation. The unsystematic nature of Origen's writings and probably also their fragmentary state preclude us from attempting any reconciliation of the divine and created aspects of his cosmic Christ. With Teilhard, however, such a reconciliation is possible, to the extent that the divine person who acts as goal of creation does so by assuming that creation as his cosmic nature. It is through his function as goal of creation that Christ in his divine nature makes contact with his cosmic nature.

Although Origen and Teilhard look at Christ's cosmic aspect from opposing vantage points, and thereby draw different conclusions about it, we can also see important points of similarity emerging in the general thrust and direction of the arguments despite those differences. Thus for example, both Origen and Teilhard see the cosmic aspect of Christ as pertaining neither to his humanity nor to his divinity in the fullest sense of that term. As we have previously indicated, that cosmic aspect is connected with the unfinished business left over from the Arian conflicts of the fourth century. If Origen, in his complete doctrine on Christ, anticipated both Nicene orthodoxy and Arianism, Teilhard in his turn wanted a new Nicaea, no longer to determine Christ's relationship to God (that was a settled question), but rather his relationship to the cosmos.

Nicaea, it is true, did have something to say about the cosmic aspect of Christ: Christ is he through whom all things are made. But, as should be obvious from this present study, that proposition is but one among not a few which concern the cosmic Christ. In any case, as a number of British theologians have pointed out, it is a proposition which has ceased to be a living article of belief in the church.[2] Nevertheless, the proposition remains, as does an array of statements about the cosmic Christ in the New Testament, not to mention a long line of teachings by theologians in an as yet scarcely explored tradition.

With so much uninvestigated and hence uncertain in cosmic Christology, we should not wonder that two authors so far apart in time and culture as Origen and Teilhard provide divergent accounts of the cosmic Christ. And yet, despite the divergence, there are also, as we have just seen, points of convergence or near convergence. What tends to bring Origen and Teilhard together is the fact that both of them are speaking out of the same Christian faith. As far as the cosmic aspect of Christ is concerned, the most readily accessible expression of that faith occurs in the New Testament. But for Origen there was also a tradition among the early Fathers of the Church; and with that tradition Teilhard was to some extent acquainted. Moreover, Teilhard also worked within a tradition handed on to him by contemporaries of his who were professional theologians.

The word 'tradition' means something handed on. That implies that something has also to be appropriated anew by each generation – indeed by each person – that receives it. Appropriation of a tradition involves bringing it into relation with other attitudes and ideas characteristic of that generation or that person. Among scholars there is a debate over what influence the Platonic background of the early Church Fathers had on the Christian faith handed down to them. One conclusion is that Platonism handicapped or even distorted their teaching of the faith.[3] Another view claims that the Fathers used Platonic notions simply as weapons for doing battle with Platonists.[4] Again, it is suggested that by taking over Platonic concepts the Fathers did not arrive at their teachings through Platonism. What they became, rather, was Platonizing Christians; Platonic concepts were the means to hand for expressing and exploring the problems implicit in the doctrines of the Christian

2. e.g. E.W. Grinfield, J.B. Lightfoot, J.R. Illingworth, W.L. Walker and W.R. Inge (see pp. 22, 24, 27, 33 and 35 respectivetively).
3. e.g. L. Dewart, *The Future of Belief,* pp. 130–70. With particular reference to Origen, see R. Arnou, Platonisme des Pères, in *Dictionnaire de théologie catholique,* tome 12:2, col. 2307–8, 2314, 2331, 2333–6.
4. e.g. H. Dörrie, 'Was ist "spätantiker Platonismus"? Uberlegungen zur Grenzziehung zwischen Platonismus und Christentum', in *Theologische Rundschau,* 36. Jahrgang, 1971, pp. 299–301.

faith which they professed.[5] Yet another position in this debate holds that, at least for the central statements of belief in the early Church, what its theologians took over was no more than the Greek technique of rational analysis. This technique consists in the establishing of an open heuristic structure which does not prejudge the precise nature of what is being spoken about. The insistence on the term 'homoousios' can be regarded in this way. It is then understood to say that what is true of the Father is also true of the Son, except only that the Father is the Father. The believer is then left free to conceive the Father in whatever way, compatible with Christian teaching about God, he may wish.[6]

Which of these approaches is best fitted to describe Origen's teaching about the cosmic aspect of Christ? It is difficult to maintain that Platonism simply distorts his theology. What he says is too directly dependent on Scripture. He is not, then, a Christian Platonist who arrives at his teaching through Platonism. As we have shown above, his conception of the Son's mediatorship in creation does not fully accord with either the emanationist or the subordinationist type of mediation which prevailed among Platonists. Nevertheless, it would not be unjust to call Origen· a Platonizing Christian. We may readily observe him employing Platonic concepts – above all, the concept of exemplarity – to articulate his faith.

Examples of the kind of open heuristic structure referred to above may be found in Origen; for example, his statement that the Father and the Son are two hypostases. What this statement does is to affirm a real distinction between Father and Son, without making a commitment to the meaning of 'hypostasis'. With regard to cosmic Christology, however, the clearest example of an open heuristic structure comes from Teilhard. His formulation of three natures in Christ does not explain the term 'nature'. It signifies only that Christ's relation to the cosmos is as real as his relation to the divine Word and to Jesus of Nazareth. Apart from this cardinal feature of Teilhard's cosmic Christology, should we call him – on the analogy of the

---

5. e.g. E. P. Meijering, 'Zehn Jahre Forschung zur Thema Platonismus und Kirchenväter', in *Theologische Rundschau* 36. Jahrgang, 1971, p. 316, and 'Wie platonistierten Christen? Zur Grenzziehung zwischen Platonismus, Kirchlichen Credo und patristischer Theologie', in *Vigiliae Christianae*, vol. 28, 1974, pp. 15–28. (Reprinted in *God Being History*, pp. 1–18 and 133–46).
6. e.g. B. J.F. Lonergan, 'The dehellenization of Dogma' in *A Second Collection*, pp. 22–7, and 'The Origins of Christian Realism', pp. 251–3.

categories of relationship between Christianity and Platonism mentioned above – a Christian evolutionist or an evolutionizing Christian? From our discussion of Teilhard's background, what appears to be of primary importance to Teilhard is that the evolving world should have a goal. Teilhard did not derive his idea of a goal from evolutionary theory; he took it from Christian eschatology and other Christian sources, Blondel and Scholasticism. Evolution is a category of thought which, in some theological contexts, he uses to provide a more fully elaborated understanding of salvation history. It seems appropriate, then, to refer to Teilhard as an evolutionizing Christian.

In their respective treatments of the cosmic Christ – a Platonizing treatment and an evolutionizing treatment – Origen and Teilhard are both putting, so to speak, the face of Christ on the Logos of the world. They agree with man's recognition through secular thought that the universe of our experience is held together by some ultimate principle. But speaking out of faith, they assert that this principle is none other than the Christ in whom Christians believe. Such is the teaching of the New Testament. And that it could find fruitful expression in the philosophical thought patterns in which Origen was nurtured is not at all surprising. In the ancient world the existence of a Logos principle was an almost universal intellectual presupposition.

But what about the modern world? Harnack, we have seen, stated that the idea of a Logos little accords with the contemporary way of thinking.[7] What Harnack said, however, cannot be treated as a universal truth about that thinking. There is no one way of thinking in the contemporary world. Even if we confine ourselves to the field of science, which has so dominated the world for the past century or more, there is no consensus. In itself, of course, science does not arrive at a Logos principle. Such a principle is a philosophical, not a scientific, concept. But some men of science, moved by what they have seen in their investigations and reflecting on it, do affirm the existence of a Logos principle. A well known popular example is the saying of Sir Arthur Eddington: 'When I look through my telescope, I see the workings of a great mind'. More recently Raymond Ruyer, a French academic concerned with the philosophy of science, has provided an extensive account of the 'Gnostics' of Princeton, a group of scientists who have elaborated a view of the universe entailing an overall immanent principle of operation.[8] Other scientists besides

7. See p. 18 above.
8. R. Ruyer, *La Gnose de Princeton*, Chs. 17 and 23.

those 'Gnostics' have recently written in similar terms.[9] What their theories amount to is the affirmation, within terms of the universe as we now know it, of a Logos principle. Such a principle is generally affirmed in a form that is immanent and pantheistic. It was to thinkers like those scientists that Teilhard addressed himself when he said that the Omega of science must turn out to be the Omega of Christian faith.

In our introductory chapter we saw that the rise of cosmic-Christ language has introduced a newly perceived issue into Christological discussion. It is a legitimate, a necessary, and an ongoing issue. It is legitimate not only because it is founded on scriptural data and continues matters that were raised in theological traditions of the past; it is also at the point where contemporary views about the universe make an impact on the Christian faith. It is a necessary issue, since it upholds the Christian belief that, however vast and strange the universe may turn out to be, it is Christ who is at the centre of all. It is an ongoing issue because the teaching Church has scarcely begun to concern itself with the cosmic Christ. The Creed acknowledges Christ's instrumental causality, while Vatican II speaks of Christ as the Lord of history. Beyond such statements, there is little else. The idea cries out for careful and sustained theological development. It is as a contribution to that end that this book has been written.

9. e.g. D. Foster, *The Intelligent Universe.*

# APPENDIX

## The Instances of 'Christ cosmique' in Teilhard's Writings

Sections A-C below list the places where Teilhard uses 'Christ cosmique'. Several instances (marked*) contain the predicative use of the adjective 'cosmique'. A selection of variant forms is given in Section D.

### A. Published Writings

(1–16) 13.3.1916–4.1.1919: *Journal*, tome 1, pp. 57 (twice), 60, 74, 77, 125, 237, 281 (twice), 282*, 283, 366 n. 2, 369*, 370, 375, 393.

(17–20) 17.4.1916: 'La Vie cosmique', *Oeuvres* 12, pp. 67, 69, 72, 81 (*ETG*, pp. 47, 48, 51, 61; *WTW*, pp. 57, 59, 62, 70).

(21) 22.12.1918: 'Forma Christi', ibid., p. 372 (*ETG*, p. 342; *WTW*, p. 256).

(22–23) 21.2.1919: 'L' Élément universel', ibid., pp. 441, 443 (*ETG*, pp. 409, 411; *WTW*, pp. 298, 300).

(24) 1.5.1921: *Journal*, [tome 2,] cahier 8, p. 76 (in Henri de Lubac (ed.), *LI*, p. 102 n. 1). (No doubt several other examples exist in this tome of the earlier journal.)

(25) 29.6.1944: 'Introduction à la Vie chrétienne', *Oeuvres* 10, p. 186 (*CE*, p. 158).

(26–27) 11.11.1945: 'Christianisme et Évolution', ibid., p. 210 (twice) (pp. 179, 180).

(28) 30.8.1946: *Journal* XIV (= 2), p. 106 (in Jacques Laberge, *Pierre Teilhard de Chardin et Ignace de Loyola*, p. 137).

(29) 24.10.1954: Lettre à André Ravier, *LI*, p. 445.

(30) 3.1955: 'Le Christique', *Oeuvres* 13, p. 109 (*HM*, p. 94).

### B. Unpublished Writings

(31–32) 23 and 28.6.1952: retreat notes in *Journal* XX (= 8), pp. 1, 2*. (No doubt several other examples exist in the later journal.)

### C. Reported Conversations

(33–35) 5. 1942–5.1945: G. M. Allegra, *My Conversations with Teilhard de Chardin on the Primacy of Christ*, pp. 66, 70, 84.

*D. Some Variant Forms*

(36) 25.7.1917: *Journal,* tome 1, p. 211 ('la Personne-Cosmique du Christ').

(37) 10.9.1918: ibid., tome 1, p. 335 ('Christ-Kosmos').

(38–40) 3 and 9.10.1918: ibid., tome 1, pp. 355, 360 (twice) ('Kosmos-Christ').

(41) 19.8.1920: ibid., [tome 2,] cahier 8, p. 44 ('Christ-Cosmos') (in Jacques Laberge, op. cit., p. 28).

(42) 30.10.1950: 'Le Coeur de la Matière', *Oeuvres* 13, p. 59 (*HM*, p. 48) ('ma vision christo-cosmique').

(43) 9.5.1951: Lettre à Pierre Leroy, *LF*, p. 99 ('Christ de Cosmos').

(44) 24.8.1954: *Carnets de retraites, 1944–1955,* Retraite 19–26.8.1954, 6e jour, p. 41 ('K- Xcentrisme' = Cosmo-Christocentrisme) (in Jacques Laberge, op. cit., p. 140).

*E. Additional Note*

The term 'Christ cosmique' disappears from Teilhard's extant writings between the mid 1920s and the mid 1940s. While this absence certainly signals shifting emphases in his thought, it is not impossible that he used the term in, say, the missing first twelve cahiers of his later journal, which he is thought to have left behind in China.

One indication that Teilhard was, in fact, employing 'Christ cosmique' during this period is its presence in a letter to him from Joseph Maréchal, 3.7.1934, *LI*, p. 287. 'Christ cosmique' is not an expression that one associates with Maréchal; there can be little doubt that he is replying to Teilhard with Teilhard's own terminology.

# BIBLIOGRAPHY

## 1. ORIGEN

A. TEXTS.

*(i) Griechischen Christlichen Schriftsteller*

| | |
|---|---|
| Vol. 1. *GCS* 2 (ed. P. Koetschau) | Exhortatio ad Martyrium |
| | Contra Celsum, Bks. I–IV |
| Vol. 2. *GCS* 3 (ed. P. Koetschau) | Contra Celsum, Bks. V–VIII |
| | De Oratione |
| Vol. 3. *GCS* 6 (ed. E. Klostermann) | Homiliae in Jermiam |
| Vol. 4. *GCS* 10 (ed. E. Preuschen) | Commentaria in Joannem |
| Vol. 5. *GCS* 22 (ed. P. Koetschau) | De Principiis |
| Vol. 6. *GCS* 29 (ed. W. A. Baehrens) | Homiliae in Genesim |
| | Homiliae in Exodum |
| | Homiliae in Leviticum |
| Vol. 7. *GCS* 30 (ed. W. A. Baehrens) | Homiliae in Numeros |
| | Homiliae in Jesum Nave |
| Vol. 8. *GCS* 33 (ed. W. A. Baehrens) | Homiliae in 1 Reges |
| | Commentaria in Canticum Canticorum |
| | Homiliae in Isaiam |
| | Homiliae in Jeremiam (Latin) |
| | Homiliae in Ezechelem |
| Vol. 9. *GCS* 49 (ed. M. Rauer) | Homiliae in Lucam |
| Vol. 10. *GCS* 40 (ed. E. Klostermann) | Commentaria in Matthaeum |
| Vol. 11. *GCS* 38 (ed. E. Klostermann) | Commentariorum Series in Matthaeum |
| Vol. 12. *GCS* 41 (ed. E. Klostermann) | Fragmenta in Matthaeum |

*(ii) Patrologia Graeca (ed. J. P. Migne)*

| | |
|---|---|
| *P.G.* 12 | Commentaria in Genesim |
| | Homiliae in Psalmos |
| | Selecta in Psalmos |

P.G. 14    Commentaria in Epistulam ad Romanos
Fragmenta in Epistulam ad Galatas
Fragmenta in Epistulam ad Colossenses
Fragmenta in Epistulam ad Titum
Fragmenta in Epistulam ad Hebraeos
P.G. 17    Expositio in Proverbia

*(iii) Other Sources*

SCHERER, J. *Entretien d'Origène avec Héraclide,* Institut Francais d'Archéologie Orientale, Cairo, 1949.

SCHERER, J. *Origène, Entretien avec Héraclide,* S. Ch. 67, Paris, 1960.

PITRA, J. B., *Analecta Sacra Spicilegio Solesmensi Parata,* tomus 2, *Patres Antenicaeni,* Typis Tusculanis, [Paris], 1884, tomus 3, Mechitaristarum Sancti Lazari, E Typographeo Veneto, 1883.

WALDIS, J. J. K., *Hieronymi Graeca in Psalmos Fragmenta untersucht und auf ihre Herkunft geprüft,* Druck der Aschendorffschen Buchdruckerei, Münster i. Westf.,1908.

CADIOU, R., *Commentaires inédits des psaumes: Étude sur les textes d'Origène contentus dans le manuscrit 'Vindobonensis 8',* Société d'édition 'Les belles lettres', Paris, 1936.

RONDEAU, M-J., 'Le Commentaire sur les Psaumes d'Evagre le Pontique', in *Orientalia Christiana Periodica,* Roma, vol. 21, 1960, pp. 307–48, especially pp. 328–48.

HARL, M. and DORIVAL, G., *La Chaîne palestinienne sur le psaume 118 (Origène, Eusèbe, Didyme, Apollinaire, Athanase, Théodoret),* Les Éditions du Cerf, Paris, 2 tomes, 1972.

SCHERER, J., *Le Commentaire d'Origène Sur Rom. III 5-V 7,* Institut Francais d'Archéologie Orientale, Cairo, 1957.

RAMSBOTHAM, H., 'The Commentary of Origen on the Epistle to the Romans', in *The Journal of Theological Studies,* Oxford, vol. 13, 1912–3, pp. 210–24, 357–68 and vol. 14, 1913–4, pp. 10–22.

JENKINS, C., 'Origen on I Corinthians, IV', in *The Journal of Theological Studies,* Oxford, vol. 10, 1908–9, pp. 29–51.

GREGG, J. A. F., 'The Commentary of Origen upon the Epistle to the Ephesians', in *The Journal of Theological Studies,* Oxford, vol. 3, 1901–2, pp. 233–44, 398–420, 554–76.

DIOBOUNIOTIS, C. and HARNACK, A., *Der Scholien-Kommentar des Origenes zur Apokalypse Johannis, nebst einem Stück aus Irenaeus, Lib. V. Graece, Texte und Untersuchungen zur Geschichte der altchristlichen Literatur,* 38. Bd., Heft 3, J.C. Hinrichs'sche Buchhandlung, Leipzig, 1911.

TURNER, C. H., 'The Text of the Newly Discovered Scholia of Origen on the Apocalypse, I. Scholia i–xxvii', *The Journal of Theological Studies,* Oxford, vol. 13, 1911–12, pp. 386–97.

CROUZEL, H. (ed.), *Grégoire le Thaumaturge, Remerciement à Origène, suivi de la lettre d'Origène à Grégoire,* S. Ch. 148, Cerf, Paris, 1969.

ROBINSON, J. A. *Origenis Philocalia,* Cambridge, 1893.

224     *Bibliography*

*Dialogus Candidi Origenis* (in Jerome, *Apol. adv. Lib. Ruf.* 2:19 (*PL* 23, col. 442C–443A)).

*Epistola Origenis ad Amicos Alexandriae* (in Rufinus, *Lib. de Adult. Lib. Orig.* (*PG* 17, col. 624A–626B); Jerome, *Apol. adv. Lib. Ruf.* 2:18 (*PL* 23, col. 440C–442C)).

JUSTINIAN, *Liber adversus Origenem ad Mennam*, Mansi, tomus 9, col. 487–534 (Greek fragments of the *De Principiis*, col. 523–34).

*(iv) Translations*

BUTTERWORTH, G. W., *Origen, On First Principles*, SPCK, London, 1936.

SIMONETTI, MANLIO, *I Principii di Origene*, Unione Tipografico-Editrice, Torinese, 1968.

*De Principiis*, Harl, Marguerite, *et al.*, *Origène, Traité des principes (peri archôn)*, Études Augustiniennes, Paris, 1976.

GÖRGEMANNS, HERWIG, and KARPP, HEINRICH, *Origenes vier Bücher von den Prinzipien*, Wissenschaftlische Buchgesellschaft, Darmstadt, 1976.

BLANC, CÉCILE (ed.), *Origène, Commentaire sur saint Jean*, tome 1, *S. Ch.* 120.

KOETSCHAU, PAUL, *Des Origenes ausgewählte Schriften aus dem Griechischen übersetzt*, 1. Bd., *Des Origenes Schriften vom Gebet und Ermahnung zum Martyrium*, Verlag Josef Kösel und Friedrich Pustet K.-G., München, 1926.

B. SECONDARY WORKS

BARDY, G., 'Origène', in *Dictionnaire de théologie catholique*, Letouzey et Ané, Paris, tome 11, 1931, col. 1489–1565.

BARDY, GUSTAVE, *Recherches sur l'histoire du texte et des versions latines du De Principiis d'Origène*, Champion, Paris, 1923.

BARNARD, L. W., 'Origen's Christology and Eschatology', in *Anglican Theological Review*, New York, vol. 46, 1964, pp. 314–19.

BERTRAND, FRÉDÉRIC, *Mystique de Jésus chez Origène*, Aubier, Paris, 1951.

CADIOU, RENÉ, *La Jeunesse d'Origène: Histoire de l'école d'Alexandrie au début du IIIe siècle*, Gabriel Beauchesne et ses fils, Paris, 1935.

CHADWICK, HENRY, 'Origen, Celsus, and the Resurrection of the Body', in *The Harvard Theological Review*, Cambridge, Massachusetts, vol. 41, 1948, pp. 83–102.

CHADWICK, HENRY, 'Origen, Celsus and the Stoa', in *The Journal of Theological Studies*, Oxford, vol. 48, 1947, pp. 34–49.

CHÊNEVERT, JACQUES, *L'Église dans le commentaire d'Origène sur le Cantique des Cantiques*, Desclée de Brouwer, Bruxelles, 1969.

CORNÉLIS, H., Les Fondements cosmologiques de l'eschatologie d'Origène, in *Revue des sciences philosophiques et théologiques*, Paris, vol. 43, 1959, pp. 32–80, 201–47: reprint, no date, pp. 1–96.

CROUZEL, HENRI, 'L'Anthropologie d'Origène dans la perspective du combat spirituel', in *Revue d'ascétique et de mystique'*, Toulouse, 31e année, 1955, pp. 364–85.

CROUZEL, HENRI, 'A Letter from Origen "To Friends in Alexandria" ', in David Neiman and Margaret Schatkin (ed.), *The Heritage of the Early Church: Essays in Honor of the Very Reverend Georges Vasilievich Florovsky*, Pontificum Institutum Studiorum Orientalium, Roma, 1973, pp. 135–50.

CROUZEL, HENRI, *Origène et la 'connaissance mystique'*, Desclée de Brouwer, Bruges, 1961.

CROUZEL, HENRI, *Origène et la philosophie*, Aubier, [Paris], 1962.

CROUZEL, HENRI, 'Les Personnes de la Trinité sont-elles de puissance inégale selon Origène, Peri Archon 1, 3, 5–8?', in *Gregorianum*, Roma, vol. 57, 1976, pp. 109–25.

CROUZEL, HENRI, *Théologie de l'image de Dieu chez Origène*, Aubier, Paris, 1956.

DANIÉLOU, JEAN, *Origen*, Sheed and Ward, New York, 1955.

DENIS, J., *De la philosophie d'Origène*, Imprimerie Nationale, Paris, 1884.

DUPUIS, JACQUES, *'L'Esprit de l'homme': Étude sur l'anthropologie religieuse d'Origène*, Desclée de Brouwer, [Bruges], 1967.

FAIRWEATHER, WILLIAM, *Origen and Greek Patristic Theology*, T. and T. Clark, Edinburgh, 1901.

FAYE, EUGENE DE, *Origen and His Work*, George Allen and Unwin Ltd., London, 1926.

FAYE, EUGÈNE DE, *Origène: Sa vie, son oeuvre, sa pensée*, Ernest Leroux, Paris, vol. 3, *La Doctrine*, 1928.

GÖGLER, ROLF, *Zur Theologie des biblischen Wortes bei Origenes*, Patmos-Verlag, Düsseldorf, 1963.

GRUBER, GERHARD, *ZΩ H: Wesen, Stufen and Mitteilung des wahren Lebens bei Origenes*, Max Hueber Verlag, München, 1962.

HANSON, RICHARD, P. C., 'Did Origen Apply the Word Homoousios to the Son?', in Jacques Fontaine and Charles Kannengiesser (ed.), *Epektasis: Mélanges patristiques offerts au Cardinal Jean Daniélou*, Beauchesne, [Paris], 1972, pp. 293–303.

HARL, MARGUERITE, *Origène et la fonction révélatrice du Verbe incarné*, Éditions du Seuil, Paris, 1958.

HUET, PIERRE DANIEL, *Origeniana*, in *PG* 17, col. 633–1284.

JUSTINIAN, *Liber adversus Origenem ad Mennam*, in Joannes Dominicus Mansi (ed.), *Sacrorum Conciliorum Nova, et Amplissima Collectio*, Expensis Antonii Zatta Veneti, Florentiae, tomus 9, 1763, col. 487–538.

KERR, HUGH T., *The First Systematic Theologian: Origen of Alexandria*, Princeton Theological Seminary, Princeton, New Jersey, 1958.

KETTLER, FRANZ HEINRICH, *Der ursprüngliche Sinn der Dogmatik des Origenes*, Verlag Alfred Töpelmann, Berlin, 1966.

KOCH, HAL, *Pronoia und Paideusis: Studien über Origenes und sein Verhältnis zum Platonismus*, Verlag von Walter de Gruyter & Co., Berlin, 1932.

LEBEAU, PAUL, 'L'Interprétation origénienne de Rm 8:19–22', in Patrick Granfield and Josef A. Jungmann (ed.), *Kyriakon: Festschrift Johannes*

*Quasten*, Verlag Aschendorff, Münster, Westfalen, 1970, vol. 1, pp. 336–45.

LIESKE, ALOISIUS, *Die Theologie der Logosmystik bei Origenes*, Aschendorffsche Verlagsbuchhandlung, Munster in Westfalen, 1938.

LOSADA, JOAQUIN, 'Una Paradoja eclesiológica conservada por Origenes', in *Miscelanea Comillas*, Comillas, vol. 47–8, 1967, pp. 65–73.

LOSADA, JOAQUIN, 'El Sacrificio de Cristo en los cielos según Orígenes', in *Miscelanea Comillas*, Comillas, vol. 50, 1968, pp. 5–19.

LOWRY, CHARLES, W., 'Did Origen Style the Son a κτίσμα?', in *The Journal of Theological Studies*, Oxford, vol. 39, 1938, pp. 39–42.

LOWRY, CHARLES, W., 'Origen as Trinitarian', in *The Journal of Theological Studies*, Oxford, vol. 37, 1936, pp. 225–40.

LUBAC, HENRI DE, *Histoire et esprit: L'intelligence de l'Écriture d'après Origène*, Aubier, Paris, 1950.

NAUTIN, PIERRE, *Origène*, tome 1, *Sa vie et son oeuvre*, Beauchesne, Paris, 1977.

NEMESHEGYI, PETER, *La Paternité de Dieu chez Origène*, Desclée & Cie, Tournai, 1960.

PAMPHILIUS, *Apologia pro Origene*, in *PG* 17, col. 521–616.

PRAT, F., *Origène: Le théologien et l'exégète*, Librairie Bloud et Cie, Paris, 1907.

REDEPENNING, ERNST RUDOLF, *Origenes: Eine Darstellung seines Lebens und seiner Lehre*, Verlag von Eduard Weber, Bonn, 2. Abtheilung, 1846.

SIMONETTI, MANLIO, 'Sull'interpretazione di un passo del *De Principiis* di Origene (1, 3, 5–8)', in *Rivista di cultura classica e medioevale*, Roma, Anno 6, 1964, pp. 15–32.

STEIDLE, BASILIUS, 'Neue Untersuchungen zu Origenes' Περὶ ἀρχῶν', in *Zeitschrift für die neutestamentliche Wissenschaft und die Kunde der älteren Kirche*, Berlin, 40. Bd., 1941, pp. 236–43.

TOWNSLEY, ASHTON, L. 'Origen's ὁ θεός, Anaximander's τὸ θεῖον and a Series of Worlds: Some Remarks', in *Orientalia Christiana Periodica*, Roma, vol. 41, 1975, pp. 140–9.

VOGT, HERMANN JOSEF, *Das Kirchenverständnis des Origenes*, Böhlau-Verlag, Köln, 1974.

WESTCOTT, BROOKE FOSS, 'Origenes', in William Smith and Henry Wace (ed.), *A Dictionary of Christian Biography, Literature, Sects and Doctrines; During the First Eight Centuries*, John Murray, London, vol. 4, 1887, pp. 96–142.

## 2. TEILHARD de CHARDIN

A. TEXTS

*(i) Published Works*

Series *Oeuvres de Pierre Teilhard de Chardin* (Paris, Éditions du Seuil)
  1. *Le phénomène humaine* (1955)

2. *L'apparition de l'homme* (1956)
3. *La vision du passé* (1957)
4. *Le milieu divin* (1957)
5. *L'avenir de l'homme* (1959)
6. *L'énergie humaine* (1962)
7. *L'activation de l'énergie* (1963)
8. *La place de l'homme dans la nature* (1956)
9. *Science et Christ* (1965)
10. *Comment je crois* (1969)
11. *Les directions de l'avenir* (1973)
12. *Écrits du temps de la guerre* (1965)
13. *Le coeur de la matière* (1976)

Series *Cahiers Pierre Teilhard de Chardin* (Paris, Éditions du Seuil)
1. *Construire la terre* (1958)
2. *Réflexions sur la bonheur* (1960)
3. *Pierrre Teilhard de Chardin et la politque africaine* (1962)
4. *La parole attendue* (1963)
5. *Le Christ évoluteur; Socialisation et religion* (1965)
6. *Le Dieu de l'évolution* (1968)
7. *Sens humain et sens divin* (1971)
8. *Terre promise* (1974)

*Accomplir l'homme* (Paris, 1968)
*Blondel et Teilhard de Chardin: Correspondance* (Paris, 1965)
*Dans le sillage des sinanthropes* (Paris, 1971)
*Écrits du temps de la guerre* (Paris (Grasset), 1956)
*Genèse d'une pensée* (Lettres 1914–1919) (Paris, 1961)
*Hymne de l'univers* (Paris, 1961)
*Journal I* (Paris, 1975)
*Lettres à Léontine Zanta* (Bruges, 1965)
*Lettres d'Hastings et de Paris* (Paris, 1965)
*Lettres de l'Égypte* (Paris, 1963)
*Lettres de voyage* (Paris, 1956)
*Lettres familières de Pierre Teilhard de Chardin, mon ami* (ed. P. Leroy) (Paris, 1976).
*Lettres intimes de Teilhard de Chardin à Auguste Valensin, Bruno de Solages, Henri de Lubac* (2nd ed., Paris, 1974)

*(ii) Unpublished or uncollected works*
*Carnet de retraites, 1944–1955*
Conversation avec F. Lafargue, 7.1954 (quoted in Claude Cuénot, *Nouveau lexique Teilhard de Chardin*, p. 147).
'Débat entre le Père Teilhard de Chardin et Gabriel Marcel', 21.1.1947.
*Journal*, cahiers I–IX, 1915–25.
*Journal*, cahiers XIII(1)–XXI(9), 1944–55.
Lettre à Claude Cuénot, 15.2.1955 (relevant part quoted in Claude Cuénot,

*Pierre Teilhard de Chardin: Les Grandes étapes de son évolution*, pp. 55–6).
Lettre à Pierre Lamare, 26.11.1929 (text, with incorrect date, in Robert Speaight, *Teilhard de Chardin: A Biography*, p. 162).
Letter to Édouard Le Roy, 19.10.1921 (quoted in Claude Cuénot, *Teilhard de Chardin: A Biographical Study*, ed. René Hague, pp. 33–4).
Lettre à Édouard Le Roy, 10.8.1929.
Lettre à Jeanne Mortier, 11.11.1953.
Lettre à François Russo, 17.11.1953.
Summary of [Lettre] à M[ar]g[uerite Teillard-Chambon], in *Journal* XVII (=5), [25.8.] 1950, p. 141.
Summary of [Lettre] à Joseph [Teilhard de Chardin], in *Journal* XIX (=7), 31.5.1953, p. 71.
Summary of [Lettre] à M[ar]g[uerite Teillard-Chambon], in *Journal* XX (=8), 22.11.1953, p. 31.
Lettre à Claude Tresmontant, 14.1.1954.
Lettre à Claude Tresmontant, 20.1.1954.
Lettre à Claude Tresmontant, 8.2.1954.
Lettre à Claude Tresmontant, 7.4.1954.
*Notes de lectures*, cahier 1, 1945.
Teilhard de Chardin, P., 'L'Homme devant les enseignements de l'Église et devant la philosophie spiritualiste', in A. d'Alès (ed.), *Dictionnaire apologétique de la foi catholique*, Gabriel Beauchesne, Paris, 4e éd., tome 2, 1911, col. 501–14.

*(iii) Translations*

*Activation of Energy* (London, 1970)
*The Appearance of Man* (London, 1965)
*Building the Earth* (London, 1965)
*Christianity and Evolution* (London, 1971)
*The Future of Man* (London, 1964)
*The Heart of Matter* (London, 1978)
*Human Energy* (London, 1969)
*Hymn of the Universe* (London, 1965)
*Let Me Explain* (London, 1970)
*Letters from Hastings* (New York, 1968)
*Letters from Paris* (New York, 1967)
*Letters from a Traveller* (London, 1962)
*Letters to Léontine Zanta* (London, 1969)
*Letters to Two Friends* (London, 1972)
*The Making of a Mind* (London, 1965)
*Man's Place in Nature* (London, 1966)
*Le Milieu Divin* (London, 1960)
*The Phenomenon of Man* (London, 1959)
*Pierre Teilhard de Chardin-Maurice Blondel: Correspondence* (New York, 1967)
*Science and Christ* (London, 1968)

*Toward the Future* (London, 1975)
*The Vision of the Past* (London, 1966)
*Writings in Time of War* (London, 1968)

B. SECONDARY WORKS

ALLEGRA, GABRIEL M., *My Conversations with Teilhard de Chardin on the Primacy of Christ, Peking, 1942–1945*, Franciscan Herald Press, Chicago, 1971.

ARMAGNAC, CHRISTIAN d', 'De Blondel à Teilhard: Nature et intériorité', in *Archives de philosophie*, Paris, tome 21, 1958, pp. 298–312.

BARBOUR, GEORGE B., *In the Field with Teilhard de Chardin*, Herder and Herder, New York, 1965.

BARTHÉLEMY-MADAULE, MADELEINE, *La Personne et le drame humain chez Teilhard de Chardin*, Éditions du Seuil, Paris, 1967.

BAUDRY, GÉRARD-HENRY, 'Les Grands axes de l'eschatologie teilhardienne (1946–1955)', in *Mélanges de science religieuse*, Lille, vol. 34, 1977, pp. 213–35; vol. 35, 1978, pp. 37–71.

BILANIUK, PETRO, 'The Christology of Teilhard de Chardin', in *Proceedings of the Teilhard Conference 1964*, Human Energetics Research Institute, Fordham University, New York, 1964, pp. 109–33.

CAIRNS, HUGH CAMPBELL, *The Identity and Originality of Teilhard de Chardin*, Thesis Presented for the Degree of Doctor of Philosophy, University of Edinburgh [Edinburgh,], 30 March 1971.

CORTE, NICOLAS, *La Vie et l'âme de Teilhard de Chardin*, Librairie Arthème Fayard, Paris, 1957 (E.T., *Pierre Teilhard de Chardin: His Life and Spirit*, Barrie and Rockliff, London, 1960).

CUÉNOT, CLAUDE, *Nouveau lexique Teilhard de Chardin*, Éditions du Seuil, Paris, 1968.

CUÉNOT, CLAUDE, *Pierre Teilhard de Chardin: Les Grandes étapes de son évolution*, Librairie Plon, Paris, 1958 (E.T., *Teilhard de Chardin: A Biographical Study*, ed. René Hague, Burns and Oates, London, 1965).

CUÉNOT, CLAUDE, 'Teilhard de Chardin et les philosophies', in *La Table ronde*, Paris, no. 90, juin 1955, pp. 36–40.

DANTINE, WILHELM, 'Zur kosmischen Stellung des Menschen nach Teilhard de Chardin: Erwägungen einer theologischen Anthropologie', in *Acta teilhardiana: Studien und Mitteilungen der Gesellschaft Teilhard de Chardin*, München, 5. Jahrgang, 1968, pp. 16–32.

DAY, MICHAEL, 'Teilhard's Rediscovery of the Cosmic Christ', in *The Teilhard Review*, London, vol. 11, 1976, pp. 109–12.

DAECKE, SIGURD MARTIN, *Teilhard de Chardin und die evangelische Theologie: Die Weltlichkeit Gottes und die Weltlichkeit der Welt*, Vandenhoeck und Ruprecht, Göttingen, 1967.

DECKERS, MARIE-CHRISTINE, *Le Vocabulaire de Teilhard de Chardin: Les éléments grecs*, J. Duculot, Gembloux, 1968.

FARICY, ROBERT L., *Teilhard de Chardin's Theology of the Christian in the World*, Sheed and Ward, New York, 1967.

FEBRAS BORRA, JOSÉ LUIS, *Les Noms du Christ dans les oeuvres de Teilhard de Chardin*, thèse presentée à. l'Institut Catholique de Paris, Paris, juin 1976.

FITZER, JOSEPH, 'Teilhard's Eucharist: A Reflection', in *Theological Studies*, Baltimore, vol. 34, 1973, pp. 251–64.

HAAS, ADOLF, *Teilhard de Chardin-Lexikon: Grundbegriffe – Erläuterungen – Texte*, Herder, Freiburg im Breisgau, 1971, A–H; I–Z.

HALE, ROBERT, *Christ and the Universe: Teilhard de Chardin and the Cosmos*, Franciscan Herald Press, Chicago, 1973.

KIM, DAI SIL, 'Irenaeus of Lyons and Teilhard de Chardin: A Comparative Study of "Recapitulation" and "Omega"', in *Journal of Ecumenical Studies*, Philadelphia, vol. 13, 1976, pp. 69–93.

KLÓSAK, KAZIMIERZ, 'Spór o Orygenesa naszych csasów' ['The Dispute about the Origen of Our Time'], in *Znak*, Kraków, vol. 12, nos 2–3, 1960, pp. 253–68.

LABERGE, JACQUES, *Pierre Teilhard de Chardin et Ignace de Loyola: Les notes de retraite (1919–1955)*, Desclée de Brouwer, [Paris], 1973.

L'ARCHEVÊQUE, PAUL, *Teilhard de Chardin: Index analytique*, Les Presses de l'Université Laval, Québec, 1967.

L'ARCHEVÊQUE, PAUL, *Teilhard de Chardin: Nouvel index analytique*, Les Presses de l'Université Laval, Québec, 1972.

LEYS, ROGER, 'Teilhard dangereux?', in *Revue Teilhard de Chardin*, Bruxelles, no 14, mars 1963, pp. 20–35.

LEYS, ROGER, 'Teilhard de Chardin et le péché originel', in Attila Szekeres (ed.), *Le Christ cosmique de Teilhard de Chardin*, Uitgeverij de Nederlandsche Boekhandel, Antwerpen, 1969.

LUBAC, HENRI de, *The Eternal Feminine: A Study on the Poem by Teilhard de Chardin, Followed by 'Teilhard and the Problems of Today'*, Collins, London, 1971.

LUBAC, HENRI de, *La Prière du Père Teilhard de Chardin*, Fayard, Paris, 1964; 2e éd., 1968 (E.T., *The Faith of Teilhard de Chardin*, Burns and Oates, London, 1965).

LUBAC, HENRI de, *The Religion of Teilhard de Chardin*, Collins, London, 1967.

LUBAC, HENRI de, *Teilhard missionnaire et apologiste*, Éditions Prière et Vie, Toulouse, 1966.

LUBAC, HENRI de, *Teilhard posthume: Réflexions et souvenirs*, Fayard, Paris, 1977.

MOONEY, CHRISTOPHER F., *Teilhard de Chardin and the Mystery of Christ*, Collins, London, 1966.

NORTH, ROBERT, *Teilhard and the Creation of the Soul*, The Bruce Publishing Company, Milwaukee, 1967.

OUINCE, RENÉ d, *Un Prophète en procès*, Aubier-Montaigne, Paris, 1970, vol. 1, *Teilhard de Chardin dans l'Église de son témps*; vol. 2, *Teilhard de Chardin et l'avenir de la pensée chrétienne*.

PHILIPPE DE LA TRINITÉ, *Teilhard de Chardin: Étude critique*, vol. 2, *Vision cosmique et christique*, La Table Ronde, Paris, 1968.

PONTET, MAURICE, *Pascal et Teilhard: Témoins de Jésus-Christ*, Desclée de Brouwer, Paris, 1968.

RABUT, OLIVIER, *Dialogue with Teilhard de Chardin*, Sheed and Ward, London, 1961.

RAVEN, CHARLES E., *Teilhard de Chardin: Scientist and Seer*, Collins, London, 1962.

RIDEAU, ÉMILE, *Teilhard de Chardin: A Guide to His Thought*, Collins, London, 1967.

SCHELLENBAUM, PETER, *Le Christ dans l'énergétique teilhardienne: Étude génétique*, Les Éditions du Cerf, Paris, 1971.

SMULDERS, PIERRE, *La Vision de Teilhard de Chardin: Essai de réflexion théologique*, Desclée de Brouwer, Paris, 3e éd., 1965.

SPEAIGHT, ROBERT, *Teilhard de Chardin: A Biography*, Collins, London, 1967.

STERN, KARL, 'Saint Augustine and Teilhard', in Neville Braybrook (ed.), *Teilhard de Chardin: Pilgrim of the Future*, Darton, Longman and Todd, London, Libra Books ed., 1965.

SZEKERES, ATTILA, 'La pensée religieuse de Teilhard de Chardin et la signification théologique de son Christ cosmique', in id. (ed.), *Le Christ cosmique de Teilhard de Chardin*, Uitgeverij de nederlandsche Boekhandel, Antwerpen, 1969, pp. 333–402.

WILDIERS, N. M., 'L'Expérience fondamentale du P. Teilhard de Chardin', in *La Table ronde*, Paris, no. 90, juin 1955, pp. 41–54.

WILDIERS, N. M., *Teilhard de Chardin*, Éditions universitaires, Paris, 1960 (E.T. from the Flemish ed., 1963, *An Introduction to Teilhard de Chardin*, Collins, London, 1968).

# INDEX

Aeby, G., 139n
Albinus, 90, 91, 96, 119
Alès, Adhémar d', 43, 44
Allegra, G. M., 44n, 72n
Ambrose, 2n, 73
Andersen, Wilhelm, 61
Anderson, J. F., 127n
Andrews, H. T., 50, 53, 55
Aquinas, Thomas, 2n, 26, 48, 73–4, 157n, 173, 174
Aristotle, 34, 165, 173
pseudo-Aristotle, 91, 92
Arius, 34, 37, 86, 111, 113, 115, 117, 198
Armagnac, C. d', 157n, 159n
Arnou, R., 216n
Athanasius, 2n, 26, 33, 111, 114
Auberlen, C. A., 14, 28
Augustine, 59, 79n, 183

Bacon, Francis, 12
Barbel, J., 139n
Bardy, G., 76n, 113n
Barnard, L. W., 77, 86n
Barth, Karl, 57
Barthélemy-Madaule, M., 40n
Beckner, M. O., 172n
Benson, R. H., 181
Benz, E., 14n
Baur, F. C., 20
Bergson, Henri, 171–2
Berkhof, Henrikus, 66–7, 69–70
Bertrand, F., 78n
Bethune-Baker, J. F., 98n
Bigg, C., 93n, 105n
Bilaniuk, Petro, 197n
Blanc, C., 139n
Blondel, Maurice, 17, 18n, 41, 147, 152n, 157, 159–68, 173–5, 177, 180, 218
Boehme, Jacob, 2n, 12, 16
Bonaventure, 2n, 26

Bookless, J. G., 63
Boulerand, E., 115n
Boyancé, P., 92n
Bréhier, E., 82n
Brière, Yves de la, 149, 151
Bruce, A. B., 29–30, 37
Bruggeman, A., 63n
Bruno, Giordano, 12
Bucke, R. M., 169
Buckham, J. W., 29, 33, 37
Bull, G., 166–17
Bultmann, Rudolf, 20
Bürkle, Horst, 60n, 61, 66
Butterworth, G. W., 107n, 111n, 132n

Cadiou, R., 105n
Cairns, H. C., 147n
Calvin, John, 25
Campbell, J. McLeod, 52
Candidus, 99n
Celsus, 84–5
Chadwick, Henry, 93n, 120n, 134n, 139n
Chênevert, J., 130n, 136n
Chossat, Marcel, 44
Clark, H. W., 50–3, 72
Clement of Alexandria, 2n, 79
Coleridge, S. T., 51–2
Congar, Yves, 63
Copernicus, 70
Cornélis, H., 109n
Corte, Nicolas, 74
Creed, J. M., 52
Crehan, J. H., 127n
Crouzel, H., 76n, 86n, 103n, 105n, 107n, 113n, 116–17, 120n, 140n
Cuénot, Claude, 41n, 61n, 176n
Cyril of Alexandria, 2n

Daecke, S. M., 60, 65
Dai Sil Kim, 79n